650 HOME PLANS

From Cottages to Mansions

HOME PLANNERS

Above: Design HPT860434, page 276

Published by Home Planners, LLC
Wholly owned by Hanley-Wood, LLC
3275 West Ina Road, Suite 110
Tucson, Arizona 85741

Distribution Center:
29333 Lorie Lane
Wixom, Michigan 48393

Jayne Fenton – *President*
Jennifer Pearce – *Vice President, Group Content*
Jan Prideaux – *Editor in Chief*
Linda B. Bellamy – *Executive Editor*
Arlen Feldwick-Jones – *Editorial Director*
Vicki Frank – *Managing Editor*
Paulette Dague – *Editor*
Ashleigh Stone and Jennifer Lowry – *Plans Editors*
Kristin Schneidler and Morenci Wodraska – *Plans Editors*
Marian E. Haggard – *Editorial Assistant*
Jay C. Walsh – *Graphic Designer*
Teralyn Morriss – *Graphic Production Artist*
Sara Lisa – *Senior Production Manager*
Brenda McClary – *Production Manager*

Photo Credits:

Front Cover: Colbert Howell
Design by William Poole Designs, Inc.
(see page 342, Design HPT860533)

Back Cover: Terrebonne Photography
Builder: Barington Homes,
Design by Frank Betz Associates, Inc.
(see page 420, Design HPT860613)

© 2002

10 9 8 7 6 5 4 3 2 1

Printed in the United States of America.

Library of Congress Catalog Card Number: 2002103146

ISBN softcover: 1-931131-04-X

Table of Contents

Design HPT860600, page 407

Design HPT860001

Square Footage: 1,429
Width: 49'-0" **Depth:** 53'-0"

This home's gracious exterior is indicative of the elegant, yet extremely livable floor plan inside. Volume ceilings that crown the family living areas combine with an open floor plan to give the modest square footage a more spacious feel. The formal dining room is set off from the foyer and vaulted family room with stately columns. The spacious family room has a corner fireplace, rear-yard door and serving bar from the open galley kitchen. A bay-windowed breakfast nook flanks the kitchen on one end, while a laundry center and wet bar/serving pantry lead to the dining room on the other. The split-bedroom plan allows the amenity-rich master suite maximum privacy. A pocket door off the family room leads to the hall housing the two family bedrooms and a full bath. Please specify crawlspace or slab foundation when ordering.

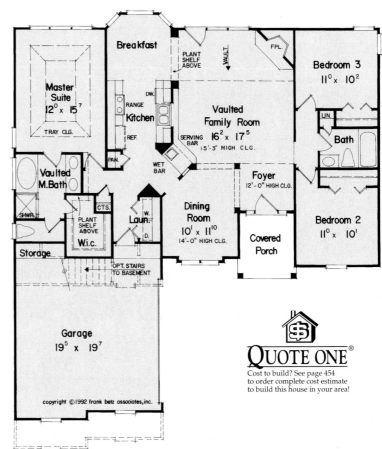

Quote One®
Cost to build? See page 454 to order complete cost estimate to build this house in your area!

Design HPT860002

First Floor: 1,171 square feet
Second Floor: 600 square feet
Total: 1,771 square feet
Width: 50'-0" **Depth:** 44'-0"

L D

There's nothing that tops gracious Southern hospitality — unless it's offered Southern farmhouse style! The entry hall opens through an archway on the right to a formal dining room. Nearby, the efficient country kitchen shares space with a bayed eating area. The two-story family/great room is warmed by a fireplace in the winter and open to outdoor country comfort in the summer via double French doors. The first-floor master suite offers a bay window and access to the porch through French doors. The second floor holds two family bedrooms that share a full bath. Plans for an optional indoor swimming pool/spa and detached garage are included.

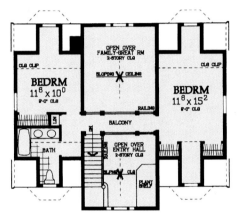

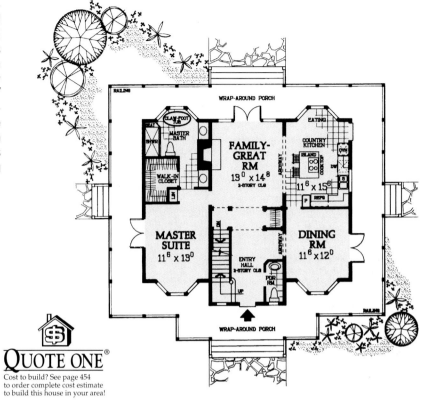

Quote One®

Cost to build? See page 454 to order complete cost estimate to build this house in your area!

5

Design HPT860003

First Floor: 1,356 square feet
Second Floor: 542 square feet
Total: 1,898 square feet
Bonus Room: 393 square feet
Width: 59'-0" **Depth:** 64'-0"

The welcoming charm of this country farmhouse is expressed by its many windows and its covered, wraparound porch. A two-story entrance foyer is enhanced by a Palladian window in a clerestory dormer above to let in natural lighting. The first-floor master suite allows privacy and accessibility. The master bath includes a whirlpool tub, separate shower, double-bowl vanity and walk-in closet. The first floor features nine-foot ceilings throughout with the exception of the kitchen area, which sports an eight-foot ceiling. The second floor provides two additional bedrooms, a full bath and plenty of storage space. The bonus room provides room to grow.

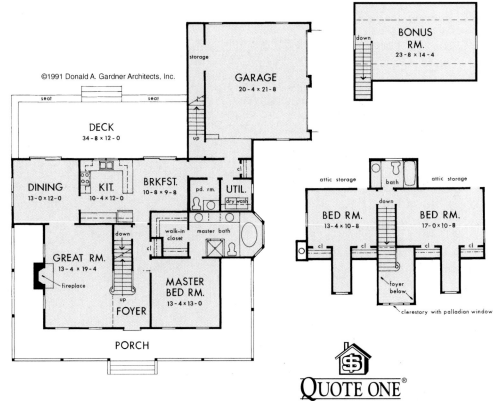

©1991 Donald A. Gardner Architects, Inc.

BONUS RM.
23-8 × 14-4

GARAGE
20-4 × 21-8

storage

DECK
34-8 × 12-0

seat   seat

DINING
13-0 × 12-0

KIT.
10-4 × 12-0

BRKFST.
10-8 × 9-8

pd. rm.

UTIL.
dry wash

GREAT RM.
13-4 × 19-4

fireplace

down

walk-in closet

master bath

cl

MASTER BED RM.
13-4 × 13-0

up

FOYER

PORCH

attic storage   bath   attic storage

BED RM.
13-4 × 10-8

down

BED RM.
17-0 × 10-8

cl   cl   cl   cl

foyer below

clerestory with palladian window

QUOTE ONE®
Cost to build? See page 454
to order complete cost estimate
to build this house in your area!

Design HPT860004

First Floor: 1,053 square feet
Second Floor: 1,053 square feet
Total: 2,106 square feet
Bonus Room: 212 square feet
Width: 52'-0" **Depth:** 34'-0"

Brick takes a bold stand with grand traditional style in this treasured design. From the front entry to the rear deck, the floor plan serves family needs in just over 2,000 square feet. The front study has a nearby full bath, making it a handy guest bedroom. The family room with a fireplace opens to a cozy breakfast area. For more formal entertaining, there's a dining room just off the entry. Upstairs, the master bedroom offers a sitting room and a giant-sized closet. This home is designed with a walkout basement foundation.

Quote One®
Cost to build? See page 454
to order complete cost estimate
to build this house in your area!

Photo courtesy of Design Basics, Inc.

This home, as shown in the photograph, may differ from the actual blueprints.
For more detailed information, please check the floor plans carefully.

Design HPT860005

First Floor: 1,653 square feet
Second Floor: 700 square feet
Total: 2,353 square feet
Width: 54'-0" **Depth:** 50'-0"

Beautiful arches and elaborate detail give the elevation of this four-bedroom home an unmistakable elegance. Inside, the floor plan is equally appealing. Note the formal dining room with a bay window, visible from the entrance hall. The large great room has a fireplace and a wall of windows with views of the rear property. A hearth room with a built-in bookcase adjoins the kitchen, which boasts a corner walk-in pantry and a spacious breakfast nook with a bay window. The first-floor master suite features His and Hers wardrobes and a large whirlpool tub.

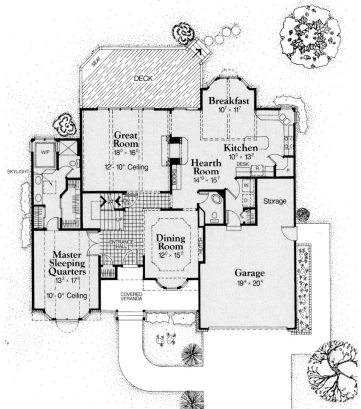

Quote One®

Cost to build? See page 454
to order complete cost estimate
to build this house in your area!

Design HPT860006

Square Footage: 3,570
Finished Basement: 2,367 square feet
Width: 84'-6" **Depth:** 69'-4"

The stone and brick exterior with multiple gables and a side-entry garage create a design that brags great curb appeal. The gourmet kitchen with an island and snack bar combine with the spacious breakfast room and hearth room to create a warm and friendly atmosphere for family living. The luxurious master bedroom with a sitting area and fireplace is complemented by a deluxe dressing room and walk-in closet. The basement level contains an office, media room, billiards room, exercise area and plenty of storage.

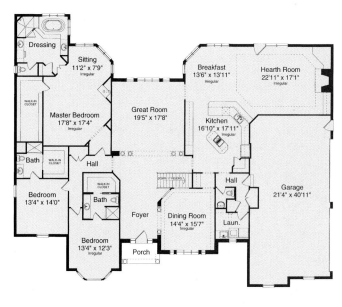

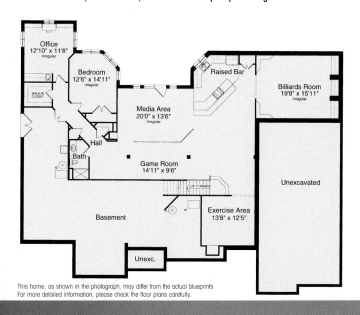

This home, as shown in the photograph, may differ from the actual blueprints
For more detailed information, please check the floor plans carefully.

Photo by Ron and Donna Kolb, Exposures Unlimited

9

Design HPT860007

Square Footage: 2,517
Width: 69'-0" **Depth:** 63'-6"

L

A graceful stucco arch supported by columns gives this home instant curb appeal. Inside, the angled foyer steps down into the living room and draws the eye to a duplicate of the exterior arch with columns. Step down again to enter the formal dining room. The kitchen features a coffered ceiling and is conveniently grouped with a sunny bayed breakfast room and the family room, the perfect place for informal gatherings. Upon entering the master suite, the master bath becomes the focal point. Columns flank the entry to this luxurious bath with a whirlpool tub as its centerpiece. Please specify crawlspace or slab foundation when ordering.

This home, as shown in the photograph, may differ from the actual blueprints
For more detailed information, please check the floor plans carefully.

Photo by Alan Mascord Design Associates, Inc ©2000

Design HPT860008

First Floor: 1,465 square feet
Second Floor: 1,103 square feet
Total: 2,568 square feet
Bonus Room: 303 square feet
Width: 63'-0" **Depth:** 48'-0"

L

With a plan that boasts excellent traffic patterns, this home will accommodate the modern family well. Formal dining and living rooms remain to one side of the house and create an elegant atmosphere for entertaining. Highlights of the front den include a bay window and built-in bookshelves. The gourmet kitchen opens into a nook and a family room. Two second-floor family bedrooms share a large hall bath along with a bonus room that's perfect for a game room. The spacious master suite has a walk-in closet and luxurious spa bath.

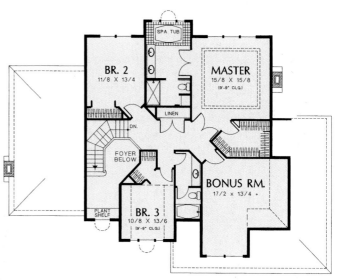

Photo courtesy of Living Concepts Home Planning

This home, as shown in the photograph, may differ from the actual blueprints.
For more detailed information, please check the floor plans carefully.

Design HPT860009

Square Footage: 2,677
Bonus Room: 319 square feet
Width: 63'-10" **Depth:** 80'-4"

A beautiful cove entry with double doors opens to a foyer with unobstructed views to the grand room. A formal dining room with a tray ceiling is to the right and the master suite fills the wing to the left. A sitting area with a bay window and entrance to the deck highlight the master bedroom. A garden tub in its own bay window and large walk-in closet enhance this area. A breakfast nook occupies a third bay window just off the U-shaped kitchen with a pass-through window to the deck. The island cooktop borders the keeping den which includes a sloped ceiling and fireplace. Two additional bedrooms each have their own bath.

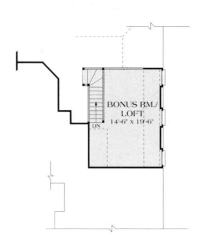

Design HPT860010

First Floor: 2,398 square feet
Second Floor: 657 square feet
Total: 3,055 square feet
Finished Basement: 1,272 square feet
Bonus Room: 374 square feet
Width: 72'-8" **Depth:** 69'-1"

Perfect for a lake or golf course setting, this home offers walls of windows in the living areas. Soak up the scenery in the sun room, which opens from the breakfast nook and leads to a rear terrace or deck. The library features a tray ceiling and an arched window, and would make an excellent home office or guest suite. Classical columns divide the great room and dining room, which has a see-through wet bar. The deluxe master suite uses defining columns between the bedroom and the lavish bath and walk-in closet. Upstairs, there are two additional suites and a bonus room. Please specify basement or crawlspace foundation when ordering.

This home, as shown in the photograph, may differ from the actual blueprints.
For more detailed information, please check the floor plans carefully.

Photo by Living Concepts Home Planning

13

Design HPT860011

First Floor: 2,642 square feet
Second Floor: 603 square feet
Total: 3,245 square feet
Bonus Room: 255 square feet
Width: 80'-0" **Depth:** 61'-0"

In this three-bedroom design, the casual areas are free-flowing, open and soaring, while the formal areas are secluded and well defined. The two-story foyer with a clerestory window leads to a quiet parlor with a vaulted ceiling and a Palladian window. The formal dining room opens from the foyer through decorative columns and is served by a spacious gourmet kitchen. The family room, defined by columns, has an angled corner hearth and is open to the kitchen and breakfast nook. The master suite is full of interesting angles, from the triangular bedroom and multi-angled walk-in closet to the corner tub in the sumptuous master bath. A nearby den has its own bathroom and could serve as a guest room. Upstairs, two additional bedrooms share a full bath and a balcony hall.

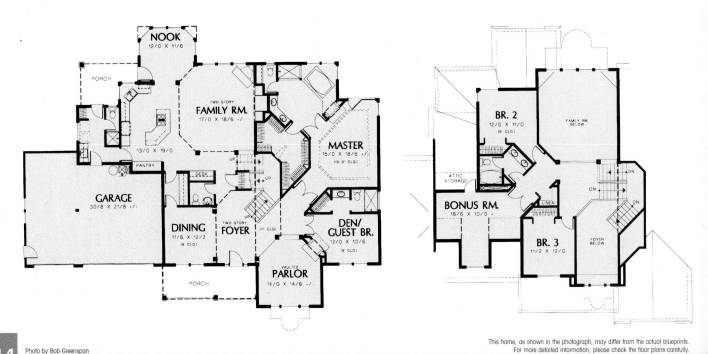

Photo by Bob Greenspan

This home, as shown in the photograph, may differ from the actual blueprints. For more detailed information, please check the floor plans carefully.

Design HPT860012

Square Footage: 3,556
Width: 85'-0" **Depth:** 85'-0"

A beautiful curved portico provides a majestic entrance to this one-story home. To the left of the foyer is a den/bedroom with a private bath, ideal for use as a guest suite. The exquisite master suite features a see-through fireplace and an exercise area with a wet bar. The family wing is geared for casual living with a powder room/patio bath, a huge island kitchen with a walk-in pantry, a glass-walled breakfast nook and a grand family room with a fireplace and media wall. Two family bedrooms share a private bath.

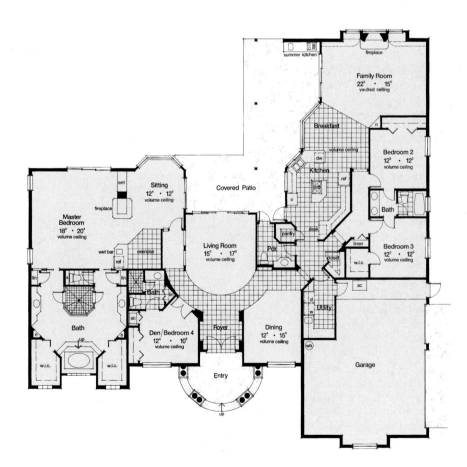

Photo by Oscar Thompson Photography

Design HPT860013

Square Footage: 4,565
Width: 88'-0" **Depth:** 95'-0"

L

A free-standing entryway is the focal point of this luxurious residence. It has an arch motif that is carried through to the rear using a gabled roof and a vaulted ceiling from the foyer out to the lanai. The kitchen, which features a cooktop island and plenty of counter space, opens to the leisure area with a handy snack bar. Two guest suites with private baths are just off this casual living area. The master wing is truly pampering, stretching the entire length of the home. The suite has a large sitting area, a corner fireplace and a morning kitchen. The bath features an island vanity, a raised tub with a curved glass wall overlooking a private garden, a sauna and separate closets. An exercise room has a curved glass wall and a pocket door to the study, where a wet bar is ready to serve up refreshment.

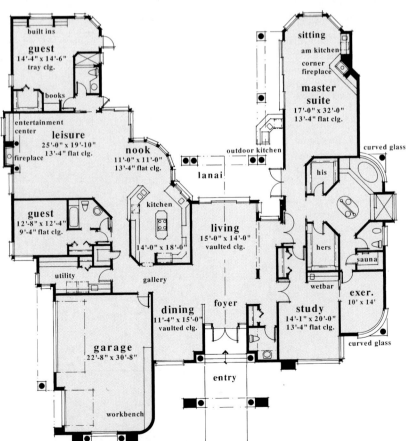

Design HPT860014

Living Quarters Square Footage: 659
Garage: 825 square feet
Width: 31'-0" **Depth:** 36'-0"

This compact home or guest house is perfect for guests or a cozy vacation retreat. The entrance is via the garage, where extra storage is provided for convenience. The living quarters reside on the second floor. A dining room is on the left side of the plan next to the kitchen, allowing for easy entertainment. To the right sits the bedroom, complete with a full bath and closet. The great room faces to the front of the plan and boasts a planter box outside its window. All rooms are vaulted, lending a spacious feel to this otherwise cozy cottage.

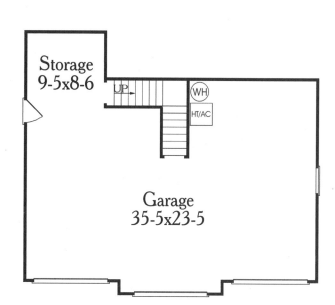

Storage
9-5x8-6

UP

WH

HT/AC

Garage
35-5x23-5

DN

Dining
9-4x13-0

Kitchen
9-11x9-3

Bedroom
10-0x13-0

Greatroom
12-5x12-4

Design HPT860016

Square Footage: 680
Unfinished Loft: 419 square feet
Width: 26'-6" **Depth:** 28'-0"

Full window walls bathe the living room and the dining room of this rustic vacation home with natural light. A full sun deck with a built-in barbecue sits just outside the living area and is accessed by sliding glass doors. The entire large living space has a vaulted ceiling to gain spaciousness and to allow for the full-height windows. The efficient U-shaped kitchen has a pass-through counter to the dining area and a corner sink with windows overlooking the side yard.

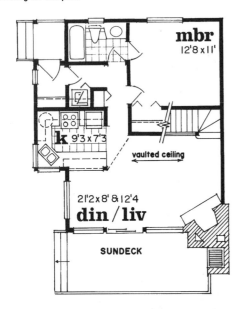

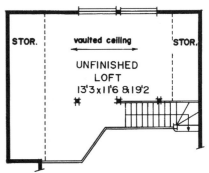

18

Design HPT860015

Square Footage: 834 (each side)
Width: 48'-0" **Depth:** 44'-0"

Two gables adorn the front of this fine duplex, while inside, matching units offer a place to call home. The foyer opens directly into the living area where there is space for both a living room and a dining area. The open kitchen offers a cheerful pass-through to the dining area. Here, sliding glass doors access the side yard, letting natural light flood the area. Two bedrooms share a full hall bath which features both a shower as well as a tub. The one-car garage offers some storage for yard equipment. This home is designed with a basement foundation.

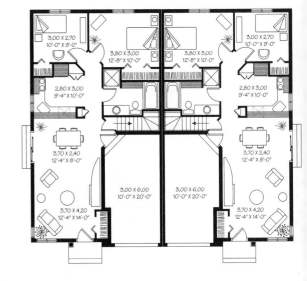

Design HPT860017

Square Footage: 920
Width: 38'-0" **Depth:** 28'-0"

Compact yet comfortable, this country cottage offers many appealing amenities. From a covered front porch that invites relaxed living, the entrance opens to the living room with access to the dining room and snack bar. Two bedrooms are secluded to the right of the plan; the kitchen, bathroom and laundry facilities are located on the left side. A second porch off the kitchen provides room for more casual dining and quiet moments. This home is designed with a basement foundation.

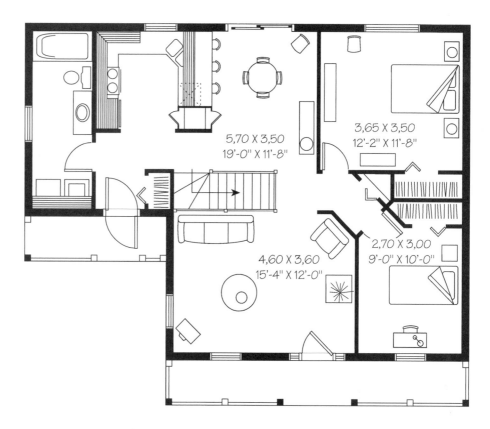

5,70 X 3,50
19'-0" X 11'-8"

3,65 X 3,50
12'-2" X 11'-8"

4,60 X 3,60
15'-4" X 12'-0"

2,70 X 3,00
9'-0" X 10'-0"

Design HPT860019

First Floor: 720 square feet
Second Floor: 203 square feet
Total: 923 square feet
Width: 32'-0" **Depth:** 38'-6"

The steeply pitched roof, shuttered windows and two full covered porches lend this two-bedroom plan great country charm. A warming fireplace, with windows on each side, is the focal point of the great room and the dining area. The master bedroom is located on the first floor and has direct access to the full bathroom. One family bedroom is nestled upstairs. Please specify basement, crawlspace or slab foundation when ordering.

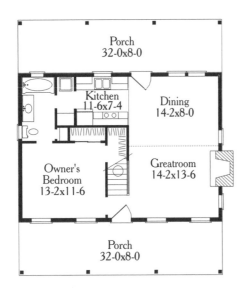

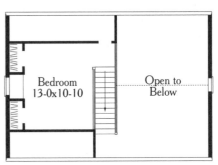

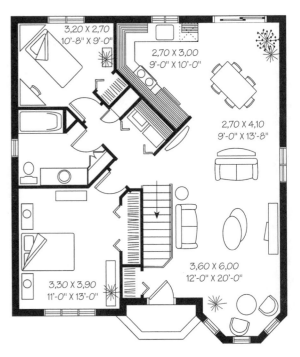

Design HPT860018

Square Footage: 972
Width: 30'-0" **Depth:** 35'-0"

An exciting floor plan makes this home a great starter. The living area is well lighted by windows in the turret and open to the dining area. A sliding door in the dining room leads to the backyard. An angled kitchen counter provides plenty of workspace. A master bedroom shares a full bath with one family bedroom. This home is designed with a basement foundation.

21

Design HPT860020

First Floor: 593 square feet
Second Floor: 383 square feet
Total: 976 square feet
Width: 22'-8" **Depth:** 26'-8"

A stunning arch-top window sets off this charming Cape Cod—perfect for a guest or vacation home. An angled entry and open planning allow a sense of spaciousness from the moment one enters the home. A voluminous bedroom on this floor adjoins a full bath. The staircase leads to a second-floor mezzanine, which overlooks the living area and may be used as a study area or an extra bedroom. This home is designed with a basement foundation.

2,80 X 3,10
9'-4" X 10'-4"

2,40 X 4,30
8'-0" X 14'-4"

3,90 X 3,60
13'-0" X 12'-0"

3,00 X 7,20
10'-0" X 24'-0"

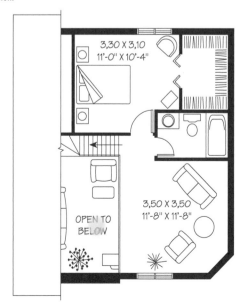

3,30 X 3,10
11'-0" X 10'-4"

3,50 X 3,50
11'-8" X 11'-8"

OPEN TO BELOW

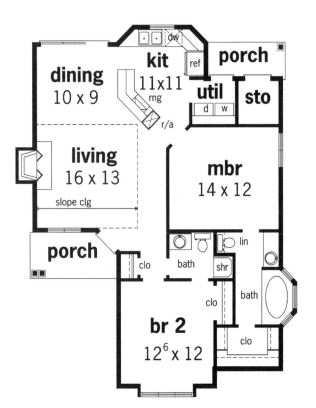

dining
10 x 9

kit
11x11
rng

porch

ref

util

d w

sto

living
16 x 13

slope clg

mbr
14 x 12

porch

clo

bath

lin

shr

bath

clo

clo

br 2
12⁶ x 12

clo

Design HPT860021

Square Footage: 984
Width: 33'-9" **Depth:** 43'-0"

This snug home uses space efficiently, with no wasted square feet. Brightened by a clerestory window, the living room features a sloped ceiling and a warming fireplace. A spacious master suite enjoys a walk-in closet and a lavish bath with a garden tub set in a bay. The secondary bedroom has access to the hall bath. Wood trim and eye-catching windows make this home charming as well as practical. Please specify crawlspace or slab foundation when ordering.

Design HPT860022

First Floor: 672 square feet
Second Floor: 401 square feet
Total: 1,073 square feet
Width: 24'-0" **Depth:** 36'-0"

This chalet plan is enhanced by a steep gable roof, scalloped fascia boards and fieldstone chimney detail. The front-facing deck and covered balcony add to outdoor living spaces. The fireplace is the main focus in the living room, separating the living room from the dining room. One bedroom is found on the first floor, while two additional bedrooms are upstairs.

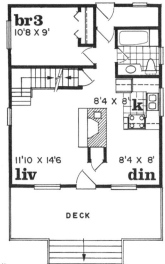

br3
10'8 x 9'

8'4 x 8'
k

11'10 x 14'6
liv

8'4 x 8'
din

DECK

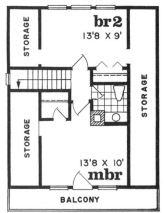

STORAGE

br2
13'8 x 9'

STORAGE

STORAGE

13'8 x 10'
mbr

BALCONY

Design HPT860023

First Floor: 814 square feet
Second Floor: 267 square feet
Total: 1,081 square feet
Width: 28'-0" **Depth:** 34'-6"

This plan easily fits into established neighborhoods, with a canted bay window, traditional trim and stucco finish. The entry leads into the living room which is complete with a warming hearth. A spacious kitchen offers a snack bar and convenient serving distance to the dining room. A second-floor bedroom with a bath overlooks the vaulted living room over a half-wall that can be finished off for more privacy. The appealing master suite features a sunny sitting area and walk-in closet. Please specify basement, crawlspace or slab foundation when ordering.

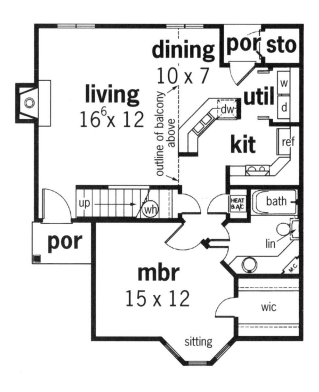

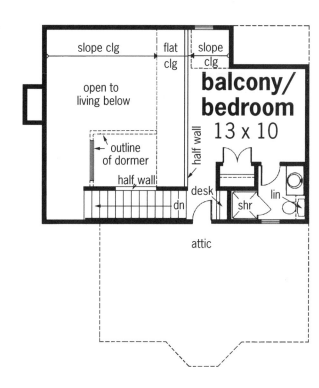

23

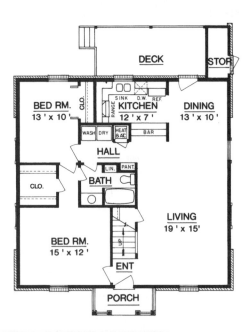

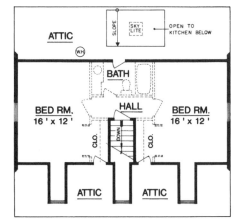

Design HPT860025

Square Footage: 1,088
Bonus Space: 580 square feet
Width: 34'-0" **Depth:** 44'-0"

The brick facade lends a rustic air to the general appearance of this cottage. The front door opens to a substantially large living room and dining room, which opens to a deck at the rear of the house. The U-shaped kitchen faces the dining room and sports a bar that overlooks the living area. Two bedrooms share a full bath—one enjoys a walk-in closet—on the first level. Upstairs, 580 square feet of unfinished space is perfect for a growing family's needs. Please specify crawlspace or slab foundation when ordering.

Design HPT860024

Square Footage: 1,150
Width: 38'-0" **Depth:** 52'-0"

A hipped roof and interesting angles give this compact home its charm. Inside, the entry leads to a galley kitchen with a breakfast bar. A dining/living room creates a feeling of spaciousness. The living room has a raised ceiling and opens to the backyard. The master suite is complete with a private bath and a sitting room for quiet contemplation. Please specify crawlspace or slab foundation when ordering.

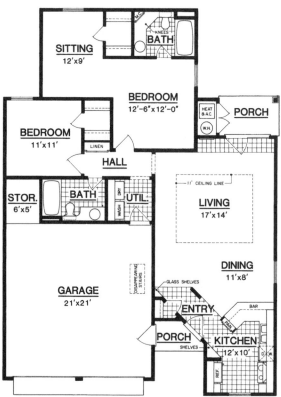

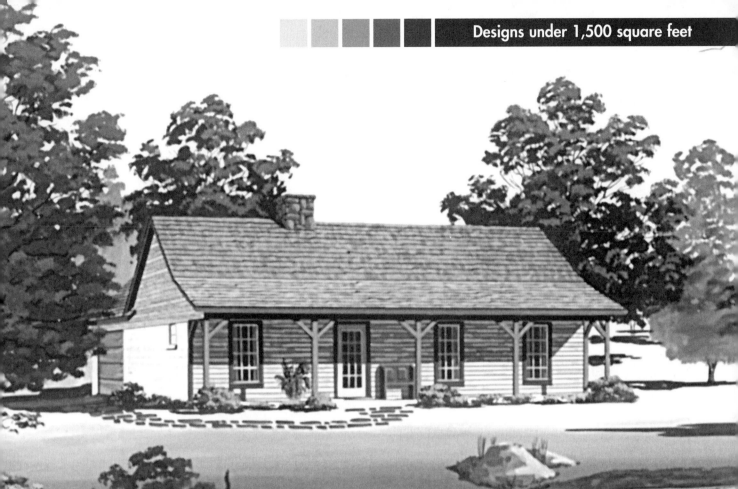

Design HPT860026

Square Footage: 1,191
Width: 44'-6" **Depth:** 59'-0"

A covered front porch gives this home country charm and makes family and guests feel welcome. Graced by a sloped ceiling and warmed by a stone fireplace, the living room provides the perfect gathering spot. The well-equipped kitchen easily serves the dining room, and adjoins a utility room that opens to the patio. The master suite offers an adjoining bath with a separate dressing area and double vanities. Two family bedrooms share a full bath. The two-car garage includes a large storage area. Please specify crawlspace or slab foundation when ordering.

GARAGE
22' x 21'

DISAPPEARING STAIRS

PATIO

STORAGE
11' x 5'

WASH.
W.H.   DRY.

UTILITY
11' x 5'

BATH

RANGE   SINK

REFRIGERATOR

DINING
12' x 12'

BEDROOM
12' x 10'

DRESS.

DISHWASHER
PANTRY   KITCHEN
BROOMS   12' x 10'

HEAT & A/C

LINEN

BATH

MASTER BEDROOM
16' x 12'

BEAM

FLAT CEILING

LIVING
18' x 16'

SLOPE CEILING

BEDROOM
12' x 10'

PORCH
42' x 5'

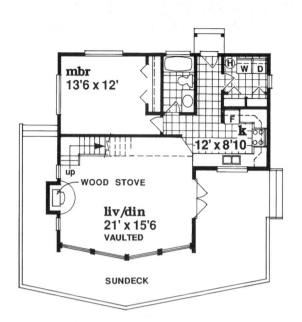

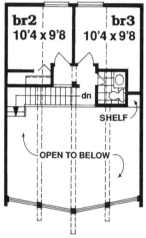

Design HPT860028

First Floor: 898 square feet
Second Floor: 358 square feet
Total: 1,256 square feet
Width: 34'-0" **Depth:** 32'-0"

A surrounding sun deck and expansive window wall capitalize on vacation-home views in this design. The full-height windows flood the living and dining room with abundant natural light and bring attention to the high vaulted ceilings. The efficient U-shaped kitchen has ample counter and cupboard space. The master bedroom sits on this floor and has a large wall closet and a full bath.

Design HPT860027

Square Footage: 1,266
Width: 40'-0" **Depth:** 64'-0"

This rustic Craftsman-style cottage provides an open interior with good outdoor flow. The front covered porch invites casual gatherings, while inside, the dining area is set for both everyday and planned occasions. A centered fireplace in the great room shares its warmth with the dining room. A rear hall leads to the master suite and a secondary bedroom, while an upstairs loft has space for computers. Please specify crawlspace or slab foundation when ordering.

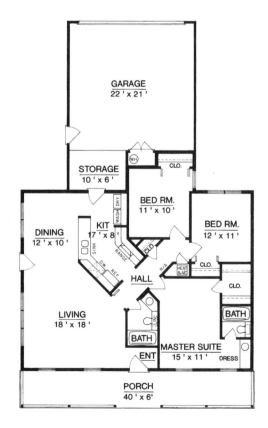

Design HPT860029

Square Footage: 1,287
Width: 66'-4" **Depth:** 48'-0"

This economical plan makes an impressive visual statement with its comfortable and well-proportioned appearance. The entrance foyer leads to all areas of the house. The great room, dining area and kitchen are all open to one another, allowing visual interaction. The great room and dining area share a dramatic cathedral ceiling and feature a grand fireplace flanked by bookshelves and cabinets. The master suite has a cathedral ceiling, walk-in closet and bath with double-bowl vanity, whirlpool tub and shower. Two family bedrooms and a full hall bath complete this cozy home.

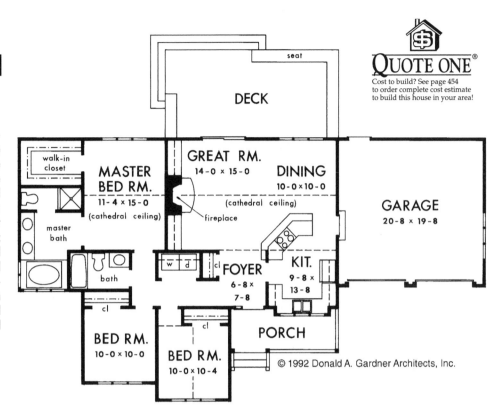

QUOTE ONE®
Cost to build? See page 454
to order complete cost estimate
to build this house in your area!

DECK

seat

GREAT RM.
14-0 × 15-0

DINING
10-0 × 10-0
(cathedral ceiling)

MASTER
BED RM.
11-4 × 15-0
(cathedral ceiling)

walk-in closet

master bath

fireplace

GARAGE
20-8 × 19-8

bath

cl

w d

cl

FOYER
6-8 ×
7-8

KIT.
9-8 ×
13-8

BED RM.
10-0 × 10-0

cl

BED RM.
10-0 × 10-4

cl

PORCH

© 1992 Donald A. Gardner Architects, Inc.

27

© 1992 Donald A. Gardner Architects, Inc.

B. NATHAN

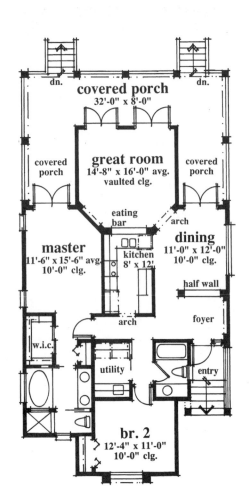

covered porch
32'-0" x 8'-0"

great room
14'-8" x 16'-0" avg.
vaulted clg.

covered porch

covered porch

eating bar

arch

dining
11'-0" x 12'-0"
10'-0" clg.

master
11'-6" x 15'-6" avg.
10'-0" clg.

kitchen
8' x 12'

half wall

foyer

arch

w.i.c.

utility

entry

br. 2
12'-4" x 11'-0"
10'-0" clg.

Design HPT860030

Square Footage: 1,288
Width: 32'-4" **Depth:** 60'-0"

Welcome home to casual, unstuffy living with this comfortable tidewater design. The heart of this home is the great room, where a put-your-feet-up atmosphere prevails, and the dusky hues of sunset can mingle with the sounds of ocean breakers. French doors open the master suite to a private area of the covered porch, where sunlight and sea breezes mingle with a spirit of *bon vivant*.

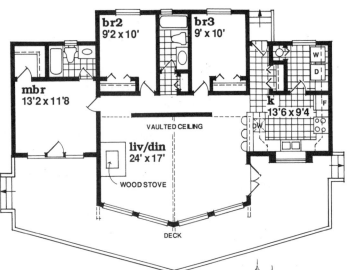

br2
9'2 x 10'

br3
9' x 10'

mbr
13'2 x 11'8

W
D

liv/din
24' x 17'

VAULTED CEILING

k
13'6 x 9'4

F

WOOD STOVE

DECK

The casual living space of this cozy home offers room to kick off your shoes or put on a bash, and is highlighted by a woodstove. The master suite nestles to the left of the living area and boasts a walk-in closet. Two secondary bedrooms allow space for guests and family members. The kitchen provides a snack counter.

Design HPT860031

Square Footage: 1,292
Width: 52'-0" **Depth:** 34'-0"

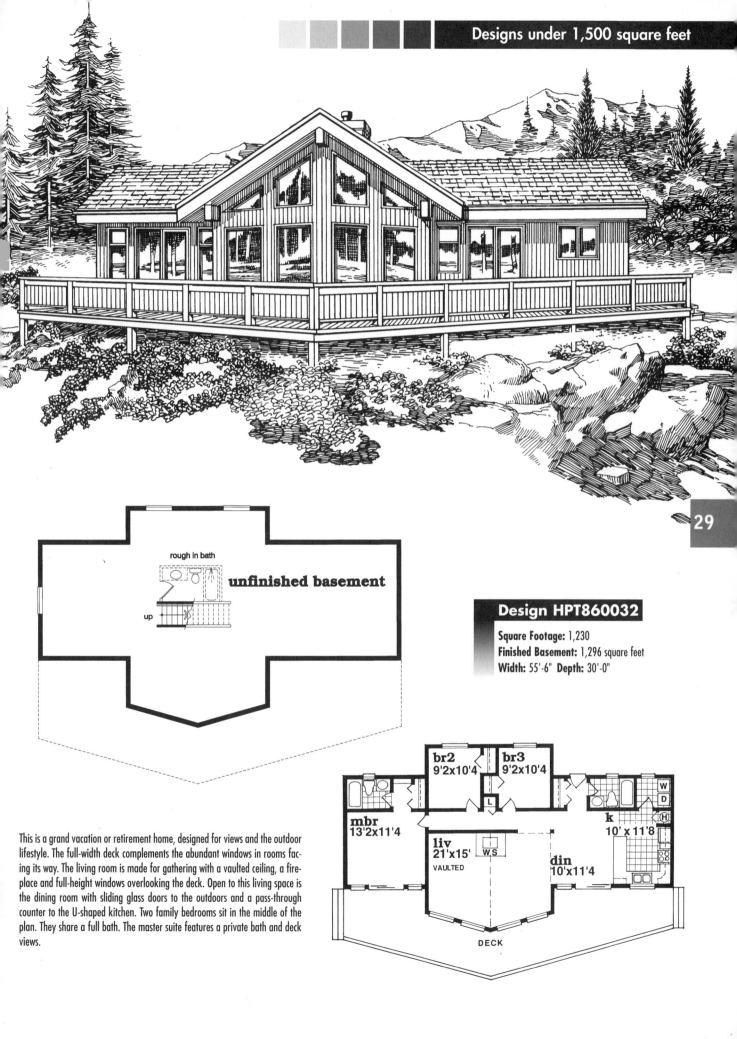

rough in bath

up

unfinished basement

Design HPT860032

Square Footage: 1,230
Finished Basement: 1,296 square feet
Width: 55'-6" **Depth:** 30'-0"

br2
9'2x10'4

br3
9'2x10'4

L

W
D

mbr
13'2x11'4

liv
21'x15'
VAULTED

W S

k
10' x 11'8

din
10'x11'4

H

DECK

This is a grand vacation or retirement home, designed for views and the outdoor lifestyle. The full-width deck complements the abundant windows in rooms facing its way. The living room is made for gathering with a vaulted ceiling, a fireplace and full-height windows overlooking the deck. Open to this living space is the dining room with sliding glass doors to the outdoors and a pass-through counter to the U-shaped kitchen. Two family bedrooms sit in the middle of the plan. They share a full bath. The master suite features a private bath and deck views.

Design HPT860033

Square Footage: 1,300 (each side)
Width: 76'-0" **Depth:** 55'-0"

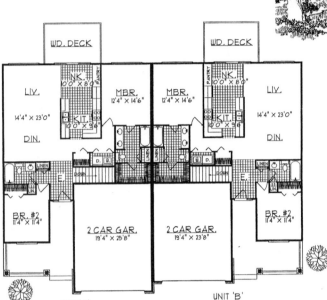

WD. DECK

NK.
10'0" X 8'0"

PANTRY

MBR.
12'4" X 14'6"

MBR.
12'4" X 14'6"

PANTRY

NK.
10'0" X 8'0"

WD. DECK

LIV.
14'4" X 23'0"

KIT.
10'0" X 9'6"

KIT.
10'0" X 9'6"

LIV.
14'4" X 23'0"

DIN.

DIN.

LINEN

LINEN

BR. #2
11'4" X 11'4"

2 CAR GAR.
19'4" X 25'8"

2 CAR GAR.
19'4" X 23'8"

BR. #2
11'4" X 11'4"

UNIT 'A'

UNIT 'B'

This attractive duplex is perfectly designed for the family just starting out, or the empty nesters who need less room now that the kids have grown and gone. A spacious living area encompasses both the living room as well as a dining area, and is conveniently located near the efficient kitchen. A wood deck is just outside the breakfast nook, providing a place for dining alfresco. The master bedroom is complete with a dual lavatory and walk-in closet. The front bedroom—or make it a cozy study—has a full bath and two linen closets available to it.

WASH   TUB   DRY

LAUNDRY
ROOM

CLOSET

D.W.   RANGE

KITCHEN & DINING
20'-0" x 8'-0"

SINK

SHOWER
BATH

REFRIG.

CLOSET

CLOSET

STORAGE

WH

LIVING ROOM
20'-0" x 19'-0"

RAILING

FIREPLACE

STONE

BEDROOM
11'-8" x 13'-0"

COATS

DN.

PORCH
36'-0" x 10'-0"

WOOD POSTS & RAILING

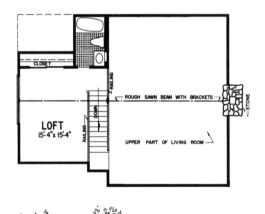

CLOSET

LOFT
15'-4" x 15'-4"

RAILING

DN.

RAILING

ROUGH SAWN BEAM WITH BRACKETS

UPPER PART OF LIVING ROOM

STONE

Quote One®

Cost to build? See page 454 to order complete cost estimate to build this house in your area!

Design HPT860034

First Floor: 1,036 square feet
Second Floor: 273 square feet
Total: 1,309 square feet
Width: 39'-0" **Depth:** 38'-0"

D

Like most vacation homes, this design features an open plan. The large living area includes a living room, a dining room and a massive stone fireplace. A partition separates the kitchen from the living room. The first floor also holds a bedroom, a full bath and a laundry room. Upstairs, a spacious sleeping loft overlooks the living room. Don't miss the large front porch—this will be a favorite spot for relaxing.

Design HPT860035

First Floor: 1,002 square feet
Second Floor: 336 square feet
Total: 1,338 square feet
Width: 36'-8" **Depth:** 44'-8"

A mountain retreat, this rustic home features covered porches at the front and rear. Enjoy open living in the great room and kitchen/dining room combination. Here, a fireplace provides the focal point and a warm welcome that continues into the L-shaped island kitchen. A cathedral ceiling graces the great room and gives an open, inviting sense of space. Two bedrooms—one with a walk-in closet—and a full bath on the first level are complemented by a master bedroom on the second floor. This suite includes a walk-in closet and deluxe bath. Attic storage is available on the second floor.

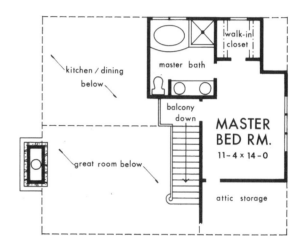

©1991 Donald A. Gardner Architects, Inc.

PORCH
33-8 × 8-0

KIT./
DINING
16-8 × 10-4

walk-in closet

BED RM.
11-4 × 10-0

w d

balcony above

bath

cl

(cathedral ceiling)

GREAT RM.
17-4 × 17-8

fireplace

cl

up

BED RM.
11-4 × 10-0

PORCH
33-8 × 8-0

kitchen / dining below

walk-in closet

master bath

balcony down

MASTER BED RM.
11-4 × 14-0

great room below

attic storage

31

©1991 Donald A. Gardner Architects, Inc.

© 1994 Donald A. Gardner Architects, Inc.

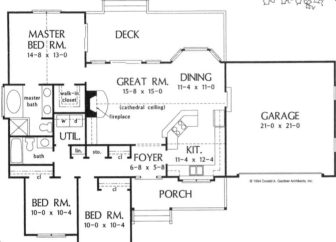

MASTER BED RM.
14-8 x 13-0

DECK

GREAT RM.
15-8 x 15-0

DINING
11-4 x 11-0

(cathedral ceiling)

master bath

walk-in closet

w d

fireplace

UTIL.

lin. sto. cl

GARAGE
21-0 x 21-0

KIT.
11-4 x 12-4

FOYER
6-8 x 5-8

bath

cl

BED RM.
10-0 x 10-4

cl

BED RM.
10-0 x 10-4

PORCH

© 1994 Donald A. Gardner Architects, Inc.

Design HPT860037

Square Footage: 1,346
Width: 65'-0" **Depth:** 44'-2"

A great room that stretches into the dining room makes this design perfect for entertaining. A cozy fireplace, stylish built-ins, and a cathedral ceiling further this casual yet elegant atmosphere. A rear deck extends living possibilities. The ample kitchen features an abundance of counter and cabinet space and an angled cooktop and serving bar that overlooks the great room. Two bedrooms, a hall bath and a handy laundry room make up the family sleeping wing while the master suite is privately located at the rear of the plan.

Design HPT860036

Square Footage: 1,347
Width: 42'-0" **Depth:** 54'-0"

From the ten-foot ceiling in the entry to the spacious great room with a fireplace, this plan expresses an open feeling. A snack bar and pantry in the kitchen complement the work area. To the left side of the plan are three bedrooms—two share a full bath. The master suite offers a box-bay window, built-in bookcase and tiered ceiling. The skylit dressing area features a double vanity, and there is a whirlpool spa in the bath.

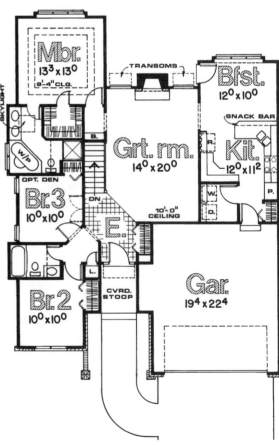

Mbr.
13³ x 13⁰
9'-4" CLG.

TRANSOMS

Bfst.
12⁰ x 10⁰

SNACK BAR

SKYLIGHT

Grt. rm.
14⁰ x 20⁰

Kit.
12⁰ x 11²

OPT. DEN

Br.3
10⁰ x 10⁰

DN

10'-0"
CEILING

W

D

P

Br.2
10⁰ x 10⁰

CVRD.
STOOP

Gar.
19⁴ x 22⁴

Design HPT860038

First Floor: 858 square feet
Second Floor: 502 square feet
Total: 1,360 square feet
Width: 35'-0" **Depth:** 29'-8"

This fine brick home features a bay-windowed sun room, perfect for admiring the view. Inside this open floor plan, a family room features a fireplace and a spacious eat-in kitchen with access to the sun room. A bedroom, full bath, and laundry facilities complete this floor. Upstairs there are two more bedrooms sharing a compartmented bath, as well as an overlook to the family room below. This home is designed with a basement foundation.

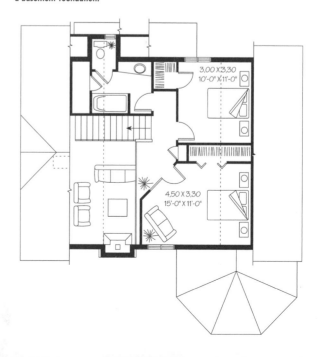

front elevation

Design HPT860039

Square Footage: 1,383
Width: 50'-0" **Depth:** 39'-0"

Three attractive gables, arch-topped windows and a covered porch add tons of charm to this fine ranch home. Inside, a vaulted ceiling in the great room and high glass windows on the rear wall combine to create an open, spacious feel. An open dining room sits just off the great room. The ample kitchen layout features a built-in pantry and easy access to the dining room. A generous walk-in closet is found in the master suite, along with a pampering bath. Two secondary suites share a hall bath. Please specify basement, slab or crawlspace foundation when ordering.

DECK/PATIO

DINING ROOM
11'-6" x 9'-4"

GREAT ROOM
16'-0" x 19'-0"

MASTER SUITE
15'-0" x 12'-0"

W.I.C.

KITCHEN
11'-6" x 11'-0"

PANT.

MASTER BATH

LAUN.

BATH

FOYER

SUITE 3
10'-0" x 10'-0"

GARAGE
20'-0" x 20'-0"

SUITE 2
11'-6" x 11'-4"

34

Design HPT860040

Square Footage: 1,389
Width: 44'-8" **Depth:** 54'-6"

L

Two elevations, one floor plan, what more could you ask? Simple rooflines and an inviting porch enhance the floor plan. A formal living room has a warming fireplace and a delightful bay window. The U-shaped kitchen shares a snack bar with the bayed family room. Note the sliding glass doors to the rear yard here. Three bedrooms include two family bedrooms served by a full bath and a lovely master suite with its own private bath.

QUOTE ONE®

Cost to build? See page 454
to order complete cost estimate
to build this house in your area!

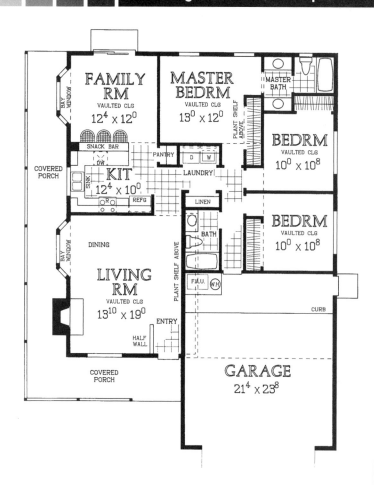

FAMILY RM
VAULTED CLG
12⁴ x 12⁰

MASTER BEDRM
VAULTED CLG
13⁰ x 12⁰

MASTER BATH

BAY WINDOW

PLANT SHELF ABOVE

SNACK BAR

PANTRY

D W

BEDRM
VAULTED CLG
10⁰ x 10⁸

COVERED PORCH

KIT
12⁴ x 10⁰

SINK

DW

REFG

LAUNDRY

LINEN

BATH

BEDRM
VAULTED CLG
10⁰ x 10⁸

BAY WINDOW

DINING

PLANT SHELF ABOVE

LIVING RM
VAULTED CLG
13¹⁰ x 19⁰

F.A.U. W.H.

CURB

ENTRY

HALF WALL

GARAGE
21⁴ x 23⁸

COVERED PORCH

alternate elevation

Design HPT860041

Square Footage: 1,395
Width: 73'-0" **Depth:** 37'-0"

Farmhouse meets Cape Cod and ranch style in this design. A welcoming covered porch leads through the foyer to the living room where classic country abounds with a beam ceiling and an expansive stone hearth with an efficient pass-through wood box. The formal dining room adjoins the kitchen where a snack bar facilitates casual eating. The master suite offers an elaborate private bath while two additional bedrooms share a second full bath. Please specify crawlspace or slab foundation when ordering.

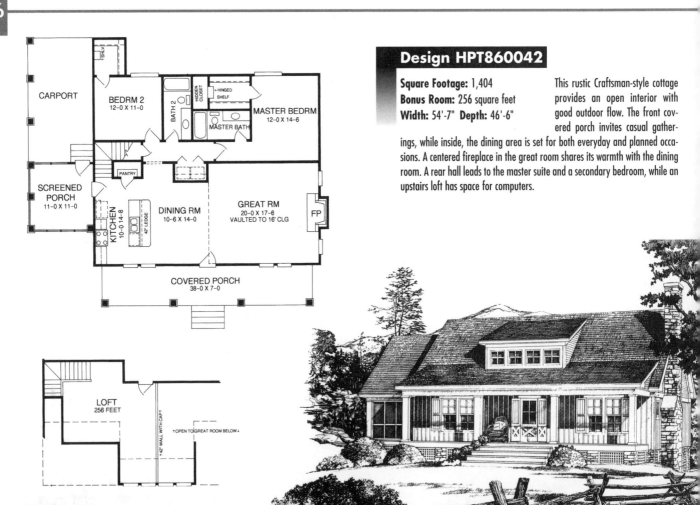

Design HPT860042

Square Footage: 1,404
Bonus Room: 256 square feet
Width: 54'-7" **Depth:** 46'-6"

This rustic Craftsman-style cottage provides an open interior with good outdoor flow. The front covered porch invites casual gatherings, while inside, the dining area is set for both everyday and planned occasions. A centered fireplace in the great room shares its warmth with the dining room. A rear hall leads to the master suite and a secondary bedroom, while an upstairs loft has space for computers.

Design HPT860043

Square Footage: 1,405
Width: 62'-0" **Depth:** 29'-0"

This three-bedroom leisure home is perfect for the family that spends casual time out of doors. An expansive wall of glass gives a spectacular view to the great room and accentuates the high vaulted ceilings throughout the design. The great room is also warmed by a wood stove and is open to the dining room and L-shaped kitchen. A triangular snack bar graces the kitchen and provides space for casual meals. Bedrooms are split, with the master bedroom on the right side of the plan and family bedrooms on the left.

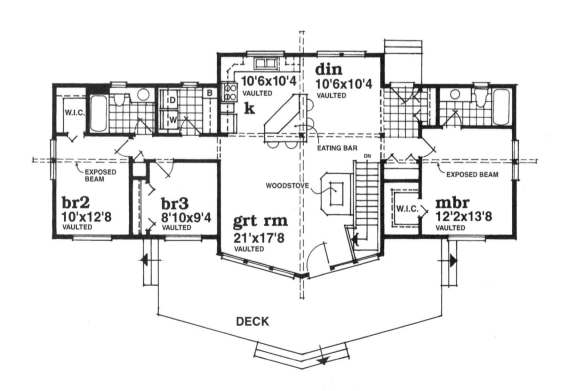

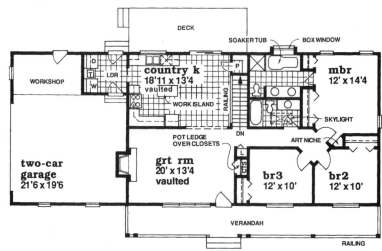

alternate master bath layout

Design HPT860045

Square Footage: 1,408
Width: 70'-0" **Depth:** 34'-0"

Vaulted ceilings lend a sense of spaciousness to this three-bedroom home. A bright country kitchen boasts an abundance of counter space and cupboards. The front entry is sheltered by a broad veranda. A box-bay window and a spa-style tub highlight the master bedroom. The two-car garage provides a workshop area.

DECK

SOAKER TUB   BOX WINDOW

WORKSHOP

LDR

country k
18'11 x 13'4
vaulted

mbr
12' x 14'4

WORK ISLAND

RAILING

SKYLIGHT

POT LEDGE
OVER CLOSETS

DN

ART NICHE

two-car garage
21'6 x 19'6

grt rm
20' x 13'4
vaulted

br3
12' x 10'

br2
12' x 10'

VERANDAH

RAILING

© 1987 Donald A. Gardner Architects, Inc.

Design HPT860044

Square Footage: 1,426
Width: 67'-6" **Depth:** 47'-8"

Rustic charm abounds in this amenity-filled, three-bedroom plan. From the central living area with its cathedral ceiling and fireplace to the sumptuous master suite, there are few features omitted. Two other bedrooms have a connecting bath with a vanity for each. The house wraps around a screened porch with skylights — a grand place for eating and entertaining. The spacious rear deck has plenty of room for a hot tub.

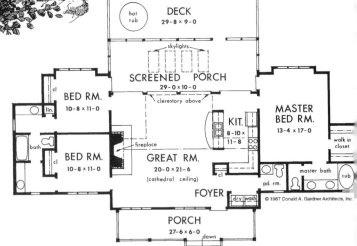

down

hot tub

DECK
29-8 x 9-0

skylights

BED RM.
10-8 x 11-0

SCREENED   PORCH
29-0 x 10-0

clerestory above

MASTER BED RM.
13-4 x 17-0

walk in closet

bath

fireplace

KIT.
8-10 x 11-8

BED RM.
10-8 x 11-0

GREAT RM.
20-0 x 21-6
(cathedral ceiling)

master bath

tub

pd. rm.

FOYER

dry   wash

© 1987 Donald A. Gardner Architects, Inc.

PORCH
27-6 x 6-0

down

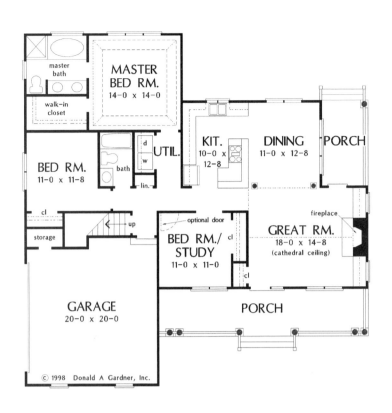

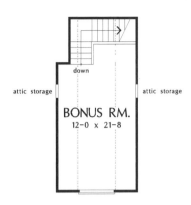

MASTER BED RM.
14-0 x 14-0

master bath

walk-in closet

BED RM.
11-0 x 11-8

UTIL.

bath

d w

lin.

KIT.
10-0 x 12-8

DINING
11-0 x 12-8

PORCH

cl

storage

up

optional door

BED RM./ STUDY
11-0 x 11-0

cl

cl

fireplace

GREAT RM.
18-0 x 14-8
(cathedral ceiling)

GARAGE
20-0 x 20-0

PORCH

© 1998 Donald A Gardner, Inc.

BONUS RM.
12-0 x 21-8

attic storage

attic storage

down

Design HPT860046

Square Footage: 1,428
Bonus Room: 313 square feet
Width: 52'-8" **Depth:** 52'-4"

Stunning arched windows framed by bold front-facing gables add to the tremendous curb appeal of this modest home. Topped by a cathedral ceiling and with porches on either side, the great room is expanded further by its openness to the dining room and kitchen. Built-ins flank the fireplace for added convenience. Flexibility, which is so important in a home this size, is found in the versatile bedroom/study as well as the bonus room over the garage. The master suite is positioned for privacy at the rear of the home, with a graceful tray ceiling, walk-in closet and private bath. An additional bedroom and a hall bath complete the plan.

© 1998 Donald A. Gardner, Inc.

Design HPT860047

Square Footage: 1,434
Width: 70'-0" **Depth:** 44'-0"

With the facade of a large, elegant home, this efficient design creates an exterior that looks much larger than it is. This plan includes formal and informal dining areas, both with direct access to the kitchen. A fireplace can be found in the living room. The isolated and spacious master suite provides a grand bath and a walk-in closet. The secondary bedrooms feature walk-in closets. The living room opens to porches via French doors to the front and back. Please specify crawlspace or slab foundation when ordering.

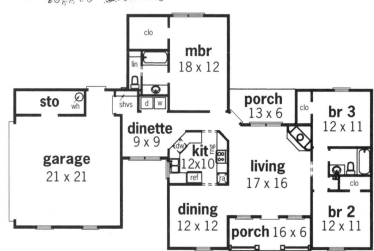

clo · mbr 18 x 12 · lin · sto · wh · shvs · d · w · dinette 9 x 9 · kit 12x10 · dw · ref · ra · garage 21 x 21 · dining 12 x 12 · living 17 x 16 · porch 13 x 6 · clo · br 3 12 x 11 · clo · br 2 12 x 11 · porch 16 x 6

Master Bedroom 13-2x15-3 · Greatroom 15-2x19-0 · Dining 9-4x10-0 · Storage 7-0x5-4 · Storage 13-0x5-0 · Kitchen 9-0x11-8 · Garage 20-4x22-0 · Bedroom 13-4x11-8 · Bedroom 12-2x13-9 · Laun. 9-0x5-5 · Porch 16-0x6-5

Ranch-style homes continue to be a popular choice all over the continent because of their casual, rustic appeal. This one is a classic, with a large great room with fireplace, a dining area and a galley-style kitchen. The two-car garage connects to the main home at an entry near the kitchen. This home features two storage areas in the two-car garage. The master bedroom features a private bath and walk-in closet. Please specify basement, crawlspace or slab foundation when ordering.

Design HPT860048

Square Footage: 1,441
Width: 67'-0" **Depth:** 34'-0"

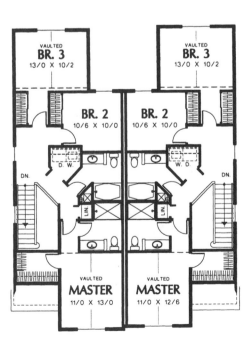

Design HPT860049

Total: 1,452 square feet (each side)
Width: 40'-0" **Depth:** 52'-6"

Two families fit nicely in this practical duplex plan in which each side is 20 feet wide and a mirror image of the other. Enter the home through the foyer or the garage to the open dining room/living room combination. The angled counter of the adjacent kitchen overlooks the living room, which has sliding doors to the outside. A powder room and two closets are also on the first floor. Upstairs, two family bedrooms share a hall bath and a walk-in closet. A linen closet and laundry facilities are located on this floor.

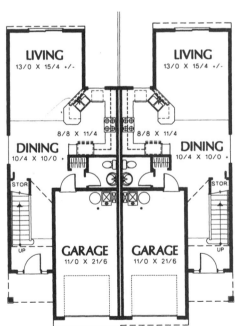

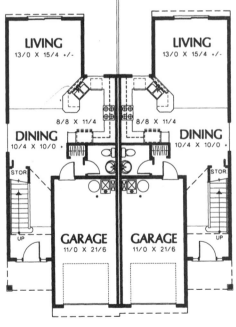

Design HPT860050

First Floor: 895 square feet
Second Floor: 565 square feet
Total: 1,460 square feet
Width: 38'-0" **Depth:** 36'-0"

12'-0" X 9'-0"

3.40 X 4.10
11'-4" X 13'-8"

7.40 X 3.70
24'-8" X 12'-4"

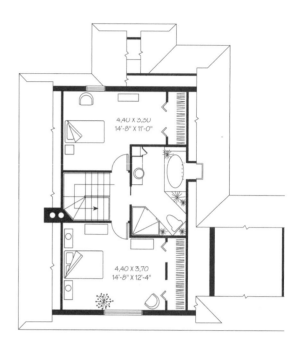

4.40 X 3.30
14'-8" X 11'-0"

4.40 X 3.70
14'-8" X 12'-4"

This four-season Cape Cod cottage is perfect for a site with great views. A sun room provides wide views and good indoor/outdoor flow. The living area boasts a corner fireplace. A well-organized kitchen serves a snack counter as well as the dining room. Upstairs, two spacious bedrooms share a lavish bath, which is complete with a separate tub and shower. This home is designed with a basement foundation.

Design HPT860051

First Floor: 895 square feet
Second Floor: 576 square feet
Total: 1,471 square feet
Width: 26'-0" **Depth:** 36'-0"

Here's a favorite waterfront home with plenty of space to kick back and relax. A lovely sun room opens from the dining room and allows great views. An angled hearth warms the living and dining areas. Three lovely windows brighten the dining space, which leads out to a stunning sun porch. The gourmet kitchen has an island counter with a snack bar. The first-floor master bedroom enjoys a walk-in closet and a nearby bath. Upstairs, a spacious bath with a whirlpool tub is thoughtfully placed between two bedrooms. A daylight basement allows a lower-level portico.

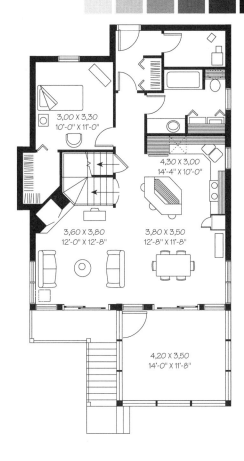

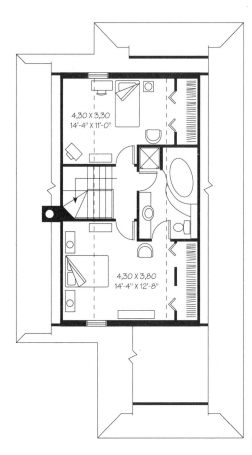

43

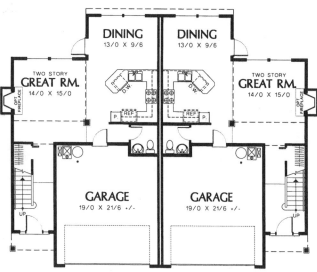

DINING
13/0 X 9/6

DINING
13/0 X 9/6

TWO STORY
GREAT RM.
14/0 X 15/0

TWO STORY
GREAT RM.
14/0 X 15/0

GARAGE
19/0 X 21/6 +/-

GARAGE
19/0 X 21/6 +/-

UP

UP

Design HPT860052

Total: 1,486 square feet (each side)
Width: 56'-0" **Depth:** 47'-0"

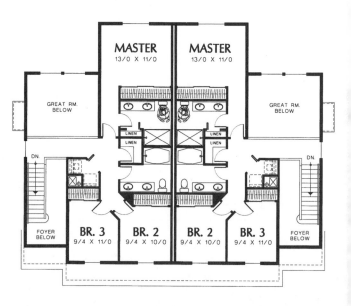

MASTER
13/0 X 11/0

MASTER
13/0 X 11/0

GREAT RM.
BELOW

GREAT RM.
BELOW

DN.

DN.

LINEN

LINEN

LINEN

LINEN

FOYER
BELOW

BR. 3
9/4 X 11/0

BR. 2
9/4 X 10/0

BR. 2
9/4 X 10/0

BR. 3
9/4 X 11/0

FOYER
BELOW

Symmetry pervades this efficient and comfortable two-story duplex. Inside each unit, a two-story great room offers a warming fireplace for those cool winter evenings. The dining room has easy access to the rear yard, as well as to the C-shaped kitchen. A powder room completes this level. Upstairs, the sleeping zone is made up of a walk-in linen closet, a master suite with a private bath, and two secondary bedrooms sharing a full hall bath that features a dual-bowl vanity.

Design HPT860053

Square Footage: 1,487
Width: 58'-0" **Depth:** 58'-0"

L

Stucco styling, elegant arches and a wealth of modern livability is presented in this compact one-story home. Inside, a great room with a vaulted ceiling opens to the lanai, offering wonderful options for either formal or informal entertaining. From the delightful kitchen savor the outdoors with a bay-window view of the lanai. Two secondary bedrooms (each with its own walk-in closet) share a full bath. Finally, enjoy the lanai from the calming master suite, which includes a pampering bath with a corner tub, separate shower and large walk-in closet.

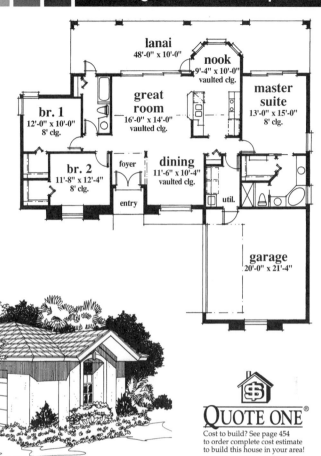

Quote One®

Cost to build? See page 454
to order complete cost estimate
to build this house in your area!

45

Design HPT860054

First Floor: 757 square feet
Second Floor: 735 square feet
Total: 1,492 square feet
Width: 47'-0" **Depth:** 42'-0"

The foyer announces the living and dining areas, defined by decorative columns. A kitchen serves both the breakfast area and the dining room. The great room opens to the rear property through a French door. The master suite provides a vaulted ceiling, garden tub with radius window, and walk-in closet. Each of two additional bedrooms offers a wide wardrobe. Please specify basement, crawlspace or slab foundation when ordering.

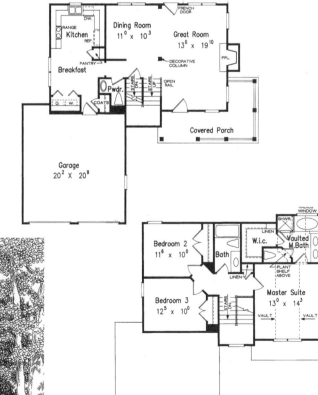

Design HPT860055

First Floor: 759 square feet
Second Floor: 735 square feet
Total: 1,494 square feet
Width: 22'-0"   **Depth:** 36'-0"

The charming front porch and the two-story turret welcome guests to this lovely home. The turret houses the living room on the first floor and the master suite on the second floor. The dining room is open to the living room and provides a box-bay window. The L-shaped kitchen features a breakfast room accessible to the backyard. A curved staircase next to the powder room leads upstairs to three bedrooms and a bath. Each family bedroom contains a walk-in closet. This home is designed with a basement foundation.

2,90 X 2,70
9'-8" X 9'-0"

3,30 X 2,70
11'-0" X 9'-0"

3,90 X 2,70
13'-0" X 9'-0"

3,50 X 4,80
11'-8" X 16'-0"

3,40 X 2,70
11'-4" X 9'-0"

3,50 X 3,30
11'-8" X11'-0"

3,50 X 4,50
11'-8" X 15'-0"

46

Design HPT860056

Square Footage: 1,495
Width: 58'-6" **Depth:** 33'-0"

This three-bedroom cottage has just the right rustic mix of vertical wood siding and stone accents. High vaulted ceilings are featured throughout the living room and master bedroom. The living room also has a fireplace and full-height windows overlooking the deck. The dining room has double-door access to the deck. A convenient kitchen includes a U-shaped work area with storage space.

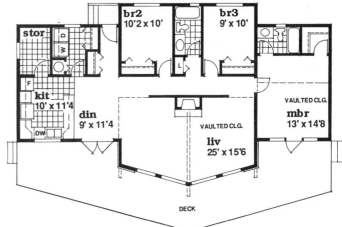

47

Design HPT860057

First Floor: 1,042 square feet
Second Floor: 456 square feet
Total: 1,498 square feet
Width: 36'-0" **Depth:** 35'-8"

With a deck to the front, this vacation home can't miss out on any outdoor fun. The living/dining room is dominated by a window wall that takes advantage of the view. A high vaulted ceiling and wood-burning fireplace create a warm atmosphere. The U-shaped kitchen, with an adjoining laundry room, is open to the dining room via a pass-through counter. Note the deck beyond the kitchen.

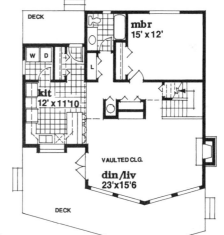

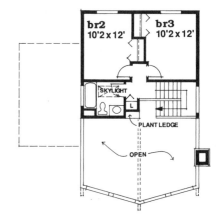

48

Design HPT860058

Square Footage: 1,498
Width: 59'-8" **Depth:** 50'-8"

This charming country home utilizes multi-pane windows, columns, dormers and a covered porch to offer a welcoming front exterior. Inside, the great room with a dramatic cathedral ceiling commands attention; the kitchen and breakfast room are just beyond a set of columns. The tier-ceilinged dining room presents a delightfully formal atmosphere for dinner parties or family gatherings. A tray ceiling in the master bedroom contributes to its pleasant atmosphere, as do the large walk-in closet and the gracious private bath with a garden tub and a separate shower. The secondary bedrooms are located at the opposite end of the house for privacy.

Design HPT860059

Square Footage: 1,500
Width: 59'-10" **Depth:** 44'-4"

A spacious interior is implied from the curb with the lofty, hipped rooflines of this economical family home. From the entry, the large living room is fully visible, as is the rear yard, through windows flanking the fireplace. The kitchen is partially open to the living room via a snack bar and offers full access to the breakfast room. A formal dining room just off the kitchen will serve entertaining needs with style. Please specify crawlspace or slab foundation when ordering.

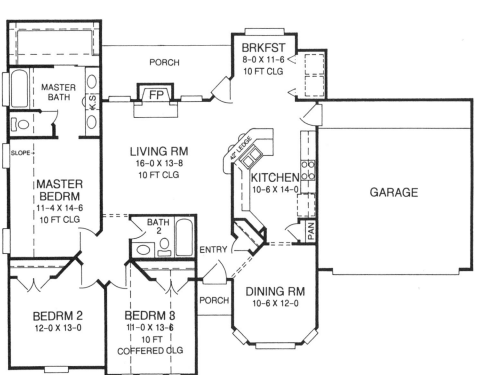

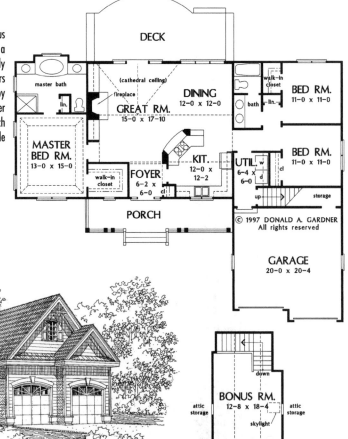

Design HPT860061

Square Footage: 1,508
Width: 60'-0" **Depth:** 47'-0"

Multiple gables and a cozy front porch welcome you to this enchanting one-level home. The grand openings between rooms create a spacious effect and the functional kitchen provides an abundance of counter space. Additional room for quick meals or serving an oversized crowd is provided at the breakfast bar. Double-hung windows and angles add light and dimension to the dining area. The bright and open floor plan of this three-bedroom ranch makes this home look and feel much larger than its actual size.

Porch

Dining Area
11'6" x 14'2"

Kitchen
18' x 10'10"

Great Room
16'6" x 17'

Master Bedroom
14' x 11'9"

Bath

Two-car Garage
20' x 22'

Foyer

Laun.

Bath   Hall

Porch

Bath

Bedroom
11' x 10'6"

Bedroom
10'6" x 10'6"

50

Design HPT860060

Square Footage: 1,517
Bonus Room: 287 square feet
Width: 61'-4" **Depth:** 48'-6"

The foyer opens to a spacious great room with a fireplace and a cathedral ceiling in this lovely traditional home. Sliding doors open to a rear deck from the great room, posing a warm welcome to enjoy the outdoors. The U-shaped kitchen features an angled peninsula counter with a cooktop. A private hall leads to the family sleeping quarters, which includes two bedrooms and a full bath with a double-bowl lavatory. Sizable bonus space above the garage provides a skylight.

DECK

master bath

(cathedral ceiling)

fireplace

GREAT RM.
15-0 x 17-10

DINING
12-0 x 12-0

walk-in closet

BED RM.
11-0 x 11-0

bath   lin.

MASTER BED RM.
13-0 x 15-0

KIT.
12-0 x 12-2

UTIL
6-4 x 6-0

BED RM.
11-0 x 11-0

w d

walk-in closet

FOYER
6-2 x 6-0

up   storage

PORCH

© 1997 DONALD A. GARDNER
All rights reserved

GARAGE
20-0 x 20-4

BONUS RM.
12-8 x 18-4

down

attic storage

attic storage

skylight

Design HPT860062

Square Footage: 1,520
Width: 40'-0" **Depth:** 59'-0"

Size doesn't always predict amenities! This one-story pier-foundation home is only 1,520 square feet, but it's packed with surprises. The spacious living room offers a huge wall of windows to show off the beach, while a fireplace offers warmth on cool winter evenings. The L-shaped kitchen features an angled work island and easily accesses the adjacent dining area. Three secondary bedrooms share a full bath and provide ample room for family or guests. The master bedroom is complete with a walk-in closet and a private bath. Please specify crawlspace or pier foundation when ordering.

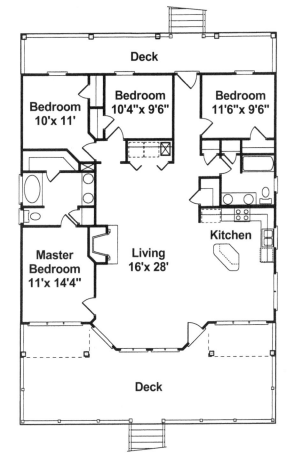

Deck

Bedroom
10'x 11'

Bedroom
10'4"x 9'6"

Bedroom
11'6"x 9'6"

Kitchen

Master
Bedroom
11'x 14'4"

Living
16'x 28'

Deck

51

Cost to build? See page 454 to order complete cost estimate to build this house in your area!

Design HPT860063

Square Footage: 1,541
Width: 87'-0" **Depth:** 44'-0"

This popular design begins with a wrap-around covered porch made even more charming with turned wood spindles. The entry opens directly into the great room, which is warmed by a woodstove. The adjoining dining room offers access to a screened porch for outdoor after-dinner leisure. A country kitchen features a center island and a breakfast bay for casual meals. Family bedrooms share a full bath that includes a soaking tub.

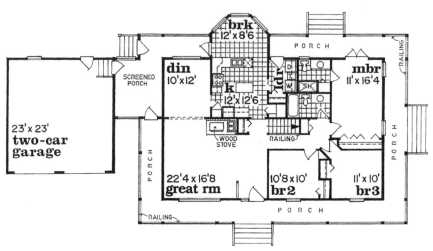

52

Design HPT860064

First Floor: 1,061 square feet
Second Floor: 482 square feet
Total: 1,543 square feet
Width: 28'-0" **Depth:** 39'-9"

A sun deck makes this design popular, but it is enhanced by views through an expansive wall of glass in the living and dining rooms. These rooms are warmed by a woodstove and enjoy vaulted ceilings as well. The kitchen is also vaulted and has a prep island and breakfast bar. Behind the kitchen is a laundry room with side-deck access. Two bedrooms and a full bath are found on the first floor. A skylit staircase leads up to the master suite and its walk-in closet and private bath on the second floor.

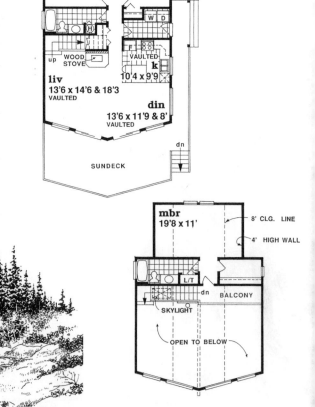

Floor Plan (HPT860066)

Bedroom 2
volume ceiling
11⁰ · 10⁰

Covered Patio
opt. summer kitchen

Master Bedroom
volume ceiling
15⁰ · 12⁰

Bath

m

opt. media center or fireplace

sh

Family Room
volume ceiling
16⁸ · 14⁴

w.i.c.

Bath

Bedroom 3
volume ceiling
11⁰ · 10⁰

pan

dw

ref

Kitchen
volume ceiling

w

d

ac

wh

Dining
11⁴ · 11⁰

Living Room
13⁶ · 11⁰
volume ceiling

ac

Double Garage

Foyer

Entry

Design HPT860066

Square Footage: 1,550
Width: 43'-0" **Depth:** 59'-0"

Enjoy resort-style living in this striking sun-country home. Guests will always feel welcome when entertained in the formal living and dining areas, but the eat-in country kitchen overlooking the family room will be the center of attention. Casual living will be enjoyed in the large family room and out on the patio with the help of an optional summer kitchen and view of the fairway. Built-in shelves and an optional media center provide decorating options. The master suite features a volume ceiling and a spacious master bath.

53

Design HPT860065

First Floor: 946 square feet
Second Floor: 604 square feet
Total: 1,550 square feet
Width: 37'-0" **Depth:** 30'-8"

This contemporary four-season cottage offers plenty of windows to take in great views. Excellent for gatherings, the living room boasts a cathedral ceiling and a cozy fireplace. The compartmented entry features a coat closet. The U-shaped kitchen includes a built-in pantry and accesses a side porch. Upstairs, two family bedrooms share a hall bath. A balcony hall leads to a sitting area with views of the front property. This home is designed with a basement foundation.

3,30 X 3,90
11'-0" X 13'-0"

8,00 X 4,00
26'-8" X 13'-4"

3,10 X 3,90
10'-4" X 13'-0"

3,10 X 3,90
10'-4" X 13'-0"

2,70 X 3,00
9'-0" X 10'-0"

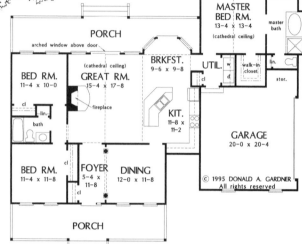

Design HPT860067

Square Footage: 1,561
Width: 60'-10" **Depth:** 51'-6"

Combining the finest country details with the most modern livability, this fine one-story home makes modest budgets really stretch. The entry foyer leads to a formal dining room defined by columns. Beyond it is the large great room with a cathedral ceiling and a fireplace. The kitchen and the breakfast room are open to the living area and include porch access. The master suite is tucked away in its own private space. It is conveniently separated from the family bedrooms which share a full bath. The two-car garage contains extra storage space.

54

Design HPT860068

Square Footage: 1,575
Width: 50'-0" **Depth:** 52'-6"

Gentle arched lintels harmonize with the high hip roof to create an elevation that is both welcoming and elegant. This efficient plan minimizes hallway space in order to maximize useable living areas. A favorite feature of this home is the "elbow-bend" galley kitchen that has easy access to the dining room and breakfast room—plus a full-length serving bar open to the great room. The master suite has a cozy sitting room and a compartmented bath. Two family bedrooms share a full hall bath. Please specify basement or crawlspace when ordering.

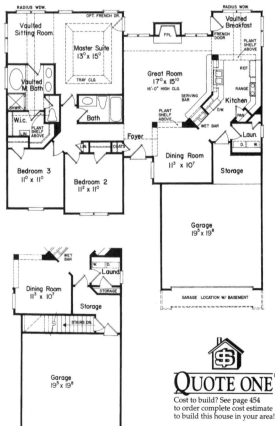

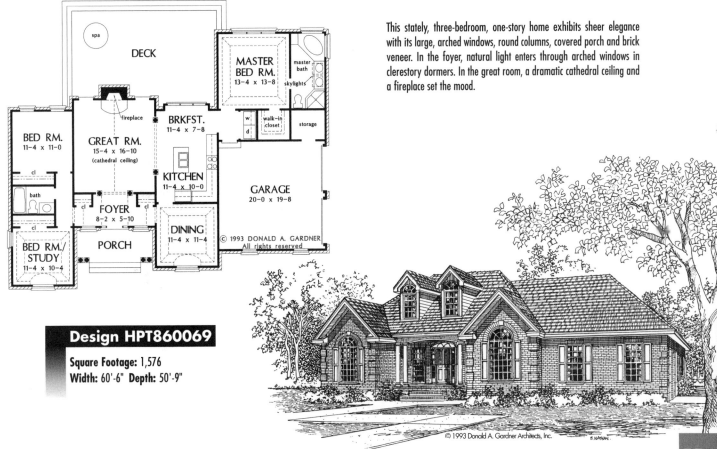

spa

DECK

MASTER BED RM.
13-4 x 13-8

master bath

skylights

BRKFST.
11-4 x 7-8

w d

walk-in closet

storage

fireplace

BED RM.
11-4 x 11-0

GREAT RM.
15-4 x 16-10
(cathedral ceiling)

cl

bath

cl

KITCHEN
11-4 x 10-0

FOYER
8-2 x 5-10

cl

GARAGE
20-0 x 19-8

BED RM./ STUDY
11-4 x 10-4

PORCH

DINING
11-4 x 11-4

This stately, three-bedroom, one-story home exhibits sheer elegance with its large, arched windows, round columns, covered porch and brick veneer. In the foyer, natural light enters through arched windows in clerestory dormers. In the great room, a dramatic cathedral ceiling and a fireplace set the mood.

Design HPT860069

Square Footage: 1,576
Width: 60'-6" **Depth:** 50'-9"

Design HPT860070

Square Footage: 1,593
Width: 60'-0" **Depth:** 48'-10"

This delightful ranch-style home offers excitement and convenience to the proud homeowner. The spacious foyer welcomes guests and introduces the great room with its corner fireplace, sloped ceiling and view to the rear yard. Separating the kitchen from the dining area is a large island with seating. An oversized pantry provides an abundance of storage space. The master bedroom has interesting ceiling details, a walk-in closet and a full bath. The two-car garage is also available for storage.

Dining
12'4" x 12'

Porch
11'4" x 10'9"

Master Bedroom
15'3" x 12
9' ceiling height

Great Room
18'2" x 17'

Kitchen
17'4" x 9'6"

Storage
7' x 14'8"

pantry

Bath

walk-in closet

Hall

Bath

Foyer

Laun.

Two-car Garage
20' x 22'

Bedroom
11' x 10'2"

Bedroom
10'6" x 11'

Porch

slope ceiling

slope ceiling

Design HPT860071

Square Footage: 1,600
Width: 75'-0" **Depth:** 37'-0"

Southern charm abounds in this one-story home with its covered porch, double dormers and combination of stone and siding. Inside, the entry opens to the living room with its beam-accented, vaulted ceiling and stone fireplace. The U-shaped kitchen adjoins the formal dining room where dividers offer privacy between the dining and living rooms. The master suite boasts a sitting room, walk-in closet and a private bath. On the left, two family bedrooms share a full bath. Please specify basement, crawlspace or slab foundation when ordering.

br 2 12 x 12
living 18 x 18
mbr 14 x 12
sitting
sto 11 x 9
beam
stone
vault
16' clg
6" drop floor
shv
garage 22 x 22
6" drop floor
divider
sew
util 9x8
br 3 12 x 12
dining 12 x 11
12x10 kit
ref
entry
porch 42 x 7
work bench
sto

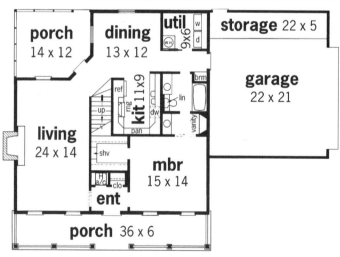

porch 14 x 12
dining 13 x 12
util 9x6
storage 22 x 5
kit 11x9
garage 22 x 21
living 24 x 14
mbr 15 x 14
ent
porch 36 x 6

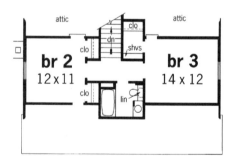

attic
br 2 12 x 11
br 3 14 x 12
attic

Design HPT860072

First Floor: 1,136 square feet
Second Floor: 464 square feet
Total: 1,600 square feet
Width: 58'-0" **Depth:** 42'-0"

This three-bedroom home is perfect for every family. A raised front porch introduces this home. The entry leads to the large living room with a warming fireplace and views of the front- and backyards. The U-shaped kitchen opens to the dining area. A first-floor master suite features private access to the entry and a luxurious bath with a separate shower and tub. Tucked on the second floor, two family bedrooms share a full bath and attic access. Please specify crawlspace or slab foundation when ordering.

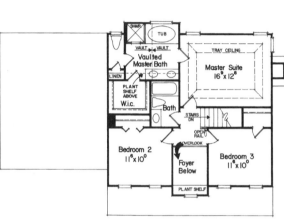

Design HPT860073

First Floor: 828 square feet
Second Floor: 772 square feet
Total: 1,600 square feet
Width: 52'-4" **Depth:** 34'-0"

Traditional farmhouse symmetry is apparent throughout this family plan. The formal dining and living rooms split off of the foyer; each has two multi-pane windows facing forward. The comfortable family room has a fireplace at the far end and a French door to the rear yard. Most notable is the spacious feeling that comes from the family room being open to the breakfast room and the kitchen. Upstairs, the master suite is detailed with a tray ceiling and a vaulted master bath. Two family bedrooms and a hall bath complete this plan. Please specify basement, slab or crawlspace foundation when ordering.

57

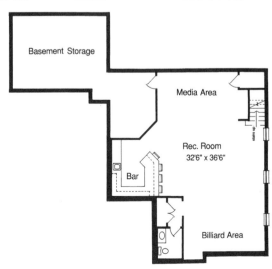

Design HPT860074

Square Footage: 1,601
Finished Basement: 990 square feet
Width: 55'-0" **Depth:** 54'-10"

This home's facade is a combination of brick, stone, and siding for interesting curb appeal. Ten-foot ceilings add volume to the great room and dining area. An impressive archway between these rooms creates the feeling of open spaciousness, while the master suite is kept separate from two secondary bedrooms for much needed privacy. The optional finished basement plan will tremendously increase playing spaces for family and guests.

Design HPT860075

Square Footage: 1,604
Width: 48'-8" **Depth:** 48'-0"

A thoughtful arrangement makes this uncomplicated three-bedroom plan comfortable. The living and working areas are grouped together for convenience—a great room with cathedral ceiling, dining room with wet bar pass-through and kitchen with breakfast room. The sleeping area features a spacious master suite with a skylit bath, whirlpool tub and large walk-in closet. Two smaller bedrooms accommodate the rest of the family. An alternate elevation is available at no extra cost.

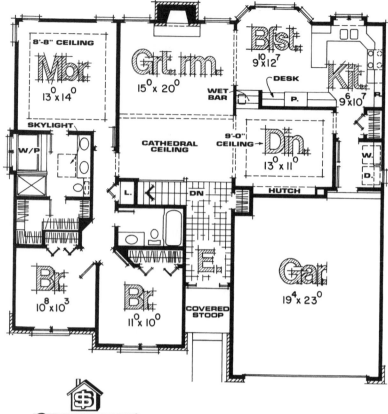

alternate elevation

QUOTE ONE®

Cost to build? See page 454
to order complete cost estimate
to build this house in your area!

Design HPT860076

First Floor: 1,027 square feet
Second Floor: 580 square feet
Total: 1,607 square feet
Width: 37'-4" **Depth:** 44'-8"

This economical, rustic, three-bedroom plan sports a relaxing country image with both front and back covered porches. The openness of the expansive great room to the kitchen/dining areas and the loft/study areas is reinforced with a shared cathedral ceiling for impressive space. The first floor provides two bedrooms, a full bath and a utility area. The master suite upstairs offers a walk-in closet and a whirlpool tub.

PORCH
34-4 × 8-0

KIT./DINING
18-0 × 11-8

bath

BED RM.
12-0 × 10-0

loft above

GREAT RM.
17-4 × 16-4

fireplace

up

BED RM.
12-0 × 12-4

PORCH
34-4 × 8-0

© 1992 Donald A. Gardner Architects, Inc.

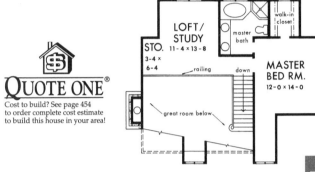

LOFT/STUDY
11-4 × 13-8

STO.
3-4 ×
6-4

walk-in closet

master bath

railing

down

MASTER BED RM.
12-0 × 14-0

great room below

Quote One®

Cost to build? See page 454 to order complete cost estimate to build this house in your area!

59

Design HPT860077

Square Footage: 1,611
Width: 66'-4" **Depth:** 43'-10"

A stone-and-siding exterior easily combines with the front covered porch on this three-bedroom ranch home. Inside, columns define the great room, which holds a warming fireplace framed by windows. The master bedroom enjoys a walk-in closet and a luxurious bath including a separate shower and a whirlpool tub. Two family bedrooms share a full bath and views of the front yard. Note the two-car side-access garage—perfect for a corner lot.

Dining
13' x 11'

Screened Porch
19' x 12'

Great Room
16' x 17'2"
48" HIGH WALL
10' CEILING HEIGHT

Master Bedroom
11'9" x 15'
10' CENTER CEILING HEIGHT

WALK-IN CLOSET

Two-Car Garage
20'8" X 21'

Kitchen
11' x 15'6"

Dressing

Foyer
10' CEILING HEIGHT

PANTRY

Laun.

Bath

Bedroom
10'8" x 11'6"

Porch

Bedroom
10'6" x 10'6"

© 1992 Donald A. Gardner Architects, Inc.

PORCH
34-6 × 8-0

KIT./ DINING
10-10 × 17-8

walk-in closet

w d

MASTER BED RM.
12-0 × 17-0

bedroom above

sto.

GREAT RM.
17-4 × 17-2

fireplace

up cl

master bath

PORCH
34-6 × 8-0

© 1992 Donald A. Gardner Architects, Inc.

Design HPT860078

First Floor: 1,039 square feet
Second Floor: 583 square feet
Total: 1,622 square feet
Width: 37'-9" **Depth:** 44'-8"

Charming and compact, this delightful two-story cabin is perfect for the small family or empty-nester. Designed with casual living in mind, the two-story great room is completely open to the dining area and the spacious island kitchen. The master suite is on the first floor for privacy and convenience. It features a roomy bath and a walk-in closet. Upstairs, two comfortable bedrooms—one includes a dormer window, the other features a balcony overlooking the great room—share a full hall bath.

BED RM.
12-6 × 13-8

bath

walk-in closet

closet

railing

down

BED RM.
12-0 × 15-8

great room below

60

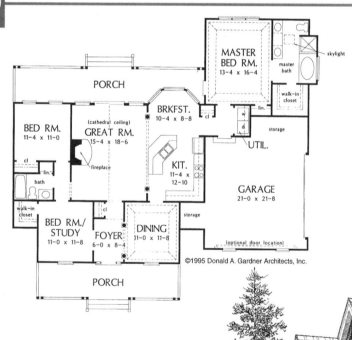

PORCH

MASTER BED RM.
13-4 × 16-4

skylight

master bath

walk-in closet

BRKFST.
10-4 × 8-8

cl

BED RM.
11-4 × 11-0

(cathedral ceiling)
GREAT RM.
15-4 × 18-6

fireplace

cl

lin.

w d

storage

UTIL.

KIT.
11-4 × 12-10

bath

walk-in closet

cl

BED RM./ STUDY
11-0 × 11-8

FOYER
6-0 × 8-4

DINING
11-0 × 11-8

storage

GARAGE
21-0 × 21-8

(optional door location)

PORCH

©1995 Donald A. Gardner Architects, Inc.

Design HPT860079

Square Footage: 1,632
Width: 62'-4" **Depth:** 55'-2"

This country home has a big heart in a cozy package. Special touches—interior columns, a bay window and dormers—add elegance. The central great room features a cathedral ceiling and a fireplace. A clerestory window splashes the room with natural light. The open kitchen easily services the breakfast area and the nearby dining room. The private master bedroom, with a tray ceiling and a walk-in closet, boasts amenities found in much larger homes. The bath features a skylight and a whirlpool tub. Two additional bedrooms share a bath. The front bedroom features a walk-in closet and would make a nice study with an optional foyer entrance.

QUOTE ONE®
Cost to build? See page 454
to order complete cost estimate
to build this house in your area!

© 1995 Donald A. Gardner Architects, Inc.

Design HPT860080

Square Footage: 1,633
Bonus Space: 595 square feet
Width: 65'-4" **Depth:** 55'-4"

This charming country home is ready to grow and change as the family's space needs evolve. For example, one of the two family bedrooms would make a fine study and the bonus room upstairs can be finished off to make a great game room or loft. A soaring cathedral ceiling and a cozy fireplace highlight the great room. The kitchen is thoughtfully set between the dining and breakfast rooms. The master bedroom features a walk-in closet.

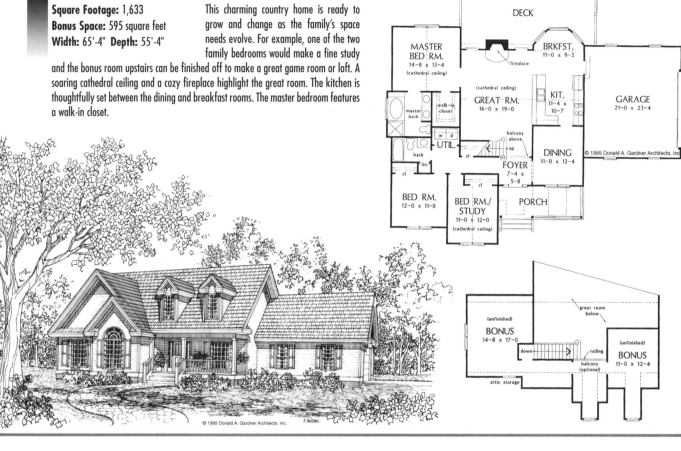

© 1995 Donald A. Gardner Architects, Inc.

© 1995 Donald A. Gardner Architects, Inc.   S. NATHAN

61

Design HPT860081

First Floor: 1,179 square feet
Second Floor: 460 square feet
Total: 1,639 square feet
Bonus Room: 350 square feet
Width: 41'-6" **Depth:** 54'-4"

With vaulted ceilings in the dining room and great room, a tray ceiling in the master suite and a sunlit two-story foyer, this inviting design offers a wealth of light and space. The counter-filled kitchen opens to a large breakfast area with backyard access. The first-floor master suite is complete with a walk-in closet and a pampering bath. Upstairs, two secondary bedrooms share a hall bath and access to an optional bonus room. Note the storage space in the two-car garage. Please specify basement or crawlspace foundation when ordering.

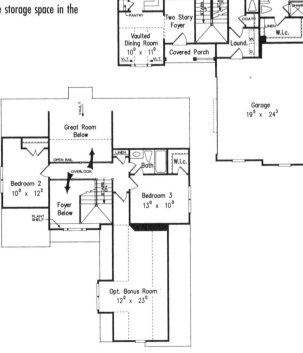

Design HPT860083

Square Footage: 1,643
Width: 62'-2" **Depth:** 51'-4"

Two covered porches lend a relaxing charm to this three-bedroom ranch home. Inside, the focal point is a warming fireplace with windows framing each side. The vaulted ceiling in the great room adds spaciousness to the adjoining kitchen and dining areas. A tray ceiling decorates the master suite, which also sports two walk-in closets. Two family bedrooms are located on the opposite side of the house. Please specify basement, crawlspace or slab foundation when ordering.

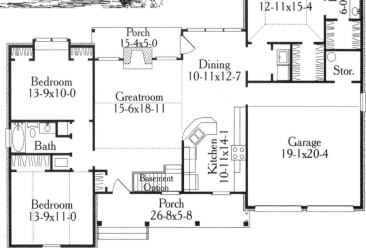

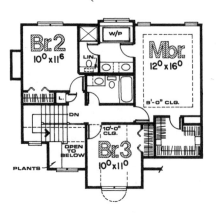

Design HPT860082

First Floor: 891 square feet
Second Floor: 759 square feet
Total: 1,650 square feet
Width: 44'-0" **Depth:** 40'-0"

This modestly sized home provides a quaint covered front porch that opens to a two-story foyer. The formal dining room features a boxed window that can be seen from the entry. A fireplace in the great room adds warmth and coziness to the attached breakfast room and the well-planned kitchen. A powder room is provided nearby for guests. Three bedrooms occupy the second floor; one of these includes an arched window under a vaulted ceiling. The deluxe master suite provides a large walk-in closet and a dressing area with a double vanity and a whirlpool tub.

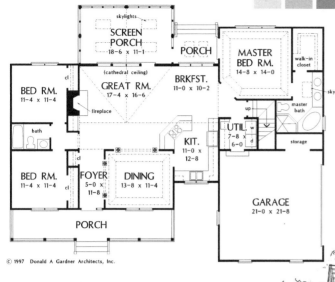

SCREEN PORCH
18-6 x 11-1

skylights

(cathedral ceiling)

PORCH

MASTER BED RM.
14-8 x 14-0

walk-in closet

skylight

GREAT RM.
17-4 x 16-6

BRKFST.
11-0 x 10-2

master bath

BED RM.
11-4 x 11-4

fireplace

up

BED RM.
11-4 x 11-4

UTIL.
7-8 x 6-0

storage

KIT.
11-0 x 12-8

FOYER
5-0 x 11-8

DINING
13-8 x 11-4

GARAGE
21-0 x 21-8

PORCH

© 1997 Donald A Gardner Architects, Inc.

BONUS RM.
14-0 x 21-8

down

attic storage

attic storage

skylights

Design HPT860084

Square Footage: 1,652
Bonus Room: 367 square feet
Width: 64'-4" **Depth:** 51'-0"

A classic country exterior enriches the appearance of this economical home, while its front porch and two skylit back porches encourage weekend relaxation. The great room features a cathedral ceiling and a fireplace with adjacent built-ins. The master suite enjoys a double-door entry, back-porch access and a tray ceiling. The master bath has a garden tub set in the corner, a separate shower, twin vanities and a skylight. Loads of storage, an open floor plan and walls of windows make this three-bedroom plan very livable.

© 1997 Donald A Gardner Architects, Inc

63

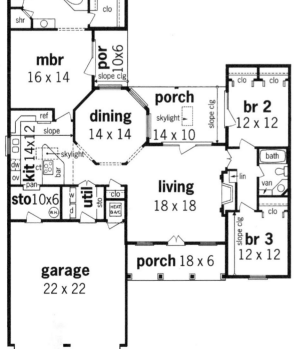

mbr
16 x 14

por
10x6

slope clg

bath

shv

clo

lin

shr

ref

slope

dining
14 x 14

porch

skylight

slope clg

br 2
12 x 12

clo clo

kit 14x12

skylight

bar

dw

ov

pan

bath

sto 10x6

util

sto

living
18 x 18

lin

van

clo

HEAT B A/C

clo

garage
22 x 22

porch 18 x 6

br 3
12 x 12

slope clg

Design HPT860085

Square Footage: 1,655
Width: 52'-0" **Depth:** 66'-0"

Elegantly arched doors and windows decorate the exterior of this fine home, which offers an intriguing floor plan. The living room features a soaring fifteen-foot ceiling and adjoins the octagonal dining room. Both rooms offer views of the skylit rear porch; a skylight also brightens the kitchen. The lavish master suite includes a walk-in closet, access to a small side porch and a full bath with a corner marble tub. Two additional bedrooms, thoughtfully placed apart from the master suite, share a full bath. Please specify crawlspace or slab foundation when ordering.

KURT KAUSS · ORLANDO

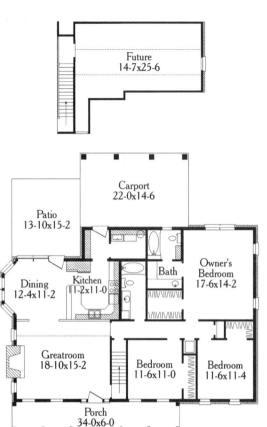

Future
14-7x25-6

Carport
22-0x14-6

Patio
13-10x15-2

Dining
12-4x11-2

Kitchen
11-2x11-0

Bath

Owner's
Bedroom
17-6x14-2

Greatroom
18-10x15-2

Bedroom
11-6x11-0

Bedroom
11-6x11-4

Porch
34-0x6-0

Design HPT860087

Square Footage: 1,656
Bonus Room: 427 square feet
Width: 52'-8" **Depth:** 54'-6"

Sit and watch the sunset on this relaxing front porch, or go inside for intimate conversations by the fireplace in the great room. A bay window in the dining area will adorn any meal with sun- or moonlight. A spacious master bedroom has a walk-in closet and a full bath. Two secondary bedrooms share a full bath with the main living areas. Please specify basement, crawlspace or slab foundation when ordering.

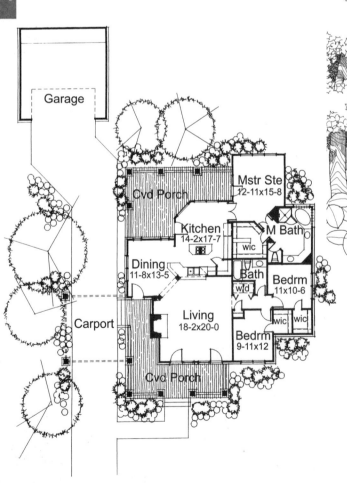

Garage

Cvd Porch

Mstr Ste
12-11x15-8

Kitchen
14-2x17-7

M Bath

wic

Dining
11-8x13-5

Bath

wld

Bedrm
11x10-6

Carport

Living
18-2x20-0

wic   wic

Bedrm
9-11x12

Cvd Porch

Design HPT860086

Square Footage: 1,657
Width: 64'-0" **Depth:** 58'-0"

Exposed rafters and stone-covered column supports hint at Craftsman style in this three-bedroom cottage. Two double doors access the living room from the covered front porch. Here, a fireplace warms the room. The dining room enjoys a wall of windows viewing the backyard and covered porch. A luxurious master suite also benefits from a private rear-porch door, and features a spacious bathroom. Two family bedrooms sharing a full bath include walk-in closets. Please specify basement, crawlspace or slab foundation when ordering.

Design HPT860089

First Floor: 1,375 square feet
Second Floor: 284 square feet
Total: 1,659 square feet
Width: 58'-0" **Depth:** 32'-0"

An expansive window wall across the great room of this home adds a spectacular view and accentuates the high ceiling. The open kitchen shares an eating bar with the dining room. Two family bedrooms sit to the back of the plan and share the use of a full bath. The master suite provides a walk-in closet and private bath. The loft on the upper level adds living or sleeping space.

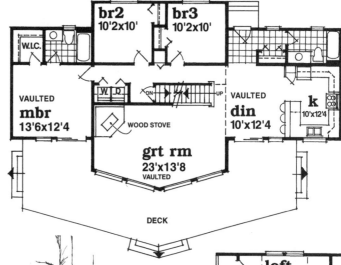

br2 10'2x10'
br3 10'2x10'
W.I.C.
VAULTED mbr 13'6x12'4
WOOD STOVE
grt rm 23'x13'8 VAULTED
VAULTED din 10'x12'4
k 10'x12'4
DECK

loft 15x16'10
STORAGE
STORAGE
42" HIGH WALL
DN
OPEN TO GREAT ROOM BELOW

65

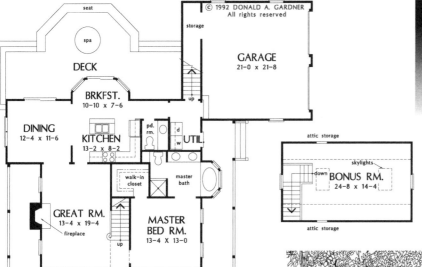

seat
spa
DECK
storage
GARAGE 21-0 x 21-8
BRKFST. 10-10 x 7-6
DINING 12-4 x 11-6
KITCHEN 13-2 x 8-2
pd. rm.
d w
UTIL.
up
walk-in closet
master bath
GREAT RM. 13-4 x 19-4
fireplace
MASTER BED RM. 13-4 X 13-0
up
PORCH

© 1992 DONALD A. GARDNER All rights reserved

at

attic storage
bath
attic storage
BED RM. 13-4 x 10-2
down
BED RM. 13-4 x 10-2
cl
cl
cl
cl

Design HPT860088

First Floor: 1,145 square feet
Second Floor: 518 square feet
Total: 1,663 square feet
Bonus Room: 380 square feet
Width: 59'-4" **Depth:** 56'-6"

Look this plan over and you'll be amazed at how much livability can be found in less than 2,000 square feet. A wraparound porch welcomes visitors to the home. Inside lies an enormous great room with a fireplace. To the rear of the home, the breakfast and dining rooms have sliding glass doors to a large deck with room for a spa. The master bedroom contains a walk-in closet and an airy bath with a whirlpool tub. Two bedrooms are found on the second floor, as well as a bonus room over the garage.

attic storage
skylights
down
BONUS RM. 24-8 x 14-4
attic storage

Quote One®
Cost to build? See page 454 to order complete cost estimate to build this house in your area!

© 1992 Donald A. Gardner Architects, Inc.

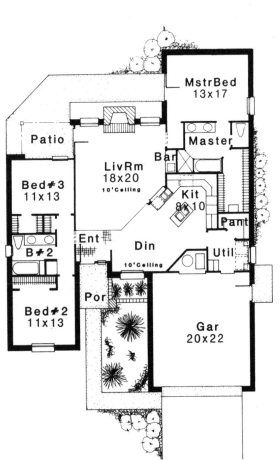

Patio

Bed #3
11x13

B #2

Bed #2
11x13

MstrBed
13x17

Master

LivRm
18x20
10'Ceiling

Bar

Kit
8x10

Pant

Ent

Din
10'Ceiling

Util

Por

Gar
20x22

Design HPT860091

Square Footage: 1,664
Width: 48'-0" **Depth:** 63'-1"

Soaring round-top windows lend excitement to the brick exterior of this traditional design. A living room with a fireplace flanked by windows opens to the kitchen and dining areas on the right and an appealing covered patio on the left. The master bedroom features double vanities and a walk-in closet. Two family bedrooms share a bath in the left wing. The utility area directly accesses the garage and a walk-in pantry.

66

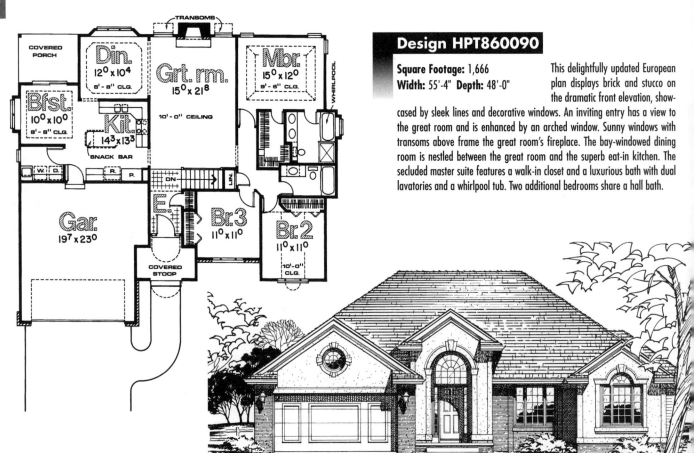

COVERED PORCH

TRANSOMS

Din.
12⁰ x 10⁴
8'- 8" CLG.

Grt. rm.
15⁰ x 21⁸
10'-0" CEILING

Mbr.
15⁰ x 12⁰
9'- 6" CLG.

WHIRLPOOL

Bfst.
10⁰ x 10⁰
8'- 8" CLG.

Kit.
14³ x 13³
SNACK BAR

W. D.

R. P.

DN.

LIN.

Gar.
19⁷ x 23⁰

Br. 3
11⁰ x 11⁰

Br. 2
11⁰ x 11⁰
10'-0" CLG.

COVERED STOOP

Design HPT860090

Square Footage: 1,666
Width: 55'-4" **Depth:** 48'-0"

This delightfully updated European plan displays brick and stucco on the dramatic front elevation, showcased by sleek lines and decorative windows. An inviting entry has a view to the great room and is enhanced by an arched window. Sunny windows with transoms above frame the great room's fireplace. The bay-windowed dining room is nestled between the great room and the superb eat-in kitchen. The secluded master suite features a walk-in closet and a luxurious bath with dual lavatories and a whirlpool tub. Two additional bedrooms share a hall bath.

Design HPT860092

First Floor: 731 square feet
Second Floor: 935 square feet
Total: 1,666 square feet
Lookout: 138 square feet
Width: 34'-0" **Depth:** 38'-0"

Perfect for a seaside abode, this pier-foundation home has an abundance of amenities to offer, not the least being the loft lookout. Here, with a 360-degree view, one can watch the storms come in over the water, or gaze with wonder on the colors of the sea. Inside the home just off the screened porch, the living room is complete with a corner gas fireplace. The spacious kitchen features a cooktop island, an adjacent breakfast nook and easy access to the dining room. From this room, a set of French doors leads out to a small deck—perfect for dining alfresco. Upstairs, the sleeping zone consists of two family bedrooms sharing a full hall bath, and a deluxe master suite.

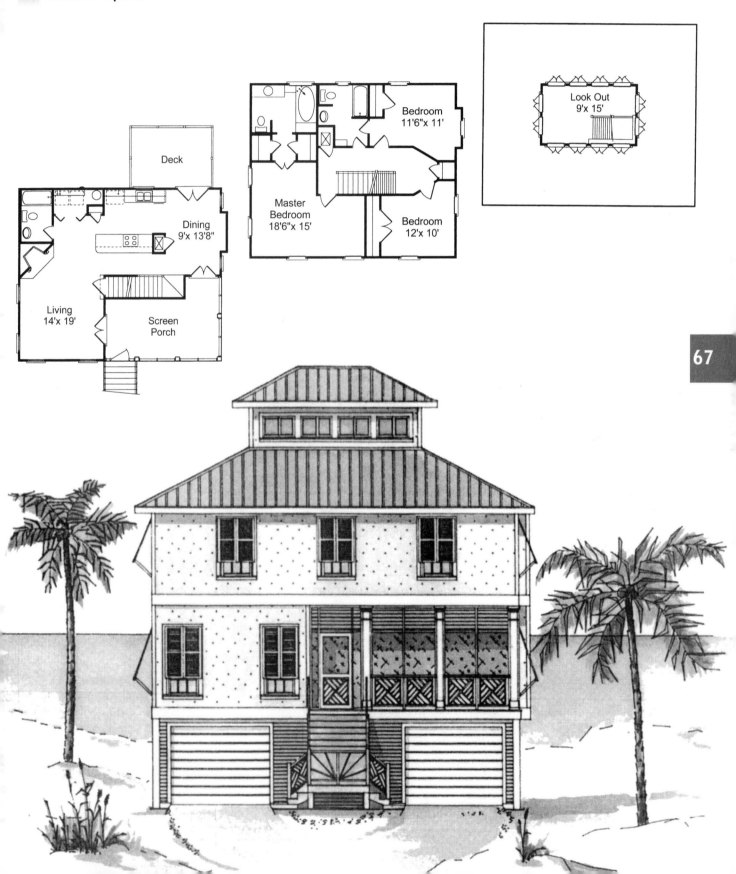

Deck

Dining
9'x 13'8"

Living
14'x 19'

Screen
Porch

Bedroom
11'6"x 11'

Master
Bedroom
18'6"x 15'

Bedroom
12'x 10'

Look Out
9'x 15'

67

QUOTE ONE®
Cost to build? See page 454
to order complete cost estimate
to build this house in your area!

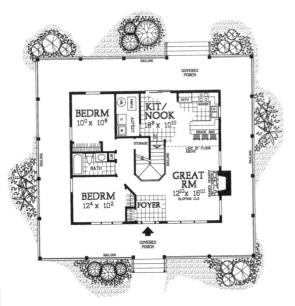

Design HPT860093

First Floor: 1,093 square feet
Second Floor: 576 square feet
Total: 1,669 square feet
Width: 52'-0" **Depth:** 46'-0"

L D

Here's a great country farmhouse with a lot of contemporary appeal. The generous use of windows—including two sets of triple muntin windows in the front—adds exciting visual elements to the exterior as well as plenty of natural light to the interior. An impressive tiled entry opens to a two-story great room with a raised hearth and views to the front and side grounds. The U-shaped kitchen conveniently combines with this area and offers a snack counter in addition to a casual dining nook with rear-porch access. The family bedrooms reside on the main level, while an expansive master suite with an adjacent study creates a resplendent retreat upstairs, complete with a private balcony, walk-in closet and bath.

68

Design HPT860094

Square Footage: 1,670
Width: 54'-0" **Depth:** 52'-0"

A grand front window display illuminates the formal dining room and the great room of this country French charmer. Open planning allows for easy access between the formal dining room, great room, vaulted breakfast nook and kitchen. Extra amenities include a decorative column, fireplace and an optional bay window in the breakfast nook. The elegant master suite is fashioned with a tray ceiling in the bedroom, a vaulted master bath and a walk-in closet. Two family bedrooms are designated in a pocket-door hall and share a large hall bath. Please specify basement, crawlspace or slab foundation when ordering.

QUOTE ONE®
Cost to build? See page 454
to order complete cost estimate
to build this house in your area!

optional basement stair location

Design HPT860095

First Floor: 1,093 square feet
Second Floor: 580 square feet
Total: 1,673 square feet
Width: 36'-0" **Depth:** 52'-0"

L **D**

Brackets and balustrades on front and rear covered porches spell old-fashioned country charm on this rustic retreat. In cooler weather, the raised-hearth fireplace will make the great room a cozy place to gather. Two family bedrooms and a full bath complete the main level. Upstairs, a master bedroom with a sloped ceiling offers a window seat and a complete bath. The adjacent loft/study overlooks the great room.

QUOTE ONE®

Cost to build? See page 454 to order complete cost estimate to build this house in your area!

69

Design HPT860096

First Floor: 1,093 square feet
Second Floor: 580 square feet
Total: 1,673 square feet
Width: 52'-0" **Depth:** 52'-0"

L **D**

Comfortable covered porches lead you into a home that's tailor-made for casual living. The foyer offers access to a front-facing great room with a raised-hearth fireplace. The great room then flows into the breakfast nook, with outdoor access, and on to the efficient kitchen. Two family bedrooms, a shared bath and a utility room complete the first floor. Curved stairs lead you to the upstairs master bedroom with its private balcony, large walk-in closet and amenity-filled bath.

QUOTE ONE®

Cost to build? See page 454 to order complete cost estimate to build this house in your area!

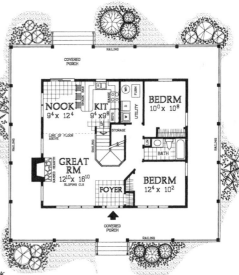

Design HPT860097

First Floor: 882 square feet
Second Floor: 793 square feet
Total: 1,675 square feet
Width: 49'-6" **Depth:** 35'-4"

This fetching country home features a second-floor room-to-grow option that is both savvy and stylish. The first floor's living area locates formal living spaces to the front of the design and casual living spaces to the rear. Upstairs, the master suite is enhanced with a private bath that contains a walk-in closet. Two secondary bedrooms share a full bath. Whether your preference is for the second-floor plan that includes a laundry room or the optional bonus room (which gains a walk-in closet, as does Bedroom 3), both provide deluxe accommodations. Please specify basement, crawlspace or slab foundation when ordering.

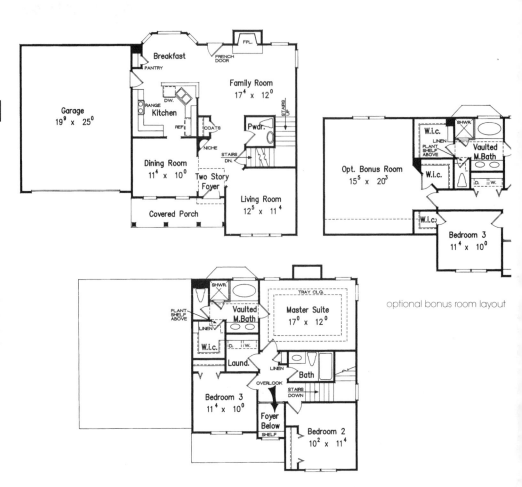

optional bonus room layout

Design HPT860098

Square Footage: 1,675
Width: 57'-5" **Depth:** 59'-6"

A fine brick presentation, this home boasts brick quoins, keystone lintels, muntin windows and a covered porch entryway. Sleeping quarters flank either end of the general living areas. On the right side of the plan are two family bedrooms, which share a full bath. On the left side, a vaulted master suite resides, complete with a garden tub and His and Hers sinks and walk-in closets. In the center of the plan is a large living room with a fireplace, a bayed nook with rear-deck access, a dining room with a pillared entrance, and a large kitchen. Storage space is provided just off the garage. Please specify basement, crawlspace or slab foundation when ordering.

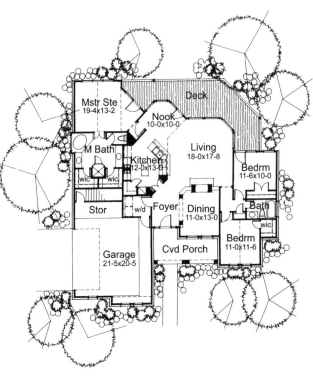

71

Design HPT860099

Square Footage: 1,675
Width: 63'-11" **Depth:** 54'-8"

A full porch of columns gives a relaxing emphasis to this country home. Inside, the great room has a cozy fireplace framed by windows. An open floor plan connects the great room, dining room and kitchen. The master suite boasts a wonderful view of the rear yard, as well as a compartmentalized bathroom with a garden tub and a separate shower. Please specify basement, crawlspace or slab foundation when ordering.

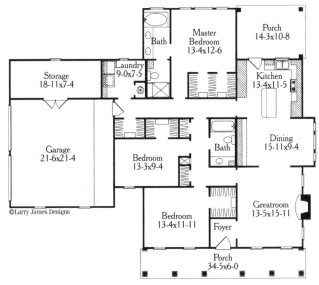

©Larry James Designs

Design HPT860101

First Floor: 1,125 square feet
Second Floor: 554 square feet
Total: 1,679 square feet
Width: 33'-9" **Depth:** 45'-0"

Three separate decks open this floor plan, creating numerous possibilities for entertaining and outdoor enjoyments. A large sun deck is found in the rear off the vaulted living room, and a second is found at the front entry, while both the dining area and the master suite open to a private balcony. An efficient L-shaped kitchen with an island workspace serves the dining area and screened deck with ease. Two bedrooms on the first floor share a full bath while the second floor is devoted solely to the master suite, which boasts twin walk-in closets, a double-sink vanity, raised tub and compartmented bath.

Design HPT860100

Square Footage: 1,680
Width: 62'-8" **Depth:** 59'-10"

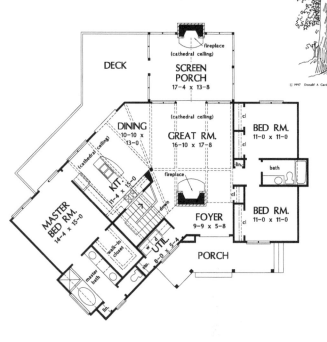

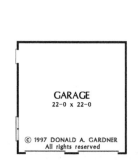

This rustic retreat is updated with contemporary angles and packs a lot of living into a small space. Start off with the covered front porch, which leads to a welcoming foyer. The beamed-ceiling great room opens directly ahead and features a fireplace, a wall of windows and access to the screened porch (with its own fireplace!) and is adjacent to the angled dining area. A highly efficient island kitchen is sure to please with tons of counter and cabinet space. Two family bedrooms, sharing a full bath, are located on one end of the plan while the master suite is secluded for complete privacy at the other end.

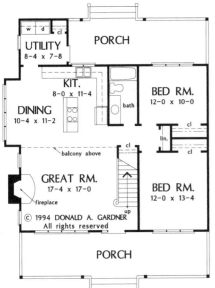

UTILITY
8-4 x 7-8

PORCH

KIT.
8-0 x 11-4

bath

BED RM.
12-0 x 10-0

DINING
10-4 x 11-2

cl
lin.
cl

balcony above

GREAT RM.
17-4 x 17-0

fireplace

BED RM.
12-0 x 13-4

up

© 1994 DONALD A. GARDNER
All rights reserved

PORCH

© 1994 Donald A. Gardner Architects, Inc.

LOFT/
STUDY
12-0 x 14-0

walk-in
closet

master
bath

MASTER
BED RM.
12-0 x 14-0

railing

down

great room
below

attic
storage

Quote One®
Cost to build? See page 454
to order complete cost estimate
to build this house in your area!

Design HPT860102

First Floor: 1,100 square feet
Second Floor: 584 square feet
Total: 1,684 square feet
Width: 36'-8" **Depth:** 45'-0"

A relaxing country image projects from the front and rear covered porches of this rustic three-bedroom home. Open planning extends to the great room, the dining room, and the efficient kitchen. A shared cathedral ceiling creates an impressive space. Completing the first floor are two family bedrooms, a full bath, and a handy utility area. The second floor contains the master suite featuring a spacious walk-in closet and a master bath with a whirlpool tub and a separate corner shower. A generous loft/study overlooks the great room below.

WORKSHOP/
STORAGE

FUTURE
FAMILY ROOM
14'-0" X 17'-6"

FUTURE
GAME ROOM
11'-4" X 1?'-6"

FUTURE
GUEST BEDROOM
11'-10" X 14'-6"

MECHANICAL

STOOP
ABOVE

UP.

FUTURE
BATH

STORAGE

SLAB ON GRADE

DECK

BREAKFAST
11'-4" X 8'-6"

BEDROOM NO. 3
11'-6" X 11'-0"

GREAT ROOM
14'-0" X 17'-6"

KITCHEN
11'-4" X 10'-0"

MASTER
BEDROOM
12'-4" X 15'-6"

BATH

FOYER
6'-6" X 5'-0"

HIS

BEDROOM NO. 2
11'-0" X 12'-2"

DINING ROOM
11'-4" X 10'-0"

PWDR.

MASTER
BATH

STOOP

DN.

LAUNDRY

HERS

HERS

TWO-CAR GARAGE
20'-4" X 19'-4"

Quote One®
Cost to build? See page 454
to order complete cost estimate
to build this house in your area!

Design HPT860103

Square Footage: 1,684
Basement: 1,684 square feet
Width: 55'-6" **Depth:** 57'-6"

Charming and compact, this one-story home is as beautiful as it is practical. The impressive arch over the double front door is repeated with an arched window in the formal dining room. This room opens to a spacious great room with fireplace and is near the kitchen and bayed breakfast area. Split sleeping arrangements put the master suite with His and Hers walk-in closets at the right of the plan and two family bedrooms at the left. This home is designed with a walkout basement foundation.

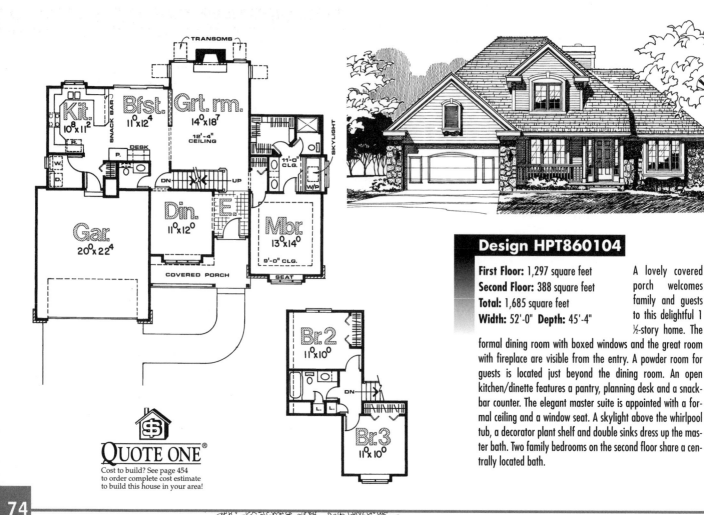

TRANSOMS

Kit.
10⁸x11²

Bfst.
11⁰x12⁴

SNACK BAR

Grt. rm.
14⁰x18⁷
12'-4" CEILING

DESK

SKYLIGHT

11'-0" CLG.

W/P

UP

DN

Gar.
20⁰x22⁴

Din.
11⁰x12⁰

Mbr.
13⁰x14⁰
9'-0" CLG.

SEAT

COVERED PORCH

Br. 2
11⁰x10⁰

DN

Br. 3
11⁰x10⁰

Design HPT860104

First Floor: 1,297 square feet
Second Floor: 388 square feet
Total: 1,685 square feet
Width: 52'-0" **Depth:** 45'-4"

A lovely covered porch welcomes family and guests to this delightful 1 ½-story home. The formal dining room with boxed windows and the great room with fireplace are visible from the entry. A powder room for guests is located just beyond the dining room. An open kitchen/dinette features a pantry, planning desk and a snack-bar counter. The elegant master suite is appointed with a formal ceiling and a window seat. A skylight above the whirlpool tub, a decorator plant shelf and double sinks dress up the master bath. Two family bedrooms on the second floor share a centrally located bath.

© 1996 Donald A. Gardner Architects, Inc.

Design HPT860105

Square Footage: 1,685
Bonus Room: 331 square feet
Width: 62'-4" **Depth:** 57'-4"

This lovely country home provides a powerful combination of well-defined formal rooms, casual living space and flexible areas. A foyer with a convenient coat closet leads to a spacious great room packed with amenities. Decorative columns announce the formal dining room, easily served by a gourmet kitchen, which boasts a breakfast area and bay window. The master bedroom offers a tray ceiling, a lovely triple window and a skylit bath. Bonus space above the garage features its own skylights and additional storage.

down

BONUS RM.
12-0 x 21-8

attic storage

skylights

skylight

**MASTER
BED RM.**
13-4 x 16-4

master bath

walk-in closet

PORCH

BED RM.
11-4 x 11-0

cl

GREAT RM.
15-4 x 18-6
(cathedral ceiling)

fireplace

BRKFST.
11-4 x 8-8

cl

w
d

up

storage

lin.

bath

walk-in closet

KIT.
11-4 x 12-10

GARAGE
21-0 x 21-8

cl

**BED RM./
STUDY**
11-0 x 11-8

FOYER
6-0 x
8-4

DINING
11-0 x 11-8

storage

PORCH

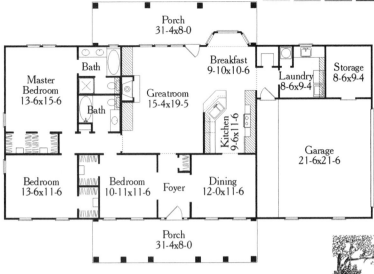

Design HPT860107

Square Footage: 1,688
Width: 70'-1" **Depth:** 48'-0"

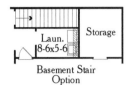

Laun. 8-6x5-6

Storage

Basement Stair
Option

Dormers and columns decorate the exterior of this three-bedroom country home. Inside, the foyer has immediate access to one family bedroom and the formal dining area. Ahead is the great room with a warming fireplace and ribbon of windows for natural lighting. The master suite is set to the back of the plan and has a lavish bath with a garden tub, separate shower and two vanities. Please specify basement, crawlspace or slab foundation when ordering.

This attractive facade presents hipped roofs, muntin windows with shutters, and a wide porch—perfect for relaxing or welcoming guests. The fireplace and built-in media center adds to the great room. Two family bedrooms occupy the right side of the plan, and share a full bath that includes a linen closet. Inside the master bedroom suite, a private bath includes a garden tub, separate shower and immense walk-in closet. Please specify basement, crawlspace or slab foundation when ordering.

Design HPT860106

Square Footage: 1,689
Width: 67'-0" **Depth:** 43'-0"

Basement
Stair Location

Owner's
Bedroom
13-2x14-3

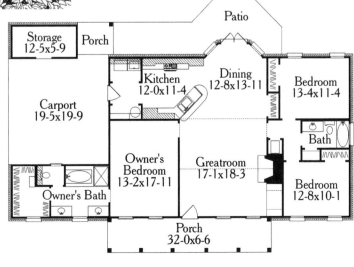

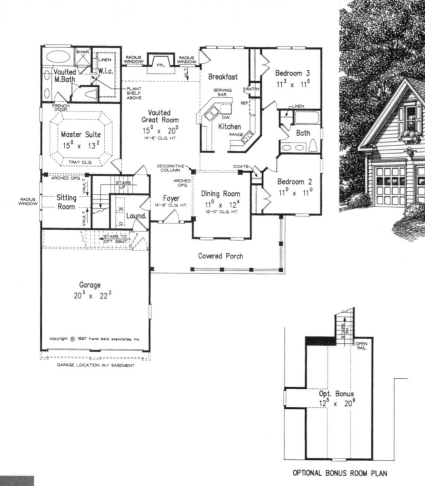

Master Suite
15⁰ x 13²
TRAY CLG.

Vaulted M.Bath

Vaulted Great Room
15⁰ x 20⁰
14'-6" CLG. HT.

Breakfast

Bedroom 3
11³ x 11⁰

Kitchen

Bath

Bedroom 2
11⁰ x 11⁰

Sitting Room

Foyer
14'-6" CLG. HT.

Dining Room
11⁰ x 12⁴
12'-0" CLG. HT.

Laund.

Covered Porch

Garage
20⁵ x 22²

copyright © 1997 frank betz associates, inc.

GARAGE LOCATION W/ BASEMENT

Opt. Bonus
12⁵ x 20⁹

OPTIONAL BONUS ROOM PLAN

Design HPT860109

Square Footage: 1,692
Bonus Room: 358 square feet
Width: 54'-0" **Depth:** 56'-6"

This cozy country cottage is enhanced with a front-facing planter box above the garage and a charming covered porch. The foyer leads to a vaulted great room, complete with a fireplace and radius windows. Decorative columns complement the entrance to the dining room, as does a decorative arch. The master suite includes a vaulted sitting room with a radius window. Please specify basement or crawlspace foundation when ordering.

Design HPT860108

First Floor: 780 square feet
Second Floor: 915 square feet
Total: 1,695 square feet
Width: 41'-0" **Depth:** 41'-0"

Columns, brickwork and uniquely shaped windows and shutters remind us of the best homes of turn-of-the-century America. The large fireplace, framed by windows, creates a lovely focal point in the great room. Upstairs, double doors lead to the lavish master suite, which features a tray ceiling. Bedrooms 2 and 3 complete this floor, with a shared bath featuring private entrances. This home is designed with a walk-out basement foundation.

QUOTE ONE®
Cost to build? See page 454 to order complete cost estimate to build this house in your area!

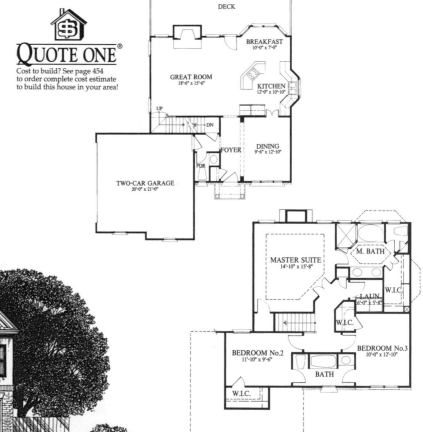

DECK

GREAT ROOM
18'-6" x 15'-6"

BREAKFAST
10'-0" x 7'-0"

KITCHEN
12'-0" x 10'-10"

FOYER

DINING
9'-6" x 12'-10"

PDR

UP

DN

TWO-CAR GARAGE
20'-0" x 21'-0"

MASTER SUITE
14'-10" x 15'-8"

M. BATH

W.I.C.

LAUN.
6'-0" x 5'-8"

W.I.C.

BEDROOM No.2
11'-10" x 9'-6"

BEDROOM No.3
10'-0" x 12'-10"

BATH

W.I.C.

Design HPT860111

Square Footage: 1,696
Width: 54'-0" **Depth:** 34'-0"

This convenient split-entry traditional home features a great room with a fireplace flanked by bookcases and a floor-to-ceiling view of the backyard. The efficient kitchen includes a sunny bay window in the breakfast area. Box ceilings grace both the breakfast nook and the formal dining room. The laundry room is strategically located near the sleeping wing. Two secondary bedrooms offer abundant closet space and a shared full bath. The deluxe master bedroom offers a vaulted ceiling, a large walk-in closet and a bath with a whirlpool tub.

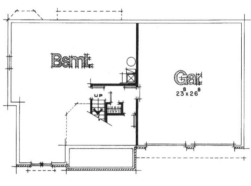

77

With sunny windows throughout and a wonderfully open living space, this plan appears larger than its modest square footage. The great room is highlighted with a corner window, a fireplace and a soaring ceiling. The dining room continues the open feeling and is easily served from the kitchen. A bayed nook complements the island kitchen that also has a stylish wraparound counter. The master bedroom suite has a lofty vaulted ceiling. Upstairs there are two family bedrooms that share a full hall bath—plus a bonus room that can be developed as needed.

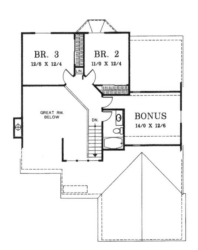

Design HPT860110

First Floor: 1,230 square feet
Second Floor: 477 square feet
Total: 1,707 square feet
Bonus Room: 195 square feet
Width: 40'-0" **Depth:** 53'-0"

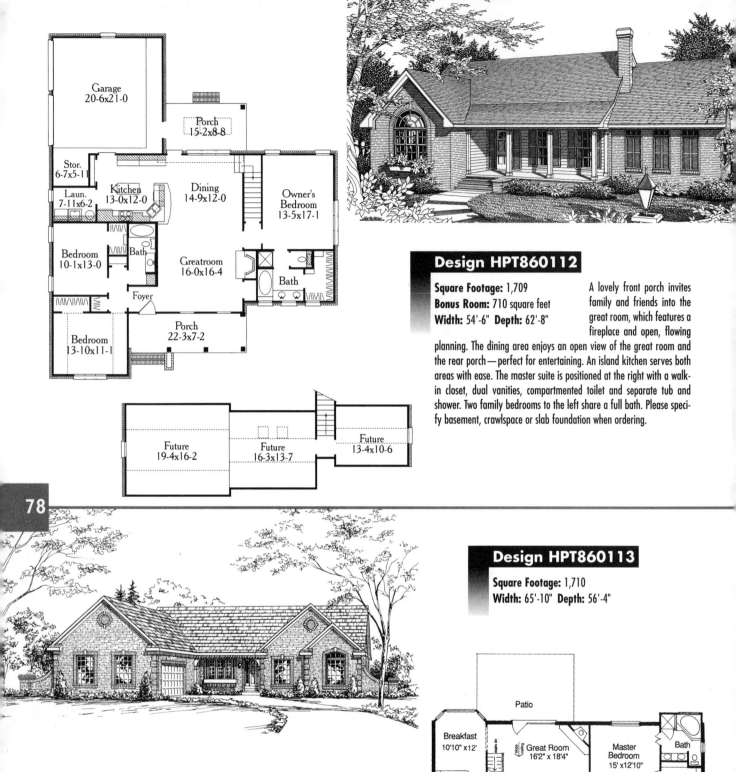

Garage
20-6x21-0

Porch
15-2x8-8

Stor.
6-7x5-11

Laun.
7-11x6-2

Kitchen
13-0x12-0

Dining
14-9x12-0

Owner's
Bedroom
13-5x17-1

Bedroom
10-1x13-0

Bath

Greatroom
16-0x16-4

Bath

Foyer

Bedroom
13-10x11-1

Porch
22-3x7-2

Future
19-4x16-2

Future
16-3x13-7

Future
13-4x10-6

Design HPT860112

Square Footage: 1,709
Bonus Room: 710 square feet
Width: 54'-6" **Depth:** 62'-8"

A lovely front porch invites family and friends into the great room, which features a fireplace and open, flowing planning. The dining area enjoys an open view of the great room and the rear porch—perfect for entertaining. An island kitchen serves both areas with ease. The master suite is positioned at the right with a walk-in closet, dual vanities, compartmented toilet and separate tub and shower. Two family bedrooms to the left share a full bath. Please specify basement, crawlspace or slab foundation when ordering.

78

Design HPT860113

Square Footage: 1,710
Width: 65'-10" **Depth:** 56'-4"

Brick and wood trim, multiple gables, and wing walls enhance the exterior of this one-level home. Sloped ceilings, a corner fireplace, windows across the rear of the great room, and a boxed window in the dining room are immediately visible as you enter the open foyer. The extra-large kitchen provides an abundance of counter space and a pantry. The breakfast area is surrounded by windows flooding the room with light. The size and amenities in the master bedroom offer a regal atmosphere to this private retreat.

Patio

Breakfast
10'10" x12'

Great Room
16'2" x 18'4"

Master
Bedroom
15' x12'10"

Bath

Kitchen
11'8" x 14' 4"

Dining Room
11' x 9'2"

Foyer

Hall

walk-in closet

Bath

Laun.

Porch

Bedroom
11' x 12'6"

Bedroom
12'6"x11'11"

Two-car Garage
22' x 20'8"

Design HPT860114

Square Footage: 1,715
Width: 55'-0" **Depth:** 51'-6"

A grand double bank of windows looking in on the formal dining room mirrors the lofty elegance of the extra-tall vaulted ceiling inside. From the foyer, an arched entrance to the great room visually frames the fireplace on the back wall. The wrap-around kitchen has plenty of counter and cabinet space, along with a handy serving bar. The luxurious master suite features a front sitting room for quiet times and a large spa-style bath. Two family bedrooms share a hall bath. Please specify basement, slab or crawlspace foundation when ordering.

Quote One®

Cost to build? See page 454 to order complete cost estimate to build this house in your area!

copyright © 1992 frank betz associates, inc.

79

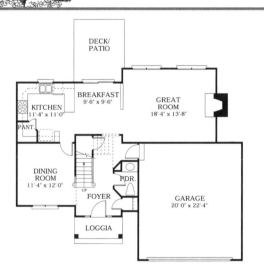

Design HPT860115

First Floor: 844 square feet
Second Floor: 875 square feet
Total: 1,719 square feet
Bonus Room: 242 square feet
Width: 45'-0" **Depth:** 37'-0"

A Palladian window adds interest to the modified gable roofline of this livable three-bedroom design. Columns and tall glass panels flank the covered entryway. A hall closet and a powder room line the foyer. The great room with its fireplace, the kitchen and the breakfast area with patio access are across the back. The master suite and two family bedrooms reside on the second floor. Please specify crawlspace or slab foundation when ordering.

Future
28-9x23-7

Garage
19-6x23-9

Patio
15-8x15-0

Porch
15-8x6-6

Breakfast
14-11x10-0

Laun.
8-4x7-3

Storage
6-5x7-3

Bedroom
10-9x12-9

Bath

Greatroom
15-6x19-5

Kitchen
12-3x11-0

Bath

Bath

Bedroom
13-0x12-0

Porch
21-11x8-0

Owner's Bedroom
13-0x15-2

Design HPT860117

Square Footage: 1,730
Bonus Room: 520 square feet
Width: 61'-0" **Depth:** 62'-0"

Three sets of double doors topped by fanlights provide a unique entry into this impressive home. The great room offers a wood-burning fireplace, a built-in entertainment center and French doors that open to a rear porch. Sleeping quarters are split, with a master suite in one wing and two family bedrooms in the other. This design is well-suited for a corner lot with its side-load garage. Please specify basement, crawlspace or slab foundation when ordering.

80

Design HPT860116

Main Level: 1,289 square feet
Lower Level: 443 square feet
Total: 1,732 square feet
Width: 43'-0" **Depth:** 40'-0"

Enter this multi-level home through the front door or through the garage on the lower floor. The family room, laundry room, powder room and unfinished space are also on the lower floor. Stairs from this level lead up to the living room, which features a vaulted ceiling and wonderful windows. Step down a few steps to the master suite with its private bath. Two family bedrooms share a bath. Please specify basement or slab foundation when ordering.

FAM. RM.
21'0" X 13'6"

UNFINISHED
18'0" X 29'8"

2 CAR GAR.
21'8" X 19'4"

W.H.

FURN

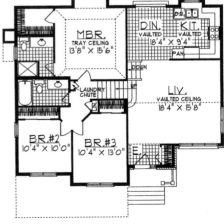

MBR
TRAY CEILING
13'8" X 15'6"

DIN.
VAULTED
18'4" X 9'4"

KIT.
VAULTED

LIV.
VAULTED CEILING
18'4" X 15'8"

LAUNDRY CHUTE

BR.#2
10'4" X 10'0"

BR.#3
10'4" X 13'0"

PORCH

BRKFST.
8-8 x 8-8

master bath

MASTER BED RM.
12-0 x 15-2

storage

GARAGE
20-4 x 24-4

KITCHEN
10-6 x 12-6

pantry

DINING RM.
12-8 x 12-0

walk-in closet

UTIL
7-8 x 8-10

d w

GREAT RM.
14-6 x 21-2
(cathedral ceiling)

fireplace

cl

cl

BED RM.
11-6 x 10-4

FOYER
8-4 x 6-8

skylights

bath

PORCH

cl

BED RM./ STUDY
11-4 x 12-0

(cathedral ceiling)

© 1994 Donald A. Gardner Architects, Inc.

Design HPT860119

Square Footage: 1,737
Width: 65'-10" **Depth:** 59'-8"

Inviting porches are just the beginning of this lovely country home. To the left of the foyer, a columned entry supplies a classic touch to a spacious great room that features a cathedral ceiling, built-in bookshelves and a fireplace that invites you to share its warmth. An octagonal dining room with a tray ceiling provides a perfect setting for formal occasions. The adjacent kitchen is designed to easily serve both formal and informal areas. It includes an island cooktop and a built-in pantry, with the sunny breakfast area just a step away. The master suite, separated from two family bedrooms by the walk-in closet and utility room, offers privacy and comfort.

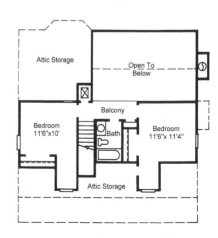

© 1994 Donald A. Gardner Architects, Inc.

Patio

Breakfast
8'10"x 11'5"

Utility

Living
20'6"x 14'

Kitchen
11'6"x 10'8"

1/2 Ba.

WIC

Dressing

Ba.

Dining
11'6"x 13'

Bedroom
11'6"x 11'4"

Porch
36'x 5'

Attic Storage

Open To Below

Balcony

Bedroom
11'6"x10'

Bath

Bedroom
11'6"x 11'4"

Attic Storage

Design HPT860118

First Floor: 1,238 square feet
Second Floor: 499 square feet
Total: 1,737 square feet
Width: 38'-4" **Depth:** 41'-0"

A nostalgic country style combined with modern livability sets this design apart from the rest. The living room, complete with a sloped ceiling and warming fireplace, opens to a bright, bay-windowed breakfast area. The nearby kitchen features wraparound cabinets and a sit-down bar. Guests will appreciate the convenient half-bath, just under the stairs. An impressive master suite, with a separate dressing area and a dual-sink vanity, opens just off the foyer. Upstairs, a balcony hall overlooks the spacious living area and connects two family bedrooms that share a bath. Please specify crawlspace or slab foundation when ordering.

Design HPT860121

Square Footage: 1,742
Width: 78'-0" **Depth:** 40'-10"

L

This traditional design welcomes family and visitors with a bay window, a Palladian window and shutters. The interior plan starts with the formal dining room and the central great room with a fireplace and access to outdoor spaces. The kitchen features an angled eating bar, a pantry and lots of cabinet and counter space. The master suite boasts a high ceiling, a deluxe bath and a walk-in closet with a window. Nearby, Bedrooms 2 and 3 share a hall bath. Please specify crawlspace or slab foundation when ordering.

82

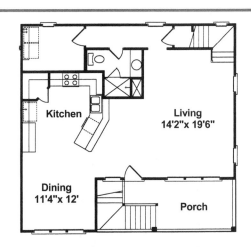

Design HPT860120

First Floor: 912 square feet
Second Floor: 831 square feet
Total: 1,743 square feet
Width: 34'-0" **Depth:** 32'-0"

With a pier foundation, this two-story home is perfect for an oceanfront lot. The main level consists of an open living area that flows into the dining area adjacent to the kitchen. Here, a walk-in pantry and plenty of counter and cabinet space will please the gourmet of the family. Upstairs, the sleeping zone is complete with two family bedrooms sharing a linen closet and a full hall bath, as well as a deluxe master bedroom.

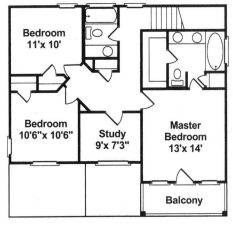

Design HPT860122

Square Footage: 1,745
Bonus Space: 741 square feet
Width: 72'-0" **Depth:** 47'-0"

This charming three-bedroom plan features plenty of amenities. A covered front porch welcomes guests to come inside and visit by the warming fireplace in the great room. The adjoining breakfast room glows with light from the bay window. Nearby, the kitchen includes a snack bar, organizing desk and access to a porch and deck—a perfect place for an outdoor barbecue. Two family bedrooms reside at the front of the house, shielding the master bedroom from any noise. The master suite enjoys a luxurious bath, walk-in closet and French-door access to a private porch. Two bonus rooms allow for expansion in the future. Please specify basement, crawlspace or slab foundation when ordering.

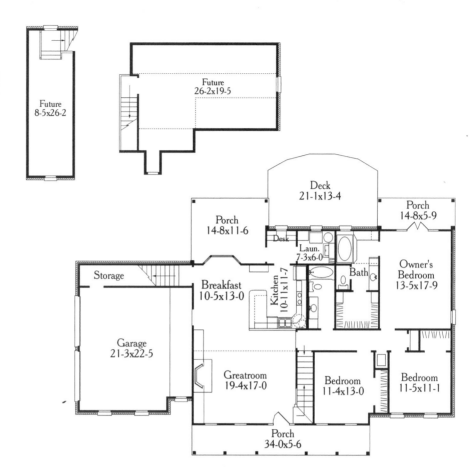

Future
8-5x26-2

Future
26-2x19-5

Deck
21-1x13-4

Porch
14-8x11-6

Porch
14-8x5-9

Desk

Laun.
7-3x6-0

Bath

Owner's
Bedroom
13-5x17-9

Storage

Breakfast
10-5x13-0

Kitchen
10-11x11-7

Garage
21-3x22-5

Greatroom
19-4x17-0

Bedroom
11-4x13-0

Bedroom
11-5x11-1

Porch
34-0x5-6

83

Design HPT860123

Square Footage: 1,751
Width: 64'-0" **Depth:** 40'-6"

This raised-porch farmhouse holds all the charisma of others of its style, but boasts a one-story floor plan. A huge living area dominates the center of the plan. It features a vaulted ceiling, built-ins and a warming fireplace. The formal dining room across the hall opens to the foyer and the living area, and is defined by a single column at its corner. Casual dining takes place in a light-filled breakfast room attached to the designer kitchen. A spectacular master suite sits behind the two-car garage. Family bedrooms at the other end of the hallway share a Jack-and-Jill bath. that includes a separate vanity area.

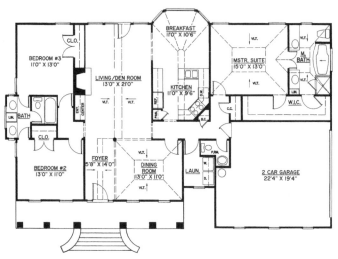

84

Design HPT860124

Square Footage: 1,755
Width: 78'-6" **Depth:** 47'-7"

A sunburst window set within a brick exterior and a multi-gabled roof lends a vibrant aura to this three-bedroom home. Conveniently placed near the garage for fast unloading, the U-shaped kitchen is sure to please. The master bedroom enjoys a walk-in closet and a luxurious bath including a whirlpool tub and twin-sink vanity.

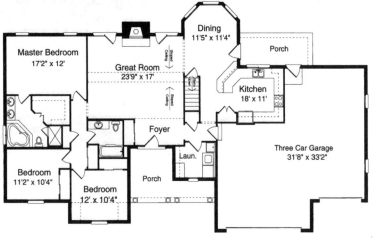

Design HPT860126

Square Footage: 1,756
Width: 57'-0" **Depth:** 58'-8"

A brick exterior and circle-top windows give this home a rich, solid look. The dramatic view from the foyer includes a corner fireplace and triple French doors. Access to the deck through the great room easily expands the entertainment area to the rear yard. The master bedroom suite with sloped ceiling and ultra bath offer the size and luxurious amenities found in today's fashionable homes.

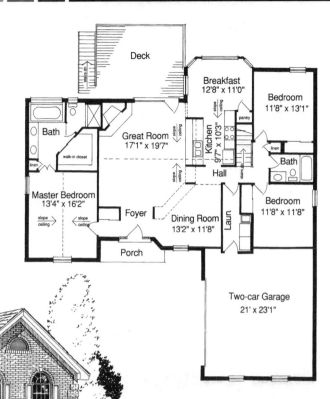

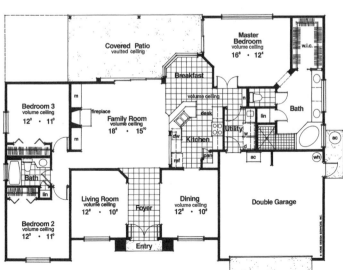

85

Design HPT860125

Square Footage: 1,758
Width: 60'-0" **Depth:** 45'-0"

The optional fourth bedroom and bath with its own private entrance to the cool covered patio will suit guest and homeowner alike. This design balances formal spaces around the foyer for even flow throughout the gathering rooms. An industrious kitchen with a built-in desk is terrific for entertaining or writing letters. Volume ceilings and enormous windows throughout the plan give the sense of expansiveness.

optional fourth bedroom layout

Design HPT860127

First Floor: 880 square feet
Second Floor: 880 square feet
Total: 1,760 square feet
Bonus Room: 256 square feet
Width: 42'-0" **Depth:** 40'-0"

6,20 X 3,40
20'-8" X 11'-4"

5,10 X 3,30
17'-0" X 11'-0"

4,60 X 6,80
15'-4" X 22'-8"

3,80 X 4,70
12'-8" X 15'-8"

4,00 X 2,70
13'-4" X 9'-0"

3,30 X 3,30
11'-0" X 11'-0"

4,70 X 4,60
15'-8" X 15'-4"

3,80 X 4,70
12'-8" X 15'-8"

This country Victorian design comes loaded with charm and amenities. The entry leads to open living space, defined by a two-sided fireplace and a large bay window. An island counter with a snack bar highlights the L-shaped kitchen. A quiet sitting area opens to the outdoors. Upstairs, the master suite allows plenty of sunlight from the turret's bay window and boasts a step-up tub, dual vanities and a separate shower. Bonus space above the garage offers room for future expansion. This home is designed with a basement foundation.

Design HPT860128

First Floor: 1,189 square feet
Second Floor: 575 square feet
Total: 1,764 square feet
Width: 46'-0" **Depth:** 44'-6"

L

An abundance of porches and a deck encourage year-round indoor/outdoor relationships in this classic two-story home. The spacious great room, with its cozy fireplace, and the adjacent dining room both offer access to the screened porch/deck area through French doors. The private master suite accesses both front and rear porches and leads into a relaxing private bath complete with dual vanities and a walk-in closet. An additional family bedroom and a loft/bedroom are also available.

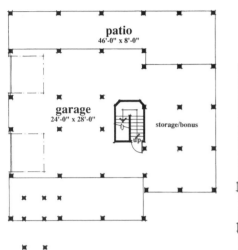

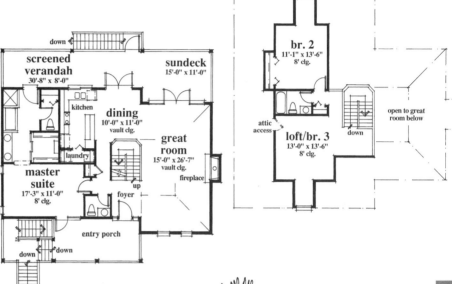

87

Design HPT860130

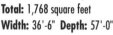

First Floor: 1,247 square feet
Second Floor: 521 square feet
Total: 1,768 square feet
Width: 36'-6" **Depth:** 57'-0"

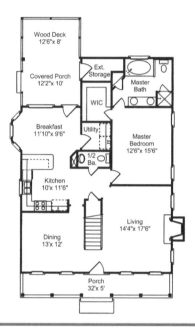

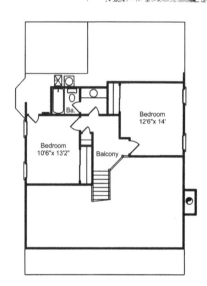

This Creole cottage has only 1,768 square feet of living space, but has the feel of a much bigger house. Natural light streaming through the full-length windows that span the entire front wall combines with the high ceiling in the front rooms to create a sense of spaciousness. The kitchen opens to a bayed breakfast room. The master bedroom features a walk-in closet. Two bedrooms occupy the second floor. Please specify crawlspace or slab foundation when ordering.

Design HPT860129

Square Footage: 1,770
Width: 64'-0" **Depth:** 48'-0"

This traditional home boasts a large receiving porch and free-flowing interior spaces. The spacious living room is open to the adjacent dining room and has a built-in fireplace and entertainment center. The master suite is isolated for privacy and is conveniently located only steps away from the kitchen. Two additional bedrooms are found on the left where they share a full bath. Please specify crawlspace or slab foundation when ordering.

Design HPT860131

Square Footage: 1,770
Width: 64'-0" **Depth:** 48'-0"

Using wood and stone for the facade, this traditional home boasts a large receiving porch and free-flowing interior spaces. The spacious living room is open to the adjacent dining room and has a built-in fireplace and entertainment center. The master suite is secluded for privacy and features a bath with a separate tub and shower and a walk-in closet. Please specify crawlspace or slab foundation when ordering.

89

Design HPT860132

First Floor: 945 square feet
Second Floor: 825 square feet
Total: 1,770 square feet
Width: 44'-0" **Depth:** 41'-4"

Shutters, window boxes and a square-columned porch add classic finishing touches to this design. The spacious great room, just past the ample foyer, features a fireplace flanked by built-in shelving and an angled border along the casual eating area. Upstairs, you'll find sleeping quarters plus a spacious study with a dormer. The generous master suite includes a walk-in closet and a large bath with separate tub, shower and toilet compartments. This home is designed with a basement foundation.

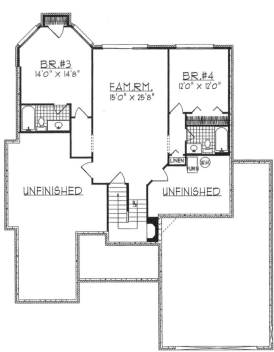

BR.#3
14'0" X 14'8"

FAM.RM.
15'0" X 25'8"

BR.#4
12'0" X 12'0"

LINEN

FURN.

W.H

UNFINISHED

UNFINISHED

Design HPT860133

Square Footage: 1,771
Finished Basement: 1,012 square feet
Width: 53'-0" **Depth:** 64'-0"

Fine brick detail, gabled rooflines and an arched window give this home plenty of class and distinction, and though it looks like a ranch home, it's actually a two-story! Inside, a tiled foyer directs traffic into the formal areas of the dining room and bayed living room. The U-shaped kitchen offers a snack counter into the sunny nook. At the front of the plan, a bedroom/study awaits with a cathedral ceiling. Located away from the family bedrooms, the master suite finished out this level with plenty of amenities. Downstairs are two bedrooms—each with a private bath—and a spacious family room. Note the abundance of unfinished space for future use.

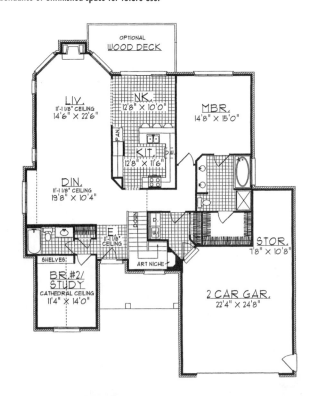

OPTIONAL
WOOD DECK

LIV.
11'-1 1/8" CEILING
14'6" X 22'6"

NK.
12'8" X 10'0"

MBR.
14'8" X 15'0"

KIT.
12'8" X 11'6"

DIN.
11'-1 1/8" CEILING
19'8" X 10'4"

STOR.
7'8" X 10'8"

SHELVES

ART NICHE

BR.#2/
STUDY
CATHEDRAL CEILING
11'4" X 14'0"

2 CAR GAR.
22'4" X 24'8"

Design HPT860134

First Floor: 1,136 square feet
Second Floor: 636 square feet
Total: 1,772 square feet
Width: 41'-9" **Depth:** 45'-0"

L

This two-story home's pleasing exterior is complemented by its warm character and decorative "widow's walk." The covered entry — with its dramatic transom window — leads to a spacious great room highlighted by a warming fireplace. To the right, the dining room and kitchen combine to provide a delightful place for mealtimes, with access to a side sun deck through double doors. Two bedrooms and a full bath complete the first floor. The luxurious master suite on the second floor features an oversized walk-in closet and a separate dressing area. The pampering master bath enjoys a relaxing whirlpool tub, double-bowl vanity and compartmented toilet. Please specify slab or pier foundation when ordering.

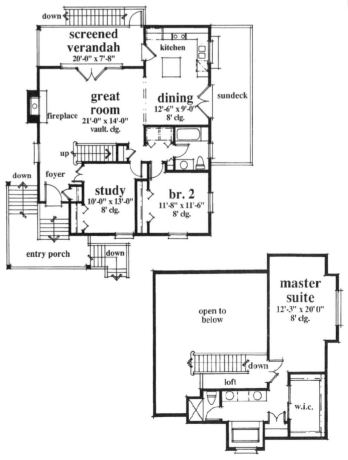

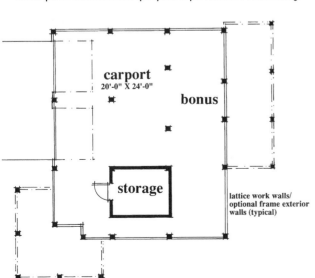

carport
20'-0" X 24'-0"

bonus

storage

lattice work walls/
optional frame exterior
walls (typical)

down

screened
verandah
20'-0" x 7'-8"

kitchen

great
room
21'-0" x 14'-0"
vault. clg.

dining
12'-6" x 9'-0"
8' clg.

sundeck

fireplace

up

down

foyer

study
10'-0" x 13'-0"
8' clg.

br. 2
11'-8" x 11'-6"
8' clg.

entry porch

down

master
suite
12'-3" x 20'0"
8' clg.

open to
below

down

loft

w.i.c.

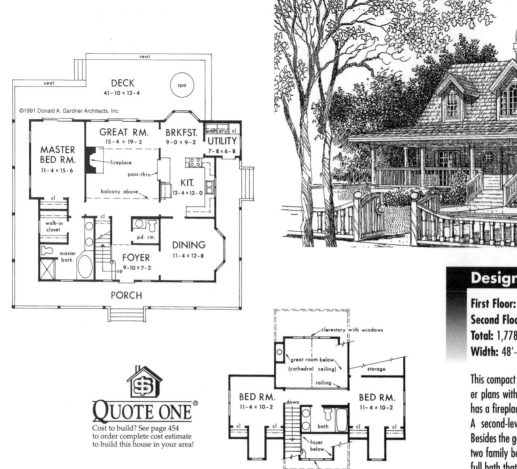

DECK
41 - 10 x 13 - 4

spa

seat

seat

©1991 Donald A. Gardner Architects, Inc.

GREAT RM.
15 - 4 x 19 - 2

BRKFST.
9 - 0 x 9 - 2

wash dry cl

UTILITY
7 - 8 x 6 - 8

MASTER BED RM.
11 - 4 x 15 - 6

fireplace

pass-thru

balcony above

KIT.
12 - 4 x 12 - 0

cl

walk-in closet

cl

pd. rm.

DINING
11 - 4 x 12 - 8

master bath

FOYER
9 - 10 x 7 - 2

up

PORCH

QUOTE ONE®

Cost to build? See page 454
to order complete cost estimate
to build this house in your area!

clerestory with windows

great room below
(cathedral ceiling)

storage

railing

BED RM.
11 - 4 x 10 - 2

BED RM.
11 - 4 x 10 - 2

cl

cl

bath

cl

cl

down

foyer below

clerestory with palladian window

Design HPT860136

First Floor: 1,325 square feet
Second Floor: 453 square feet
Total: 1,778 square feet
Width: 48'-4" **Depth:** 51'-10"

This compact design has all the amenities available in larger plans with little wasted space. The spacious great room has a fireplace, a cathedral ceiling and clerestory windows. A second-level balcony overlooks this gathering area. Besides the generous master suite with a full bath, there are two family bedrooms located on the second level sharing a full bath that offers a double vanity.

Design HPT860135

First Floor: 907 square feet
Second Floor: 872 square feet
Total: 1,779 square feet
Width: 34'-0" **Depth:** 30'-0"

Two stories and still up on a pier foundation! A covered front porch leads to two sets of French doors—one to the spacious living room and one to the dining area. An L-shaped kitchen features a work island, a nearby utility room and plenty of counter and cabinet space. A sun room finishes off this floor with class. Upstairs, the sleeping zone consists of two family bedrooms—one with access to a balcony—a full bath and a master suite.

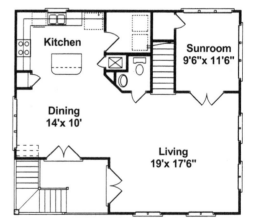

Kitchen

Sunroom
9'6"x 11'6"

Dining
14'x 10'

Living
19'x 17'6"

Bedroom
11'x 9'4"

Bedroom
11'x 9'2"

Master Bedroom
19'x 13'4"

Balcony

Floor Plan — Design HPT860138

Covered Porch

Vaulted Sitting Area

Breakfast
TRAY CLG.

FRENCH DOOR

FPL.

Bedroom 2
12⁸ x 10⁴

RANGE
Kitchen
D.W.
SERVING BAR

Vaulted Family Room
15⁰ x 20⁷
14'-0" HIGH CEILING

Master Suite
17⁰ x 13⁰
TRAY CLG.

PANTRY
REF.

Bath

Foyer
14'-0" HIGH CLG.

NICHE

DECORATIVE COLUMNS

COATS

K.S.

Vaulted M.Bath
PLANT SHELF ABOVE
W.i.c.
LINEN
SHWR.

Laund.
W.
D.

PLANT SHELF ABOVE

Dining Room
12⁵ x 12⁷
14'-0" HIGH CEILING

Bedroom 3
10⁶ x 12⁰

LIN.

Covered Entry

Garage
22⁵ x 20²

copyright © 1995 frank betz associates, inc.

GARAGE LOCATION W/ BASEMENT

Vaulted M.Bath
PLANT SHELF ABOVE
W.i.c.
LINEN
SHWR.

SINK

Laund.
W.
D.

STAIRS DN.

COATS

Garage
22⁵ x 20²

optional basement stair location

Design HPT860138

Square Footage: 1,779
Width: 57'-0" **Depth:** 56'-4"

European style shines from this home's facade in the form of its stucco detailing, hipped rooflines, fancy windows and elegant entryway. Inside, decorative columns and a plant shelf define the formal dining room, which works well with the vaulted family room. The efficient kitchen offers a serving bar to both the family room and the deluxe breakfast room. Located apart from the family bedrooms for privacy, the master suite is sure to please with its many amenities, including a vaulted sitting area and a private covered porch. The two secondary bedrooms share a full hall bath. Please specify basement or crawlspace foundation when ordering.

Floor Plan — Design HPT860137

BONUS RM.
14-2 x 17-10

storage

down

SCREEN PORCH

BRKFST.
8-6 x 9-6

master bath

MASTER BED RM.
12-4 x 15-2
(cathedral ceiling)

GARAGE
20-4 x 24-4

DINING
12-8 x 12-0

KITCHEN
10-6 x 13-6
pantry

walk-in closet

d w

UTIL.

© 1994 DONALD A. GARDNER
All rights reserved

cl

GREAT RM.
14-6 x 21-2
(cathedral ceiling)
fireplace

cl

BED RM.
10-6 x 11-4

FOYER
up

bath

skylights

PORCH

BED RM./ STUDY
11-8 x 12-0
(cathedral ceiling)

walk-in closet

Design HPT860137

Square Footage: 1,787
Bonus Room: 326 square feet
Width: 66'-2" **Depth:** 66'-8"

Cathedral ceilings bring a feeling of spaciousness to this home. The great room features a fireplace, cathedral ceilings and built-in bookshelves. The kitchen is designed for efficient use with its food preparation island and pantry. The master suite provides a welcome retreat with a cathedral ceiling, a walk-in closet and a luxurious bath. Two additional bedrooms, one with a walk-in closet, share a skylit bath. A second-floor bonus room is perfect for a study or a play area.

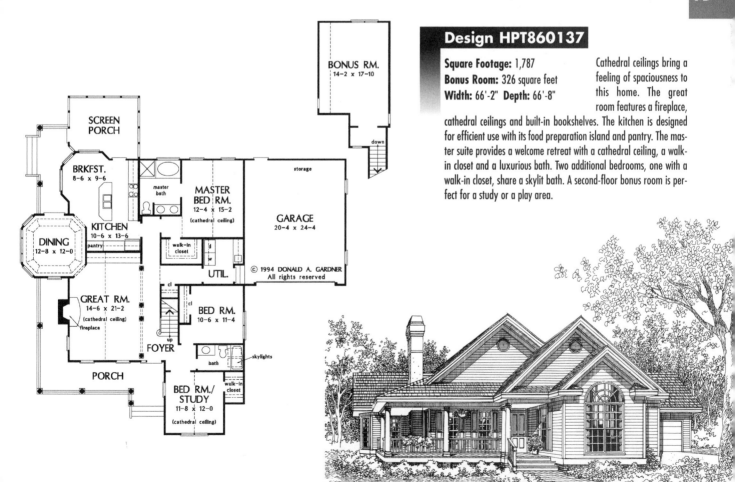

© 1994 Donald A. Gardner Architects, Inc.

Design HPT860139

First Floor: 959 square feet
Second Floor: 833 square feet
Total: 1,792 square feet
Bonus Room: 344 square feet
Width: 52'-6" **Depth:** 42'-8"

Active families will enjoy the great room that opens to the island kitchen and breakfast bay. Accessed from either the kitchen or the foyer, the dining room features a bay window. The master suite, located on the second floor, contains a walk-in closet and a bath with a garden tub. Two additional bedrooms, one with a walk-in closet, share a full bath. An easily accessible bonus room adds extra versatility for growth.

©1995 Donald A. Gardner Architects, Inc.

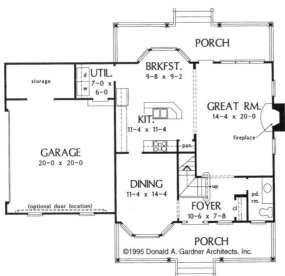

PORCH

UTIL.
7-0 x 6-0

storage

BRKFST.
9-8 x 9-2

KIT.
11-4 x 11-4

GREAT RM.
14-4 x 20-0

fireplace

pan.

GARAGE
20-0 x 20-0

DINING
11-4 x 14-4

up

(optional door location)

FOYER
10-6 x 7-8

pd. rm.

cl

PORCH

©1995 Donald A. Gardner Architects, Inc.

attic storage

BONUS RM.
20-0 x 14-2

BED RM.
10-4 x 10-0

bath

MASTER BED RM.
13-6 x 15-8

cl

down

walk-in closet

master bath

attic storage

BED RM.
11-4 x 11-10

walk-in closet

Design HPT860140

Square Footage: 1,792
Width: 68'-0" **Depth:** 62'-0"

Light dazzles through arched transoms, and double columns add a Mediterranean aura to this three-bedroom home. The living and dining rooms open to a rear porch, a deck and a patio area. Two family bedrooms share a full bath to the right of the living room. Secluded to the left of the plan, the spacious master suite enjoys a cathedral ceiling, walk-in closet and luxurious bath. A cozy eating area adjoins the kitchen, which shares a serving bar with the dining room. Please specify basement, crawlspace or slab foundation when ordering.

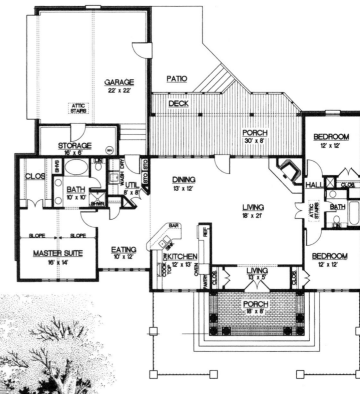

GARAGE
22' x 22'

ATTIC STAIRS

PATIO

DECK

PORCH
30' x 8'

BEDROOM
12' x 12'

STORAGE
16' x 6'

WASH DRY

LIN

STO STO

DINING
13' x 12'

HALL

CLOS

CLOS

BATH

BATH
10' x 10'

UTIL
8' x 8'

LIVING
18' x 21'

ATTIC STAIRS

SLOPE

SLOPE

BAR

REF

MASTER SUITE
16' x 14'

EATING
10' x 12'

KITCHEN
12' x 13'

PANTRY

OPEN

CLOS

LIVING
15' x 5'

BEDROOM
12' x 12'

PORCH
18' x 8'

Design HPT860141

First Floor: 1,157 square feet
Second Floor: 638 square feet
Total: 1,795 square feet
Width: 36'-0" **Depth:** 40'-0"

This leisure home is perfect for outdoor living, with French doors opening to a large sun deck and sunken spa. The open-beam, vaulted ceiling and high window wall provide views for the living and dining rooms, which are decorated with wood columns and warmed by a fireplace. The step-saving U-shaped kitchen has ample counter space and a bar counter to the dining room. The master suite on the first floor features a walk-in closet and a private bath. A convenient mudroom with an adjoining laundry room accesses a rear deck. Two bedrooms on the second floor share a full bath.

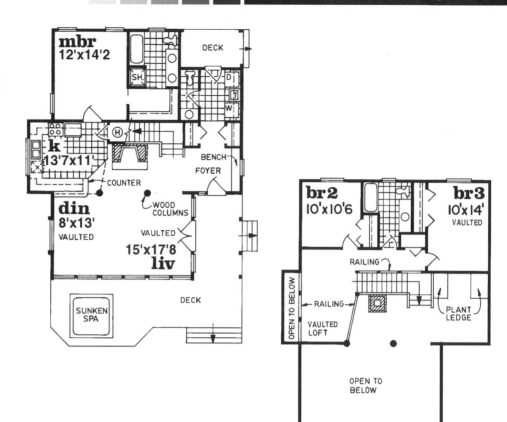

95

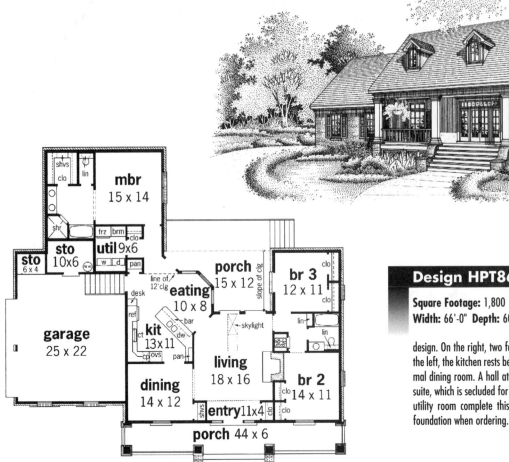

Floor Plan — Design HPT860142

- **mbr** 15 x 14
- shvs, clo, lin
- shr, frz, brm, clo
- **sto** 10x6
- **sto** 6 x 4
- **util** 9x6
- w / d, pan
- line of 12'clg
- desk, ref, ct
- **kit** 13 x 11
- cp, ovs, bar, dw
- pan
- **garage** 25 x 22
- **eating** 10 x 8
- **porch** 15 x 12 — slope of clg
- **br 3** 12 x 11 — clo, clo
- lin, lin
- skylight
- **living** 18 x 16
- **dining** 14 x 12
- **br 2** 14 x 11 — clo, clo
- shvs, **entry** 11x4, clo, clo
- **porch** 44 x 6

Design HPT860142

Square Footage: 1,800
Width: 66'-0" **Depth:** 60'-0"

The romance of a Colonial plantation is resurrected in this charming design. On the right, two family bedrooms share a full hall bath. To the left, the kitchen rests between the bayed eating area and the formal dining room. A hall at the rear of the plan leads to the master suite, which is secluded for privacy. A two-car garage, storage and a utility room complete this plan. Please specify basement or slab foundation when ordering.

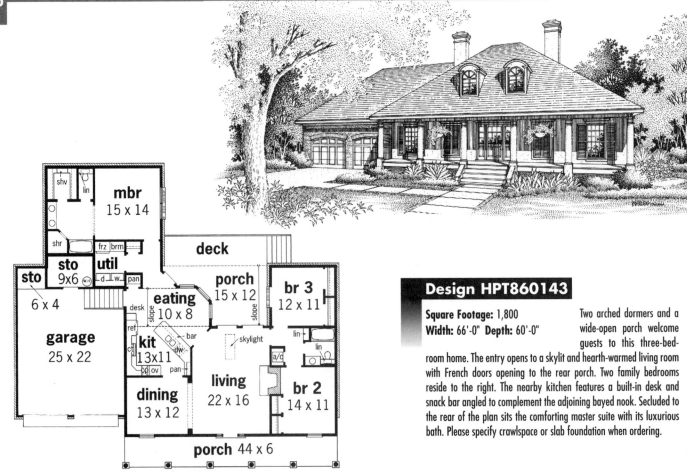

Floor Plan — Design HPT860143

- **mbr** 15 x 14
- shv, lin
- shr, frz, brm
- **sto** 9x6
- **sto** 6 x 4
- **util**
- d, w, pan
- desk, ref, ct
- **kit** 13x11
- dw, bar, pan
- ov
- **garage** 25 x 22
- **deck**
- **eating** 10 x 8 — slope, slope
- **porch** 15 x 12
- **br 3** 12 x 11
- lin, lin
- a/c
- skylight
- **living** 22 x 16
- **dining** 13 x 12
- **br 2** 14 x 11
- **porch** 44 x 6

Design HPT860143

Square Footage: 1,800
Width: 66'-0" **Depth:** 60'-0"

Two arched dormers and a wide-open porch welcome guests to this three-bedroom home. The entry opens to a skylit and hearth-warmed living room with French doors opening to the rear porch. Two family bedrooms reside to the right. The nearby kitchen features a built-in desk and snack bar angled to complement the adjoining bayed nook. Secluded to the rear of the plan sits the comforting master suite with its luxurious bath. Please specify crawlspace or slab foundation when ordering.

© 1994 Donald A. Gardner Architects, Inc.

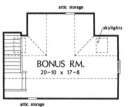

attic storage

BONUS RM.
20-10 x 17-8

skylights

attic storage

QUOTE ONE®
Cost to build? See page 454
to order complete cost estimate
to build this house in your area!

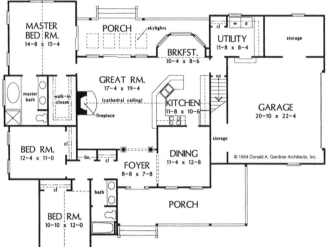

MASTER BED RM.
14-8 x 15-4

PORCH

skylights

UTILITY
11-8 x 8-4

storage

BRKFST.
10-4 x 8-6

master bath

walk-in closet

GREAT RM.
17-4 x 19-4

(cathedral ceiling)

fireplace

KITCHEN
11-8 x 10-6

up

GARAGE
20-10 x 22-4

BED RM.
12-4 x 11-0

lin.

cl

storage

DINING
11-4 x 12-8

FOYER
8-8 x 7-8

© 1994 Donald A. Gardner Architects, Inc.

bath

BED RM.
10-10 x 12-0

PORCH

Design HPT860145

Square Footage: 1,807
Bonus Room: 419 square feet
Width: 70'-8" **Depth:** 52'-8"

This comfortable country home begins with a front porch that opens to a columned foyer. To the right, enter the formal dining room. Dectorative columns define the central great room, which boasts wide views of the outdoors. A breakfast nook nearby accommodates casual dining. The master suite and the great room open to the rear porch. Family bedrooms share a full bath with double lavatories.

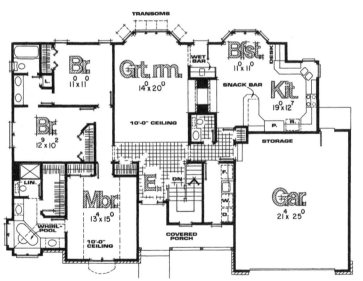

TRANSOMS

Br.
11 x 11

Grt. rm.
14⁰ x 20⁰

10'-0" CEILING

WET BAR

Bfst.
11⁰ x 11⁰

DESK

SNACK BAR

Kit.
19⁰ x 12⁷

Br.
12⁰ x 10²

P.

R.

STORAGE

LIN.

DN

Mbr
13⁴ x 15⁰

WHIRL-POOL

10'-0" CEILING

F.

W.

D.

Gar
21⁴ x 25⁰

COVERED PORCH

Design HPT860144

Square Footage: 1,808
Width: 64'-0" **Depth:** 44'-0"

Discriminating buyers will love the refined yet inviting look of this three-bedroom home plan.
A tiled entry with a ten-foot ceiling leads into the spacious great room with a large bay window. An open-hearth fireplace warms both the great room and the kitchen. The sleeping area features a spacious master suite with a dramatic arched window and a bath with a whirlpool tub, twin vanities and a walk-in closet. Two secondary bedrooms each have private access to the shared bath. Don't miss the storage space in the oversized garage.

PORCH

BREAKFAST
10'-0" X 10'-0"

GREAT ROOM
16'-0" X 18'-0"

MASTER BEDROOM
15'-0" X 14'-0"

W.I.C.

MASTER BATH

POWDER

KITCHEN
14'-0" X 11'-4"

DINING ROOM
10'-6" X 13'-0"

FOYER
5'-0" X 9'-0"

BEDROOM
NO. 3
10'-6" X 10'-0"

BEDROOM NO. 2
11'-2" X 11'-0"

BATH

LAUND
5'-2" X
10'-6"

DN

TWO CAR GARAGE
20'-4" X 19'-4"

QUOTE ONE®

Cost to build? See page 454
to order complete cost estimate
to build this house in your area!

Design HPT860147

Square Footage: 1,815
Width: 60'-0" **Depth:** 58'-6"

Inside, the foyer of this lovely European home opens into the great room with a vaulted ceiling and a dining room defined by columns. Kitchen tasks are made easy with this home's step-saving kitchen and breakfast bar. Nestled away at the opposite end of the home, the master suite combines perfect solitude with elegant luxury. Features include a double-door entry, tray ceiling, and niche details. Two family bedrooms share a private bath. This home is designed with a walkout basement foundation.

© 1994 Donald A. Gardner Architects, Inc.

B. URBAN

QUOTE ONE®

Cost to build? See page 454
to order complete cost estimate
to build this house in your area!

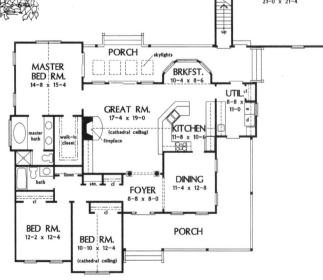

attic stor.

skylights

BONUS RM.
24-8 x 11-10

down

© 1994 DONALD A. GARDNER
All rights reserved

GARAGE
21-0 x 21-4

storage

up

PORCH

skylights

MASTER
BED RM.
14-8 x 15-4

BRKFST.
10-4 x 8-6

UTIL.
8-8 x
11-0

w d

GREAT RM.
17-4 x 19-0

(cathedral ceiling)

KITCHEN
11-8 x 10-6

master
bath

walk-in
closet

fireplace

DINING
11-4 x 12-8

linen

sto.

bath

cl

FOYER
8-8 x 8-0

cl

BED RM.
12-2 x 12-4

BED RM.
10-10 x 12-4
(cathedral ceiling)

PORCH

Design HPT860146

Square Footage: 1,815
Bonus Room: 336 square feet
Width: 70'-8" **Depth:** 70'-2"

Dormers, arched windows and covered porches lend this home its country appeal. Inside, the foyer opens to the dining room on the right and leads through a columned entrance to the great room. The open kitchen easily serves the great room, the breakfast area and the dining room. A cathedral ceiling graces the master suite.

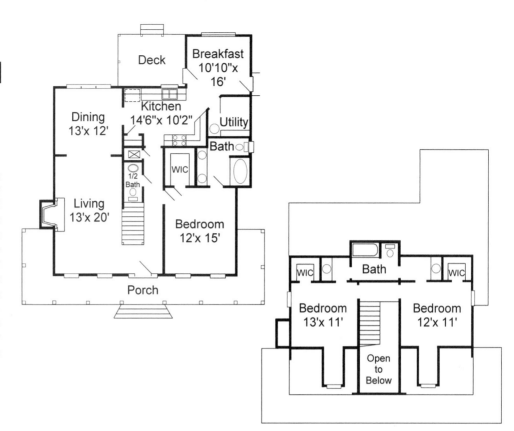

Design HPT860148

First Floor: 1,242 square feet
Second Floor: 577 square feet
Total: 1,819 square feet
Width: 43'-0" **Depth:** 47'-0"

This petite and efficient home offers a charming floor plan with a stunning front porch. The first floor provides a formal living room with a fireplace and an opening to the dining area. The kitchen opens to the breakfast room, which overlooks the rear deck. Secluded on the first floor for privacy, the master bedroom includes a spacious walk-in closet and a bathroom with a whirlpool tub. Upstairs, two secondary bedrooms with walk-in closets share a bathroom. Please specify crawlspace or slab foundation when ordering.

This home, as shown in the photograph, may differ from the actual blueprints. For more detailed information, please check the floor plans carefully.

Photo courtesy of Chatham Home Planning Inc. Chris A. Little of Atlanta

99

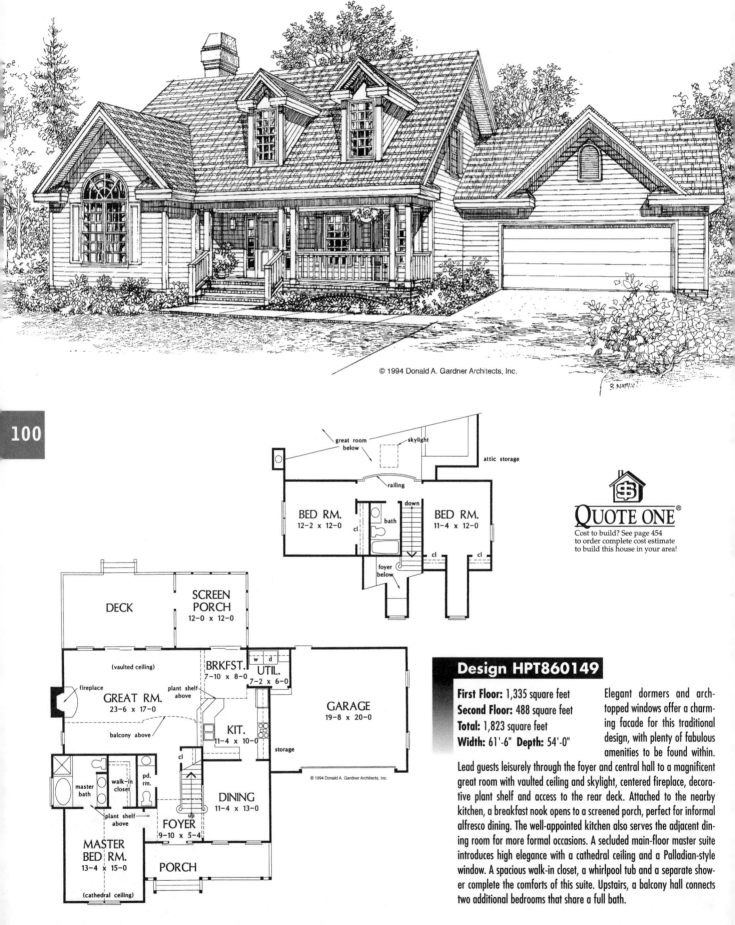

© 1994 Donald A. Gardner Architects, Inc.

B. NATHAN

great room below   skylight

attic storage

railing

BED RM.
12-2 x 12-0

bath

cl

down

BED RM.
11-4 x 12-0

cl

cl

foyer below

DECK

SCREEN
PORCH
12-0 x 12-0

(vaulted ceiling)

BRKFST.
7-10 x 8-0

w   d

UTIL.
7-2 x 6-0

fireplace

GREAT RM.
23-6 x 17-0

plant shelf
above

balcony above

KIT.
11-4 x 10-0

GARAGE
19-8 x 20-0

storage

© 1994 Donald A. Gardner Architects, Inc.

master
bath

walk-in
closet

pd.
rm.

cl

plant shelf
above

FOYER
9-10 x 5-4

up

DINING
11-4 x 13-0

MASTER
BED RM.
13-4 x 15-0

PORCH

(cathedral ceiling)

Design HPT860149

First Floor: 1,335 square feet
Second Floor: 488 square feet
Total: 1,823 square feet
Width: 61'-6" **Depth:** 54'-0"

Elegant dormers and arch-topped windows offer a charming facade for this traditional design, with plenty of fabulous amenities to be found within. Lead guests leisurely through the foyer and central hall to a magnificent great room with vaulted ceiling and skylight, centered fireplace, decorative plant shelf and access to the rear deck. Attached to the nearby kitchen, a breakfast nook opens to a screened porch, perfect for informal alfresco dining. The well-appointed kitchen also serves the adjacent dining room for more formal occasions. A secluded main-floor master suite introduces high elegance with a cathedral ceiling and a Palladian-style window. A spacious walk-in closet, a whirlpool tub and a separate shower complete the comforts of this suite. Upstairs, a balcony hall connects two additional bedrooms that share a full bath.

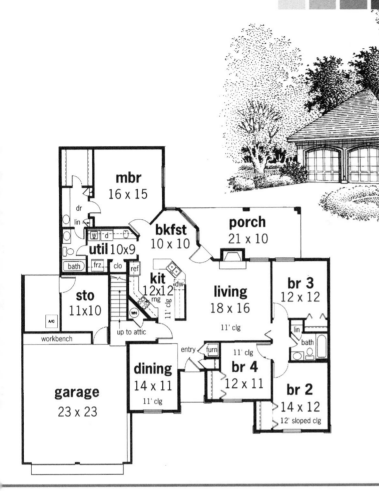

mbr 16 x 15

dr

lin

bkfst 10 x 10

porch 21 x 10

W d

util 10x9

bath · frz · clo

ref

kit 12x12
rng
11' clg
dw

WH

living 18 x 16

11' clg

br 3 12 x 12

lin

bath

sto 11x10

A/C

up to attic

workbench

entry · furn

11' clg

br 4 12 x 11

garage 23 x 23

dining 14 x 11

11' clg

br 2 14 x 12

12' sloped clg

Design HPT860150

Square Footage: 1,828
Width: 64'-0" **Depth:** 62'-0"

Quoins, sunburst windows and a hipped roof lend this four-bedroom home a European feel. Privacy is assured in this split-bedroom plan with the master suite accessed from the breakfast area. Warm yourself by the living room fireplace or step out onto the porch to enjoy the outdoor view. Three family bedrooms complete this plan, all located on the right side of the house. Please specify basement, crawlspace or slab foundation when ordering.

101

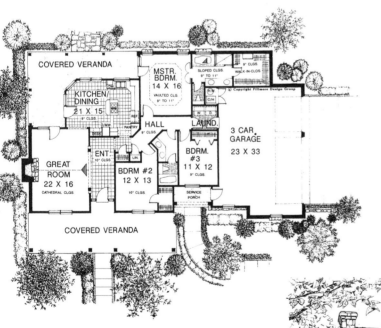

COVERED VERANDA

MSTR. BDRM. 14 X 16
VAULTED CLG 9' TO 11'

SLOPED CLGS 9' TO 11'

WALK-IN-CLOS

KITCHEN/ DINING 21 X 15
9" CLGS

REF
PANTRY

HALL 9' CLGS

LAUND.

W D

C/H

© Copyright Fillmore Design Group

3 CAR GARAGE 23 X 33

GREAT ROOM 22 X 16
CATHEDRAL CLGS

ENT 10" CLGS

LIN

BDRM #2 12 X 13
10" CLGS

BDRM. #3 11 X 12
9" CLGS

SERVICE PORCH

COVERED VERANDA

Design HPT860151

Square Footage: 1,830
Width: 75'-0" **Depth:** 52'-3"

Characteristics that include a cupola, shutters, arched transoms and an exterior of combined stone and lap siding give this one-story home its country identity. To the left of the entry, the great room's cathedral ceiling and fireplace extend an invitation for family and friends alike to relax and enjoy themselves. The kitchen and dining room are located nearby. Kitchen amenities include an island cooktop, built-in planning desk and pantry, while the multi-windowed dining room overlooks and provides access to the covered veranda. A hall leads to sleeping quarters that include two secondary bedrooms and a luxurious master suite.

Design HPT860153

Square Footage: 1,831
Width: 59'-0" **Depth:** 55'-4"

A two-story entry, varying rooflines and multi-pane windows add to the spectacular street appeal of this three-bedroom home. To the right, off the foyer, is the dining room surrounded by elegant columns. The family room includes plans for an optional fireplace and accesses the covered porch. The master bedroom is tucked in the back of the home and features a walk-in closet. Two additional bedrooms share a full bath.

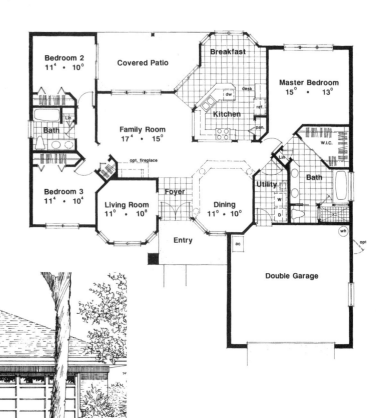

102

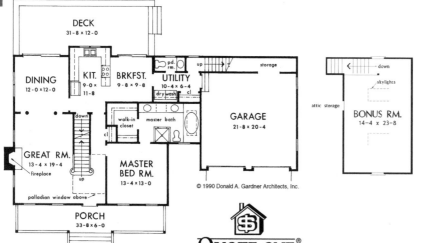

© 1990 Donald A. Gardner Architects, Inc.

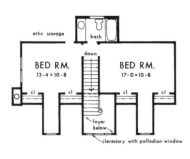

QUOTE ONE®

Cost to build? See page 454 to order complete cost estimate to build this house in your area!

Design HPT860152

First Floor: 1,289 square feet
Second Floor: 542 square feet
Total: 1,831 square feet
Bonus Room: 393 square feet
Width: 66'-4" **Depth:** 50'-4"

This cozy country cottage is perfect for the growing family — offering both an unfinished basement option and a bonus room. Enter through the two-story foyer with a Palladian window in a clerestory dormer above. The master suite is on the first floor for privacy and accessibility. Its accompanying bath boasts a whirlpool tub with a skylight above and a double-bowl vanity. The second floor contains two bedrooms, a full bath and plenty of storage.

© 1990 Donald A. Gardner Architects, Inc.

Design HPT860155

Square Footage: 1,832
Bonus Room: 425 square feet
Width: 65'-4" **Depth:** 62'-0"

This plan rises with a cathedral ceiling in the great room and dormer windows shedding light on the foyer, front bedroom and the formal dining room. The kitchen is completely open to the great room and features a stylish snack-bar island and a bay window at the breakfast nook. The master suite has a tray ceiling and a skylit bath. Two secondary bedrooms are split for privacy and share a full hall bath. Bonus space may be developed over the garage.

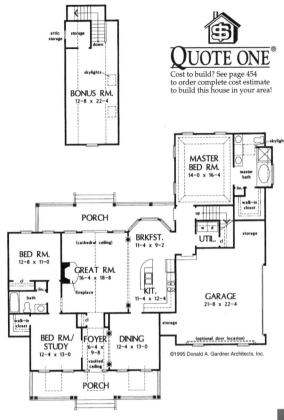

Quote One®
Cost to build? See page 454 to order complete cost estimate to build this house in your area!

© 1995 Donald A. Gardner Architects, Inc.

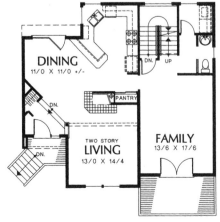

Design HPT860154

First Floor: 1,022 square feet
Second Floor: 813 square feet
Total: 1,835 square feet
Width: 36'-0" **Depth:** 33'-0"

L

This house not only accommodates a narrow lot, but it also fits a sloping site. The angled corner entry gives way to a two-story living room with a tiled hearth. The dining room enjoys easy service from the efficient kitchen. The family room offers double doors to a balcony.

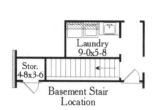

Laundry
9-0x5-8

Stor.
4-8x3-6

Basement Stair
Location

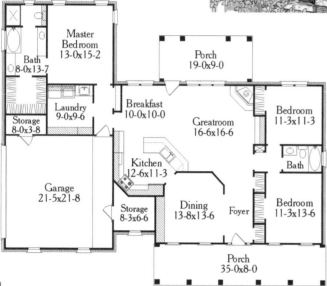

Master
Bedroom
13-0x15-2

Bath
8-0x13-7

Laundry
9-0x9-6

Storage
8-0x3-8

Garage
21-5x21-8

Storage
8-3x6-6

Breakfast
10-0x10-0

Kitchen
12-6x11-3

Dining
13-8x13-6

Foyer

Porch
19-0x9-0

Greatroom
16-6x16-6

Bedroom
11-3x11-3

Bath

Bedroom
11-3x13-6

Porch
35-0x8-0

Design HPT860157

Square Footage: 1,836
Width: 65'-8" **Depth:** 55'-0"

Pillars, beautiful transoms and sidelights set off the entry door and draw attention to this comfortable home. The foyer leads to a formal dining room and a great room with a ribbon of windows pouring in light. Privacy is assured with a master suite set in its own section of the L-shaped plan. A large walk-in closet and full bath with shower and separate large tub add to the pleasure of this wing. Two family bedrooms occupy the right side of the design and share a full bath. Please specify basement, crawlspace or slab foundation when ordering.

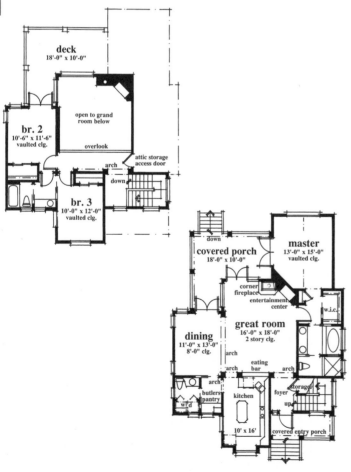

deck
18'-0" x 10'-0"

open to grand
room below

br. 2
10'-6" x 11'-6"
vaulted clg.

overlook

attic storage
access door

arch

br. 3
10'-0" x 12'-0"
vaulted clg.

down

down

covered porch
18'-0" x 10'-0"

master
13'-0" x 15'-0"
vaulted clg.

corner
fireplace

entertainment
center

w.i.c.

dining
11'-0" x 13'-0"
8'-0" clg.

great room
16'-0" x 18'-0"
2 story clg.

arch

arch

eating
bar

arch

foyer

storage

up

butlers
pantry

w/d

kitchen

10' x 16'

covered entry porch

Design HPT860156

First Floor: 1,290 square feet
Second Floor: 548 square feet
Total: 1,838 square feet
Width: 38'-0" **Depth:** 51'-0"

Horizontal siding complements a metal roof to create a charming look to this two-story home. Inside, cozy interior spaces and great outdoor views through wide windows and French doors prevail. At the heart of the home, the two-story great rooms features a corner fireplace, an entertainment center and an eating bar shared with the gourmet kitchen. A first-floor master suite offers privacy, while two family bedrooms reside upstairs.

Design HPT860159

Square Footage: 1,845
Bonus Space: 409 square feet
Width: 56'-0" **Depth:** 60'-0"

The stucco exterior and combination rooflines give a stately appearance to this traditional home. Inside, the well-lit foyer leads to an elegant living room with a vaulted ceiling, fireplace, radius window and French door that opens to the rear property. Two family bedrooms share a full bath on the right side of the home, while an impressive master suite resides to the left for privacy. A formal dining room and an open kitchen with plenty of counter space complete the plan. Please specify basement or crawlspace foundation when ordering.

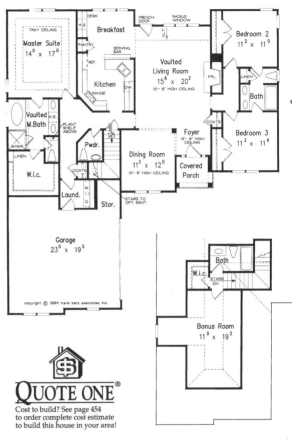

Quote One®

Cost to build? See page 454 to order complete cost estimate to build this house in your area!

105

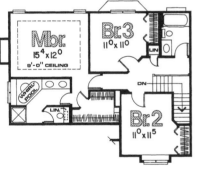

Design HPT860158

First Floor: 1,042 square feet
Second Floor: 803 square feet
Total: 1,845 square feet
Width: 48'-0" **Depth:** 40'-0"

This classic two-story home is perfect for a variety of lifestyles. To the right of the entry is a formal living room with a ten-foot ceiling. Nearby, the formal dining room enjoys a bright window. Serving the dining room and bright bayed dinette, the kitchen features a pantry, Lazy Susan and window sink. Off the breakfast area, step down into the family room with a handsome fireplace and a wall of windows. Upstairs, two secondary bedrooms share a hall bath. The private master bedroom contains a boxed ceiling, walk-in closet and a pampering dressing area with a double vanity and whirlpool tub.

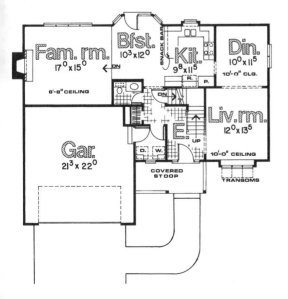

Design HPT860160

First Floor: 919 square feet
Second Floor: 927 square feet
Total: 1,846 square feet
Width: 44'-0" **Depth:** 40'-0"

This wonderful design begins with the wraparound porch. Explore further and find a two-story entry with a coat closet and plant shelf above and a strategically placed staircase alongside. The island kitchen with a boxed window over the sink is adjacent to a large bay-windowed dinette. The great room includes many windows and a fireplace. A powder room and laundry room are both conveniently placed on the first floor. Upstairs, the large master suite contains His and Hers walk-in closets, corner windows and a bath area featuring a double vanity and whirlpool tub. Two pleasant secondary bedrooms have interesting angles, and a third bedroom in the front features a volume ceiling and an arched window.

Quote One®
Cost to build? See page 454
to order complete cost estimate
to build this house in your area!

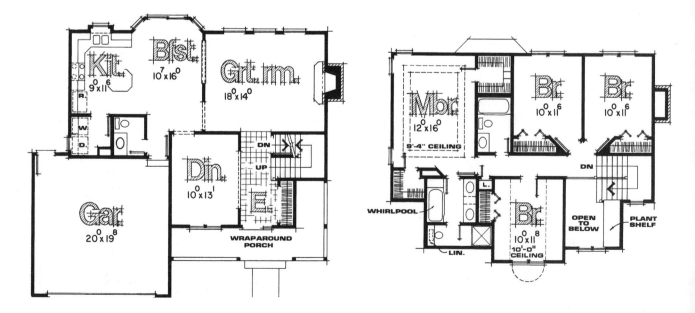

Design HPT860161

First Floor: 1,342 square feet
Second Floor: 511 square feet
Total: 1,853 square feet
Width: 44'-0" **Depth:** 40'-0"

Amenities abound in this delightful two-story home. The foyer opens directly into the fantastic grand room, which offers a warming fireplace and two sets of double doors to the rear deck. The dining room also accesses this deck and a second deck shared with Bedroom 2. A convenient kitchen and another bedroom also reside on this level. Upstairs the master bedroom reigns supreme. Entered through double doors, it pampers with a luxurious bath, walk-in closet, morning kitchen and private observation deck.

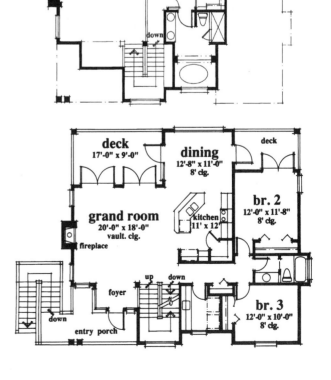

observation deck

master
13'-0" x 14'-0"
vault. clg.

am kitchen

open to grand room below

down

deck
17'-0" x 9'-0"

dining
12'-8" x 11'-0"
8' clg.

deck

grand room
20'-0" x 18'-0"
vault. clg.

kitchen
11' x 12'

br. 2
12'-0" x 11'-8"
8' clg.

fireplace

up   down

foyer

br. 3
12'-0" x 10'-0"
8' clg.

down

entry porch

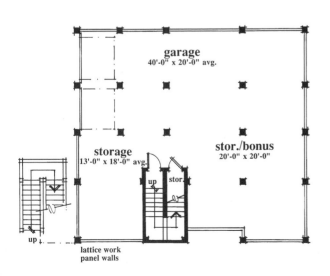

garage
40'-0" x 20'-0" avg.

storage
13'-0" x 18'-0" avg.

stor./bonus
20'-0" x 20'-0"

up   stor.

up

lattice work
panel walls

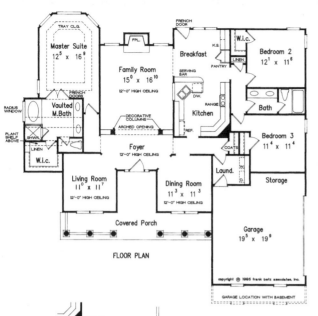

FLOOR PLAN

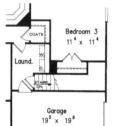

optional basement stair location

QUOTE ONE®

Cost to build? See page 454
to order complete cost estimate
to build this house in your area!

Design HPT860162

Square Footage: 1,856
Width: 59'-0" **Depth:** 54'-6"

The smart addition of a front gable crowns a delightful covered porch with a recessed entry. Extra-high ceilings in the foyer and family room complement a fireplace flanked by windows. An efficiently designed kitchen features a serving bar to the breakfast nook. The master suite is split from the two family bedrooms for privacy—a perfect owner's retreat. Please specify basement, crawlspace or slab foundation when ordering.

Design HPT860163

Square Footage: 1,858
Bonus Room: 499 square feet
Width: 83'-0" **Depth:** 50'-10"

This elegant exterior reveals a charming, open floor plan. French doors in the breakfast room open to a covered rear porch and a brick patio. The master suite provides a sitting bay and a bath with a garden tub. A laundry room is thoughtfully placed near a full bath and two family bedrooms. The kitchen shares a gently curved snack bar with the great room and breakfast room. The staircase in the foyer leads to a bonus room with skylights. Please specify basement, crawlspace or slab foundation when ordering.

Design HPT860164

First Floor: 1,336 square feet
Second Floor: 523 square feet
Total: 1,859 square feet
Bonus Room: 225 square feet
Width: 45'-0" **Depth:** 53'-0"

Twin dormers and a well-planned layout characterize this elegant home. From the shelter of the front porch, the foyer leads to the stairway or directly ahead to the great room. A fireplace, a cathedral ceiling and access to the rear porch highlight the great room. The kitchen offers a pass-through to the great room and a window sink. The master suite features a wall of windows, a walk-in closet and a compartmented bath with a double-bowl vanity.

© 1998   Donald A Gardner, Inc.

Design HPT860165

Square Footage: 1,860
Width: 62'-0" **Depth:** 64'-0"

All the comforts of modern living accent the interior of this home. A full kitchen revealing twin Lazy Susans, a pantry, and a built-in desk is easily accessible for entertaining. A spacious living room offers a corner fireplace. The master bedroom with luxury bath is a perfect retreat, plus, two additional bedrooms provide increased sleeping space. Double storage closets are available behind the carport. Please specify crawlspace or slab foundation when ordering.

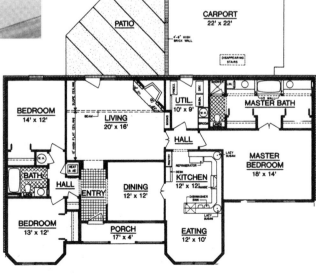

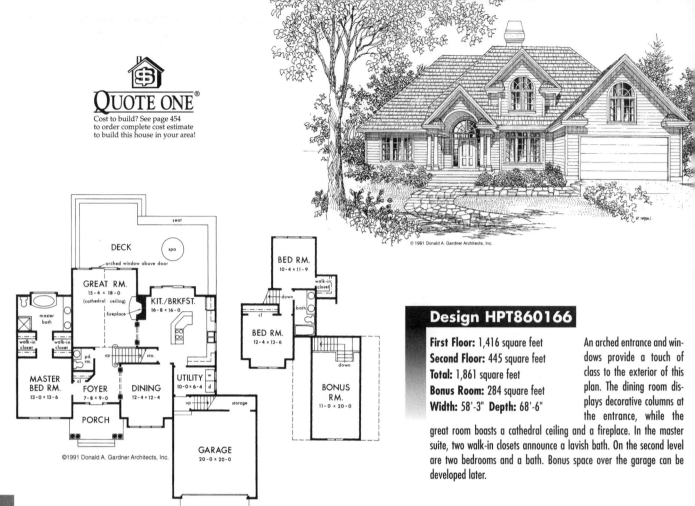

© 1991 Donald A. Gardner Architects, Inc.

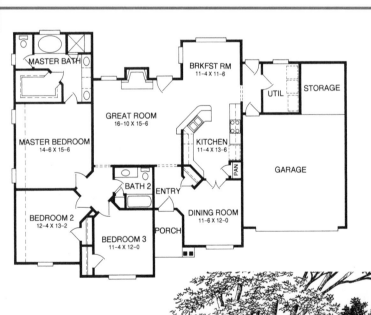

DECK

seat

spa

arched window above door

GREAT RM.
15-4 x 18-0
(cathedral ceiling)

KIT./BRKFST.
16-8 x 16-0

fireplace

BED RM.
10-4 x 11-9

walk-in closet

down

cl

bath

BED RM.
12-4 x 13-6

master bath

walk-in closet   walk-in closet

pd. rm.

up

sto.

down

MASTER BED RM.
13-0 x 13-6

FOYER
7-8 x 9-0

DINING
12-4 x 12-4

UTILITY
10-0 x 6-4

w
d

BONUS RM.
11-0 x 20-0

up

storage

PORCH

GARAGE
20-0 x 20-0

©1991 Donald A. Gardner Architects, Inc.

Design HPT860166

First Floor: 1,416 square feet
Second Floor: 445 square feet
Total: 1,861 square feet
Bonus Room: 284 square feet
Width: 58'-3" **Depth:** 68'-6"

An arched entrance and windows provide a touch of class to the exterior of this plan. The dining room displays decorative columns at the entrance, while the great room boasts a cathedral ceiling and a fireplace. In the master suite, two walk-in closets announce a lavish bath. On the second level are two bedrooms and a bath. Bonus space over the garage can be developed later.

MASTER BATH

BRKFST RM
11-4 X 11-6

UTIL

STORAGE

GREAT ROOM
16-10 X 15-6

KITCHEN
11-4 X 13-6

MASTER BEDROOM
14-6 X 15-6

PAN

GARAGE

BATH 2

ENTRY

BEDROOM 2
12-4 X 13-2

DINING ROOM
11-6 X 12-0

BEDROOM 3
11-4 X 12-0

PORCH

Design HPT860167

Square Footage: 1,862
Width: 65'-0" **Depth:** 46'-2"

This traditional home offers all the amenities of a larger plan in a compact layout. Ten-foot ceilings give this home an expansive feel. An angled eating bar separates the kitchen and the great room, while leaving these areas open for family gatherings and entertaining. The master bedroom includes a huge walk-in closet and a superior master bath with a whirlpool and a separate shower. Please specify crawlspace or slab foundation when ordering.

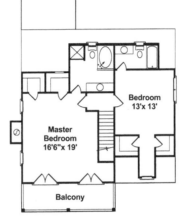

Design HPT860169

First Floor: 1,056 square feet
Second Floor: 807 square feet
Total: 1,863 square feet
Width: 33'-0" **Depth:** 54'-0"

Run up a flight of stairs to an attractive four-bedroom home! The living room features a fireplace and easy access to the L-shaped kitchen. Here, a work island makes meal preparation a breeze. Two family bedrooms share a full bath and access to the laundry facilities. Upstairs, a third bedroom offers a private bath and two walk-in closets. The master suite is complete with a pampering bath, two walk-in closets and a large private balcony. Please specify crawlspace or pier foundation when ordering.

111

Design HPT860168

Square Footage: 1,864
Bonus Room: 420 square feet
Width: 70'-4" **Depth:** 56'-4"

Quaint and cozy on the outside with porches front and back, this three-bedroom country home surprises with an open floor plan featuring a large great room with a cathedral ceiling. The privately located master suite has a cathedral ceiling and access to the deck. Two secondary bedrooms share a full hall bath. A bonus room makes expanding easy.

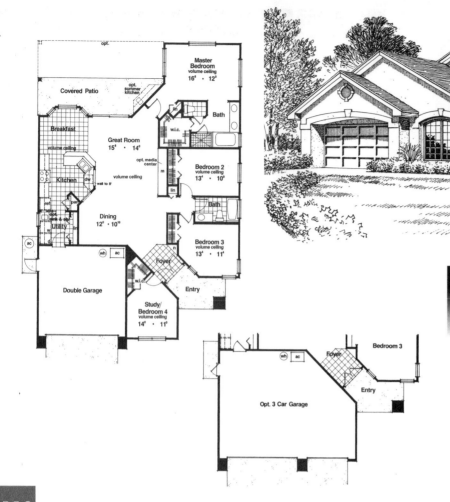

Master Bedroom
volume ceiling
16⁸ · 12⁰

opt.

Covered Patio

opt. summer kitchen

Bath

Breakfast
volume ceiling

Great Room
15⁴ · 14⁴

w.i.c.

Kitchen
volume ceiling

volume ceiling

opt. media center

wall to 9'

Bedroom 2
volume ceiling
13⁴ · 10⁰

Bath

Dining
12⁰ · 10¹⁰

ref.
opt. dble & etc.
par.

Utility

lin

Bedroom 3
volume ceiling
13⁴ · 11⁰

ac

Double Garage

wh   ac

Foyer

w.i.c.

Entry

Study/
Bedroom 4
volume ceiling
14⁸ · 11⁰

Bedroom 3

wh   ac

Foyer

Entry

Opt. 3 Car Garage

Design HPT860171

Square Footage: 1,865
Width: 45'-0" **Depth:** 66'-0"

This innovative plan features an angled entry into the home, lending visual impact to the facade and giving the interior floor plan space for a fourth bedroom. A fabulous central living area with a volume ceiling includes a dining area with kitchen access, a great room with a built-in media center, and access to the rear covered patio. The bayed breakfast area with another volume ceiling shares natural light with the tiled kitchen. The kitchen and breakfast nook overlook the outdoor living space which even offers an optional summer kitchen—great for entertaining. A plush master suite opens from the great room through a privacy door and offers vistas to the rear and side grounds.

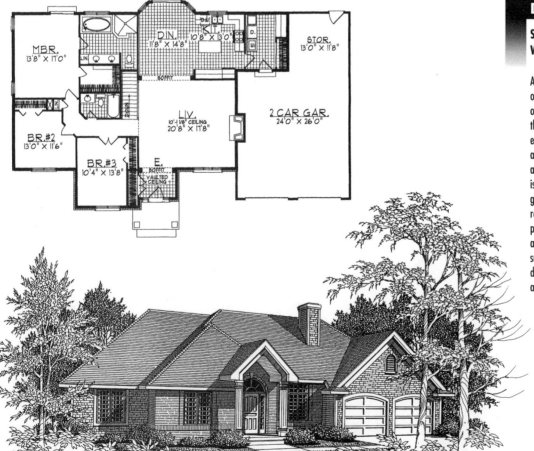

M.B.R.
13'8" X 17'0"

DIN.
11'8" X 14'8"

KIT.
10'8" X 13'0"

STOR.
13'0" X 11'8"

LIN

SOFFIT

B.R. #2
13'0" X 11'6"

LIV.
10'-1 1/8" CEILING
20'8" X 17'8"

2 CAR GAR.
24'0" X 26'0"

B.R. #3
10'4" X 13'8"

E.

VAULTED CEILING

Design HPT860170

Square Footage: 1,868
Width: 72'-0" **Depth:** 42'-0"

A large living area dominates the center of this contemporary-flavored traditional one-story. It opens off of a vaulted foyer through a doorway with soffit. At one end is a warming hearth; at the other, another soffitted opening to the dining area and island kitchen. The dining area is enhanced by a bay window with sliding glass doors to the outdoors. The bedrooms are at the opposite end of the plan and include two family bedrooms and a master suite. Accents in the master suite: a corner shower, whirlpool tub, double sinks, a large walk-in closet and a sliding glass door to the rear yard.

Design HPT860173

Square Footage: 1,868
Width: 62'-0" **Depth:** 64'-0"

Fanlights and transoms help to fill this home with natural light, enhancing the open planning of the interior design. The formal dining room to the right of the foyer is delightfully defined with a series of columns and arches opening to the glorious living room, which enjoys a sloped ceiling accentuated with two skylights. Here the fireplace is impressively flanked by sliding-glass doors that open to the rear patio. The kitchen accesses the dining room via French doors while adjoining the casual eating area to the front and the utility room to the back. Please specify crawlspace or slab foundation when ordering.

113

QUOTE ONE®

Cost to build? See page 454 to order complete cost estimate to build this house in your area!

Design HPT860172

First Floor: 1,421 square feet
Second Floor: 448 square feet
Total: 1,869 square feet
Width: 52'-0" **Depth:** 47'-4"

Always a welcome sight, the covered front porch of this home invites investigation of its delightful floor plan. Living areas to the back of the house include the great room with a see-through fireplace to the bayed dinette and kitchen with a large corner walk-in pantry. A split-bedroom sleeping plan puts the master suite, with a whirlpool tub, on the first floor away from two second-floor bedrooms and a shared full bath.

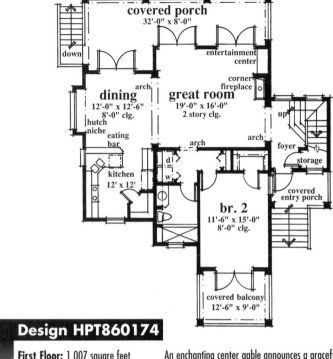

covered porch
32'-0" x 8'-0"

entertainment
center

dining
12'-0" x 12'-6"
8'-0" clg.

arch

corner
fireplace

great room
19'-0" x 16'-0"
2 story clg.

up

hutch
niche

eating
bar

arch

arch

foyer

storage

kitchen
12' x 12'

d
w

covered
entry porch

br. 2
11'-6" x 15'-0"
8'-0" clg.

down

covered balcony
12'-6" x 9'-0"

stair tower

down

open to grand
room below

br. 3
11'-0" x 10'-6"
8'-0" clg.

overlook

up

down

w.i.c.

master
11'-6" x 14'-6"
8'-0" clg.

covered balcony

Design HPT860174

First Floor: 1,007 square feet
Second Floor: 869 square feet
Total: 1,876 square feet
Width: 43'-8" **Depth:** 53'-6"

An enchanting center gable announces a graceful, honest architecture that's at home with the easygoing nature of this coastal design. A columned porch and romantic fretwork lend balance and proportion outside. The great room, featuring double doors, arches, a built-in entertainment center and a warming fireplace, is the heart of this home. The kitchen is adjoined to the dining room (with French doors) by an eating bar and provides a walk-in pantry. The foyer stairs lead to a master suite with a spacious bedroom and a lavish private bath.

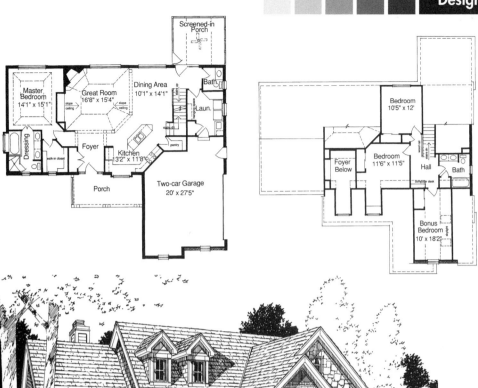

Design HPT860175

First Floor: 1,348 square feet
Second Floor: 528 square feet
Total: 1,876 square feet
Bonus Room: 195 square feet
Width: 56'-2" **Depth:** 48'-0"

Greeted by the cozy front porch and richly abundant exterior detailing, this home welcomes you in a warm and fashionable manner. The corner fireplace and multiple windows across the rear create an aura of excitement in the great room. The deluxe master suite is located on the first floor, offering privacy. If you're looking for a home that grows with your family, this home easily becomes a four-bedroom home by accessing the second-floor bonus room. The location of the rear stairs with wood banisters, a computer desk on the second floor, a spacious first-floor laundry room and a screened-in porch are amenities that create an exciting package.

Design HPT860176

Square Footage: 1,879
Bonus Room: 965 square feet
Width: 45'-0" **Depth:** 62'-0"

A sunburst over the entry door, columns supporting the covered porch, three dormers and shutters give this home a comforting air. Inside, the living room contains a warming fireplace framed by windows. Sunshine or moonlight fills the formal dining room through bay windows. The kitchen adjoins the dining room with a snack bar and shares the natural lighting of both the sun room and the dining area. Nearby, the master suite has a private bath with a walk-in closet, separate shower, large oval tub and two-sink vanity. Two bedrooms share a full bath. Please specify basement, crawlspace or slab foundation when ordering.

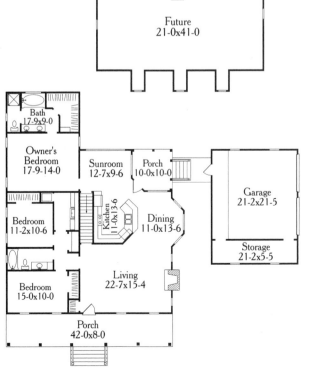

Design HPT860178

First Floor: 1,230 square feet
Second Floor: 649 square feet
Total: 1,879 square feet
Width: 38'-0" **Depth:** 53'-6"

The tiled foyer of this two-story home opens to a living/dining space with a soaring ceiling, a fireplace in the living room and access to a covered patio that invites outdoor livability. The kitchen has an oversized, sunny breakfast area with a volume ceiling. The master bedroom offers privacy with its sumptuous bath; a corner soaking tub, dual lavatories and a compartmented toilet lend character to the room. Upstairs, a loft overlooking the living spaces could become a third bedroom. One of the family bedrooms features a walk-in closet. Both bedrooms share a generous hall bath.

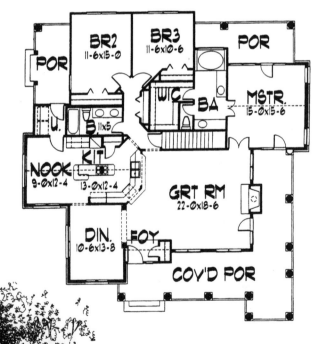

Design HPT860177

Square Footage: 1,883
Width: 55'-11" **Depth:** 58'-0"

Two pedimented dormers look out over the sturdy columns of the front porch of this three-bedroom home. Inside the foyer, the great room welcomes guests and family to sit before a roaring fire, or chat about the day. One of three porches is accessed only via the master suite. The master suite also has access to the front porch. Please specify basement, crawlspace or slab foundation when ordering.

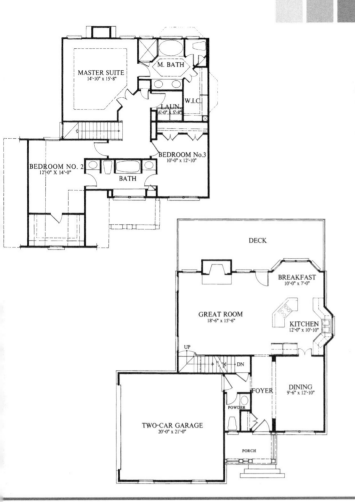

Design HPT860180

First Floor: 830 square feet
Second Floor: 1,060 square feet
Total: 1,890 square feet
Width: 41'-0"   **Depth:** 40'-6"

The pleasing character of this house does not stop behind its facade. The foyer opens to a great room with a fireplace and also to the eat-in kitchen. Stairs lead from the great room to the second floor, where a laundry room is conveniently placed near the bedrooms. The master suite spares none of the amenities: a full bath with a double vanity, shower, tub and walk-in closet. Bedrooms 2 and 3 share a full bath. This home is designed with a walkout basement foundation.

117

Design HPT860179

Square Footage: 1,890
Width: 65'-10"   **Depth:** 53'-5"

This classic home exudes elegance and offers sophisticated amenities in a compact size. A generous living room with a sloped ceiling, built-in bookcases and a centerpiece fireplace offers views as well as access to the rear yard. The nearby breakfast room shares an informal eating counter with the ample kitchen, which serves the coffer-ceilinged dining room through French doors. Three bedrooms include a sumptuous master suite and two family bedrooms that share a full bath. Please specify slab or crawlspace foundation when ordering.

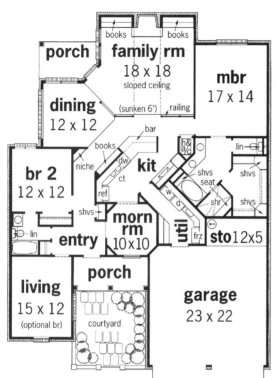

Design HPT860181

Square Footage: 1,891
Width: 49'-0" **Depth:** 64'-0"

The gated entry leading to a private courtyard is a unique design feature that increases the personality of this home. The open interior consists of a vaulted and sunken family room, a brilliantly sunny dining room and a cleverly angled kitchen. An optional bedroom, study or studio can replace the formal living room. Please specify crawlspace or slab foundation when ordering.

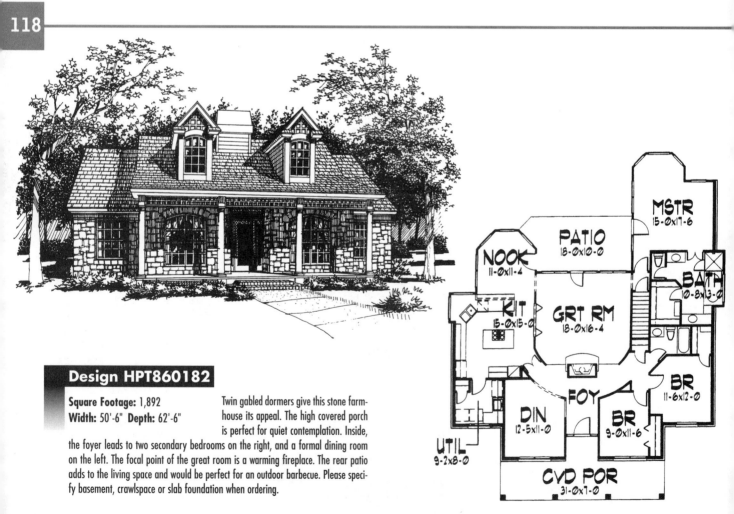

Design HPT860182

Square Footage: 1,892
Width: 50'-6" **Depth:** 62'-6"

Twin gabled dormers give this stone farmhouse its appeal. The high covered porch is perfect for quiet contemplation. Inside, the foyer leads to two secondary bedrooms on the right, and a formal dining room on the left. The focal point of the great room is a warming fireplace. The rear patio adds to the living space and would be perfect for an outdoor barbecue. Please specify basement, crawlspace or slab foundation when ordering.

Design HPT860184

Square Footage: 1,894
Width: 68'-0" **Depth:** 56'-6"

Elegant pillars and multi-pane windows give this design classy curb appeal. The galley kitchen leads to a breakfast area with a ribbon of windows. The great room will draw people in to watch a crackling fire or look out two windows framing the fireplace. Walk-in closets and extra storage space in the master suite are sure to please, not to mention the privacy created by the split-bedroom floor plan. Please specify basement, crawlspace or slab foundation when ordering.

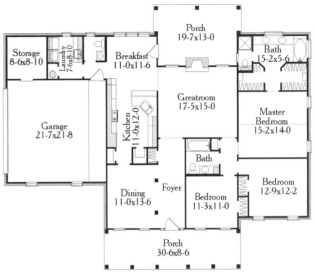

Porch
19-7x13-0

Storage
8-6x8-10

Laundry
7-6x8-10

Breakfast
11-0x11-6

Bath
15-2x5-6

Garage
21-7x21-8

Kitchen
11-0x12-0

Greatroom
17-5x15-0

Master
Bedroom
15-2x14-0

Bath

Dining
11-0x13-6

Foyer

Bedroom
11-3x11-0

Bedroom
12-9x12-2

Porch
30-6x8-6

Laun.
7-6x5-5

Basement Stair
Location

119

PATIO

KITCHEN
13'x12'

STORAGE
9'x8'

EATING
9'x9'

MASTER
BEDROOM
17'x12'-6"

BATH

DRESS.

VAULTED CEILING

FALSE
BEAMS

DINING
12'x10'

GARAGE
21'x21'

FAMILY
21'x20'

2'-8" HIGH WALL
WITH SPINDLES

LIVING
13'x12'

ENTRY

BEDROOM
14'x11'-6"

DRESS.

BEDROOM
15'x13'

BATH

PORCH
18'x5'

Design HPT860183

Square Footage: 1,898
Width: 72'-0" **Depth:** 42'-0"

A lovely spindled porch frames the living-room picture window, and a quaint cupola gives Victorian flavor to this home. Inside, the family room has a dramatic vaulted ceiling with false beams. The fireplace is centered between two sets of long windows, one of which is actually a door to the rear patio. The master bedroom has a private bath, dressing room and walk-in closet. Please specify crawlspace or slab foundation when ordering.

Design HPT860186

First Floor: 1,422 square feet
Second Floor: 477 square feet
Total: 1,899 square feet
Width: 51'-8" **Depth:** 40'-6"

Arched windows ornament the facade of this traditional design, while a front gable and spacious front porch add country appeal. Inside, find a two-story family room with a fireplace, an island kitchen with an adjacent breakfast bay, and a formal dining room. Sleeping quarters include the first-floor master suite, with a private bath, walk-in closet and porch access. Upstairs, two additional bedrooms—one with a bay window—share a storage area, a full bath and a balcony that overlooks the family room. Please specify basement, crawl-space or slab foundation when ordering.

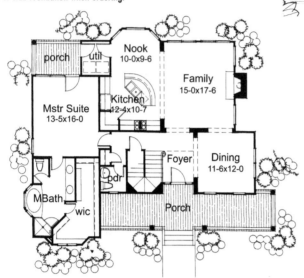

Design HPT860185

First Floor: 1,097 square feet
Second Floor: 807 square feet
Total: 1,904 square feet
Width: 40'-0" **Depth:** 45'-0"

The combination of rafter tails, stone and siding, and gabled rooflines give this home plenty of curb appeal. The Craftsman styling on this three-bedroom bungalow is highly attractive. A spacious, vaulted great room features a fireplace and is near the formal dining room, providing entertaining ease. Upstairs, two family bedrooms share a hall bath, while the master suite features a private bath.

Design HPT860187

First Floor: 1,028 square feet
Second Floor: 878 square feet
Total: 1,906 square feet
Bonus Space: 315 square feet
Width: 55'-4" **Depth:** 33'-0"

Colonial symmetry is accented by fine detailing on the exterior of this elegant three-bedroom home. Inside, the formal living room is to the right of the two-story foyer, while the formal dining room offers direct access to the efficient kitchen. Family living takes place at the rear of the home in the spacious family room, which is enhanced by a warming fireplace. Upstairs, two family bedrooms—each with a walk-in closet—share a full hall bath. The lavish master suite is rife with amenities. Please specify basement, crawlspace or slab foundation when ordering.

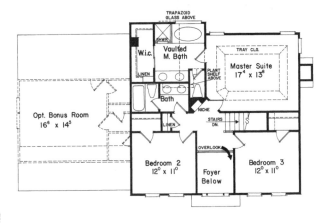

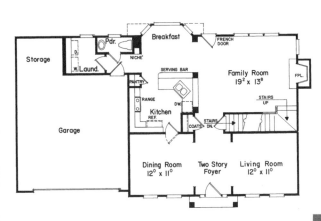

121

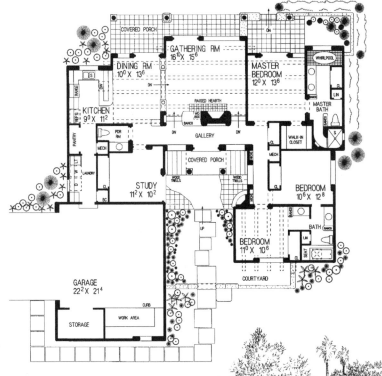

Design HPT860188

Square Footage: 1,907
Width: 61'-6" **Depth:** 67'-4"

Graceful curves welcome you into the courtyard of this Santa Fe home. Inside, a gallery directs traffic to the work zone on the left or the sleeping zone on the right. The wide covered rear porch is accessible from the dining room, gathering room (with fireplace) and secluded master bedroom. The master bath features a whirlpool tub, separate shower, double vanity and a spacious walk-in closet. Two additional bedrooms share a full bath, with separate vanities. Extra storage space is provided in the two-car garage.

Quote One®

Cost to build? See page 454 to order complete cost estimate to build this house in your area!

Design HPT860190

First Floor: 1,100 square feet
Second Floor: 808 square feet
Total: 1,908 square feet
Width: 34'-0" **Depth:** 32'-0"

L D

This Cape Cod home contains a very livable floor plan. The first floor centers around the huge country kitchen, which includes a raised-hearth fireplace, a window seat and backyard access. The living room and the private study are to the front of the plan. Three bedrooms and two full baths reside upstairs.

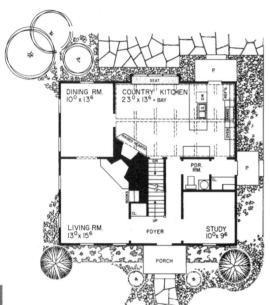

QUOTE ONE®
Cost to build? See page 454 to order complete cost estimate to build this house in your area!

122

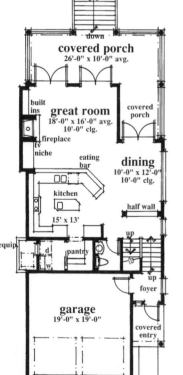

Design HPT860189

First Floor: 873 square feet
Second Floor: 1,037 square feet
Total: 1,910 square feet
Width: 27'-6" **Depth:** 64'-0"

This ultra-charming Saltbox design provides three bedrooms and two full baths, plus a handy powder room on the first floor. The great room offers a fireplace, built-in shelves and an art niche. French doors open the interior to the outdoors, extending the living spaces. A flexible dining space offers the possibility of a sitting area and leads out to the rear covered porch. Upstairs, a secondary bedroom easily converts to a study or home office. The master suite opens to a sun deck and features an angled corner shower and a garden tub.

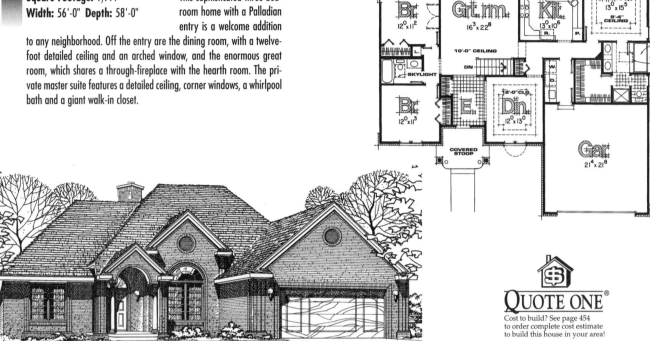

Design HPT860191

Square Footage: 1,911
Width: 56'-0" **Depth:** 58'-0"

This sophisticated three-bed-room home with a Palladian entry is a welcome addition to any neighborhood. Off the entry are the dining room, with a twelve-foot detailed ceiling and an arched window, and the enormous great room, which shares a through-fireplace with the hearth room. The private master suite features a detailed ceiling, corner windows, a whirlpool bath and a giant walk-in closet.

QUOTE ONE®

Cost to build? See page 454
to order complete cost estimate
to build this house in your area!

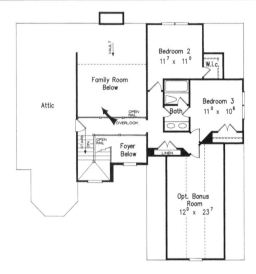

Design HPT860192

First Floor: 1,398 square feet
Second Floor: 515 square feet
Total: 1,913 square feet
Width: 48'-0" **Depth:** 50'-10"

Varied rooflines, keystones and arches set off a stucco exterior that's highlighted by a stone turret. Inside, the formal dining room leads to a private cov-ered porch. The central kitchen boasts a built-in planning desk, an ample pantry and an angled counter that overlooks the breakfast room. Sleeping quarters include a first-floor master suite with a vaulted bath, and two sec-ond-floor family bedrooms that share a balcony overlook and a full bath. Please specify basement, crawlspace or slab foundation when ordering.

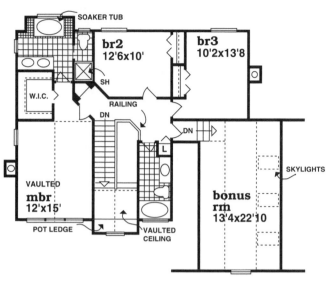

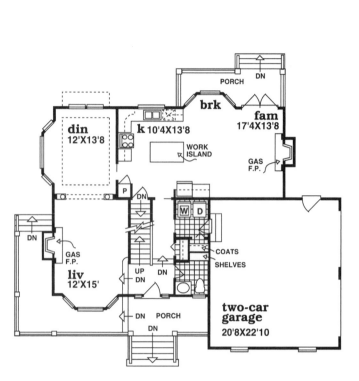

Design HPT860193

First Floor: 1,007 square feet
Second Floor: 917 square feet
Total: 1,924 square feet
Bonus Room: 325 square feet
Width: 53'-0" **Depth:** 44'-0"

This charming country exterior conceals an elegant interior, starting with formal living and dining rooms, each with a bay window. The gourmet kitchen features a work island and a breakfast area with its own bay window. A fireplace warms the family room, which opens to the rear porch through French doors. Second-floor sleeping quarters include a master suite with a whirlpool tub and a walk-in closet.

Design HPT860194

Square Footage: 1,925
Width: 78'-0" **Depth:** 52'-0"

This three-bedroom traditional beauty has all the features of a modern home but with the quaint look of a more established design. The living room features a fireplace, a sloped ceiling and a rear porch accessible via a French door. The kitchen boasts an ample pantry and easily serves a casual eating area as well as a formal dining room. Please specify crawlspace or slab foundation when ordering.

125

Design HPT860195

Square Footage: 1,927
Bonus Room: 400 square feet
Width: 64'-0" **Depth:** 56'-0"

A beautiful Palladian window and enchanting front porch lend this cottage country charm. Built-in cabinets flank the fireplace in the vaulted great room. The master bedroom offers a full bath with two walk-in closets and private access to a covered rear porch. Two family bedrooms each provide a walk-in closet and share a bath that offers separate vanities. The kitchen contains built-in cabinets and a serving counter that allows access to the dining room. Notice the two-car garage that boasts a separate entrance and a compact storage area. Please specify basement, crawlspace or slab foundation when ordering.

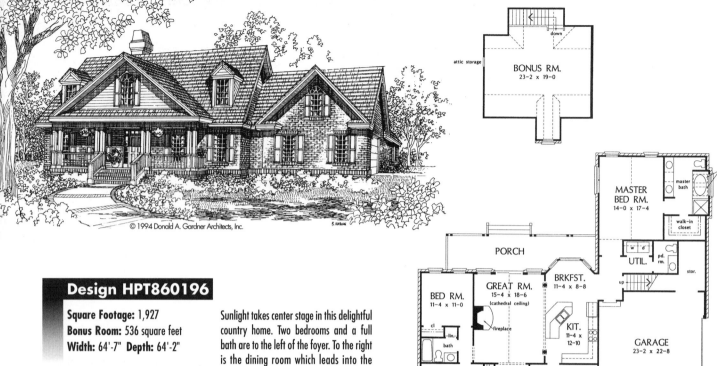

© 1994 Donald A. Gardner Architects, Inc.

B. Kincaid

BONUS RM.
23-2 x 19-0

attic storage

down

MASTER BED RM.
14-0 x 17-4

master bath

walk-in closet

PORCH

BRKFST.
11-4 x 8-8

UTIL.

w d

pd. rm.

stor.

BED RM.
11-4 x 11-0

GREAT RM.
15-4 x 18-6
(cathedral ceiling)

fireplace

KIT.
11-4 x 12-10

GARAGE
23-2 x 22-8

lin.

bath

BED RM.
13-8 x 11-8

FOYER
7-4 x 11-8

DINING
14-8 x 11-8

cl

up

© 1994 Donald A. Gardner Architects, Inc.

PORCH

Design HPT860196

Square Footage: 1,927
Bonus Room: 536 square feet
Width: 64'-7"   **Depth:** 64'-2"

Sunlight takes center stage in this delightful country home. Two bedrooms and a full bath are to the left of the foyer. To the right is the dining room which leads into the L-shaped kitchen, featuring a peninsular cooktop and connecting bayed breakfast area. The central great room offers a cathedral ceiling, a fireplace and access to the rear porch. The master suite is separated for privacy and features a lovely display of windows, a large walk-in closet and a luxurious whirlpool bath with skylights. Additional storage space is available in the garage and in the attic.

126

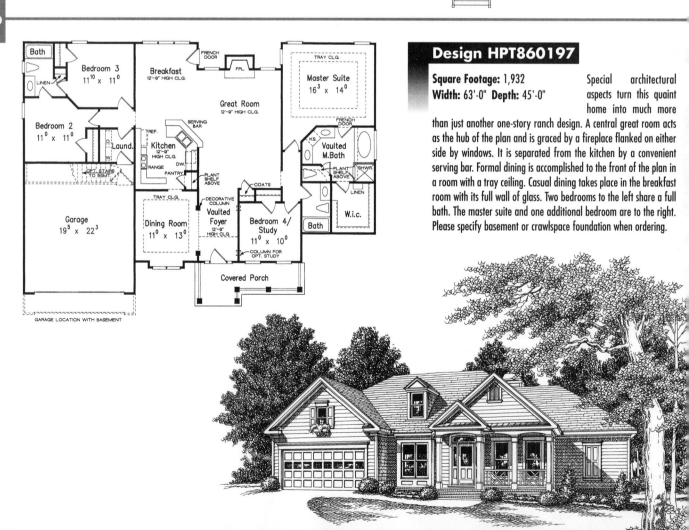

Bath

Bedroom 3
11¹⁰ x 11⁰

LINEN

Breakfast
12'-9" HIGH CLG.

FRENCH DOOR

FPL.

TRAY CLG.

Master Suite
16³ x 14⁰

Bedroom 2
11⁰ x 11⁰

D.

W.

Laund.

REF.

SERVING BAR

Great Room
12'-9" HIGH CLG.

KS.

FRENCH DOOR

Vaulted M.Bath

Kitchen
12'-9" HIGH CLG.

RANGE

DW.

PANTRY

PLANT SHELF ABOVE

PLANT SHELF ABOVE

SHWR

LINEN

OPT. STAIRS TO BSMT.

COATS

COVES

W.i.c.

Garage
19⁵ x 22³

TRAY CLG.

Dining Room
11⁰ x 13⁰

DECORATIVE COLUMN

Vaulted Foyer
12'-9" HIGH CLG.

Bedroom 4/ Study
11⁰ x 10⁰

Bath

COLUMN FOR OPT. STUDY

Covered Porch

GARAGE LOCATION WITH BASEMENT

Design HPT860197

Square Footage: 1,932
Width: 63'-0"   **Depth:** 45'-0"

Special architectural aspects turn this quaint home into much more than just another one-story ranch design. A central great room acts as the hub of the plan and is graced by a fireplace flanked on either side by windows. It is separated from the kitchen by a convenient serving bar. Formal dining is accomplished to the front of the plan in a room with a tray ceiling. Casual dining takes place in the breakfast room with its full wall of glass. Two bedrooms to the left share a full bath. The master suite and one additional bedroom are to the right. Please specify basement or crawlspace foundation when ordering.

Design HPT860199

Square Footage: 1,932
Width: 53'-5" **Depth:** 65'-10"

Enter this beautiful home through graceful archways and columns. The foyer, dining room and living room are one open space, defined by a creative room arrangement. The living room opens to the breakfast room and porch. The bedrooms are off a small hall reached through an archway. Two family bedrooms share a bath, while the master suite enjoys a private bath with a double-bowl vanity. Please specify slab or crawlspace foundation when ordering.

127

Design HPT860198

First Floor: 1,025 square feet
Second Floor: 911 square feet
Total: 1,936 square feet
Bonus Room: 410 square feet
Width: 53'-8" **Depth:** 67'-8"

The exterior of this three-bedroom home is enhanced by its many gables, arched windows and wraparound porch. A great room with an impressive fireplace leads to both the dining room and the screened porch with access to the deck. An open kitchen offers a country-kitchen atmosphere. The second-floor master suite has two walk-in closets and an impressive bath. Two family bedrooms share a full bath and plenty of storage. There is also bonus space over the garage.

Quote One®

Cost to build? See page 454 to order complete cost estimate to build this house in your area!

©1991 Donald A. Gardner Architects, Inc.

Design HPT860200

Square Footage: 1,937
Bonus Room: 414 square feet
Width: 76'-4" **Depth:** 73'-4"

L

Gables, dormers and an old-fashioned covered porch create a winsome, country look for this transitional exterior. Inside, an upscale, educated floor plan starts with the great room, which offers a sloped ceiling, a fireplace with an extended hearth, and built-in shelves for an entertainment center. Gourmet features in the kitchen include a cooktop island counter, easy-care ceramic tile flooring and a divided sink. A split bedroom plan allows a separate wing for the master suite.

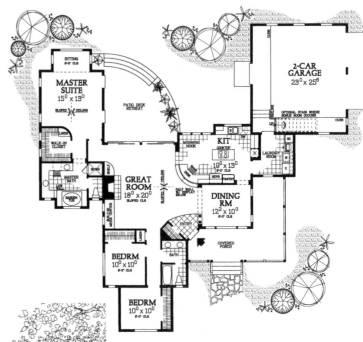

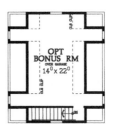

OPT BONUS RM OVER GARAGE 14⁰ x 22⁰

128

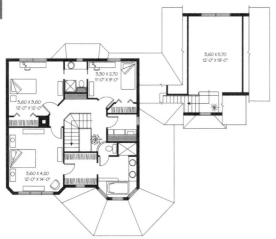

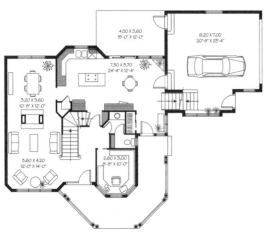

Design HPT860201

First Floor: 1,044 square feet
Second Floor: 894 square feet
Total: 1,938 square feet
Bonus Room: 228 square feet
Width: 58'-0" **Depth:** 43'-6"

This charming country traditional home provides a well-lit home office, harbored in a beautiful bay with three windows. The second-floor bay brightens the master bath, which has a double-bowl vanity, a step-up tub and a dressing area. The living and dining rooms share a two-sided fireplace. The gourmet kitchen has a cooktop island counter and enjoys outdoor views through sliding glass doors in the breakfast area. A sizable bonus room above the two-car garage can be developed into hobby space or a recreation room. This home is designed with a basement foundation.

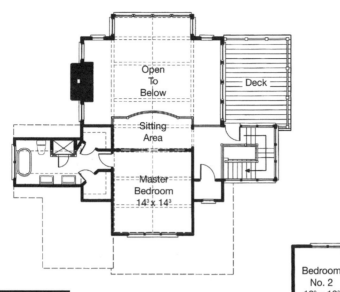

Design HPT860202

First Floor: 1,341 square feet
Second Floor: 598 square feet
Total: 1,939 square feet
Width: 50'-3" **Depth:** 46'-3"

Horizontal siding, plentiful windows and a wraparound porch grace this comfortable home. The great room is aptly named, with a fireplace, built-in seating and access to the rear deck. Meal preparation is a breeze with a galley kitchen designed for efficiency. A screened porch is available for sipping lemonade on warm summer afternoons. The first floor contains two bedrooms and a unique bath to serve family and guests. The second floor offers a private get-away with a master suite that supplies panoramic views from its adjoining sitting area. A master bath with His and Hers walk-in closets and a private deck completes the second floor.

129

Design HPT860204

Square Footage: 1,945
Width: 56'-6" **Depth:** 52'-6"

Corner quoins and keystones above graceful window treatments have long been a hallmark of elegant European-style exteriors—this home has all that and more. This becomes apparent upon entering the foyer, which is beautifully framed by columns in the dining room and the entrance to the vaulted great room. The left wing holds three secondary bedrooms—one doubles as a study—and a full bath. To the right of the combined kitchen and vaulted breakfast room, you will find the private master suite. A relaxing master bath and a large walk-in closet complete this splendid retreat. Please specify basement or crawlspace foundation when ordering.

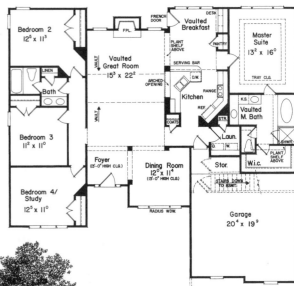

Cost to build? See page 454 to order complete cost estimate to build this house in your area!

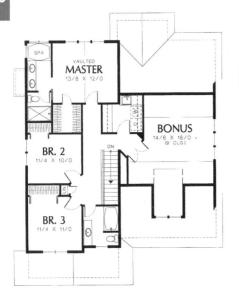

Design HPT860203

First Floor: 1,082 square feet
Second Floor: 864 square feet
Total: 1,946 square feet
Bonus Room: 358 square feet
Width: 40'-0" **Depth:** 52'-0"

Elements of the Craftsman style are evident in this gracious two-story home. A spacious living area designed for comfortable gatherings serves as the heart of this home. A gourmet kitchen boasts a food prep island and a morning nook with views of the back property. The second floor includes the vaulted master suite and two family bedrooms, which share a full bath. The connecting hall leads to a sizable bonus room.

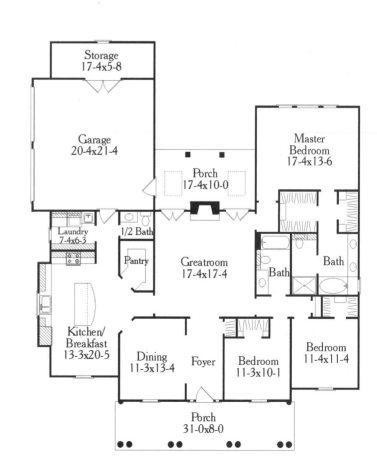

Design HPT860205

Square Footage: 1,955
Width: 56'-4" **Depth:** 67'-4"

Double pillars, beautiful transoms and sidelights set off the entry door and draw attention to this comfortable home. The foyer leads to a formal dining room and a great room with a pair of French doors framing a warming fireplace. The kitchen enjoys a large island/snack bar and walk-in pantry. Privacy is assured in the master suite—a large walk-in closet and full bath with a separate shower and large tub add to the pleasure of this wing. Two family bedrooms share a full bath at the front of the design. Please specify basement, crawlspace or slab foundation when ordering.

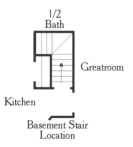

1/2 Bath
Greatroom
Kitchen
Basement Stair Location

Design HPT860206

First Floor: 1,113 square feet
Second Floor: 835 square feet
Total: 1,948 square feet
Opt. Second Floor: 1,080 square feet
Width: 54'-0" **Depth:** 34'-8"

The covered porch on the charming two-story home provides a place to relax and enjoy peaceful summer evenings. Warmed by the fireplace and lit by a bay window and glass door, the rear of this home becomes a favorite gathering place for family activities. The island kitchen offers a pantry. The option of a three- or four-bedroom second floor is available with this plan. Choose the plan that best fits your family's needs and you will receive the same master bedroom suite with a luxurious bath and walk-in closet. A balcony overlooks the entry in both options providing added excitement to the family-size home.

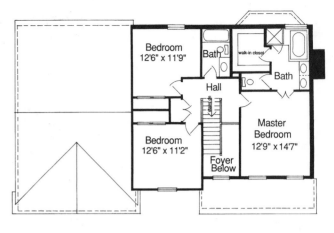

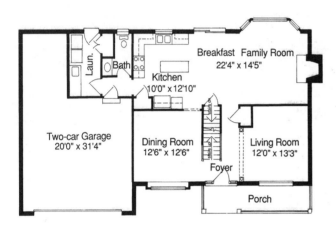

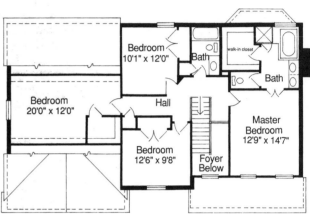

optional seocnd floor layout

132

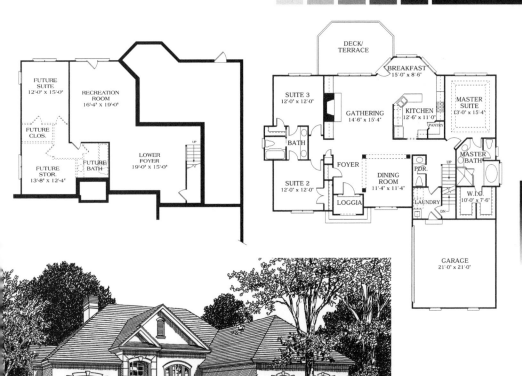

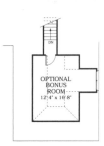

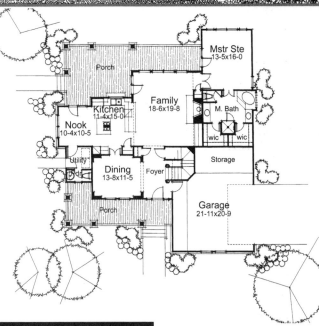

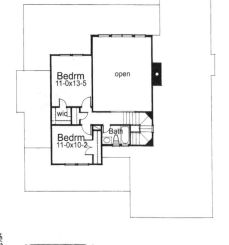

Design HPT860207

Square Footage: 1,950
Bonus Room: 255 square feet
Width: 59'-4" **Depth:** 61'-4"

Cost-effective design makes this a very attractive and sought-after house plan. An open formal dining room and spacious gathering room provide an inviting atmosphere for entertaining. The kitchen features a walk-in pantry and large breakfast bay. The master suite has a tray ceiling and full bath with His and Hers walk-in closets. Two additional bedrooms, one with a walk-in closet, share a full bath. An optional bonus room allows space for expansion.

133

Design HPT860208

First Floor: 1,510 square feet
Second Floor: 442 square feet
Total: 1,952 square feet
Width: 54'-7" **Depth:** 60'-3"

A stone chimney lends a sturdy appearance to this attractive country design, while a Palladian window offers elegance. The lavish master suite—with a fireplace, private patio, two closets and a luxurious bath—is the highlight of the floor plan. Other special features include another fireplace, flanked by two sets of French doors, in the living room; a gourmet kitchen with an island cooktop and walk-in pantry; and a sunny nook with access to the rear deck. Three second-floor bedrooms and a full bath complete the plan. Please specify basement, crawlspace or slab foundation when ordering.

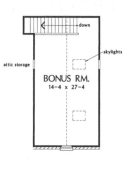

attic storage

down

skylights

BONUS RM.
14-4 x 27-4

Quote One®

Cost to build? See page 454
to order complete cost estimate
to build this house in your area!

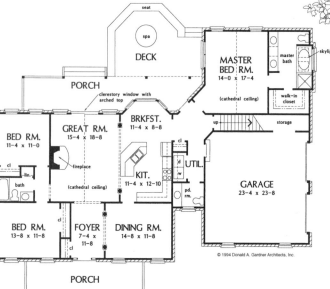

seat

spa

DECK

PORCH

clerestory window with
arched top

MASTER
BED RM.
14-0 x 17-4

(cathedral ceiling)

master
bath

skylights

walk-in
closet

BED RM.
11-4 x 11-0

GREAT RM.
15-4 x 18-8

BRKFST.
11-4 x 8-8

up

storage

cl

fireplace

(cathedral ceiling)

KIT.
11-4 x 12-10

d
w

UTIL.

GARAGE
23-4 x 23-8

lin.

bath

cl

BED RM.
13-8 x 11-8

FOYER
7-4 x
11-8

DINING RM.
14-8 x 11-8

pd.
rm.

cl

PORCH

© 1994 Donald A. Gardner Architects, Inc.

Design HPT860209

Square Footage: 1,954
Bonus Room: 436 square feet
Width: 71'-3" **Depth:** 62'-6"

This beautiful brick country home offers style and comfort for an active family. Two covered porches and a rear deck with a spa invite enjoyment of the outdoors. A cathedral ceiling soars above the central great room, warmed by an extended-hearth fireplace and by sunlight through an arch-top clerestory window. The splendid master suite enjoys its own secluded wing and provides a skylit whirlpool bath, a cathedral ceiling and private access to the deck.

Design HPT860210

Square Footage: 1,947
Bonus Room: 255 square feet
Width: 59'-4" **Depth:** 62'-2"

Twin columns frame the arched entry to this three-bedroom single-level home. Three additional columns define the formal dining room to the right of the entry foyer. The large gathering room, with a fireplace and built-in bookshelves, opens to the breakfast area, which accesses the rear deck/terrace. The master suite features a sloped ceiling, oval garden tub and His and Hers walk-in closets.

DECK/
TERRACE

BREAKFAST
15'-0" x 8'-6"

SUITE 3
12'-0" x 12'-0"

GATHERING
14'-6" x 15'-4"

KITCHEN
12'-6" x 11'-0"

MASTER
SUITE
13'-0" x 15'-4"

PANTRY

BATH

FOYER

MASTER
BATH

SUITE 2
12'-0" x 12'-0"

DINING
ROOM
11'-4" x 11'-4"

PDR.

UP

LOGGIA

LAUNDRY

W.I.C.
10'-0" x 7'-6"

OPT.
DN

GARAGE
21'-0" x 21'-0"

DN

OPTIONAL
BONUS
ROOM
12'-4" x 16'-8"

Design HPT860211

Square Footage: 1,955
Width: 65'-0" **Depth:** 58'-8"

A finely detailed covered porch and arch-topped windows announce a scrupulously designed interior, replete with amenities. Clustered sleeping quarters to the left include a deluxe master suite with a sloped ceiling, corner whirlpool bath and walk-in closet. Picture windows flanking a centered fireplace lend plenty of natural light to the great room. Please specify crawlspace or slab foundation when ordering.

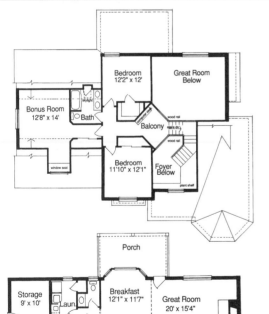

Design HPT860212

First Floor: 1,420 square feet
Second Floor: 549 square feet
Total: 1,969 square feet
Bonus Room: 268 square feet
Width: 58'-0" **Depth:** 44'-4"

An octagonal tower, covered porch, arched trim and boxed window decorate this home's exterior. Interior highlights include an elaborate wood rail staircase in the foyer, great room with fireplace, and large expanses of glass overlooking the backyard. The first-floor master suite offers privacy, while upstairs, two family bedrooms share a hall bath and access to a bonus room.

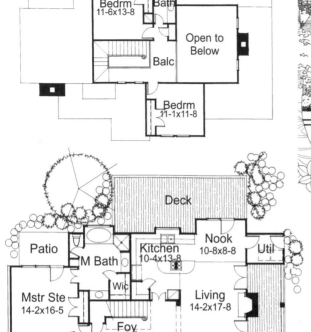

Second floor plan labels: Bedrm 11-6x13-8, Bath, Open to Below, Balc, Bedrm 11-1x11-8

First floor plan labels: Deck, Patio, M Bath, Kitchen 10-4x13-8, Nook 10-8x8-8, Util, Wic, Living 14-2x17-8, Mstr Ste 14-2x16-5, Foy, Pdr, Cvd Porch, Dining 13-5x11-8, Cvd Porch

Design HPT860213

First Floor: 1,427 square feet
Second Floor: 545 square feet
Total: 1,972 square feet
Width: 59'-6" **Depth:** 40'-6"

This gabled two-story farmhouse features a covered front porch flanked by two commanding stone chimneys. Inside, the foyer leads to the living and dining rooms. The living room provides a fireplace and double French doors to the side porch. The kitchen and eating nook are open and easily serve the living area. A private bath pampers the master suite. Two additional bedrooms share a full bath and a balcony space on the second floor. Please specify basement, crawlspace or slab foundation when ordering.

Design HPT860214

Square Footage: 1,974
Width: 72'-0" **Depth:** 55'-2"

A Palladian window brightens the dining room of this attractive home. The great room offers a fireplace and a built-in entertainment center; double doors lead to a covered rear porch with skylights. The master suite, conveniently near the laundry room, features a full bath, a large walk-in closet and easy access to the back porch and patio. An island kitchen shares an eating bar with the breakfast area. A full hall bath is shared by two family bedrooms, one with double doors opening to the porch. Please specify basement, crawlspace or slab foundation when ordering.

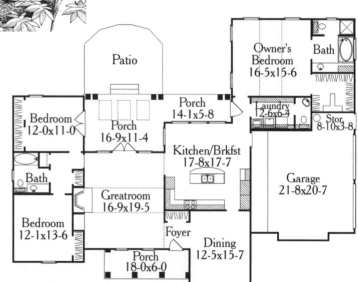

Floor plan labels: Patio, Owner's Bedroom 16-5x15-6, Bath, Bedroom 12-0x11-0, Porch 16-9x11-4, Porch 14-1x5-8, Laundry 12-6x6-4, Stor 8-10x3-8, Bath, Kitchen/Brkfst 17-8x17-7, Garage 21-8x20-7, Greatroom 16-9x19-5, Bedroom 12-1x13-6, Foyer, Dining 12-5x15-7, Porch 18-0x6-0

Design HPT860216

First Floor: 924 square feet
Second Floor: 1,052 square feet
Total: 1,976 square feet
Width: 44'-8" **Depth:** 36'-0"

This magnificent European adaptation is highlighted by hip roofs, plenty of windows, cornice detailing and an elegant entrance door adjacent to an impressive two-story turret. Inside are a magnificent living/dining area, U-shaped kitchen, breakfast bar and comfortable family room. A gracious staircase leads upstairs to a deluxe master suite lavish in its efforts to pamper you. A well-lit home office and two secondary bedrooms share this level with a full bath. This home is designed with a basement foundation.

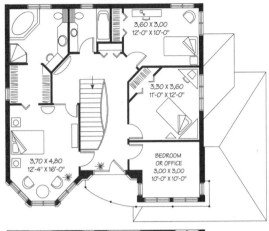

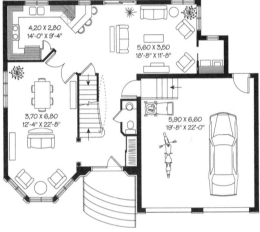

137

Design HPT860215

Square Footage: 1,977
Bonus Room: 430 square feet
Width: 69'-8" **Depth:** 67'-6"

A two-story foyer with a Palladian window above sets the tone for this sunlit home. Columns mark the passage from the foyer to the great room, where a central fireplace and built-in cabinets are found. A screened porch with four skylights above and a wet bar provides a pleasant place to start the day or wind down after work. The kitchen is flanked by the formal dining room and the breakfast room. Hidden quietly in the rear, the master suite includes a bath with dual vanities and skylights. Two family bedrooms (one an optional study) share a bath that has twin sinks.

QUOTE ONE®
Cost to build? See page 454 to order complete cost estimate to build this house in your area!

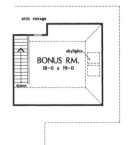

© 1994 Donald A. Gardner Architects, Inc.

GARAGE
28/2 X 29/10

UP

Design HPT860217

Main Level: 1,106 square feet
Upper Level: 872 square feet
Total: 1,978 square feet
Width: 38'-0" **Depth:** 35'-0"

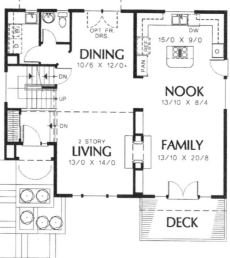

D/W

OPT. FR. DRS.

DINING
10/6 X 12/0+

DN

UP

DN

2 STORY
LIVING
13/0 X 14/0

PAN REF

15/0 X 9/0

DW

NOOK
13/10 X 8/4

FAMILY
13/10 X 20/8

DECK

BR. 3
11/0 X 10/8

BR. 2
11/0 X 10/0

DN

SHELVES

LOFT

FOYER
BELOW

LIN

LIVING
BELOW

VAULTED
MASTER
15/2 X 12/0

Though this home gives the impression of the Northwest, it will be the winner of any neighborhood. From the foyer, the two-story living room is just a couple of steps up and features a through-fireplace. The U-shaped kitchen has a cooktop work island, an adjacent nook and easy access to the formal dining room. A spacious family room shares the fireplace with the living room, is enhanced by built-ins and also offers a quiet deck for stargazing. The upstairs consists of two family bedrooms sharing a full bath and a vaulted master suite complete with a walk-in closet and sumptuous bath. A two-car, drive-under garage has plenty of room for storage. Please specify basement or slab foundation when ordering.

Design HPT860219

First Floor: 1,060 square feet
Second Floor: 927 square feet
Total: 1,987 square feet
Bonus Room: 267 square feet
Width: 55'-8" **Depth:** 32'-0"

Brick and siding combine to give this home a fine, sturdy look. Inside, the sunken great room creates a charming first impression. A formal dining room offers room for entertaining, and the spacious kitchen and breakfast area function well for everyday activities. The second floor offers three bedrooms, highlighted by a spacious master suite with a nine-foot raised ceiling and deluxe bath. Taking advantage of all usable space, a computer center is neatly provided at the top of the stairs where the balcony overlooks the foyer.

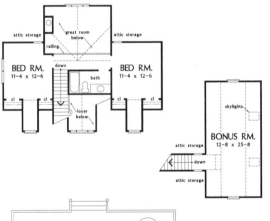

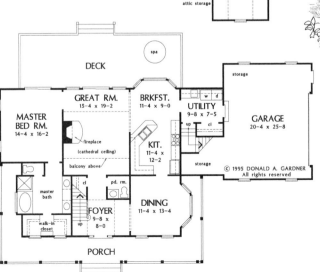

© 1995 DONALD A. GARDNER
All rights reserved

© 1995 Donald A. Gardner Architects, Inc.

Design HPT860218

First Floor: 1,480 square feet
Second Floor: 511 square feet
Total: 1,991 square feet
Bonus Room: 363 square feet
Width: 73'-0" **Depth:** 51'-10"

This farmhouse has plenty to offer, from its covered front porch to its rear deck with a spa. Inside, the amenities continue, including a bayed formal dining room, a great room—with both a fireplace and direct access to the rear deck—and a bayed breakfast nook. A nearby kitchen is spacious and shares a snack bar with the breakfast/great room area. A deluxe master bedroom pampers you with access to the rear deck and a luxurious bath. Upstairs, two family bedrooms share a full hall bath and a balcony overlooking the great room.

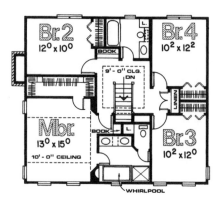

Design HPT860220

First Floor: 1,000 square feet
Second Floor: 993 square feet
Total: 1,993 square feet
Width: 56'-0" **Depth:** 30'-0"

At less than 2,000 square feet, this plan captures the heritage and romance of an authentic Colonial home with many modern amenities. A central hall leads to the formal rooms at the front where the homeowner can display showpiece furnishings. For daily living, the informal rooms can't be beat. The master suite shows further evidence of tasteful design. A volume ceiling, large walk-in closet and whirlpool tub await the fortunate homeowner. Each secondary bedroom includes bright windows to add natural lighting and comfort.

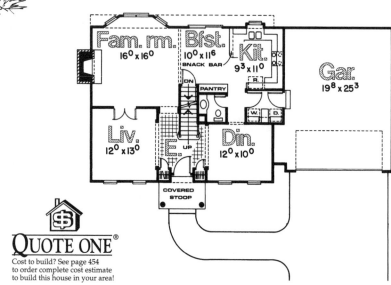

Quote One®
Cost to build? See page 454
to order complete cost estimate
to build this house in your area!

Design HPT860221

First Floor: 1,071 square feet
Second Floor: 924 square feet
Total: 1,995 square feet
Bonus Room: 280 square feet
Width: 55'-10" **Depth:** 38'-6"

Move-up buyers can enjoy all the luxuries of this two-story home highlighted by an angled staircase separating the dining room from casual living areas. A bay window and built-in desk in the breakfast area are just a few of the plan's amenities. The sleeping zone occupies the second floor—away from everyday activities—and includes a master suite and two secondary bedrooms. Please specify basement or crawlspace foundation when ordering.

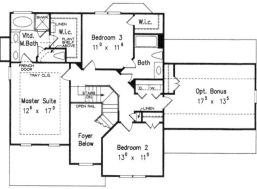

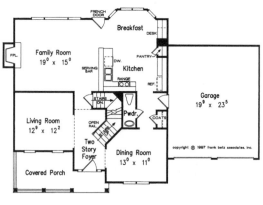

Design HPT860223

First Floor: 916 square feet
Second Floor: 1,080 square feet
Total: 1,996 square feet
Width: 44'-8" **Depth:** 36'-0"

A lovely recessed porch with a curved balcony above lends a touch of classic design to this two-story brick home. The breakfast bar—with sliding glass doors to the rear yard—is adjacent to the family room. The U-shaped kitchen shares a snack bar with the family room. Bedrooms on the second floor include two family bedrooms and the master suite with a bath that offers a corner whirlpool tub and separate shower. This home is designed with a basement foundation.

141

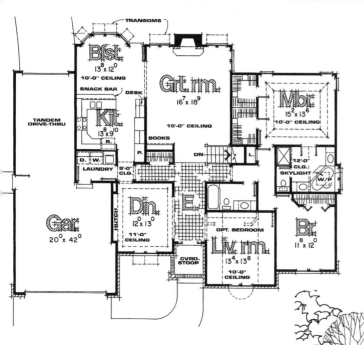

Design HPT860222

Square Footage: 1,996
Width: 64'-0" **Depth:** 50'-0"

Practical, yet equipped with a variety of popular amenities, this pleasant ranch home is an excellent choice for empty-nesters or small families. The front living room can become a third bedroom if you choose. The great room with a dramatic fireplace serves as the main living area. A luxurious master suite features a ten-foot tray ceiling and a large bath with a whirlpool tub and twin vanities. The kitchen with a breakfast room serves both the dining and great rooms. Please specify basement or slab foundation when ordering.

QUOTE ONE®

Cost to build? See page 454
to order complete cost estimate
to build this house in your area!

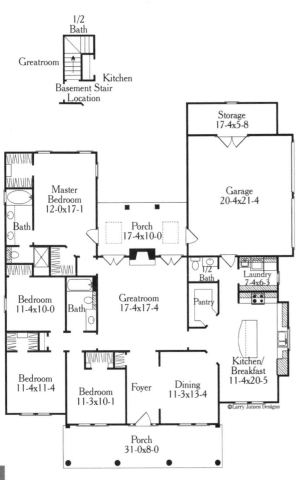

1/2 Bath

Greatroom

Kitchen

Basement Stair Location

Storage
17-4x5-8

Master Bedroom
12-0x17-1

Garage
20-4x21-4

Bath

Porch
17-4x10-0

Bedroom
11-4x10-0

Bath

1/2 Bath

Laundry
7-4x6-3

Greatroom
17-4x17-4

Pantry

Kitchen/Breakfast
11-4x20-5

Bedroom
11-4x11-4

Bedroom
11-3x10-1

Foyer

Dining
11-3x13-4

©Larry James Designs

Porch
31-0x8-0

Design HPT860225

Square Footage: 1,997
Width: 56'-4" **Depth:** 67'-4"

The curved front steps, columned porch and symmetrical layout give this charming home a Georgian appeal. The central great room offers radiant French doors on both sides of the fireplace. The large kitchen with its adjoining walk-in pantry will gratify any cook. Three family bedrooms share a hall bath, while the master suite features a pampering bath and two walk-in closets. Please specify basement, crawlspace or slab foundation when ordering.

Design HPT860224

Square Footage: 1,997
Bonus Room: 310 square feet
Width: 64'-4" **Depth:** 63'-0"

The center of the hub of this charming plan is the spacious kitchen with an island and serving bar. The nearby breakfast nook accesses the greenhouse. A built-in media center beside a warming fireplace is the focal point of the family room. Bedroom 2 shares a full bath with the den/study, which might also be a third bedroom. The master suite features a lavish bath and a walk-in closet. Please specify basement, crawlspace or slab foundation when ordering.

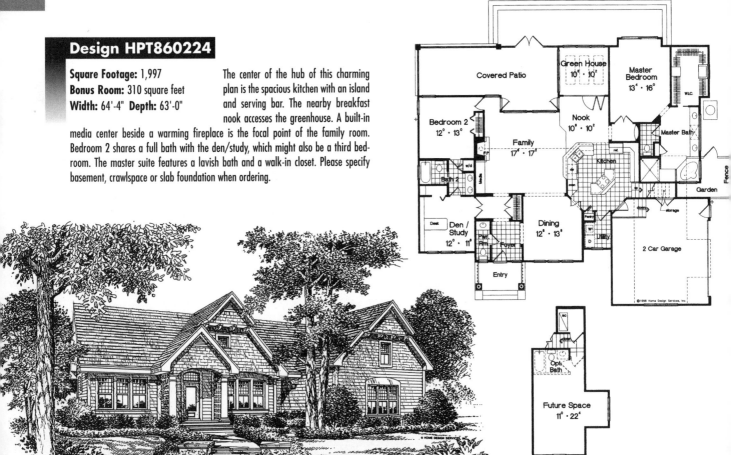

Covered Patio

Green House
10⁸·10⁰

Master Bedroom
13⁴·16⁰

W.I.C.

Bedroom 2
12⁰·13⁰

Nook
10⁰·10⁰

Master Bath

Family
17⁸·17⁸

Kitchen

Bath 2

Garden

Fence

Den/Study
12⁰·11⁰

Dining
12⁸·13⁰

2 Car Garage

storage

Entry

Foyer

©1998 Home Design Services, Inc.

Opt. Bath

Future Space
11⁰·22⁴

Design HPT860226

First Floor: 1,421 square feet
Second Floor: 578 square feet
Total: 1,999 square feet
Width: 52'-0" **Depth:** 47'-4"

Growing families will love this unique plan, which combines all the essentials with an abundance of stylish touches. Start with the living area—a spacious great room with high ceilings, windows overlooking the backyard, a through-fireplace to the kitchen and access to the rear yard. The master suite, with a whirlpool tub and walk-in closet, is found downstairs while three family bedrooms are upstairs. Please specify basement or slab foundation when ordering.

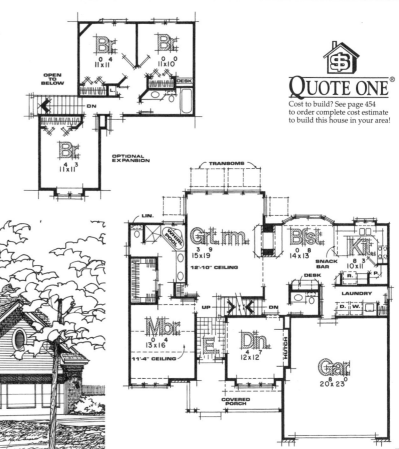

Quote One®
Cost to build? See page 454 to order complete cost estimate to build this house in your area!

143

Design HPT860227

First Floor: 1,421 square feet
Second Floor: 578 square feet
Total: 1,999 square feet
Width: 52'-0" **Depth:** 47'-4"

Victorian details and a covered veranda lend a peaceful flavor to the elevation of this popular home. A volume entry hall views the formal dining room and luxurious great room. Imagine the comfort of relaxing in the great room, which features a high ceiling and abundant windows. The kitchen and breakfast area include a through-fireplace, snack bar, walk-in pantry and wrapping counters. The secluded master suite features a vaulted ceiling, luxurious dressing/bath area and corner whirlpool tub. Upstairs, the family sleeping quarters contain special amenities unique to each.

Design HPT860228

First Floor: 1,530 square feet
Second Floor: 469 square feet
Total: 1,999 square feet
Width: 59'-6" **Depth:** 53'-0"

Stone porch supports and wide pillars lend a Craftsman look to this design. An octagonal home office is just to the left of the entry, and a formal dining room sits to the right. The central great room offers a fireplace and a wall of windows that overlooks the deck; the nearby island kitchen includes a walk-in pantry and adjoins the breakfast bay. Access the greenhouse from the expansive side deck. Double doors open to the master bedroom, which provides a private bath with an angled soaking tub; two family bedrooms are found upstairs. Please specify basement, crawlspace or slab foundation when ordering.

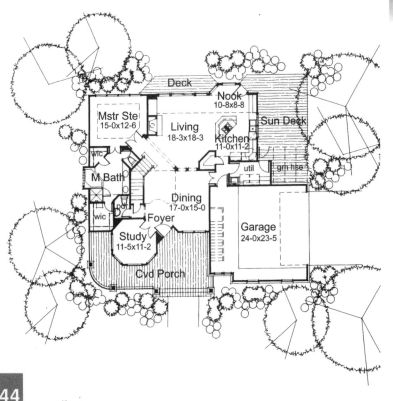

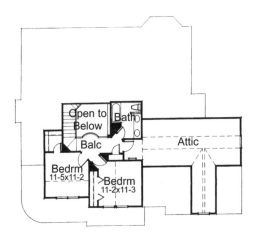

Design HPT860229

Square Footage: 2,000
Width: 65'-10" **Depth:** 51'-11"

An arched entrance, a sunburst and side-lights around the four-panel door provide a touch of class to this European-style home. An angled bar opens the kitchen and breakfast room to the living room with bookcases and a fireplace. The master suite boasts a sloped ceiling and private bath with a five-foot turning radius, dual vanity, and a separate tub and shower. Two family bedrooms provide ample closet space and share a full hall bath and linen closet. Don't miss the two-car garage located to the far right of the plan.

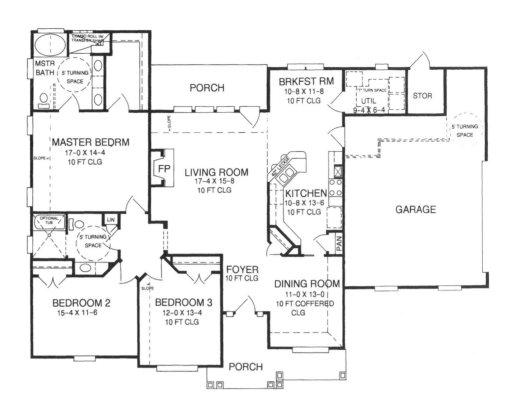

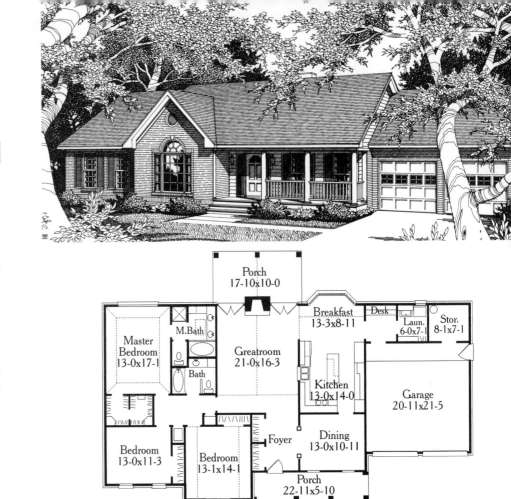

Design HPT860231

Square Footage: 2,018
Width: 74'-11" **Depth:** 49'-2"

This ranch home is highlighted by a front-facing covered porch, a mixture of brick and siding, and a Palladian window set into a front-facing gable. The dining room, on the right, includes accent columns and convenient kitchen service. The great room offers twin French doors that access the rear porch. The master suite is set to the rear and features a walk-in closet made for two, dual vanities and a compartmented toilet. Please specify basement, crawlspace or slab foundation when ordering.

Design HPT860230

Square Footage: 2,019
Loft: 384 square feet
Width: 56'-0" **Depth:** 56'-3"

This design takes inspiration from the casual fishing cabins of the Pacific Northwest and interprets it for modern livability. It offers three options for a main entrance. One door opens to a mud porch, while two French doors on the side porch open into a dining room with bay-window seating. Another porch entrance opens directly into the great room. The secluded master bedroom features a bath with a clawfoot tub and twin pedestal sinks. Two more bedrooms share a bath.

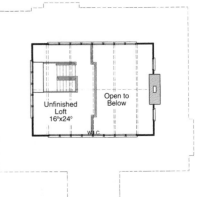

Design HPT860232

Square Footage: 2,023
Width: 73'-0" **Depth:** 66'-0"

Contemporary elegance is yours for the taking in this charming ranch plan. The exterior is adorned with large brick quoins set against a stucco facade, keystone lintels, a prominent front-facing pediment and multiple rooflines. Special features include twelve-foot ceilings in the kitchen and dining and living rooms. The kitchen/eating area accesses the courtyard, while the living room accesses the rear porch. The master suite is located on the left side of the plan, where it indulges in a walk-in closet and full bath with a garden tub and separate shower. Two additional bedrooms are on the right side and share a full bath. Please specify crawlspace or slab foundation when ordering.

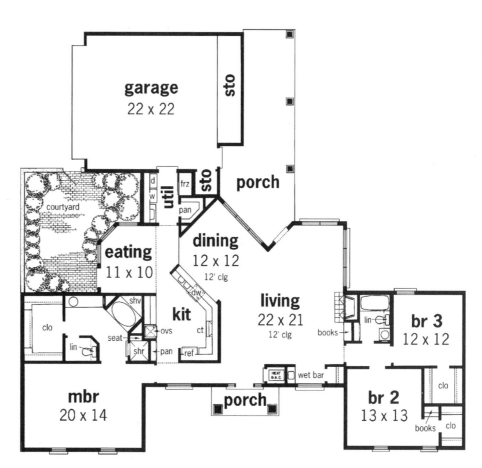

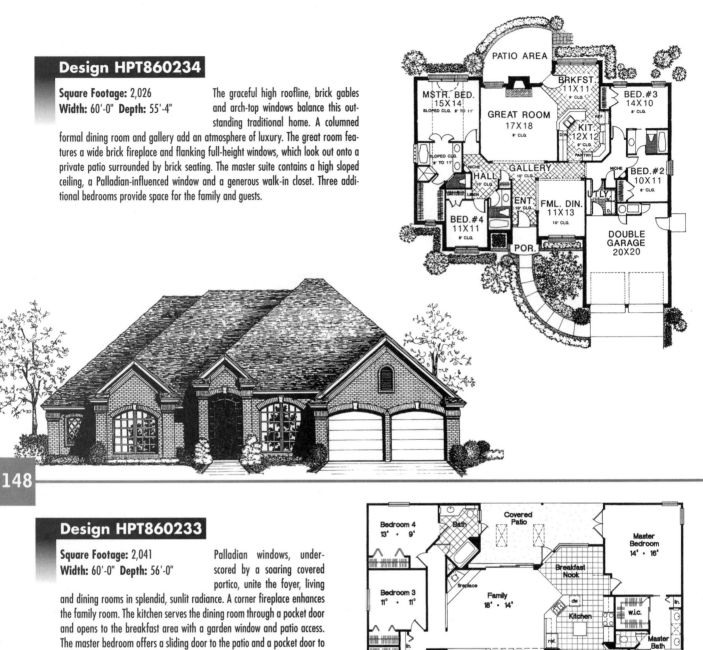

Design HPT860234

Square Footage: 2,026
Width: 60'-0" **Depth:** 55'-4"

The graceful high roofline, brick gables and arch-top windows balance this outstanding traditional home. A columned formal dining room and gallery add an atmosphere of luxury. The great room features a wide brick fireplace and flanking full-height windows, which look out onto a private patio surrounded by brick seating. The master suite contains a high sloped ceiling, a Palladian-influenced window and a generous walk-in closet. Three additional bedrooms provide space for the family and guests.

148

Design HPT860233

Square Footage: 2,041
Width: 60'-0" **Depth:** 56'-0"

Palladian windows, underscored by a soaring covered portico, unite the foyer, living and dining rooms in splendid, sunlit radiance. A corner fireplace enhances the family room. The kitchen serves the dining room through a pocket door and opens to the breakfast area with a garden window and patio access. The master bedroom offers a sliding door to the patio and a pocket door to a full bath with a walk-in closet and spa tub.

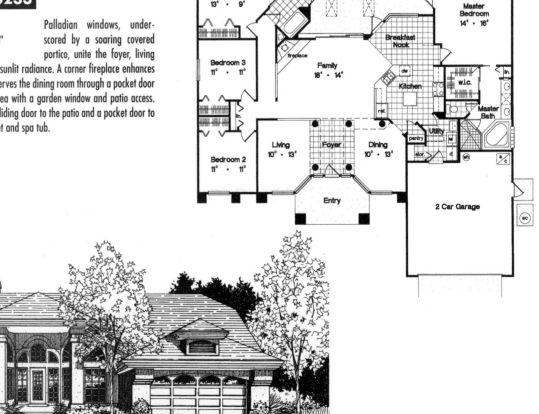

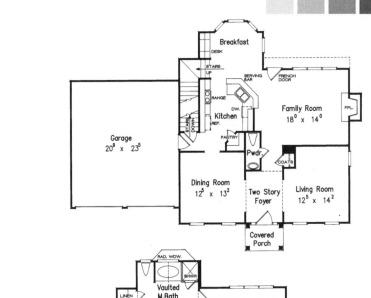

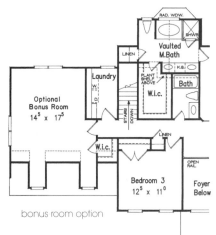

Design HPT860235

First Floor: 1,068 square feet
Second Floor: 977 square feet
Total: 2,045 square feet
Bonus Room: 412 square feet
Width: 56'-4" **Depth:** 43'-0"

Two upper-level floor plan options are included with this delightful design. Both options include space for two family bedrooms, a full bath and a master suite with a tray ceiling and a lavish private bath. The second option adds an upper-level laundry room and a bonus room with a walk-in closet. Downstairs, the large family room, bayed breakfast room and efficient kitchen cater to comfort. Please specify basement or crawlspace foundation when ordering.

bonus room option

149

Design HPT860237

Square Footage: 2,046
Width: 68'-2" **Depth:** 57'-4"

Curb appeal abounds in this three-bedroom farmhouse with its columned porch, keystone lintel windows and stucco facade. A warming fireplace with adjacent built-ins in the great room can be viewed from the foyer and breakfast area. Light pours in from the rear porch with windows at every turn. Please specify basement, crawlspace or slab foundation when ordering.

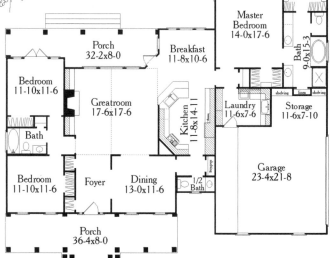

Design HPT860236

Square Footage: 2,061
Width: 60'-0" **Depth:** 57'-1"

This one-living-area plan is perfect for the contemporary family with a taste for classic design. The traditional exterior presents a combination of brick and stone. The large great room is open to the kitchen and breakfast room. Full-view doors lead to a large covered patio. Off the entry, a home office/study provides plenty of built-ins. The master bedroom features a sloped ceiling from eight feet to eleven feet and a large walk-in closet.

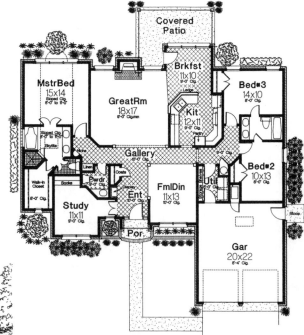

Design HPT860239

First Floor: 1,546 square feet
Second Floor: 512 square feet
Total: 2,058 square feet
Width: 46'-0" **Depth:** 65'-0"

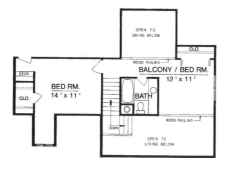

Columns, shutters and French doors give this New Orleans-style home great appeal. The living room features plenty of windows and French-door access to the rear porch. The modified galley kitchen easily serves the bay-windowed informal dining area and the formal dining room. The master suite enjoys seclusion on the first level. Two bedrooms sharing a full bath are tucked upstairs. Please specify basement, crawlspace or slab foundation when ordering.

151

Design HPT860238

Square Footage: 2,065
Width: 60'-0" **Depth:** 65'-10"

Two elevations are available for this delightful one-story home. Brick, shutters and corner quoins provide European ambiance, while gables and horizontal wood siding offer a more traditional elevation—the choice is yours. With an eleven-foot ceiling, unobstructed rear views, a warming fireplace and built-in bookcases, the great room will certainly be the family's favorite. A nook opens to the patio area near a convenient U-shaped kitchen.

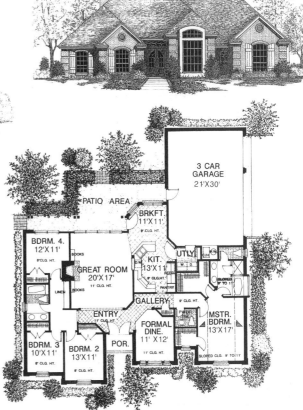

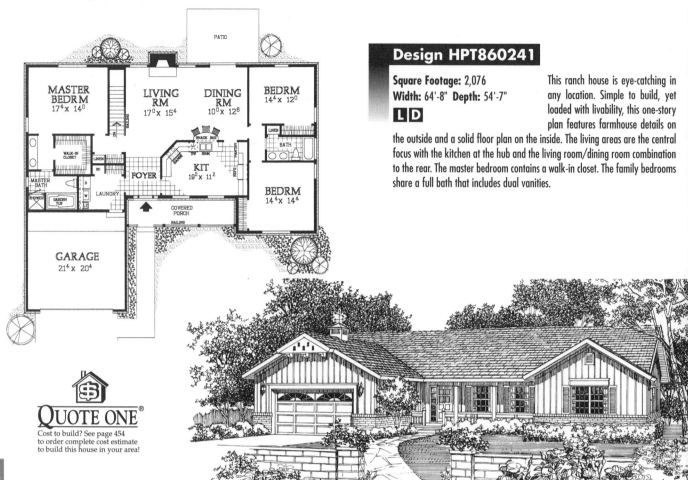

MASTER BEDRM 17⁴ x 14⁰

LIVING RM 17⁰ x 15⁴

DINING RM 10⁰ x 12⁶

BEDRM 14⁴ x 12⁰

WALK-IN CLOSET

LINEN

BATH

MASTER BATH

SHOWER

GARDEN TUB

LAUNDRY

FOYER

KIT 19⁰ x 11²

SNACK BAR

DW SINK

BEDRM 14⁴ x 14⁴

COVERED PORCH

RAILING

GARAGE 21⁴ x 20⁴

PATIO

Design HPT860241

Square Footage: 2,076
Width: 64'-8" **Depth:** 54'-7"

L **D**

This ranch house is eye-catching in any location. Simple to build, yet loaded with livability, this one-story plan features farmhouse details on the outside and a solid floor plan on the inside. The living areas are the central focus with the kitchen at the hub and the living room/dining room combination to the rear. The master bedroom contains a walk-in closet. The family bedrooms share a full bath that includes dual vanities.

Quote One®

Cost to build? See page 454 to order complete cost estimate to build this house in your area!

152

Design HPT860240

Square Footage: 2,078
Width: 75'-0" **Depth:** 47'-10"

Colonial style meets farmhouse style, furnishing old-fashioned charisma with a flourish. Off the dining room is a large island kitchen that easily serves both formal and informal areas. Nearby is the spacious great room, warmed by a center fireplace and large windows. The secluded master suite, with its vaulted ceiling, is tucked behind the three-car garage. The master bath contains a relaxing tub, double-bowl vanity, separate shower and compartmented toilet.

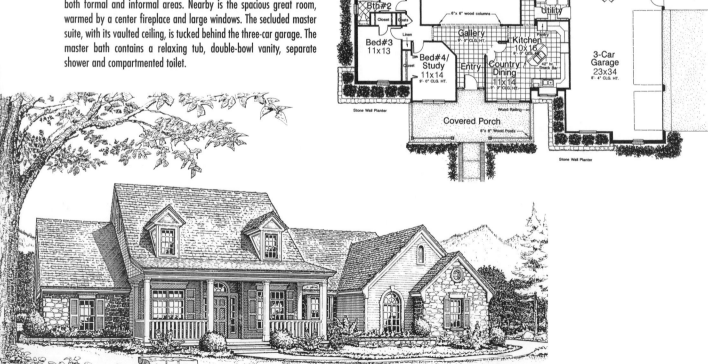

Covered Patio

Bed#2 13x12

Great Room 24x16 9'-0" CLG.HT.

MasterBed 18x13 VAULTED CEILING FROM 8'-0" TO 10'-0"

MstrBth 10'-0" CLG. HT.

Bth#2

Bed#3 11x13

Gallery

Kitchen 10x16

Utility

Walk-In Closet

Bed#4/ Study 11x14 9'-0" CLG.HT.

Entry

Country Dining 11x14

3-Car Garage 23x34 8'-4" CLG. HT.

Covered Porch

Stone Wall Planter

Stone Wall Planter

G. MacDonald

153

Design HPT860242

First Floor: 1,113 square feet
Second Floor: 965 square feet
Total: 2,078 square feet
Width: 46'-0" **Depth:** 41'-5"

Elegant detailing, a charming veranda and a tall brick chimney make a pleasing facade on this four-bedroom, two-story Victorian home. From the large, bayed parlor with a sloped ceiling to the sunken gathering room with a fireplace, there's plenty to appreciate about this floor plan. The formal dining room opens to the parlor for convenient entertaining. An L-shaped kitchen with an attached breakfast room sits nearby. Upstairs quarters include a master suite with a private dressing area and a whirlpool tub, and three family bedrooms.

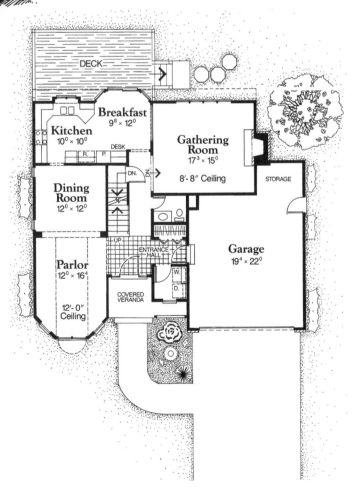

Quote One®

Cost to build? See page 454
to order complete cost estimate
to build this house in your area!

Design HPT860244

First Floor: 1,524 square feet
Second Floor: 558 square feet
Total: 2,082 square feet
Bonus Room: 267 square feet
Width: 60'-0" **Depth:** 50'-4"

A multi-textured exterior provides a rich, solid look to this extraordinary home.

From the foyer, view the cozy fireplace and stylish French doors of the great room. A grand entry into the formal dining room pulls these two rooms together for a spacious feeling. Split stairs lead to the second floor where a balcony overlooking the foyer directs you to two secluded bedrooms or to a computer area with a desk and bookshelves.

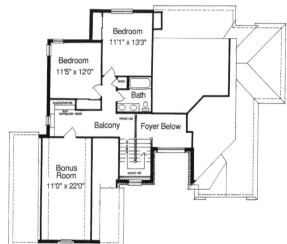

154

QUOTE ONE®

Cost to build? See page 454 to order complete cost estimate to build this house in your area!

Design HPT860243

Square Footage: 2,086
Width: 82'-0" **Depth:** 58'-4"

L

This home contains dual-use space in the wonderful sunken living room and media area. A raised-hearth fireplace further accents this area. The kitchen and the breakfast bay look over the snack bar to the sunken family area. A few steps from the island kitchen and functioning well with the upper patio is the formal dining room. Two family bedrooms share a full bath. The private master suite includes a sitting area and French doors that open to a private covered patio.

This beautiful three-bedroom home boasts many attractive features. Two covered porches will entice you outside, while inside, a special sun room on the first floor brings the outdoors in. The foyer opens on the right to a comfortable family room that may be used as a home office. On the left, the living area is warmed by the sun room and a cozy corner fireplace. A formal dining area lies adjacent to an efficient kitchen with a central island and breakfast nook overlooking the back porch. The second level offers two family bedrooms served by a full bath. A spacious master suite with a walk-in closet and luxurious bath completes the second floor. This home is designed with a daylight basement.

Design HPT860245

First Floor: 1,146 square feet
Second Floor: 943 square feet
Total: 2,089 square feet
Bonus Room: 324 square feet
Width: 56'-0" **Depth:** 38'-0"

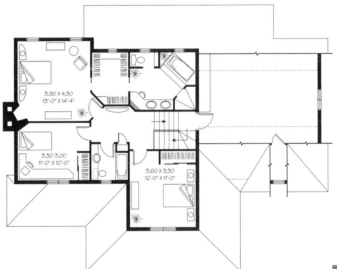

155

Design HPT860246

Square Footage: 2,089
Width: 61'-8" **Depth:** 50'-4"

This four-bedroom, three-bath home offers the finest in modern amenities. The huge family room, which opens up to the patio, has space for a fireplace and media equipment. The master suite, located just off the kitchen and nook, is private yet easily accessible. It has a double-door entry and a bed wall with glass above. Bedrooms 3 and 4 share their own bath while Bedroom 2 has a private bath.

Design HPT860247

Square Footage: 2,089
Future Space: 878 square feet
Width: 63'-10" **Depth:** 64'-7"

Clean lines and classic country features are found inside and out of this lakeside home. The fireplace framed by French doors will certainly draw attention to the wonderfully spacious great room. The efficient kitchen design serves the dining room and the breakfast nook easily. Two family bedrooms share a full bath while the master suite has a private compartmented bath. The rear porch supplies additional living space. Please specify basement, crawlspace or slab foundation when ordering.

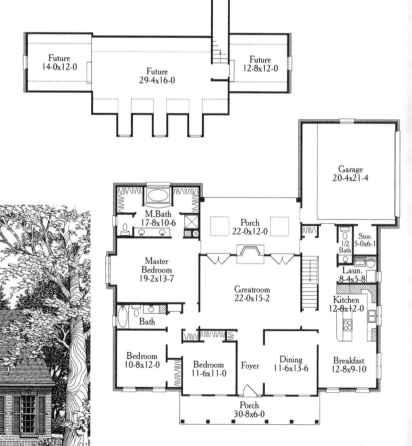

Quote One®
Cost to build? See page 454 to order complete cost estimate to build this house in your area!

© Stephen Fuller, Inc.

Porch

Master Bath

Master Bedroom
16⁴ x 13⁶

Breakfast
13⁴ x 9⁰

Bedroom/ Office
10⁴ x 11⁰

Kitchen
13⁴ x 10⁶

Great Room
17⁰ x 17⁸

Bedroom #2
10⁴ x 12⁰

Dining Room
11⁴ x 12¹⁰

Bedroom/ Study
11² x 12⁰

Two Car Garage
20⁶ x 19⁶

Porch

Design HPT860249

Square Footage: 2,090
Width: 61'-0" **Depth:** 70'-6"

This traditional home features board-and-batten and cedar shingles in a well-proportioned exterior. The foyer opens to the dining room and leads to the great room, which offers French doors to the rear columned porch. An additional bedroom or study shares a full bath with a family bedroom, while the lavish master suite enjoys a luxurious private bath. This home is designed with a walkout basement foundation.

Quote One®
Cost to build? See page 454 to order complete cost estimate to build this house in your area!

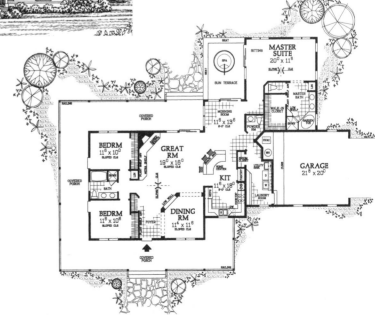

MASTER SUITE
20⁰ x 11⁸

GREAT RM
19⁰ x 18⁰

BEDRM
11⁰ x 10⁰

BEDRM
11⁸ x 10⁸

DINING RM
11⁴ x 11⁶

KIT
11⁸ x 9⁰

GARAGE
21⁸ x 20⁰

Design HPT860248

Square Footage: 2,090
Width: 84'-6" **Depth:** 64'-0"

L D

This classic farmhouse enjoys a wraparound porch that's perfect for enjoyment of the outdoors. The formal dining room is defined by a low wall and graceful archways set off by decorative columns. The tiled kitchen has a center island counter with a snack bar and adjoins a laundry area. Two family bedrooms reside to the side of the plan; each enjoys private access to the covered porch. A secluded master suite features a sitting area with access to the rear terrace and spa.

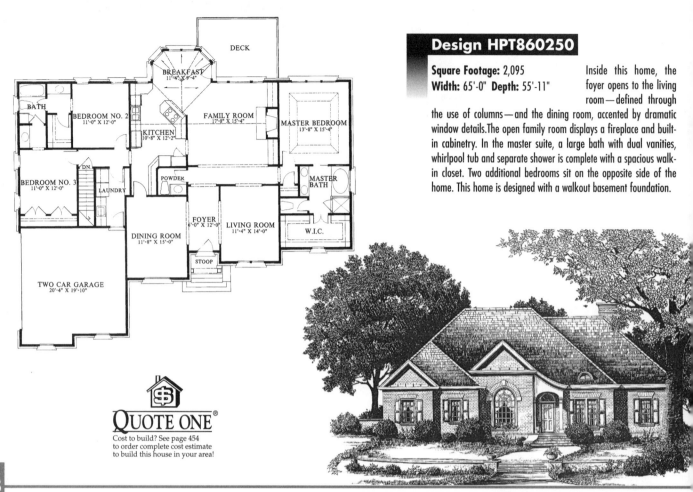

DECK

BREAKFAST
11'-4" X 9'-4"

BATH

BEDROOM NO. 2
11'-0" X 12'-0"

KITCHEN
10'-8" X 12'-2"

FAMILY ROOM
17'-8" X 15'-4"

MASTER BEDROOM
13'-8" X 15'-4"

DN

BEDROOM NO. 3
11'-0" X 12'-0"

LAUNDRY

POWDER

MASTER
BATH

DINING ROOM
11'-8" X 15'-0"

FOYER
6'-0" X 12'-0"

LIVING ROOM
11'-4" X 14'-0"

W.I.C.

STOOP

TWO CAR GARAGE
20'-4" X 19'-10"

QUOTE ONE®

Cost to build? See page 454
to order complete cost estimate
to build this house in your area!

158

Design HPT860250

Square Footage: 2,095
Width: 65'-0" **Depth:** 55'-11"

Inside this home, the foyer opens to the living room—defined through the use of columns—and the dining room, accented by dramatic window details. The open family room displays a fireplace and built-in cabinetry. In the master suite, a large bath with dual vanities, whirlpool tub and separate shower is complete with a spacious walk-in closet. Two additional bedrooms sit on the opposite side of the home. This home is designed with a walkout basement foundation.

QUOTE ONE®

Cost to build? See page 454
to order complete cost estimate
to build this house in your area!

PATIO

WHIRLPOOL TUB

fam
18'x15'
SUNKEN

SH

brk
13'6x8'

HALF WALL

DESK

k
11'2x14'

PLANT SHELF OVER

FOYER

TRAY CEILING

**12'x10'
din**

H F

T W D

**12'x14'
mbr**

PORCH

WALL LINE OVER

**21'6 x 22'
two~car
garage**

Design HPT860251

First Floor: 1,445 square feet
Second Floor: 652 square feet
Total: 2,097 square feet
Width: 56'-8" **Depth:** 48'-4"

A portico entry, graceful arches and brick detailing create an appealing low-maintenance exterior for this design. A half-circle transom over the entry lights the two-story foyer. A plant shelf lines the hallway to the family room, which features a vaulted ceiling, a masonry fireplace and French-door access to the railed patio. The nearby kitchen has a center prep island and a built-in desk, which overlooks the family room.

DESK

OPEN TO FAMILY ROOM

br 4
11'4 x10'4

HALF WALL

OPEN

PLANT SHELF

FOYER
BELOW

10'x11'4
br 2

10'10x12'
br 3

DESK

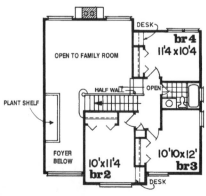

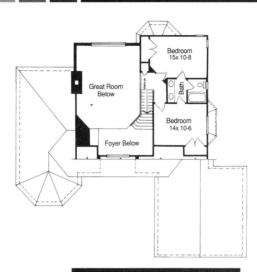

Design HPT860253

First Floor: 1,626 square feet
Second Floor: 475 square feet
Total: 2,101 square feet
Width: 59'-0" **Depth:** 60'-8"

An exterior with a rich solid look and an exciting roofline is very important to the discriminating buyer. An octagonal and vaulted master bedroom with a vaulted ceiling and a sunken great room with a balcony above provide this home with all the amenities. The island kitchen is easily accessible to both the breakfast area and the bayed dining area. The tapered staircase leads to two family bedrooms, each with their own access to a full dual-vanity bath. Both bedrooms have a vast closet area with double doors.

159

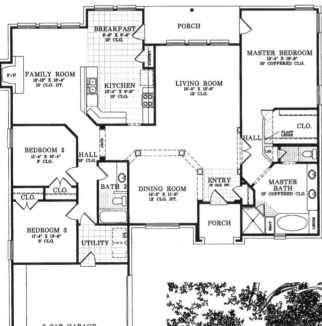

Design HPT860252

Square Footage: 2,109
Width: 57'-8" **Depth:** 67'-0"

L

A traditional exterior combined with an open design and amenities normally found in a larger home makes this plan a popular choice. The dining room is defined by three columns connected by arches and adds elegance to the home. The split-bedroom plan separates the master bedroom from Bedrooms 2 and 3 to allow privacy. With ten-foot ceilings and a luxury bath, the master suite offers it all. The family room, breakfast area and kitchen are open to one another for informal family use.

QUOTE ONE®

Cost to build? See page 454
to order complete cost estimate
to build this house in your area!

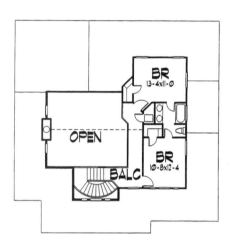

Design HPT860255

First Floor: 1,598 square feet
Second Floor: 514 square feet
Total: 2,112 square feet
Width: 52'-0" **Depth:** 53'-0"

A sweeping wraparound porch, a Palladian window and an interesting variation in rooflines spice up this spacious, well-lit country plan. The foyer opens to a winding staircase and to the spacious living room. The formal dining room is set off by graceful columns and features a pocket door to the kitchen. The master suite is a sumptuous affair with full bath and secluded position. Two family bedrooms complete the second floor. Please specify basement, crawlspace or slab foundation when ordering.

MSTR 16-0x17-4
BATH 12-0x11-4
CVD POR 9' WIDE
UTIL 7-8x5-8
KIT 12-6x12-6
NOOK 11-6x12-6
GRT RM 19-4x18-8
DIN 10-8x13-8
FOY
CVD POR 8' WIDE

BR 13-4x11-0
OPEN
BR 10-8x12-4
BALC

Design HPT860254

Square Footage: 2,123
Bonus Room: 556 square feet
Width: 58'-0" **Depth:** 71'-0"

This three-bedroom home features a country facade with dormers and a columned covered porch. The heart of this home is the living room with a fireplace, built-in bookshelf and access to the rear sun porch with skylights. The spacious kitchen provides plenty of counter space and an eating area. The master bedroom boasts His and Hers walk-in closets and a sumptuous private bath. Please specify basement, crawlspace or slab foundation when ordering.

dn
open to living rm below
unfinished attic
15 x 30

garage 22 x 21
sto 11x7
porch 20 x 11
skylt skylt
mbr 20 x 14
entry
util 8x8
up
living 21 x 15
books
books
br 2 12 x 12
kit 14 x 11
w. d
dwl ov
ref
rng
bar
r/a
eating 13 x 12
dining 12 x 12
foy
br 3 12 x 12
lin
porch 30 x 8

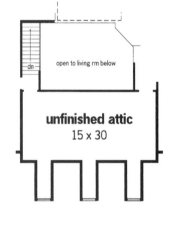

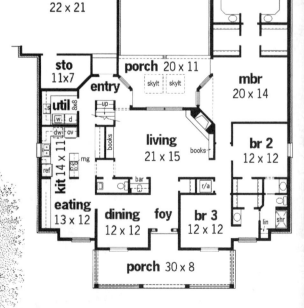

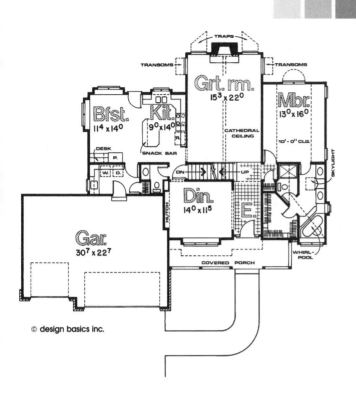

© design basics inc.

Farmhouse style is updated and improved by a high roofline and a central arched window. Many windows, lap siding and a covered porch give this elevation a welcoming country flair. The formal dining room with hutch space is conveniently located near the island kitchen. A main-floor laundry room with a sink is discreetly located next to the bright breakfast area with a desk and pantry. Highlighting the spacious great room are a raised-hearth fireplace, a cathedral ceiling and trapezoid windows. Special features in the master suite include a large dressing area with a double vanity, skylight, step-up corner whirlpool tub and generous walk-in closet. Upstairs, the three secondary bedrooms are well separated from the master bedroom and share a hall bath.

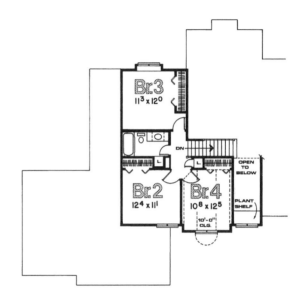

Design HPT860256

First Floor: 1,505 square feet
Second Floor: 610 square feet
Total: 2,115 square feet
Width: 64'-0" **Depth:** 52'-0"

QUOTE ONE®

Cost to build? See page 454
to order complete cost estimate
to build this house in your area!

161

Design HPT860258

First Floor: 1,581 square feet
Second Floor: 534 square feet
Total: 2,115 square feet
Bonus Room: 250 square feet
Width: 53'-0" **Depth:** 43'-4"

Behind the gables and arched windows of this fine traditional home lies a great floor plan. The two-story foyer leads past a formal dining room defined by decorative pillars to a vaulted family room with a fireplace. The L-shaped kitchen is open to the sunny breakfast nook and provides access to the rear property. The lavish master suite is separated from the two upper-level bedrooms. Please specify basement or crawlspace foundation when ordering.

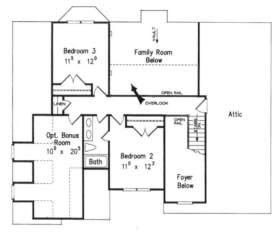

162

Design HPT860257

Square Footage: 2,120
Width: 62'-0" **Depth:** 62'-6"

Arched lintels and fanlight windows act as graceful accents for this design. The formal dining room is to the front of the plan and is open to the entry foyer. A private den also opens off the foyer with double doors. Bedrooms are split, with the master suite to the right side of the design and family bedrooms to the left. This home is designed with a walkout basement foundation.

QUOTE ONE®
Cost to build? See page 454 to order complete cost estimate to build this house in your area!

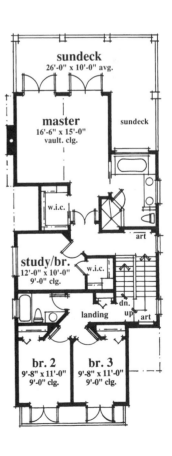

Design HPT860259

First Floor: 878 square feet
Second Floor: 1,245 square feet
Total: 2,123 square feet
Width: 27'-6" **Depth:** 64'-0"

Key West Conch style blends Old World charm with New World comfort in this picturesque design. A glass-paneled entry lends a warm welcome and complements a captivating front balcony. Reminiscent of the Caribbean "shotgun" houses, the narrow floor plan works well. Two sets of French doors open the great room to wide views and extend the living areas to the back covered porch. A gourmet kitchen is prepared for any occasion with a prep sink, plenty of counter space, an ample pantry and an eating bar. The mid-level landing leads to two additional bedrooms, a full bath and a windowed art niche. Double French doors open the upper-level master suite to a sun deck.

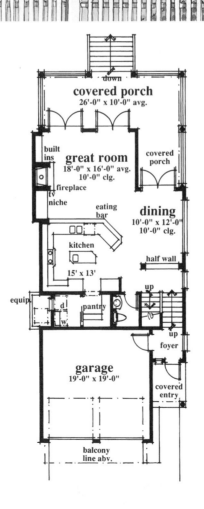

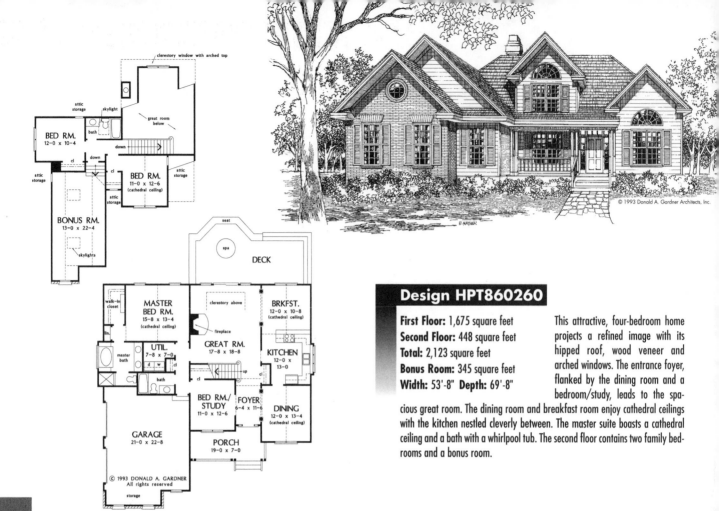

Design HPT860260

First Floor: 1,675 square feet
Second Floor: 448 square feet
Total: 2,123 square feet
Bonus Room: 345 square feet
Width: 53'-8" **Depth:** 69'-8"

This attractive, four-bedroom home projects a refined image with its hipped roof, wood veneer and arched windows. The entrance foyer, flanked by the dining room and a bedroom/study, leads to the spacious great room. The dining room and breakfast room enjoy cathedral ceilings with the kitchen nestled cleverly between. The master suite boasts a cathedral ceiling and a bath with a whirlpool tub. The second floor contains two family bedrooms and a bonus room.

Design HPT860261

Square Footage: 2,125
Width: 65'-0" **Depth:** 56'-8"

A luxurious master suite is just one of the highlights offered with this stunning plan — an alternate plan for this suite features a sitting room, wet bar and fireplace. Two family bedrooms to the right of the plan share a full bath that includes a dual vanity. Tile adds interest to the living area and surrounds the spacious great room, which offers a fireplace and access to the rear patio. A formal dining room and a secluded den or study flank the foyer.

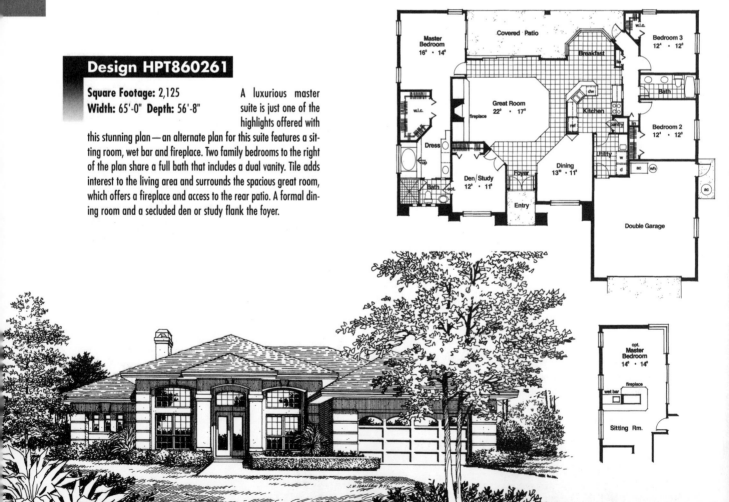

Design HPT860262

First Floor: 1,583 square feet
Second Floor: 543 square feet
Total: 2,126 square feet
Bonus Room: 251 square feet
Width: 53'-0" **Depth:** 47'-0"

Here's a new country home with a fresh face and a dash of Victoriana. Inside, decorative columns help define an elegant dining room, but the heart of the home is the vaulted family room with a radius window and a French door to the rear property. The first-floor master suite features a private bath with a vaulted ceiling and a whirlpool tub set off with a radius window. Please specify basement, slab or crawlspace foundation when ordering.

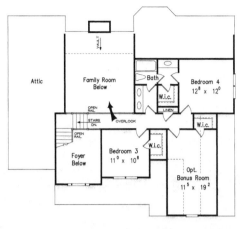

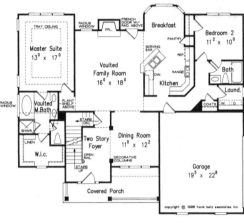

165

Design HPT860263

Square Footage: 2,127
Expandable Area: 338 square feet
Width: 62'-0" **Depth:** 62'-6"

Three arched windows provide just the right touch of elegance and give this home a picturesque appeal. The great room with a corner fireplace is located near the breakfast area and kitchen. Ten-foot ceilings in all major living areas give the plan an open, spacious feel. The master suite includes a luxury bath with a coffered ceiling, large His and Hers closets and a whirlpool tub. Please specify crawlspace or slab foundation when ordering.

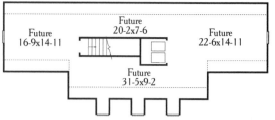

Future
16-9x14-11

Future
20-2x7-6

Future
22-6x14-11

Future
31-5x9-2

Storage
4-11x12-6

Garage
21-7x21-5

Porch
9-0x21-6

Bath

Desk

Laun.
5-5x6-0

Owner's
Bedroom
14-3x15-11

Greatroom
18-7x15-11

Breakfast
12-7x10-1

Bedroom
13-3x11-0

Kitchen
12-7x11-3

Bath

Bath

Bonus Room
12-7x12-7

Foyer

Dining
12-7x11-2

Bedroom
13-3x10-2

Porch
32-8x6-0

Design HPT860264

Square Footage: 2,127
Future Space: 1,095 square feet
Width: 69'-0" **Depth:** 67'-4"

This home's facade employs an elegant balance of country comfort and traditional grace. Inside, the foyer opens to the formal dining room. Straight ahead, the great room offers a warm fireplace. Two secondary bedrooms and a full bath can be found just off the kitchen. The private master bath enjoys dual vanities, two walk-in closets and a compartmented toilet. Upstairs, unfinished space is ready for expansion. Please specify basement, crawlspace or slab foundation when ordering.

166

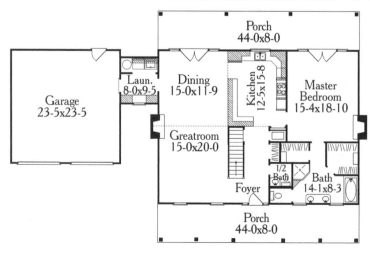

Design HPT860265

First Floor: 1,501 square feet
Second Floor: 631 square feet
Total: 2,132 square feet
Width: 76'-0" **Depth:** 48'-4"

This home reveals its rustic charm with a metal roof, dormers and exposed column rafters. The full-length porch is an invitation to comfortable living inside. The great room shares a fireplace with the spacious dining room that offers rear-porch access. The kitchen is this home's focus, with plenty of counter and cabinet space, a window sink and an open layout. Please specify basement, crawlspace or slab foundation when ordering.

Porch
44-0x8-0

Laun.
8-0x9-5

Dining
15-0x11-9

Kitchen
12-5x15-8

Master
Bedroom
15-4x18-10

Garage
23-5x23-5

Greatroom
15-0x20-0

1/2
Bath

Bath
14-1x8-3

Foyer

Porch
44-0x8-0

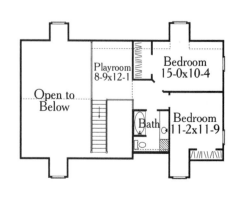

Open to
Below

Playroom
8-9x12-1

Bedroom
15-0x10-4

Bath

Bedroom
11-2x11-9

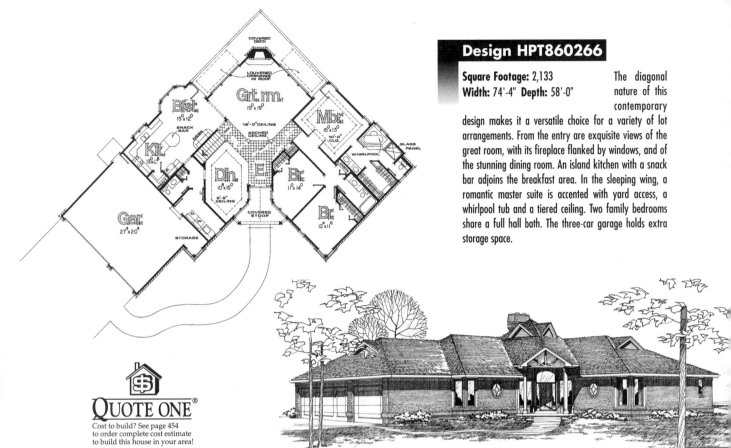

Design HPT860266

Square Footage: 2,133
Width: 74'-4" **Depth:** 58'-0"

The diagonal nature of this contemporary design makes it a versatile choice for a variety of lot arrangements. From the entry are exquisite views of the great room, with its fireplace flanked by windows, and of the stunning dining room. An island kitchen with a snack bar adjoins the breakfast area. In the sleeping wing, a romantic master suite is accented with yard access, a whirlpool tub and a tiered ceiling. Two family bedrooms share a full hall bath. The three-car garage holds extra storage space.

Quote One®

Cost to build? See page 454 to order complete cost estimate to build this house in your area!

167

Design HPT860267

First Floor: 1,050 square feet
Second Floor: 1,085 square feet
Total: 2,135 square feet
Width: 50'-8" **Depth:** 39'-4"

This lovely country design features a stunning wrapping porch and plenty of windows to provide the interior with natural light. The living room boasts a centered fireplace, which helps to define this spacious, open area. The casual living room leads outdoors to a rear porch. Upstairs, four bedrooms cluster around a central hall. The master suite sports a walk-in closet and a deluxe bath. This home is designed with a basement foundation.

Bedroom #3
11⁶ x 11⁰

Bedroom #2
11³ x 11⁰

Sun Room
12' x 13⁹

Porch

Master Bedroom
13³ x 15⁶

Porch

Breakfast
10' x 9⁰

Kitchen
12' x 13³

Great Room
18⁰ x 14⁰

Dining Room
10' x 10⁷

Den/Guest Room
13⁴ x 14⁸

Two Car Garage
20⁸ x 21⁸

Design HPT860269

Square Footage: 2,140
Width: 62'-0" **Depth:** 60'-6"

Imagine the luxurious living you'll enjoy in this beautiful home! The natural beauty of stone combined with sophisticated window detailing represents the good taste you'll find carried throughout the design. Common living areas include the great room with a fireplace, the sun room and the breakfast area, plus rear and side porches. The master suite features private access to the rear porch and a wonderfully planned bath. This home is designed with a walkout basement foundation.

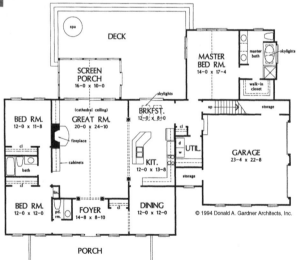

spa

DECK

SCREEN PORCH
16-0 x 10-0

MASTER BED RM.
14-0 x 17-4

master bath

skylights

walk-in closet

skylights

BED RM.
12-0 x 11-8

GREAT RM.
20-0 x 24-10
(cathedral ceiling)

fireplace

cabinets

BRKFST.
12-0 x 8-0

skylights

up

storage

UTIL.

GARAGE
23-4 x 22-8

KIT.
12-0 x 13-8

storage

BED RM.
12-0 x 12-0

bath

pd. rm.

FOYER
14-8 x 8-10

DINING
12-0 x 12-0

PORCH

© 1994 Donald A. Gardner Architects, Inc.

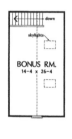

down

skylights

BONUS RM.
14-4 x 26-4

Design HPT860268

Square Footage: 2,136
Bonus Room: 405 square feet
Width: 76'-4" **Depth:** 64'-4"

The spacious great room of this elegant country home features built-in cabinets, a fireplace and a cathedral ceiling that continues into the adjoining screened porch. An island kitchen is conveniently grouped with the great room, the dining room and the skylit breakfast area for the cook who enjoys conversation while preparing meals. The master suite features a cathedral ceiling, a large walk-in closet and a relaxing master bath with a skylit whirlpool tub and separate shower. Two secondary bedrooms share a full bath.

© 1994 Donald A. Gardner Architects, Inc.

QUOTE ONE®
Cost to build? See page 454 to order complete cost estimate to build this house in your area!

Design HPT860270

Square Footage: 2,150
Finished Basement: 2,150 square feet
Width: 64'-0" **Depth:** 60'-4"

From the arched covered entry to the jack-arch window, this house retains the distinction of a much larger home. From the foyer and across the spacious great room, French doors and large side windows give a generous view of the covered rear porch. A bay window in the keeping room allows natural light to flow through the kitchen and breakfast area. This home is designed with a walkout basement foundation.

Quote One®
Cost to build? See page 454 to order complete cost estimate to build this house in your area!

169

Design HPT860271

Square Footage: 2,150
Width: 62'-0" **Depth:** 59'-8"

Open, casual living space is offset by a quiet den or study with its own fireplace in this casual Colonial-style home. The dining room features French doors that access the front porch. Nearby, the gourmet kitchen enjoys a breakfast area convenient to the family bedrooms. A bright sun room opens to the covered rear porch through French doors. A corner whirlpool tub highlights the master suite. This home is designed with a walkout basement foundation.

Design HPT860273

First Floor: 1,628 square feet
Second Floor: 527 square feet
Total: 2,155 square feet
Bonus Room: 207 square feet
Width: 54'-0" **Depth:** 46'-10"

Multiple rooflines, charming stonework and a covered entryway all combine to give this home plenty of curb appeal. Inside, the two-story foyer leads to either the formal dining room or the spacious, vaulted great room. An efficient kitchen offers an abundance of counter and cabinet space, plus a vaulted breakfast room and a nearby keeping room. Please specify basement or crawlspace foundation when ordering.

170

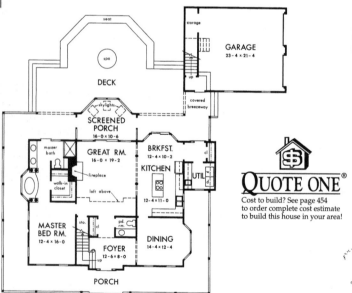

QUOTE ONE®

Cost to build? See page 454 to order complete cost estimate to build this house in your area!

Design HPT860272

First Floor: 1,526 square feet
Second Floor: 635 square feet
Total: 2,161 square feet
Bonus Room: 355 square feet
Width: 76'-4" **Depth:** 74'-2"

Clerestory windows with arched tops enhance the exterior both front and back, as well as allowing natural light to penetrate into the foyer and the great room. A kitchen with an island counter and a breakfast area is open to the great room. The master suite includes a walk-in closet and a lush master bath. The second level contains two bedrooms sharing a full bath and a loft/study area overlooking the great room.

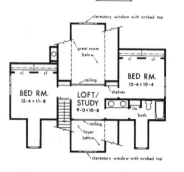

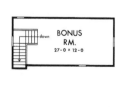

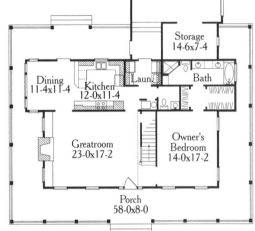

Bedroom
17-10x11-10

Bedroom
17-10x11-8

Garage
20-4x20-4

Storage
14-6x7-4

Laun.

Bath

Dining
11-4x11-4

Kitchen
12-0x11-4

Greatroom
23-0x17-2

Owner's
Bedroom
14-0x17-2

Porch
58-0x8-0

Design HPT860275

First Floor: 1,339 square feet
Second Floor: 823 square feet
Total: 2,162 square feet
Width: 58'-0" **Depth:** 67'-2"

Charming dormer windows and a wraparound porch make this country home a prize. The great room offers porch views and a fireplace to warm guests and family alike. The dining room features a bumped-out wall of windows and easy service from the nearby kitchen. The master suite is pampered by a walk-in closet and lavish bath. Upstairs, two family bedrooms enjoy plenty of closet space and share a full bath. Please specify basement, crawlspace or slab foundation when ordering.

Design HPT860274

First Floor: 1,499 square feet
Second Floor: 665 square feet
Total: 2,164 square feet
Bonus Room: 380 square feet
Width: 69'-8" **Depth:** 40'-6"

The grand foyer leads to a two-story great room with an extended-hearth fireplace and access to the rear deck and spa. Open planning allows the bayed breakfast nook and gourmet kitchen to enjoy the view of the fireplace, while the secluded formal dining room basks in natural light from two multi-pane windows. The master suite offers deck access and a bath that includes twin vanities and a windowed, whirlpool tub.

© 1994 Donald A. Gardner Architects, Inc.

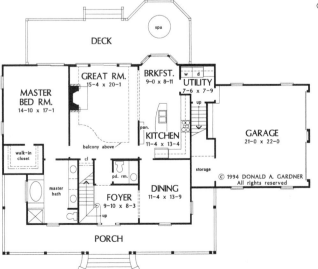

DECK

spa

GREAT RM.
15-4 x 20-1

BRKFST.
9-0 x 8-11

w   d

UTILITY
7-6 x 7-9

MASTER
BED RM.
14-10 x 17-1

balcony above

pan.

KITCHEN
11-4 x 13-4

up

GARAGE
21-0 x 22-0

walk-in
closet

cl

master
bath

pd. rm.

FOYER
9-10 x 8-3

DINING
11-4 x 13-9

storage

up

PORCH

© 1994 Donald A. GARDNER
All rights reserved

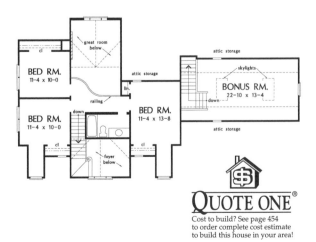

great room
below

cl

BED RM.
11-4 x 10-0

attic storage

attic storage

skylights

BONUS RM.
22-10 x 13-4

BED RM.
11-4 x 10-0

railing

down

lin.

BED RM.
11-4 x 13-8

attic storage

down

foyer
below

cl

cl

QUOTE ONE®

Cost to build? See page 454
to order complete cost estimate
to build this house in your area!

BATH

BEDROOM NO. 3
11'-6" X 11'-0"

BEDROOM NO. 2
11'-4" X 11'-0"

SUN ROOM
12'-0" X 13'-8"

PORCH

MASTER
BATH

W.I.C.

PORCH

BREAKFAST
10'-0" X 9'-0"

FAMILY ROOM
18'-0" X 14'-0"

MASTER BEDROOM
13'-4" X 15'-6"

LAUNDRY

KITCHEN
12'-0" X 13'-2"

STORAGE

BATH

TWO CAR GARAGE
20'-4" X 19'-8"

DINING ROOM
11'-4" X 11'-4"

FOYER
6'-8" X 11'-10"

DEN/GUEST
BEDROOM
11'-4" X 14'-0"

PORCH

QUOTE ONE®

Cost to build? See page 454
to order complete cost estimate
to build this house in your area!

Design HPT860277

Square Footage: 2,170
Width: 62'-0" **Depth:** 61'-6"

This classic cottage boasts a stone-and-wood exterior with a welcoming arch-top entry. An extended-hearth fireplace is the focal point of the family room, while a nearby sun room opens up the living area to the outdoors. Sleeping quarters include a master wing with a spacious, angled bath and a sitting room or den that has its own full bath. On the opposite side of the plan, two family bedrooms share a full bath. This home is designed with a walkout basement foundation.

172

QUOTE ONE®

Cost to build? See page 454
to order complete cost estimate
to build this house in your area!

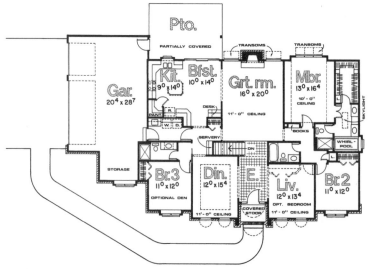

Pto.

PARTIALLY COVERED

TRANSOMS

TRANSOMS

Gar.
20'4 x 28'7

Kit.
9'0 x 14'0

Bfst.
10'0 x 14'0

Grt. rm.
16'0 x 20'0

11'-0" CEILING

Mbr.
13'0 x 16'4

10'-0"
CEILING

SKYLIGHT

DESK

SERVERY

STORAGE

WHIRL-
POOL

BOOKS

Br. 3
11'0 x 12'0

OPTIONAL DEN

Din.
12'0 x 15'4

E.

11'-0" CEILING

COVERED
STOOP

Liv.
12'0 x 13'4

11'-0" CEILING

OPT.
BEDROOM

Br. 2
11'0 x 12'0

Design HPT860276

Square Footage: 2,172
Width: 76'-0" **Depth:** 46'-0"

This one-story home holds a most convenient floor plan. The great room with a fireplace complements a front-facing living room. The formal dining room is convenient to the kitchen. An island, pantry, breakfast room and patio are highlights in the kitchen. A bedroom at this end of the house works fine as an office or guest bedroom. Two additional bedrooms are to the right of the plan: a master suite and an additional family bedroom.

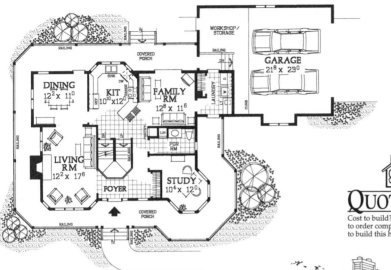

Quote One®

Cost to build? See page 454
to order complete cost estimate
to build this house in your area!

Design HPT860279

First Floor: 1,186 square feet
Second Floor: 988 square feet
Total: 2,174 square feet
Width: 72'-0" **Depth:** 50'-10"

L D

A Palladian window, fish-scale shingles and turret-style bays set off this country-style Victorian exterior. An impressive tile entry opens to the formal rooms, which nestle to the left side of the plan. The turret houses a secluded study on the first floor and provides a sunny bay window for a family bedroom upstairs. The second-floor master suite features its own fireplace, a dressing area with a walk-in closet, and a lavish bath.

173

Design HPT860278

First Floor: 1,580 square feet
Second Floor: 595 square feet
Total: 2,175 square feet
Bonus Room: 290 square feet
Width: 48'-6" **Depth:** 70'-11"

Multi-pane windows and ink-black shutters stand out against the rich brick-and-horizontal-clapboard backdrop. Inside, the spacious foyer leads directly to a large vaulted great room with its handsome fireplace. The dining room to the right of the foyer features a dramatic vaulted ceiling. In the privacy and quiet of the rear of the home is the master suite with its luxury bath and walk-in closet. This home is designed with a walkout basement foundation.

Quote One®

Cost to build? See page 454
to order complete cost estimate
to build this house in your area!

Design HPT860281

First Floor: 1,696 square feet
Second Floor: 479 square feet
Total: 2,175 square feet
Width: 86'-0" **Depth:** 54'-8"

Elements of country living grace this comfortable home. Inside, sit in the bay-windowed seating area of the study and read a book. The family room, with separate access to the porch, has a warming fireplace with built-ins. Just a step away is the L-shaped island kitchen and its attached breakfast nook with rear-deck access. Two family bedrooms upstairs share a full bath, while the master suite is secluded downstairs. Please specify basement, crawlspace or slab foundation when ordering.

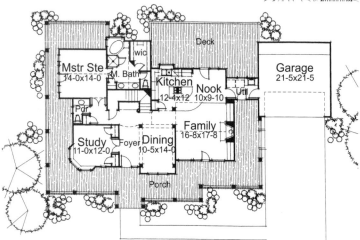

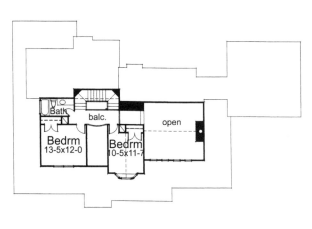

174

Design HPT860280

First Floor: 1,580 square feet
Second Floor: 595 square feet
Total: 2,175 square feet
Width: 48'-0" **Depth:** 69'-6"

Traditional formality asks for well-defined rooms, while the demands of sophisticated lifestyles call for wide-open spaces that bend to patterns of living. The formal dining room opens through decorative pillars to the two-story great room, which features a fireplace. French doors lead from the bayed breakfast area to the private master suite, a retreat with a lavish bath featuring an angled whirlpool tub, glass-enclosed shower and twin vanities. Two family bedrooms share a bath upstairs. This home is designed with a walkout basement foundation.

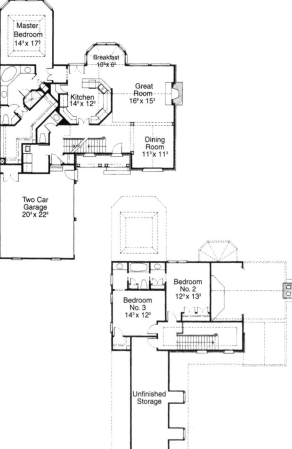

Design HPT860282

Square Footage: 2,177
Width: 61'-0" **Depth:** 77'-0"

Corner quoins, sidelights and a sunburst over the glass entry door lend a European appeal to this three-bedroom home. Sit by the warming fireplace in the living room or contemplate the view through a ribbon of windows facing the backyard. Two family bedrooms sharing a full bath feature walk-in closets. The master suite enjoys a sitting room, walk-in closet and sumptuous bath with an angled tub and a separate shower. Please specify basement, crawlspace or slab foundation when ordering.

175

Design HPT860283

Square Footage: 2,184
Future Space: 572 square feet
Width: 68'-0" **Depth:** 62'-0"

The front porch of this Colonial design is accented with stately columns and graceful full-length stairs. Three sets of French doors make the entry a stunning display of style. The great room features a central fireplace, while the breakfast room offers patio views. The secluded master suite enjoys two walk-in closets and a private bath. Two secondary bedrooms, to the left of the great room, share a bath. Please specify basement, crawlspace or slab foundation when ordering.

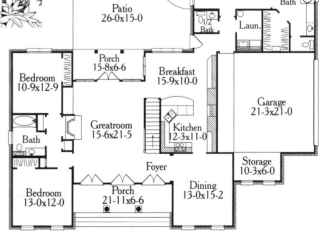

Design HPT860284

First Floor: 1,586 square feet
Second Floor: 601 square feet
Total: 2,187 square feet
Width: 50'-0" **Depth:** 44'-0"

Lattice walls, pickets and horizontal siding complement a relaxed Key West design that's perfect for waterfront properties. The grand room with a fireplace, the dining room and Bedroom 2 open through French doors to the veranda. The master suite occupies the entire second floor and features access to a private balcony through double doors. This pampering suite also includes a spacious walk-in closet and a full bath with a whirlpool tub. Enclosed storage/bonus space and a garage are available on the lower level. This home is designed with a pier foundation.

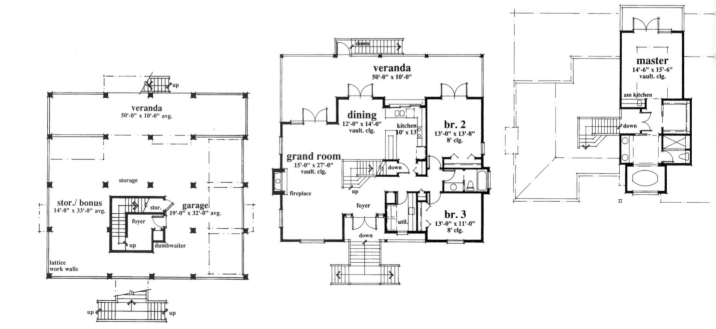

Design HPT860286

Square Footage: 2,189
Width: 56'-0" **Depth:** 72'-0"

L

Simplicity is the key to the stylish good looks of this home's facade. Inside, the kitchen opens directly off the foyer and contains an island counter and a work counter with eating space on the living-area side. The master suite sports sliding glass doors to the terrace. Its dressing area is enhanced with double walk-in closets and lavatories. A whirlpool tub and seated shower are additional amenities. Two family bedrooms are found on the opposite side of the house.

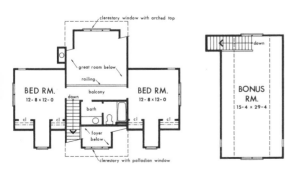

QUOTE ONE®
Cost to build? See page 454
to order complete cost estimate
to build this house in your area!

177

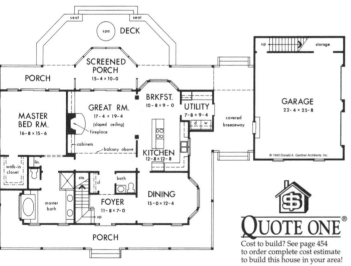

QUOTE ONE®
Cost to build? See page 454
to order complete cost estimate
to build this house in your area!

Design HPT860285

First Floor: 1,618 square feet
Second Floor: 570 square feet
Total: 2,188 square feet
Bonus Room: 495 square feet
Width: 87'-0" **Depth:** 57'-0"

The entrance foyer and great room enjoy Palladian clerestory windows which allow natural light to enter the well-planned interior of this country home. The spacious great room boasts a fireplace and built-in cabinets. The kitchen has a cooktop island counter and is placed conveniently between the breakfast room and the formal dining room. A generous first-floor master suite offers plenty of closet space and a lavish bath. Upstairs, two family bedrooms share a full bath. Bonus space over the garage awaits later development.

Design HPT860287

Square Footage: 2,190
Width: 58'-0" **Depth:** 54'-0"

The dramatic arched entry of this Southampton-style cottage borrows freely from its Southern coastal past. The foyer and central hall open to the grand room. The kitchen is flanked by the dining room and the morning nook, which opens to the lanai. On the left side of the plan, the master suite also accesses the lanai. Two walk-in closets and a compartmented bath with a separate tub and shower and a double-bowl vanity complete this opulent retreat. The right side of the plan includes two secondary bedrooms and a full bath.

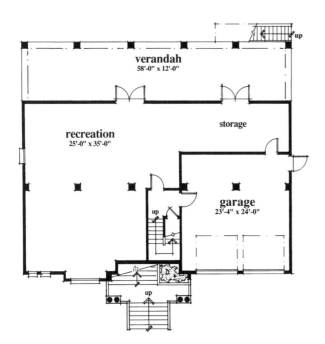

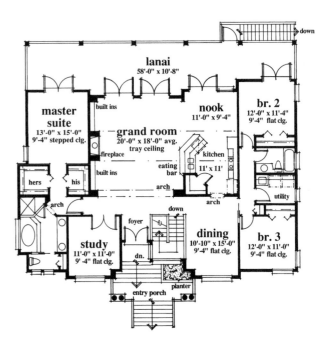

178

Design HPT860289

Square Footage: 2,190
Finished Basement: 1,376 square feet
Width: 58'-0" **Depth:** 54'-0"

A dramatic set of stairs leads to the entry of this home. The foyer opens to an expansive grand room with a fireplace and built-in bookshelves. For formal meals, a front-facing dining room offers plenty of space and a bumped-out bay. A study and three bedrooms make up the rest of the floor plan. Two secondary bedrooms share a full bath. The master suite contains two walk-in closets and a full bath.

QUOTE ONE®

Cost to build? See page 454 to order complete cost estimate to build this house in your area!

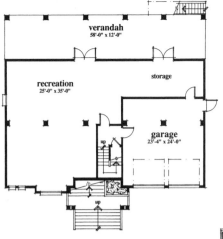

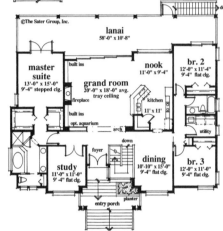

179

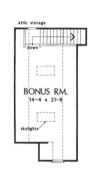

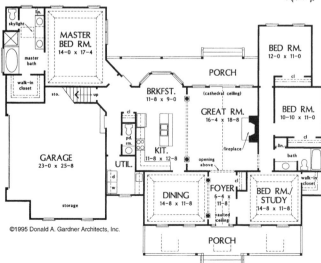

Design HPT860288

Square Footage: 2,192
Bonus Room: 390 square feet
Width: 74'-10" **Depth:** 55'-8"

Exciting volumes and nine-foot ceilings add elegance to a comfortable and open plan. Sunlight fills the airy foyer from a vaulted dormer and streams into the great room. A dining room, delineated from the foyer by columns, features a tray ceiling. Family bedrooms share a full bath complete with a linen closet. The front bedroom doubles as a study for extra flexibility. The master bedroom suite sits to the left rear of the plan.

©1995 Donald A. Gardner Architects, Inc.

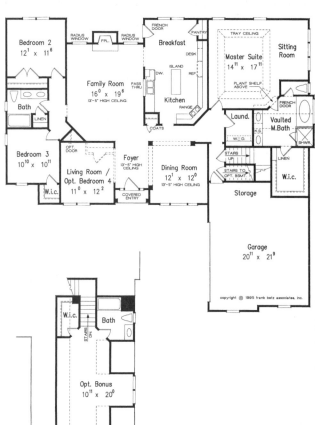

Design HPT860291

Square Footage: 2,193
Bonus Room: 400 square feet
Width: 64'-6" **Depth:** 59'-0"

From the hipped and gabled roof to the gracious entryway, class is a common element in the makeup of this home. Inside, the foyer is flanked by a formal living room (or make it a guest bedroom) and a formal dining room, defined by columns. Directly ahead lies the spacious family room, offering a warming fireplace. The sleeping quarters are split for privacy. The master suite has a lavish bath and tray ceiling. Please specify basement, crawlspace or slab foundation when ordering.

Design HPT860290

Square Footage: 2,200
Width: 56'-0" **Depth:** 74'-0"

A versatile swing room highlights this charming French-style home. At the center of the plan is a spacious living room with a warming fireplace and a built-in entertainment center. French doors open to the rear porch. Enjoy entertaining in this elegant tray-ceilinged dining room, complete with columns and arches at the entry. The master suite furnishes a spacious bath and a giant walk-in closet. Two secondary bedrooms offer walk-in closets and private baths. Please specify crawlspace or slab foundation when ordering.

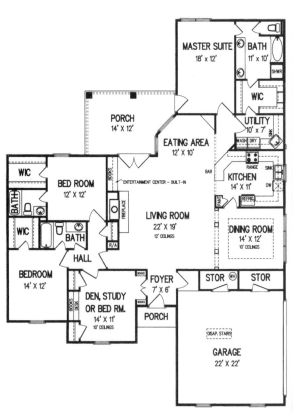

Design HPT860292

First Floor: 1,169 square feet
Second Floor: 1,034 square feet
Total: 2,203 square feet
Bonus Room: 347 square feet
Width: 55'-4" **Depth:** 52'-0"

This fashionable farmhouse shows off the height of style, but never at the expense of comfort. Clapboard siding sets off a light-hearted symmetry on this country elevation that braces an Early American flavor with new spirit. Inside, formal rooms flank the foyer and lead to casual living space. An expansive family room with a focal-point fireplace opens to a wide-open breakfast area and gourmet kitchen. The rear covered porch invites enjoyment of the outdoors and adjoins an entertainment porch. Upstairs, the lavish master suite offers twin vanities and a generous walk-in closet. Two additional bedrooms share a hall bath. A sizable bonus room includes a walk-in closet.

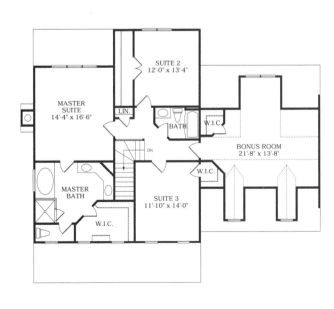

QUOTE ONE®

Cost to build? See page 454
to order complete cost estimate
to build this house in your area!

Design HPT860294

Square Footage: 2,203
Width: 77'-2" **Depth:** 46'-6"

L

Nothing completes a traditional-style home quite as well as a country kitchen with a fireplace and a built-in wood box. Notice also the second fireplace (with a raised hearth) and the sloped ceiling in the living room. The nearby dining room has an attached porch and separate dining terrace. Aside from two family bedrooms with a shared full bath, there is also a marvelous master suite with rear-terrace access.

Design HPT860293

Square Footage: 2,207
Bonus Room: 435 square feet
Width: 76'-1" **Depth:** 50'-0"

A quaint covered porch, twin dormers and arch-top windows lend charm to this stylish country home. Inside, decorative pillars announce the formal dining room, which enjoys easy service from the adjoining kitchen. A cathedral ceiling opens up the living area, while a large clerestory window brings in natural light. The master bedroom leads out to the rear deck and spa, and offers a lavish bath with an oversized whirlpool tub. Two family bedrooms and a fourth bedroom or study share a full bath.

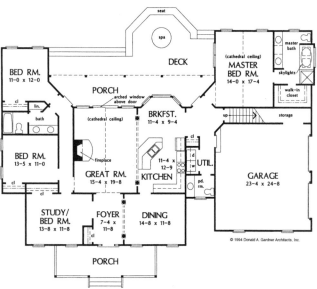

© 1994 Donald A. Gardner Architects, Inc.

QUOTE ONE®

Cost to build? See page 454
to order complete cost estimate
to build this house in your area!

© 1994 Donald A. Gardner Architects, Inc.

The brick trim, sidelights and transom window at the front entry of this home say welcome in an elegant and stylish manner. A high ceiling through the foyer and great room showcases the staircase, while the warmth of the fireplace and a built-in entertainment center make the great room a favorite gathering place. The modern kitchen serves the formal dining room and breakfast area with equal efficiency. The master suite is located on the first floor and positioned for privacy. The second floor of this home is more than an additional sleeping area—a study loft, walk-in closets in the bedrooms and a bonus room combine to create a very exciting home.

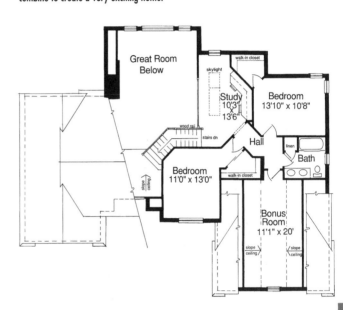

Design HPT860295

First Floor: 1,542 square feet
Second Floor: 667 square feet
Total: 2,209 square feet
Bonus Room: 236 square feet
Width: 58'-6" **Depth:** 49'-0"

Design HPT860296

First Floor: 1,165 square feet
Second Floor: 1,050 square feet
Total: 2,215 square feet
Bonus Room: 265 square feet
Width: 58'-0" **Depth:** 36'-0"

No detail is left to chance in this classically designed two-story home. A formal entry opens to the living and dining rooms through graceful arches. The family room provides ample space for large gatherings and features a fireplace and access to the rear deck through double doors. A triple window bathes the breakfast area in natural light. The L-shaped kitchen handles any occasion with ease. Upstairs, the master suite runs the width of the house and includes a generous walk-in closet and a bath. This home is designed with a walkout basement foundation.

Quote One®

Cost to build? See page 454
to order complete cost estimate
to build this house in your area!

Design HPT860297

Square Footage: 2,224
Width: 58'-6" **Depth:** 74'-0"

Arches crowned by a gentle, hipped roof provide Italianate charm in this bright family-oriented plan. A covered entry leads to the foyer that presents the angular, vaulted living and dining rooms. A kitchen includes a walk-in pantry and looks out over the breakfast nook and family room. The master suite features a sitting area, two walk-in closets and a full bath. A roomy bedroom opens off the family room and works perfectly as a guest room. Two additional bedrooms share a full bath.

185

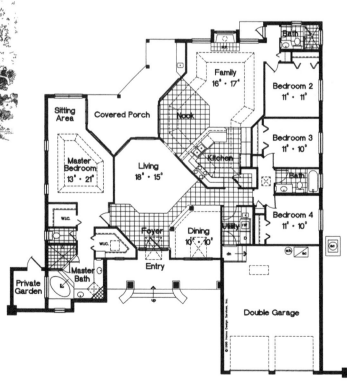

Design HPT860298

Square Footage: 2,224
Width: 58'-6" **Depth:** 72'-0"

Stone accents and two dormer windows add style to this home's facade. Inside, columns separate the cozy dining room from the tiled entry. A fireplace and a tray ceiling highlight the family room. Three family bedrooms sit to the right of the plan, while the master suite to the left features a private sitting area and a lavish bath.

QUOTE ONE®
Cost to build? See page 454
to order complete cost estimate
to build this house in your area!

Design HPT860300

Square Footage: 2,226
Width: 103'-1" **Depth:** 71'-11"

L

The impressive, double-door entry to the walled courtyard sets the tone for this Santa Fe masterpiece home. The expansive great room shows off its casual style with a centerpiece fireplace. Joining the great room is the formal dining room. The large gourmet kitchen has an eat-in snack bar. Family-room extras include a fireplace and entertainment built-ins. Just off the family room are the two large family bedrooms. The relaxing master suite is located off the great room and has double doors to the back patio.

Design HPT860299

First Floor: 1,701 square feet
Second Floor: 534 square feet
Total: 2,235 square feet
Bonus Room: 274 square feet
Width: 65'-11" **Depth:** 43'-5"

Columns, gables, multi-pane windows and a stone and stucco exterior give this home its handsome appearance. The formal rooms are to the right and left of the foyer. The family room, with a cathedral ceiling, fireplace, built-ins and access to the rear patio, is open to the breakfast room. On the opposite side of the plan, the master suite offers two walk-in closets and a compartmented bath. Two family bedrooms on the second floor share a bath.

Design HPT860301

First Floor: 1,569 square feet
Second Floor: 682 square feet
Total: 2,251 square feet
Bonus Room: 332 square feet
Width: 64'-8" **Depth:** 43'-4"

The wide porch across the front and the deck off the great room in back allow as much outdoor living as the weather permits. The foyer opens through columns off the front porch to the dining room, with a nearby powder room, and to the great room. The breakfast room is open to the great room and the adjacent kitchen. The utility room adjoins this area and accesses the garage. On the opposite side of the plan, the master suite offers a compartmented bath and two walk-in closets. A staircase leads upstairs to two family bedrooms—one at each end of a balcony that overlooks the great room. Each bedroom contains a walk-in closet, a dormer window and private access to the bath through a private vanity area.

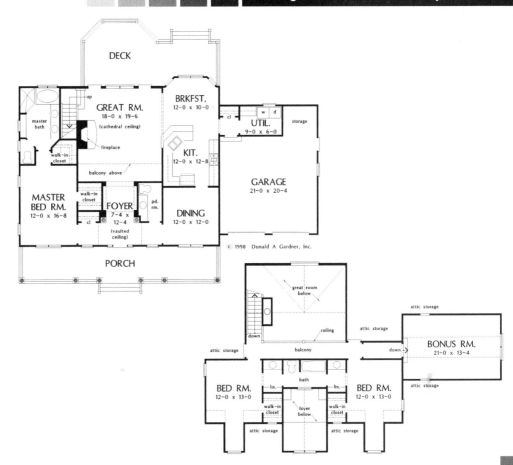

© 1998 Donald A Gardner, Inc.

© 1998 Donald A Gardner, Inc.

Design HPT860303

First Floor: 1,358 square feet
Second Floor: 894 square feet
Total: 2,252 square feet
Bonus Room: 300 square feet
Width: 58'-0" **Depth:** 58'-4"

From the wraparound covered porch, enter this attractive home to find the roomy master suite on the left and the formal dining room on the right. Leading through double doors from the dining area is a sunlit, U-shaped kitchen with a breakfast island, which flows into a comfortable family room featuring a fireplace. The second floor is reserved for three family bedrooms that share a full bath. This home is designed with a basement foundation.

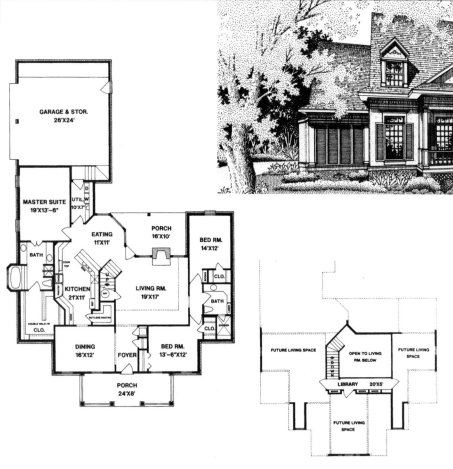

Design HPT860302

First Floor: 2,159 square feet
Second Floor: 96 square feet
Total: 2,255 square feet
Future Expansion Space: 878 square feet
Width: 59'-0" **Depth:** 86'-0"

This plan charms instantly with its muntin windows, decorative French-style shutters, stucco exterior and steeply sloping roof with dormers. The kitchen is replete with luxuries: a desk, butler's pantry and plenty of counter space. An adjacent eating area boasts a bay window and looks out to the rear property. The luxurious master suite is complete with double walk-in closets, His and Hers sinks, a garden tub and a separate shower. Please specify basement, crawlspace or slab foundation when ordering.

Design HPT860304

First Floor: 1,074 square feet
Second Floor: 884 square feet
Third Floor: 299 square feet
Total: 2,257 square feet
Width: 50'-10" **Depth:** 47'-0"

This attractive multi-level home is rich with exterior detail and offers early-century charm coupled with modern amenities. Formal and informal spaces are provided, with the open hearth room, kitchen and breakfast area serving as an exciting gathering place for family members. The first-floor mudroom or laundry provides a buffer to the garage and outdoors. Split stairs, graced with wood banisters, lead to the second floor. The lavish master bedroom is topped with a tray ceiling and offers a deluxe bath and a large walk-in closet. A front bedroom can be converted to an open loft overlooking the stairway. Continuing to the third floor, a bonus room provides optional space and a full bath allows this to be a private bedroom retreat.

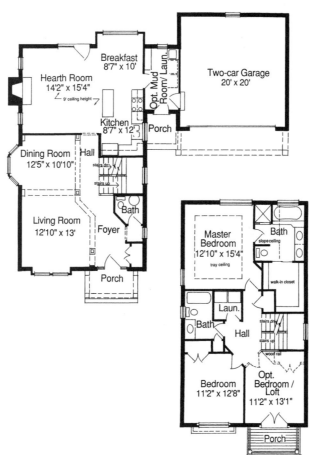

Design HPT860305

Square Footage: 2,258
Width: 66'-0" **Depth:** 73'-4"

Columns add the finishing touches to this dazzling plan. The double-door entry opens to the foyer, which leads to the vaulted living room with sliding glass doors to the covered patio. The kitchen is open to both the living room and the bayed nook. A bow window and a fireplace define the family room. The master bedroom features access to the covered patio and provides dual walk-in closets and a spa tub. Two additional bedrooms share a full bath.

Design HPT860306

First Floor: 1,274 square feet
Second Floor: 983 square feet
Total: 2,257 square feet
Width: 50'-0" **Depth:** 46'-0"

Special attention to exterior details and interior nuances gives this relaxed farmhouse fine distinction. From the large covered porch, enter to find a roomy, well-zoned plan. A striking central staircase separates the first-floor living area, which boasts a cathedral ceiling in the living room. The second floor includes a master suite, two bedrooms that share a full bath, and a flexible upstairs sitting area. The master suite contains a bath with double-bowl vanities and a walk-in closet. This home has a daylight basement.

191

Design HPT860307

First Floor: 1,633 square feet
Second Floor: 629 square feet
Total: 2,262 square feet
Width: 55'-0" **Depth:** 55'-7"

High gables, a dramatic entry and corner quoins lend an extra dash of distinction to this fine traditional home. Formal and informal living areas are clearly defined. To the left of the entry you will find the formal dining room. Casual gatherings will be enjoyed in the family room, enhanced with a fireplace and open to the dinette and U-shaped kitchen. A sloped-ceiling master bedroom comprises the right portion of the plan and accesses the backyard. Upstairs, three family bedrooms share a full bath.

QUOTE ONE®

Cost to build? See page 454
to order complete cost estimate
to build this house in your area!

Design HPT860308

First Floor: 1,720 square feet
Second Floor: 545 square feet
Total: 2,265 square feet
Bonus Room: 365 square feet
Width: 50'-0" **Depth:** 53'-6"

Style abounds in this English country cottage. Accented by a fireplace and built-in bookcases, the family room with a ribbon of windows is an excellent setting for family gatherings. The central staircase leads to the balcony overlook and a bath serving two family bedrooms. Another bedroom and bath on this level can be completed later. This home is designed with a walkout basement foundation.

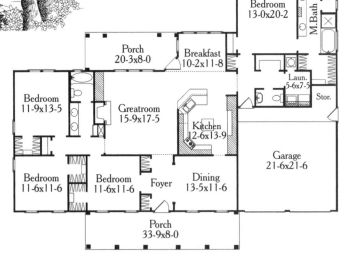

Design HPT860309

Square Footage: 2,267
Width: 71'-2" **Depth:** 62'-0"

Six columns and a steeply pitched roof lend elegance to this four-bedroom home. To the right of the foyer, the dining area sits conveniently near the efficient kitchen. Escape to the relaxing master suite, with its luxurious bath set between His and Hers walk-in closets. The great room is at the center of this L-shaped plan, and is complete with a warming fireplace and built-ins. Please specify basement, crawlspace or slab foundation when ordering.

Design HPT860310

First Floor: 1,150 square feet
Second Floor: 1,120 square feet
Total: 2,270 square feet
Width: 46'-0" **Depth:** 48'-0"

Lap siding, special windows and a covered porch enhance the elevation of this popular-style home. The spacious two-story entry surveys the formal dining room, which includes hutch space. An entertainment center, a through-fire-place and bayed windows add appeal to the great room. Families will love the spacious kitchen with its breakfast and hearth rooms. Comfortable secondary bedrooms and a sumptuous master bedroom feature privacy by design. Bedroom 3 is highlighted by a half-round window, volume ceiling and double closets, while Bedroom 4 contains a built-in desk. The master suite possesses a vaulted ceiling, large walk-in closet, His and Hers vanities and an oval whirlpool tub.

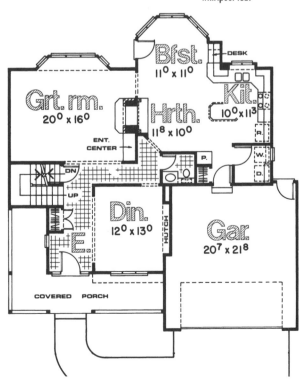

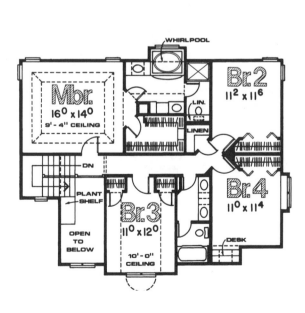

Design HPT860312

First Floor: 1,572 square feet
Second Floor: 700 square feet
Total: 2,272 square feet
Bonus Room: 212 square feet
Width: 70'-0" **Depth:** 38'-5"

A charming porch wraps around the front of this farmhouse, whose entry opens to a formal dining room. The island kitchen and sun-filled breakfast area are located nearby. The family room is warmed by a fireplace flanked by windows. Located for privacy, the first-floor master bedroom features its own covered patio and a private bath designed for relaxation. The second floor contains three family bedrooms—each with a walk-in closet—a full bath and a bonus room.

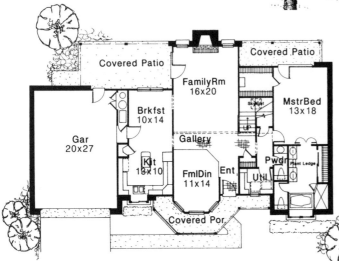

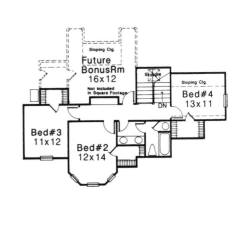

194

© 1997 Donald A. Gardner Architects, Inc.

B. NATHAN

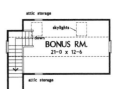

Design HPT860311

Square Footage: 2,273
Bonus Room: 342 square feet
Width: 74'-8" **Depth:** 75'-10"

An exciting blend of styles, this home features the wrapping porch of a country farmhouse with a brick-and-siding exterior, for a uniquely pleasing effect. The great room shares its cathedral ceiling with an open kitchen while the octagonal dining room is complemented by a tray ceiling. Built-ins flank the great room's fireplace for added convenience.

Design HPT860313

First Floor: 1,290 square feet
Second Floor: 985 square feet
Total: 2,275 square feet
Bonus Room: 186 square feet
Width: 45'-0" **Depth:** 43'-4"

This casually elegant European country-style home offers more than just a slice of everything you've always wanted: this plan is designed with room to grow. Formal living and dining rooms are defined by decorative columns and open from a two-story foyer, which leads to open family space. A two-story family room offers a fireplace and shares a French door to the rear property with the breakfast room. A gallery hall with a balcony overlook connects two sleeping wings upstairs. The master suite boasts a vaulted bath, while the family hall leads to bonus space. Please specify basement, crawlspace or slab foundation when ordering.

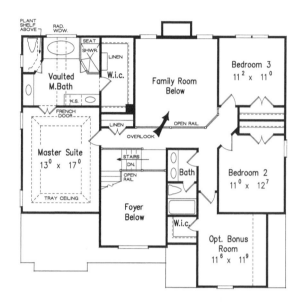

195

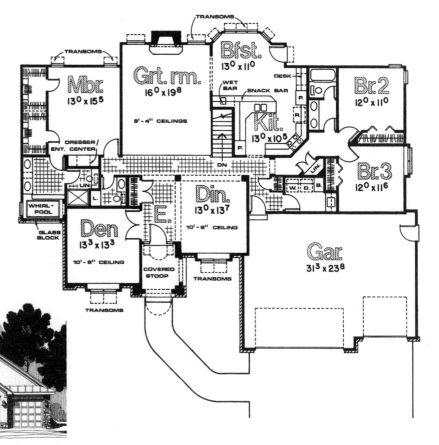

Design HPT860314

Square Footage: 2,276
Width: 72'-0" **Depth:** 56'-0"

Drama and harmony are expressed in this plan by utilizing a variety of elegant exterior materials. The great room with a window-framed fireplace is conveniently located next to the eat-in kitchen with bayed breakfast area. Two secluded secondary bedrooms enjoy easy access to a compartmented bath with a twin vanity. His and Hers closets and a built-in armoire grace the master suite where a private bath features glass blocks over the whirlpool, double sinks and an extra linen storage cabinet. An alternate elevation is provided at no extra cost.

alternate elevation

Design HPT860315

First Floor: 1,371 square feet
Second Floor: 916 square feet
Total: 2,287 square feet
Width: 43'-0" **Depth:** 69'-0"

The decorative pillars and the wrap-around porch give a perfect introduction to this charming bungalow. Inside, the foyer offers an angled stairway that leads to the second floor. French doors lead to the den, which shares a see-through fireplace with the family room. Upstairs, the master suite is a real treat with its French-door access, vaulted ceiling and luxurious bath. Two secondary bedrooms and a full bath complete the second floor.

QUOTE ONE®
Cost to build? See page 454 to order complete cost estimate to build this house in your area!

197

Design HPT860316

Square Footage: 2,287
Width: 63'-4" **Depth:** 62'-4"

Low-pitched roofs and a grand, columned entry introduce a floor plan designed to carry over into the next millennium. Ceramic tiles lead from the foyer to the breakfast area and roomy kitchen, which offers an angled wrapping counter and overlooks the family room. French doors open off the foyer to a secluded den or guest suite, which complements the nearby master suite. A gallery hall off the breakfast nook leads to family sleeping quarters, which share a full bath.

Design HPT860317

First Floor: 1,246 square feet
Second Floor: 1,046 square feet
Total: 2,292 square feet
Width: 58'-0" **Depth:** 40'-0"

Stone accents enhance the exterior of this two-story farmhouse. A country kitchen opens to the wraparound front porch and the back porch, and is conveniently located near the dining room. Upstairs, the master bedroom contains a private luxurious bath, a walk-in closet, a fireplace and a sitting area. Two additional bedrooms upstairs complete the sleeping zone. This home is designed with a basement foundation.

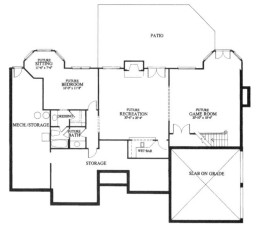

198

Design HPT860318

Square Footage: 2,295
Width: 69'-0" **Depth:** 49'-6"

The abundance of details in this plan make it the finest in one-story living. The great room and formal dining room have an open, dramatic sense of space. The kitchen with a preparation island shares the right side of the plan with a bayed breakfast area and a keeping room with a fireplace. Sleeping accommodations to the left of the plan include a master suite and two family bedrooms. This home is designed with a walkout basement foundation.

QUOTE ONE®
Cost to build? See page 454 to order complete cost estimate to build this house in your area!

Design HPT860319

First Floor: 1,743 square feet
Second Floor: 555 square feet
Total: 2,298 square feet
Bonus Room: 350 square feet
Width: 77'-11" **Depth:** 53'-2"

A lovely arch-top window and a wraparound porch set off this country exterior. Inside, formal rooms open off the foyer, which leads to a spacious great room. This living area provides a fireplace and access to a screened porch with a cathedral ceiling. Bay windows allow natural light into the breakfast area and formal dining room. The master suite features a spacious bath and access to a private area of the rear porch. Two second-floor bedrooms share a bath and a balcony hall that offers an overlook to the great room.

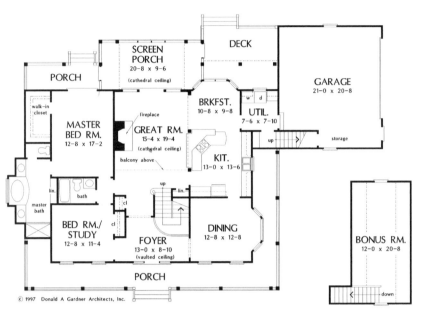

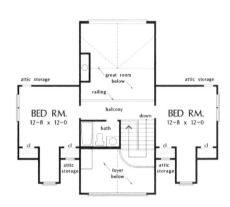

© 1997 Donald A Gardner Architects, Inc.

199

© 1997 Donald A Gardner Architects, Inc.

Design HPT860321

First Floor: 1,067 square feet
Second Floor: 1,233 square feet
Total: 2,300 square feet
Width: 58'-0" **Depth:** 33'-0"

A wraparound porch and a second-floor deck add to the warmth and livability of this splendid two-story Victorian home. A large angled kitchen with an adjoining dining area is the hub around which all activity will revolve. A delightful fireplace adds warmth to the living room where French doors lead to the front porch. The family room resides on the second-floor landing and shares the deck with the master suite. This home is designed with a basement foundation.

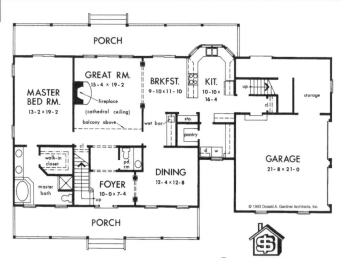

© 1993 Donald A. Gardner Architects, Inc.

QUOTE ONE®
Cost to build? See page 454
to order complete cost estimate
to build this house in your area!

Design HPT860320

First Floor: 1,632 square feet
Second Floor: 669 square feet
Total: 2,301 square feet
Bonus Room: 528 square feet
Width: 72'-6" **Depth:** 46'-10"

This open country plan boasts front and rear covered porches and a bonus room for future expansion. The entrance foyer has a Palladian window clerestory to allow natural light in. The great room has a fireplace, cathedral ceiling and a clerestory with arched windows. A U-shaped kitchen provides the ideal layout for food preparation. For flexibility, access is provided to the bonus room from both the first and second floors.

Design HPT860322

Square Footage: 2,311
Bonus Room: 425 square feet
Width: 61'-0" **Depth:** 64'-4"

With elegant hipped rooflines, stucco-and-brick detailing, arched windows and gabled roofs, this home presents its European heritage with pride. The covered entryway leads to a formal dining room defined by graceful columns and arched openings. Columns and arched openings also lead into the vaulted family room, where a welcoming fireplace waits to warm cool evenings and radius windows flood the room with light. The kitchen is sure to please with its angled counter and accessibility to the vaulted breakfast nook. Two family bedrooms are to the right of the design while the master suite is to the left. Please specify basement or crawlspace foundation when ordering.

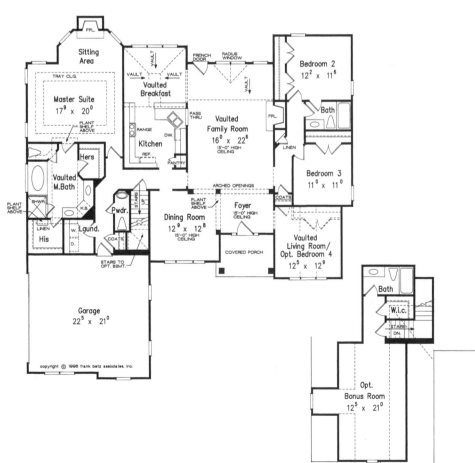

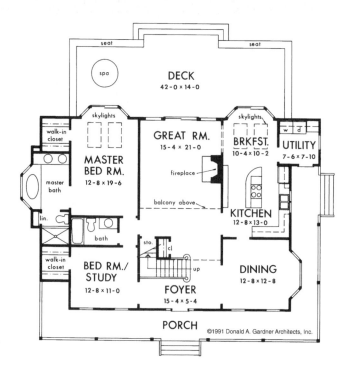

seat   seat

DECK
42-0 x 14-0

spa

skylights   skylights

walk-in
closet

GREAT RM.   **BRKFST.**   **UTILITY**
15-4 x 21-0   10-4 x 10-2   7-6 x 7-10

w d

**MASTER
BED RM.**
12-8 x 19-6

master
bath   fireplace

lin.   balcony above

bath

KITCHEN
12-8 x 13-0

walk-in
closet   sto.   cl

**BED RM./
STUDY**
12-8 x 11-0

up

DINING
12-8 x 12-8

FOYER
15-4 x 5-4

PORCH

©1991 Donald A. Gardner Architects, Inc.

QUOTE ONE®

Cost to build? See page 454
to order complete cost estimate
to build this house in your area!

Design HPT860323

First Floor: 1,756 square feet
Second Floor: 565 square feet
Total: 2,321 square feet
Width: 56'-8" **Depth:** 54'-4"

A wraparound covered porch at the front and sides of this house and an open deck at the back provide plenty of outside living area. The spacious great room features a fireplace, cathedral ceiling and clerestory with arched window. The island kitchen has an attached skylit breakfast room complete with a bay window. The first-floor master bedroom contains a generous closet and a master bath with a garden tub, double-bowl vanity and shower. The second floor sports two bedrooms and a full bath with a double-bowl vanity. An elegant balcony overlooks the great room.

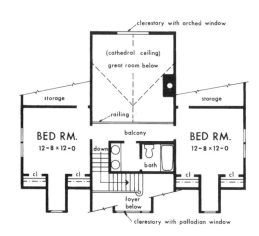

clerestory with arched window

(cathedral ceiling)

great room below

storage   storage

railing

BED RM.   balcony   **BED RM.**
12-8 x 12-0   12-8 x 12-0

down

bath

cl   cl   cl   cl

foyer
below

clerestory with palladian window

© 1991 Donald A. Gardner Architects, Inc.

B. NATHAN

Design HPT860325

Square Footage: 2,322
Bonus Room: 370 square feet
Width: 60'-0" **Depth:** 76'-8"

Grand Palladian windows create a classic look for this sensational stucco home. A magnificent view from the living room provides unlimited vistas of the rear grounds through a wall of glass. The kitchen, breakfast nook and family room comprise the family wing. Two secondary bedrooms share a bath and provide complete privacy to the master suite located on the opposite side of the plan. The lavish master bath impresses with a soaking tub and a compartmented toilet.

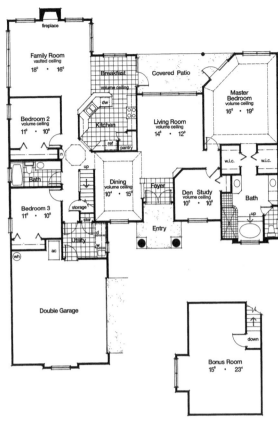

203

Design HPT860324

Square Footage: 2,322
Width: 62'-0" **Depth:** 61'-0"

An eclectic mix of building materials—stone, stucco and siding—sings in tune with the European charm of this one-story home. Decorative columns set off the formal dining room and foyer from the vaulted family room, while the formal living room is quietly tucked behind French doors. The master suite has an elegant tray ceiling, bay sitting area and a lush bath. Please specify basement, crawlspace or slab foundation when ordering.

QUOTE ONE®
Cost to build? See page 454
to order complete cost estimate
to build this house in your area!

Design HPT860327

First Floor: 1,660 square feet
Second Floor: 665 square feet
Total: 2,325 square feet
Bonus Room: 240 square feet
Width: 64'-0" **Depth:** 48'-6"

This European design is filled with space for formal and informal occasions. Informal areas include an open kitchen, breakfast room and family room with a fireplace. Formal rooms surround the foyer, with the living room on the left and dining room on the right. The master suite is conveniently placed on the first floor, with a gorgeous private bath and a walk-in closet. This home is designed with a walkout basement foundation.

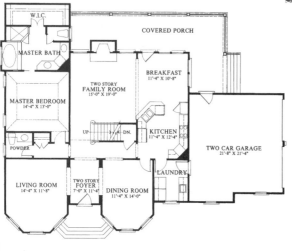

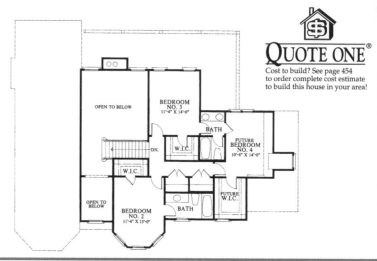

Quote One®
Cost to build? See page 454 to order complete cost estimate to build this house in your area!

Design HPT860326

First Floor: 1,660 square feet
Second Floor: 665 square feet
Total: 2,325 square feet
Bonus Room: 240 square feet
Width: 64'-0" **Depth:** 48'-6"

Stately brick and jack-arch detailing create an exterior that looks established and possesses a floor plan that offers 21st-Century livability. A dramatic two-story entry is framed by formal living and dining areas. The breakfast nook allows rear covered-porch access and opens to the kitchen. A coffered ceiling, sumptuous bath and walk-in closet highlight the master suite. Upstairs, two additional bedrooms, an optional fourth bedroom and two baths complete the plan. This home is designed with a walkout basement foundation.

Quote One®
Cost to build? See page 454 to order complete cost estimate to build this house in your area!

© Stephen Fuller, Inc.

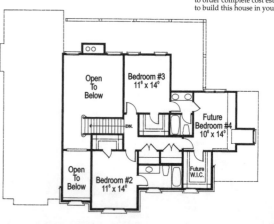

Design HPT860328

First Floor: 1,685 square feet
Second Floor: 648 square feet
Total: 2,333 square feet
Width: 77'-0" **Depth:** 50'-10"

Decorative columns create an exceptional exterior on this traditional cottage. Comfort in grand style awaits in a spacious living area, complete with a centered fireplace and French doors opening to the rear covered porch. The plush master suite features a spacious bath loaded with amenities. Walk from this bedroom and through a hall bath to a guest bedroom or study. Two family bedrooms upstairs offer private dressing areas and share a bath that includes twin lavatories. The balcony hallway leads to an unfinished area that can be used as a game room or study. Please specify crawlspace or slab foundation when ordering.

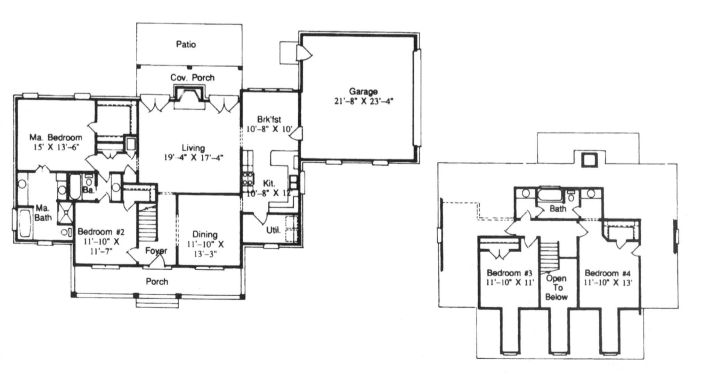

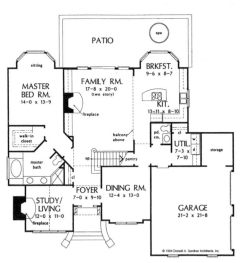

PATIO

spa

sitting

MASTER BED RM. 14-0 x 13-9

FAMILY RM. 17-8 x 20-0 (two story)

fireplace

BRKFST. 9-6 x 8-7

KIT. 13-11 x 8-10

walk-in closet

master bath

balcony above

up

pantry

pd. rm.

cl

UTIL. 7-3 x 7-10

w d

storage

FOYER 7-0 x 9-10

DINING RM. 12-4 x 13-0

GARAGE 21-2 x 21-8

STUDY/ LIVING 12-0 x 11-0

fireplace

© 1994 Donald A. Gardner Architects, Inc.

© 1994 Donald A. Gardner Architects, Inc.

B. NATHAN

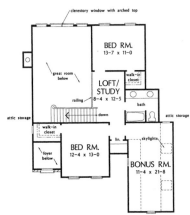

clerestory window with arched top

great room below

attic storage

railing

down

walk-in closet

foyer below

BED RM. 13-7 x 11-0

LOFT/ STUDY 8-4 x 12-5

walk-in closet

bath

attic storage

BED RM. 12-4 x 13-0

lin.

skylights

BONUS RM. 11-4 x 21-8

Quote One®

Cost to build? See page 454 to order complete cost estimate to build this house in your area!

Design HPT860329

First Floor: 1,715 square feet
Second Floor: 620 square feet
Total: 2,335 square feet
Bonus Room: 265 square feet
Width: 58'-6" **Depth:** 50'-3"

With a delightful flavor, this two-story home features family living at its best. The foyer opens to a study or living room on the left. The dining room on the right offers large proportions and full windows. The family room remains open to the kitchen and the breakfast room. Here, sunny meals are guaranteed with a bay window overlooking the rear yard. In the master suite, a bayed sitting area, a walk-in closet and a pampering bath are sure to please. Upstairs, two family bedrooms flank a loft or study area.

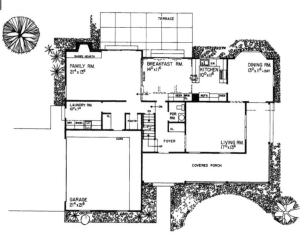

TERRACE

RAISED HEARTH

FAMILY RM. 21⁴ x 13⁶

BREAKFAST RM. 14⁰ x 11⁶

KITCHEN 10⁰ x 11⁰

DINING RM. 13⁰ x 11⁴ + BAY

LAUNDRY RM. 10⁰ x 7⁴

PANTRY

POR.

FOYER

LIVING RM. 17⁰ x 13⁶

COVERED PORCH

GARAGE 21⁴ x 21⁸

BEDROOM/ STUDY 11⁰ x 13²

BATH

DRESS. RM.

VANITY

MASTER BEDROOM 13⁰ x 13²

BATH

BEDROOM 10⁰ x 10⁶

BEDROOM 13⁰ x 10⁶

ROOF

ROOF

ATTIC 29⁴ x 26⁴ (HEADROOM 29⁴ x 10⁴)

ROOF

Design HPT860330

First Floor: 1,370 square feet
Second Floor: 969 square feet
Total: 2,339 square feet
Attic: 969 square feet
Width: 59'-8" **Depth:** 44'-0"

L D

Here's a great farmhouse adaptation with all the most up-to-date features. The quiet corner living room opens to the sizable dining room which enjoys views from a bay window. The gourmet kitchen features many built-ins and a pass-through to the beamed-ceiling nook. Sliding glass doors to the terrace are found in both the family room and the nook. The second floor holds three family bedrooms, which share a full bath and a pampering master bedroom. The master retreat enjoys a private bath.

Quote One®

Cost to build? See page 454 to order complete cost estimate to build this house in your area!

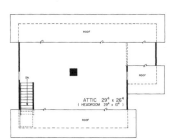

Design HPT860331

First Floor: 1,761 square feet
Second Floor: 580 square feet
Total: 2,341 square feet
Bonus Room: 276 square feet
Width: 56'-0" **Depth:** 47'-6"

Decorative arches and quoins give this home a wonderful curb appeal that matches its comfortable interior. The two-story foyer is bathed in natural light as it leads to the formal dining room and beyond to the counter-filled kitchen and the vaulted breakfast nook. A den, or possible fourth bedroom, is tucked away at the rear for privacy and includes a full bath. Located on the first floor, also for privacy, is a spacious master suite with a luxurious private bath. Two family bedrooms and a full bath reside on the second floor, as well as a balcony that looks down to the family room and the foyer. An optional bonus room is available for expanding at a later date. Please specify basement, crawlspace or slab foundation when ordering.

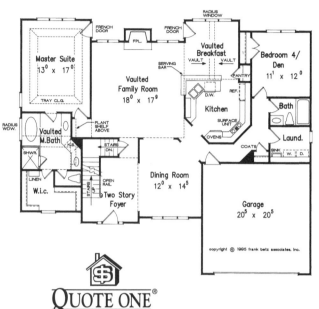

copyright © 1995 frank betz associates, Inc.

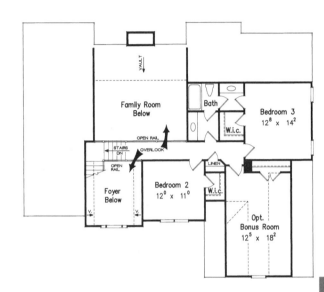

QUOTE ONE®

Cost to build? See page 454
to order complete cost estimate
to build this house in your area!

207

Design HPT860332

First Floor: 1,000 square feet
Second Floor: 1,345 square feet
Total: 2,345 square feet
Width: 57'-4" **Depth:** 30'-0"

An arched entry, shutters and a brick facade highlight the exterior of this two-story modern Colonial home. Living and dining rooms at the front of the plan accommodate formal occasions. The rear of the plan is designed for informal gatherings, such as the generous family room, which includes a warming fireplace and bayed conversation area. The bright breakfast area is open to an efficient U-shaped kitchen with a snack bar. Bright windows and French doors add appeal to the living room. Upstairs, a U-shaped balcony hall overlooks the entry below and connects four bedrooms, including a master suite. This retreat features a private sitting room, two walk-in closets, a compartmented bath, separate vanities and a window-brightened whirlpool tub.

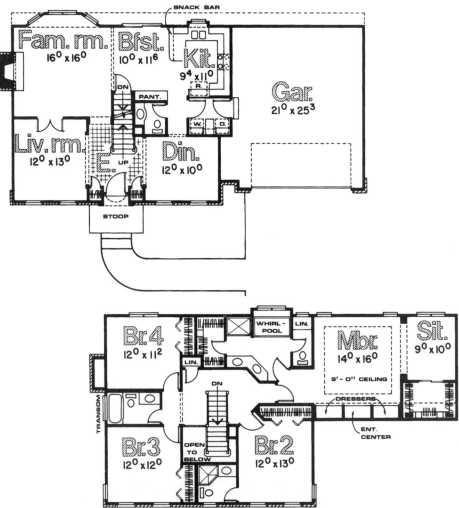

Design HPT860334

Square Footage: 2,348
Future Space: 860 square feet
Width: 70'-10" **Depth:** 65'-4"

Arched windows and a front door with sidelights give this home classic style. Columns accent the dining room to the right of the foyer. The great room offers a fireplace and looks out on a rear porch brightened by three skylights. The master suite includes a sitting area and an amenity-filled bath featuring a garden tub with a view. Upstairs, a balcony overlooks the great room enhanced by floor-to-ceiling windows. Please specify basement, crawlspace or slab foundation when ordering.

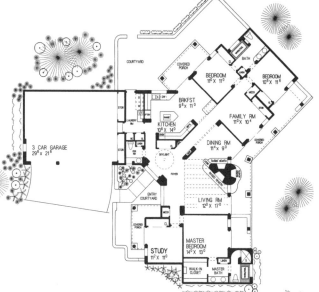

209

Design HPT860333

Square Footage: 2,350
Width: 92'-7" **Depth:** 79'-0"

L

Santa Fe styling creates interesting angles in this one-story home. A grand entrance leads through a courtyard into the foyer with a circular skylight. Turn right to the master suite with a deluxe bath and a bedroom close at hand — perfect for a nursery, home office or exercise room. Two more family bedrooms are placed quietly in the far wing of the house. Make note of the island range in the kitchen and the covered porches on two sides.

QUOTE ONE®
Cost to build? See page 454 to order complete cost estimate to build this house in your area!

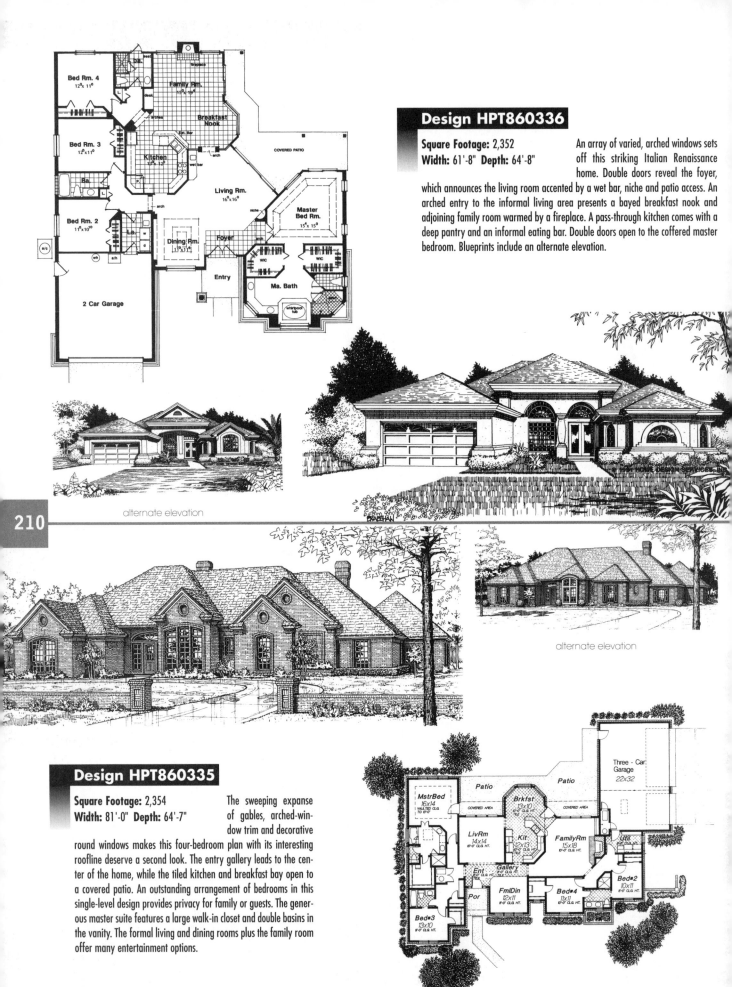

Design HPT860336

Square Footage: 2,352
Width: 61'-8" **Depth:** 64'-8"

An array of varied, arched windows sets off this striking Italian Renaissance home. Double doors reveal the foyer, which announces the living room accented by a wet bar, niche and patio access. An arched entry to the informal living area presents a bayed breakfast nook and adjoining family room warmed by a fireplace. A pass-through kitchen comes with a deep pantry and an informal eating bar. Double doors open to the coffered master bedroom. Blueprints include an alternate elevation.

alternate elevation

alternate elevation

Design HPT860335

Square Footage: 2,354
Width: 81'-0" **Depth:** 64'-7"

The sweeping expanse of gables, arched-window trim and decorative round windows makes this four-bedroom plan with its interesting roofline deserve a second look. The entry gallery leads to the center of the home, while the tiled kitchen and breakfast bay open to a covered patio. An outstanding arrangement of bedrooms in this single-level design provides privacy for family or guests. The generous master suite features a large walk-in closet and double basins in the vanity. The formal living and dining rooms plus the family room offer many entertainment options.

Design HPT860337

First Floor: 1,236 square feet
Second Floor: 1,120 square feet
Total: 2,356 square feet
Bonus Room: 270 square feet
Width: 56'-0" **Depth:** 38'-0"

L

This gracious home integrates timeless traditional styling with a functional, cost-effective plan. An interesting feature is the two-story nook area with a bay window and a desk, set between the gourmet kitchen and the large family room. Warming fireplaces occupy both the family room and living area. Across from the bottom of the staircase sits a den with French doors. Upstairs, two bedrooms share a full bath that includes dual sinks. A conveniently located door in the upper hallway opens to the large bonus room over the two-car garage. Rounding out the upper floor, a sumptuous master suite makes its own private retreat over the entry with an enormous bath that contains a spa and separate shower.

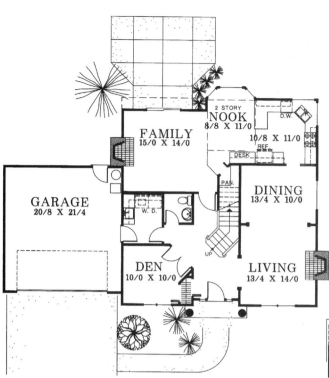

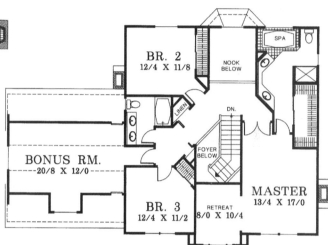

211

Design HPT860338

First Floor: 1,492 square feet
Second Floor: 865 square feet
Total: 2,357 square feet
Bonus Room: 285 square feet
Width: 66'-10" **Depth:** 49'-7"

This roomy country design features two covered porches and an island kitchen with a breakfast area. The long foyer leads to the living room with a fireplace and to the stunning master suite with an oversized tub, glass shower, toilet compartment and His and Hers walk-in closets. The island kitchen is flanked by the formal dining room and a breakfast area with a sunny bay window. Upstairs, a balcony overlooks the living area and leads to three additional bedrooms and two full baths. Please specify crawlspace or slab foundation when ordering.

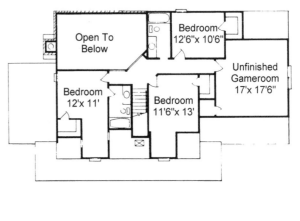

Design HPT860339

First Floor: 1,765 square feet
Second Floor: 595 square feet
Total: 2,360 square feet
Width: 68'-0" **Depth:** 74'-0"

Dormer windows and a covered front porch lend a Southern country flavor to the exterior of this fine home. The open living areas are comprised of a formal dining room, a family room with a sloped ceiling and fireplace, and a kitchen with an eating area. The master suite features a sitting area and large garden tub. The second floor holds two family bedrooms and a full bath. Please specify basement, crawlspace or slab foundation when ordering.

This home, as shown in the photograph, may differ from the actual blueprints.
For more detailed information, please check the floor plans carefully.

Photo courtesy of Design Basics, Inc.

213

Design HPT860340

First Floor: 1,188 square feet
Second Floor: 1,172 square feet
Total: 2,360 square feet
Width: 58'-0" **Depth:** 40'-0"

Beginning with the interest of a wraparound porch, there's a feeling of country charm in this two-story plan. Formal dining and living rooms, visible from the entry, offer ample space for gracious entertaining. The large family room is truly a place of warmth and welcome with its gorgeous bay window, fireplace and French doors to the living room. The kitchen, with an island counter, pantry and desk, makes cooking a delight. Upstairs, the secondary bedrooms share an efficient compartmented bath. The expansive master bedroom has its own luxury bath with a double vanity, whirlpool tub, walk-in closet and dressing area.

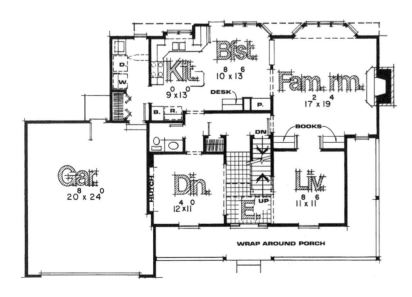

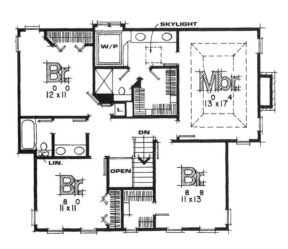

Design HPT860342

First Floor: 1,294 square feet
Second Floor: 1,067 square feet
Total: 2,361 square feet
Bonus Room: 168 square feet
Width: 54'-4" **Depth:** 37'-6"

A graceful front porch with a French-door entry welcomes guests to this traditional three-bedroom home. Living quarters downstairs include a well-designed eat-in kitchen with a great deal of counter space, a formal dining area, spacious family room, laundry room and powder room. All three bedrooms reside upstairs. The master bedroom features a vast walk-in closet and a grand private bath with two vanities, a shower stall and a separate tub. The additional bedrooms each have considerable closets and share a bathroom. Please specify basement or crawlspace foundation when ordering.

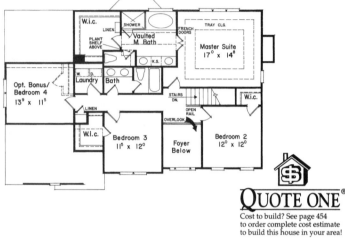

214

Design HPT860341

Square Footage: 2,362
Width: 76'-0" **Depth:** 49'-0"

Delicate elongated windows add a lovely contrast to the rustic textures of this charming ranch home. The great room features a wall of windows to the rear, a fireplace flanked by built-in cabinets, and archways to the hall and kitchen, where a large island and additional built-ins provide ample work space. Across the breakfast nook and through double doors is a convenient and comfortable office with built-in cabinets.

Design HPT860343

First Floor: 1,337 square feet
Second Floor: 1,025 square feet
Total: 2,362 square feet
Width: 50'-6" **Depth:** 72'-6"

This Victorian design is far more than just a pretty face. The turret houses a spacious den with built-in cabinetry on the first floor and provides a sunny bay window for the family bedroom upstairs. Just off the foyer, the formal living and dining rooms create an elegant open space for entertaining, while a focal-point fireplace with an extended hearth warms up the spacious family area. The cooktop-island kitchen and morning nook lead to a powder room and laundry area. Two second-floor bedrooms share a full bath, while the master suite offers a private bath with an oversized whirlpool tub, twin vanities and a walk-in closet.

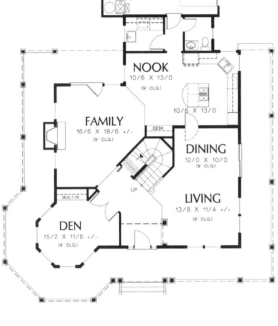

215

Design HPT860344

First Floor: 1,205 square feet

Second Floor: 1,160 square feet

Total: 2,365 square feet

Bonus Room: 350 square feet

Width: 52'-6" **Depth:** 43'-6"

This charming exterior conceals a perfect family plan. The formal dining and living rooms reside on either side of the foyer. At the rear of the home is a family room with a fireplace and access to a deck and veranda. The modern kitchen features a sunlit breakfast area. The second floor provides four bedrooms, one of which may be finished at a later date and used as a guest suite. Note the extra storage space in the two-car garage. This home is designed with a walkout basement foundation.

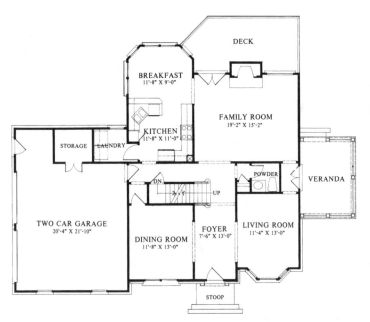

Quote One®

Cost to build? See page 454 to order complete cost estimate to build this house in your area!

Quote One®

Cost to build? See page 454
to order complete cost estimate
to build this house in your area!

Design HPT860346

First Floor: 1,736 square feet
Second Floor: 640 square feet
Total: 2,376 square feet
Bonus Space: 840 square feet
Width: 54'-0" **Depth:** 44'-0"

L

Character prevails in this delightful coastal home. Double doors flank a fireplace in the spacious great room. An adjacent dining room provides views of the rear grounds and space for formal and informal entertaining. Bedrooms 2 and 3, a full bath and an island kitchen complete the first floor. The second floor holds the master suite. Here you will find a private deck and a bath with an arched whirlpool tub. The lower level supplies room for storage and bonus space.

217

Quote One®

Cost to build? See page 454
to order complete cost estimate
to build this house in your area!

Design HPT860345

Square Footage: 2,377
Width: 69'-0" **Depth:** 49'-6"

One-story living takes a lovely traditional turn in this brick home. The entry foyer opens to the formal dining room and the great room through graceful columned archways. The open gourmet kitchen, bayed breakfast nook and keeping room with a fireplace will be a magnet for family activity. Sleeping quarters offer two family bedrooms and a hall bath and a rambling master suite with a bayed sitting area and a sensuous bath. This home is designed with a walkout basement foundation.

Design HPT860347

First Floor: 1,223 square feet
Second Floor: 1,163 square feet
Total: 2,386 square feet
Bonus Room: 204 square feet
Width: 50'-0" **Depth:** 48'-0"

Classic capstones and arched windows complement rectangular shutters and pillars on this traditional facade. The family room offsets a formal dining room and shares a see-through fireplace with the keeping room. The gourmet kitchen boasts a food-preparation island with a serving bar, a generous pantry and French-door access to the rear property. Upstairs, a sensational master suite—with a tray ceiling and a vaulted bath with a plant shelf, whirlpool spa and walk-in closet—opens from a gallery hall with a balcony overlook. Bonus space offers the possibility of an adjoining sitting room. Three additional bedrooms share a full bath. Please specify basement or crawlspace foundation when ordering.

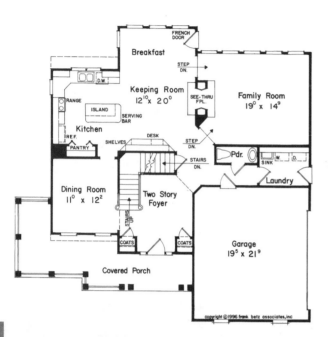

218

Design HPT860348

First Floor: 1,303 square feet
Second Floor: 1,084 square feet
Total: 2,387 square feet
Width: 54'-0" **Depth:** 42'-0"

It's hard to get beyond the covered front porch of this home, but doing so reveals a bright two-story entry open to the central hall. Just to the left, a living room features French doors connecting to the family room. The efficient kitchen with a snack bar and pantry is open to the bay-windowed breakfast area. The second-floor master bedroom features a raised ceiling and an arched window. Three family bedrooms and a hall bath complete this level.

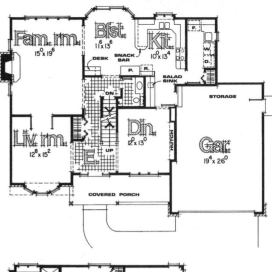

Design HPT860349

Square Footage: 2,387
Bonus Room: 377 square feet
Width: 69'-6" **Depth:** 68'-11"

This three-bedroom home brings the past to life with Tuscan columns, dormers and fanlight windows. The entrance is flanked by the dining room and study. The great room boasts cathedral ceilings and a fireplace. The spacious kitchen adjoins a breakfast nook and accesses the rear covered veranda. The master bedroom enjoys a sitting area, access to the covered veranda, and a spacious bathroom. This home is complete with two family bedrooms.

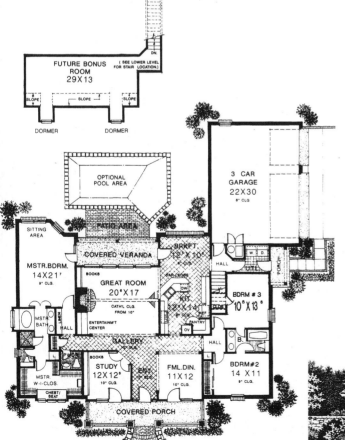

Here is a truly elegant home with a striking exterior and an interior that uses diagonals to create comfort and space. The two-story foyer opens to the formal living/sitting room, which has a vaulted ceiling. A secluded master suite offers two walk-in closets and a vaulted bath with an angled corner tub. The family room reaches to the second story, where two bedrooms and an optional bonus room complete the plan.

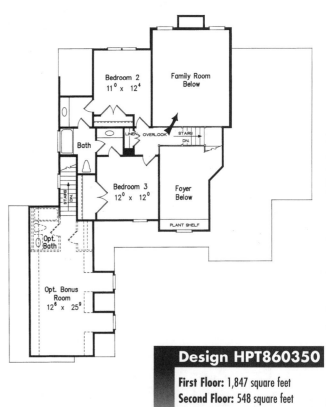

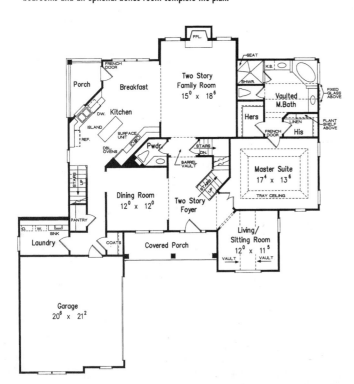

Design HPT860350

First Floor: 1,847 square feet
Second Floor: 548 square feet
Total: 2,395 square feet
Bonus Room: 395 square feet
Width: 60'-0" **Depth:** 66'-4"

Design HPT860351

Square Footage: 2,397
Width: 60'-0" **Depth:** 71'-8"

Low-slung, hipped rooflines and an abundance of glass enhance the unique exterior of this sunny one-story home. Inside, the use of soffits and tray ceilings heightens the distinctive style of the floor plan. To the left, double doors lead to the private master bedroom, which is bathed in natural light. Convenient planning of the gourmet kitchen places everything at minimal distances and serves the outdoor summer kitchen, breakfast nook and family room with equal ease.

221

Design HPT860352

Square Footage: 2,397
Width: 73'-2" **Depth:** 73'-2"

Dramatic rooflines and a unique entrance set the mood of this contemporary home. Double doors lead into the foyer, which opens directly to the formal living/dining rooms. The kitchen features a large cooktop work island and plenty of counter and cabinet space. The spacious family room expands this area. Two secondary bedrooms share a full bath. The master suite includes a lavish bath and a deluxe walk-in closet, as well as access to the covered patio.

Bedroom 4
11' x 10¹⁰

Vaulted
M. Bath

Master Suite
13' x 17⁰

Bath

Bedroom 3
11⁰ x 12⁷

Bedroom 2
13' x 12⁵

Foyer Below

Bedroom 4
11' x 10¹⁰

Bonus Room
17⁰ x 18⁵

Bath

Bedroom 3
11⁰ x 12⁷

Vaulted
Family Room
15⁰ x 19⁴

Living Room
14⁰ x 20⁰
12'-5" HIGH CEILING

Kitchen

optional basement stair location

Kitchen
Breakfast
Family Room
22' x 15⁰

Garage
20⁹ x 23⁵

Pantry

Laundry

Dining Room
13⁵ x 11⁰

Living Room
13' x 13⁵

Two Story
Foyer

Covered Porch

Design HPT860354

First Floor: 1,290 square feet
Second Floor: 1,108 square feet
Total: 2,398 square feet
Bonus Room: 399 square feet
Width: 67'-4" **Depth:** 38'-6"

A grand columned porch, shuttered windows and brick detailing all proclaim this home to be of true quality. The two-story foyer is flanked by the formal areas of the dining room and living room. A large island kitchen has plenty of storage and a walk-in pantry. The deluxe master suite is enhanced by a tray ceiling, a vaulted bath with a corner tub, and a spacious walk-in closet. Please specify crawlspace or basement foundation when ordering.

222

Design HPT860353

Square Footage: 2,403
Bonus Room: 285 square feet
Width: 60'-0" **Depth:** 67'-0"

Asymmetrical gables, pediments and tall arch-top windows accent a European-style exterior, while inside, an unrestrained floor plan expresses its independence. A spider-beam ceiling and a centered fireplace framed by shelves refocus the open area of the family room to cozy space. The vaulted breakfast nook enjoys a radius window and a French door that leads outside. Split sleeping quarters lend privacy to the luxurious master suite. Please specify basement or crawlspace foundation when ordering.

W.i.c.

Opt. Bonus
11³ x 12⁰

Opt. Bath

Vaulted
Breakfast

Bedroom 2
12⁵ x 11⁰

Kitchen

Bath

Bedroom 3
11³ x 12⁰

Pwdr.

Laund.

optional basement stair location

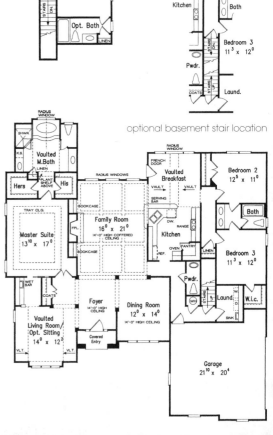

Vaulted
M. Bath

Hers

His

Master Suite
13¹⁰ x 17⁰

Family Room
16' x 21⁰
14'-0" HIGH COFFERED CEILING

Vaulted
Breakfast

Bedroom 2
12⁵ x 11⁰

Kitchen

Bath

Bedroom 3
11³ x 12⁰

Pwdr.

Laund.

W.i.c.

Foyer
14'-0" HIGH CEILING

Dining Room
12⁰ x 14⁰
14'-0" HIGH CEILING

Vaulted
Living Room/
Opt. Sitting
14⁰ x 12⁵

Covered Entry

Garage
21¹⁰ x 20⁴

Design HPT860355

First Floor: 1,566 square feet
Second Floor: 837 square feet
Total: 2,403 square feet
Apartment: 506 square feet
Width: 116'-3" **Depth:** 55'-1"

L

Be the owner of your own country estate—this two-story home gives the look and feel of grand-style living without the expense of large square footage. The entry leads to a massive foyer and great hall, worthy of your estate lifestyle. There's space enough here for living and dining areas. Two window seats in the great hall overlook the rear veranda. One fireplace warms the living area, while another looks through the dining room to the kitchen and breakfast nook. A screened porch offers casual dining space for warm weather. The master suite has another fireplace and a window seat and adjoins a luxurious master bath with a separate tub and shower. The second floor contains three family bedrooms and two full baths. A separate apartment over the garage includes its own living room, kitchen and bedroom.

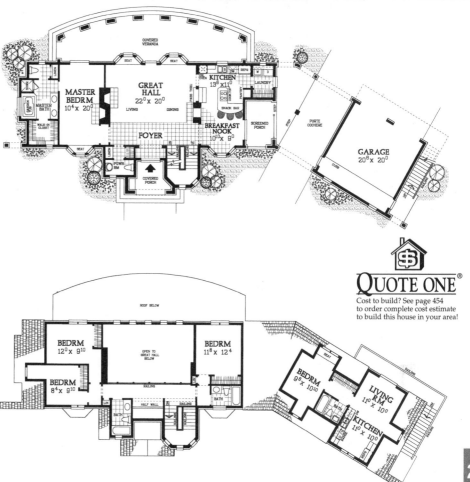

QUOTE ONE®
Cost to build? See page 454 to order complete cost estimate to build this house in your area!

223

Design HPT860356

First Floor: 1,796 square feet
Second Floor: 610 square feet
Total: 2,406 square feet
Width: 65'-9" **Depth:** 64'-9"

Eye-catching details create an elegant entry for this Southern cottage. The interior is just as inviting. Walk through the foyer to a two-story family room with a dramatic sloped ceiling. The family room opens to a large kitchen and an informal eating area with access to a guest bath. Upstairs, a balcony hall overlooks the stunning family room and leads to two large family bedrooms that share a bath. Please specify crawlspace or slab foundation when ordering.

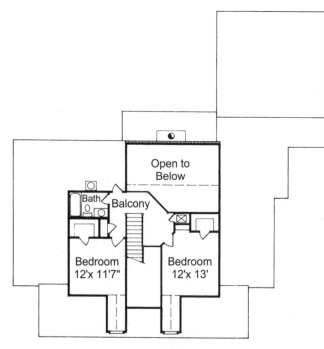

Design HPT860358

Square Footage: 2,410
Future Space: 1,123 square feet
Width: 64'-4" **Depth:** 77'-4"

Three dormers in a row bring charm while the porch colonnade adds elegance to this home. The dining room has plenty of room for formal gatherings and provides ease of service with the island kitchen close by. A bumped-out sitting bay, twin walk-in closets, dual vanities and a compartmented toilet highlight the spacious master suite. Please specify basement, crawlspace or slab foundation when ordering.

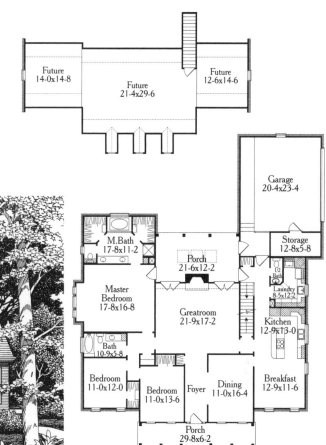

Future 14-0x14-8
Future 21-4x29-6
Future 12-6x14-6

Garage 20-4x23-4
Storage 12-8x5-8
M.Bath 17-8x11-2
Porch 21-6x12-2
1/2 Bath
Master Bedroom 17-8x16-8
Greatroom 21-9x17-2
Laundry 8-5x12-2
Kitchen 12-9x13-0
Bath 10-9x5-8
Bedroom 11-0x12-0
Bedroom 11-0x13-6
Foyer
Dining 11-0x16-4
Breakfast 12-9x11-6
Porch 29-8x6-2

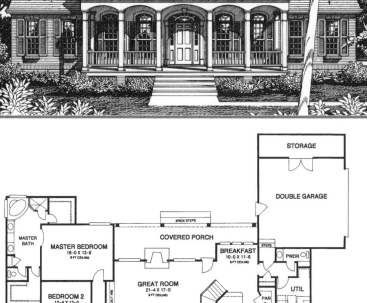

STORAGE
DOUBLE GARAGE
BRICK STEPS
COVERED PORCH
MASTER BATH
MASTER BEDROOM 16-0 X 13-6 9 FT CEILING
BREAKFAST 10-0 X 11-6 9 FT CEILING
PWDR
BEDROOM 2 12-4 X 12-0 9 FT CEILING
GREAT ROOM 21-4 X 17-0 9 FT CEILING
UTIL
PAN
BATH 2
BEDROOM 3 13-0 X 11-6 9 FT CEILING
FOYER 9 FT CEILING
DINING ROOM 13-4 X 14-0 9 FT CEILING
KITCHEN 14-6 X 16-0 9 FT CEILING
PORCH

Design HPT860357

Square Footage: 2,409
Bonus Space: 709 square feet
Width: 85'-8" **Depth:** 68'-4"

The great room of this charming Colonial home provides a large masonry fireplace. Built-ins are included on one wall for entertainment equipment and books. The master suite is located to the rear of the house and features a luxury bath that includes two large walk-in closets. The kitchen, equipped with a snack bar, walk-in pantry and desk, is well designed for the busy cook. From the kitchen area, the staircase rises to an expandable second floor. Please specify basement, crawlspace or slab foundation when ordering.

FUTURE GAME RM 16-2 X 15-0
FUTURE BEDRM 11-6 X 13-0

Quote One®
Cost to build? See page 454 to order complete cost estimate to build this house in your area!

Design HPT860359

Square Footage: 2,412
Lower Entry: 130 square feet
Width: 60'-0" **Depth:** 59'-0"

This is a gorgeous design that would easily accommodate a sloping lot. A grand great room sets the tone for this fabulous floor plan, with an elegant tray ceiling and French doors to a private front balcony. With windows and glass panels to take in the view, this design would make an exquisite seaside resort. The formal dining room is off the center of the plan for privacy and is served by a nearby gourmet kitchen. Three steps up from the foyer, the sleeping level includes a spacious master suite with a sizable private bath. Each of the two additional bedrooms privately accesses a shared bath with two vanities.

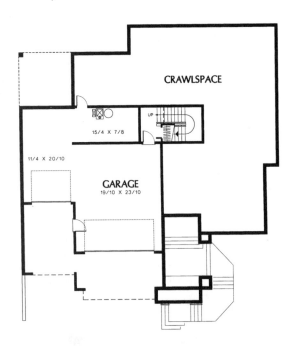

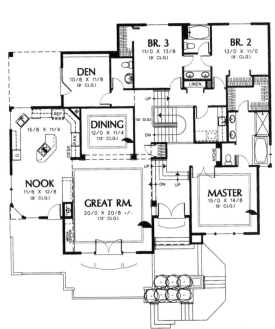

Design HPT860360

First Floor: 1,724 square feet
Second Floor: 700 square feet
Total: 2,424 square feet
Width: 47'-10" **Depth:** 63'-8"

All the charm of gables, stonework and multi-level rooflines combine to create this home. To the left of the foyer, you will see the dining room highlighted by a tray ceiling and expansive windows with transoms. The gourmet kitchen holds a work island, oversized pantry and adjoining octagonal breakfast room. The great room features a pass-through wet bar, a fireplace and bookcases. The master suite enjoys privacy at the rear of the home. An open-rail loft above the foyer leads to two additional bedrooms. This home is designed with a walkout basement foundation.

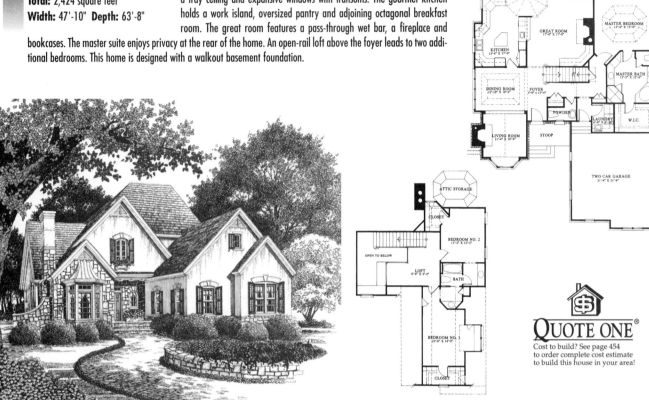

Quote One®
Cost to build? See page 454
to order complete cost estimate
to build this house in your area!

227

Design HPT860361

Square Footage: 2,424
Width: 68'-2" **Depth:** 67'-6"

Columns on the front of this home mark it with grace and style and dress up its sunny stucco facade. The floor plan holds open living areas: a great room with a fireplace, a dining room, a U-shaped kitchen and a breakfast room. Family bedrooms on the right side of the plan are separated by a full bath. The master suite is tucked away behind the garage and contains a huge walk-in closet and bath with a whirlpool tub. Please specify crawlspace or slab foundation when ordering.

Design HPT860362

First Floor: 1,533 square feet
Second Floor: 895 square feet
Total: 2,428 square feet
Width: 45'-10" **Depth:** 48'-5"

This classic two-story farmhouse offers two porches for outdoor living. Inside, an elegant dining room is accented with twin columns. The expansive kitchen is nestled between the sunny breakfast area and the dining room, with a half-bath and utility room close at hand. The living room delights with a window wall, corner fireplace and access to the rear porch. The master suite pampers with two walk-in closets, a double-sink vanity and a separate shower and tub. Three bedrooms on the second floor share a full bath.

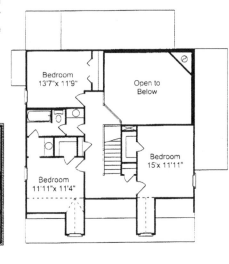

Design HPT860363

First Floor: 1,415 square feet
Second Floor: 1,015 square feet
Total: 2,430 square feet
Bonus Room: 169 square feet
Width: 54'-0" **Depth:** 43'-4"

This disarming design is reminiscent of the grand homes of the past century. Its wood siding and covered porch are complemented by shuttered windows and a glass-paneled entry. Historic design is updated in the floor plan to include a vaulted living room, a two-story family room and a den that doubles as a guest suite on the first floor. Second-floor bedrooms feature a master suite with a tray ceiling and vaulted bath. Please specify basement or crawlspace foundation when ordering.

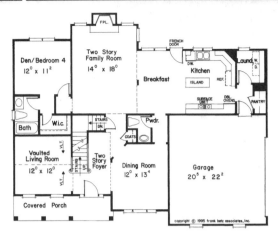

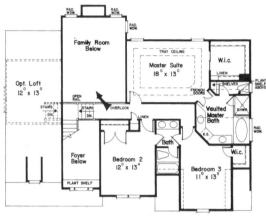

229

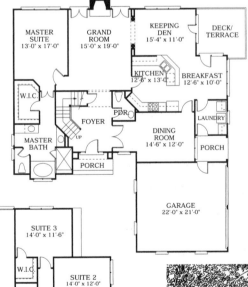

Design HPT860364

First Floor: 1,777 square feet
Second Floor: 657 square feet
Total: 2,434 square feet
Bonus Room: 340 square feet
Width: 52'-4" **Depth:** 59'-10"

The floor plan of this cottage beauty provides several living areas. An open keeping den/kitchen combination allows for close family communication. The two-story grand room features a fireplace and two sets of French doors opening to the outside. A covered side porch is located between the laundry and garage. The spacious master suite provides an impressive walk-in closet and dual vanities in the bath. Follow the dramatic angled foyer staircase upstairs and across a balcony to two additional suites and an oversized bonus room.

Design HPT860366

First Floor: 1,841 square feet
Second Floor: 594 square feet
Total: 2,435 square feet
Bonus Room: 391 square feet
Width: 82'-2" **Depth:** 48'-10"

Spaciousness and lots of amenities earmark this design as a family favorite. The front wraparound porch leads to the foyer where a bedroom/study and dining room open. The central great room presents a warming fireplace, a cathedral ceiling and access to the rear porch. In the master suite, a walk-in closet and a private bath with a bumped-out tub are extra enhancements. Bonus space over the garage could become a fine home office.

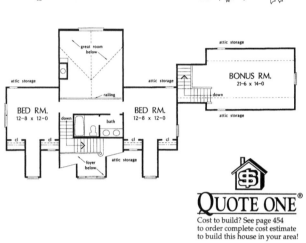

© 1994 Donald A. Gardner Architects, Inc.

© 1994 Donald A. Gardner Architects, Inc.

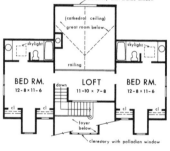

Quote One®
Cost to build? See page 454 to order complete cost estimate to build this house in your area!

230

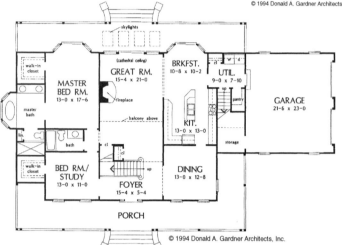

© 1992 Donald A. Gardner Architects, Inc.

Quote One®
Cost to build? See page 454 to order complete cost estimate to build this house in your area!

Design HPT860365

First Floor: 1,766 square feet
Second Floor: 670 square feet
Total: 2,436 square feet
Width: 93'-10" **Depth:** 62'-0"

This farmhouse celebrates sunlight with a Palladian window dormer, a skylit screened porch and a rear arched window. The clerestory window in the foyer throws natural light across the loft to a great room with a fireplace and a cathedral ceiling. The central island kitchen and the breakfast area are open to the great room. The master suite is a calm retreat and opens to the screened porch through a bay area. Upstairs, a loft overlooking the great room connects two family bedrooms, each with a private bath.

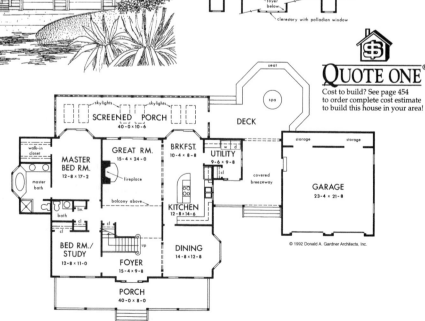

© 1992 Donald A. Gardner Architects, Inc.

Design HPT860367

First Floor: 1,293 square feet
Second Floor: 1,154 square feet
Total: 2,447 square feet
Bonus Room: 426 square feet
Width: 50'-0" **Depth:** 90'-0"

Louvered shutters, circle-head windows and a courtyard are images from the Charleston Row past brought up-to-date in a floor plan for today's lifestyles. From the great room, three sets of French doors open to the covered porch and sundeck. The U-shaped kitchen includes a central island and adjoins the dining bay. The second floor includes two family bedrooms, a master suite, and a bonus room with a private bath, walk-in closet and morning kitchen. A covered balcony is accessible from the master suite and Bedroom 3.

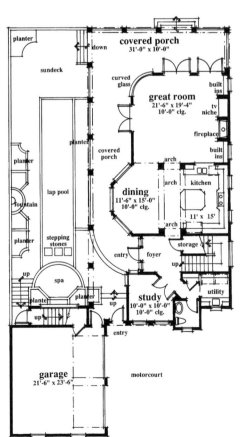

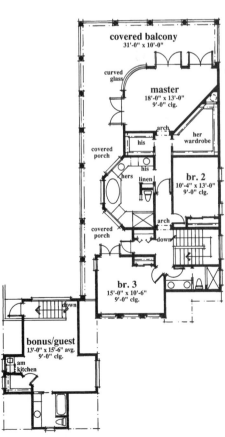

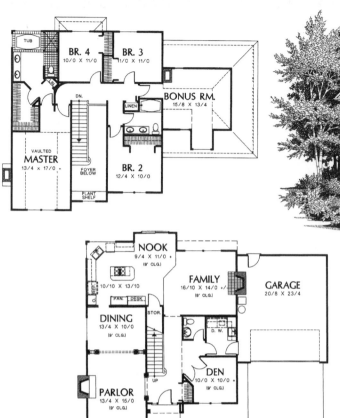

Design HPT860368

First Floor: 1,308 square feet
Second Floor: 1,141 square feet
Total: 2,449 square feet
Bonus Room: 266 square feet
Width: 56'-0" **Depth:** 42'-0"

L

Quietly stated elegance is the key to this home's attraction. The floor plan allows plenty of space for formal and informal occasions. The rear of the first floor is devoted to an open area serving as the family room, breakfast nook and island kitchen. This area is complemented by a formal parlor and dining room. A private den could function as a guest room with the handy powder room nearby. There are four bedrooms on the second floor. The bonus room over the garage could become an additional bedroom or study.

Design HPT860369

Square Footage: 2,456
Width: 66'-0" **Depth:** 68'-0"

Gently tapered columns set off an elegant arched entry framed by multi-pane windows. Inside, an open great room features a wet bar, fireplace, tall transom windows and access to a covered porch. The gourmet kitchen boasts a food-preparation island and a snack bar. Double doors open to the master suite, where French doors lead to a private bath with an angled whirlpool tub. One of two nearby family bedrooms could serve as a den, with optional French doors opening to a hall central to the sleeping wing.

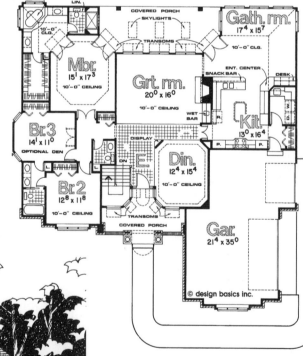

© design basics inc.

QUOTE ONE®
Cost to build? See page 454
to order complete cost estimate
to build this house in your area!

Design HPT860370

First Floor: 1,907 square feet
Second Floor: 551 square feet
Total: 2,458 square feet
Width: 58'-10" **Depth:** 83'-7"

Straight from the South, this home sets a country tone. This Southern Colonial design boasts decorative two-story columns and large windows that enhance the front porch and balcony. Enter through the foyer—notice that the formal dining room on the left connects to the island kitchen. The kitchen opens to a breakfast room, which accesses a side porch that's perfect for outdoor grilling. The great room features a warming fireplace and accesses a rear porch. The master bedroom also includes a fireplace, as well as a private bath with a whirlpool tub and a walk-in closet. A home office, laundry room and carport complete the first floor. Upstairs, two additional bedrooms share a full hall bath. Please specify crawlspace or slab foundation when ordering.

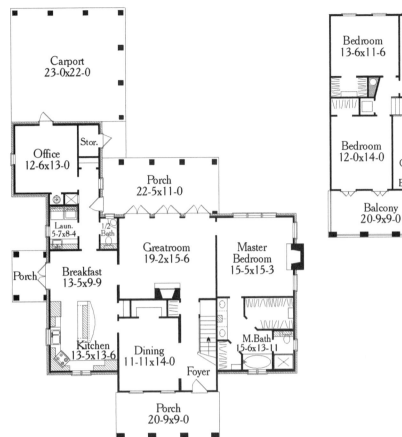

Carport
23-0x22-0

Office
12-6x13-0

Stor.

Laun.
5-7x8-4

1/2 Bath

Porch
22-5x11-0

Porch

Breakfast
13-5x9-9

Kitchen
13-5x13-6

Greatroom
19-2x15-6

Master Bedroom
15-5x15-3

M.Bath
15-6x13-11

Dining
11-11x14-0

Foyer

Porch
20-9x9-0

Bedroom
13-6x11-6

Bath

Bedroom
12-0x14-0

Open to Below

Balcony
20-9x9-0

Design HPT860372

First Floor: 1,205 square feet
Second Floor: 1,254 square feet
Total: 2,459 square feet
Width: 71'-6" **Depth:** 56'-6"

With details reminiscent of Victorian design, this home is graced by a wraparound covered veranda and an elegant bay window. The vaulted foyer introduces an octagonal staircase. Details in the living room include a tray ceiling and an adjoining dining room with a beam ceiling. A country kitchen offers a spacious walk-in pantry, a center prep island and a breakfast bay. The master bedroom upstairs is graced by a bayed sitting area. Bedrooms 2, 3 and 4 share the use of a full hall bath.

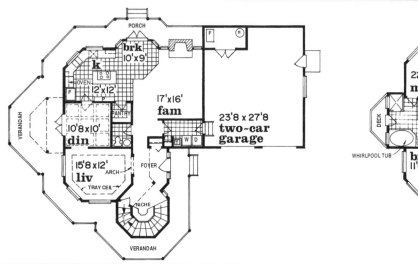

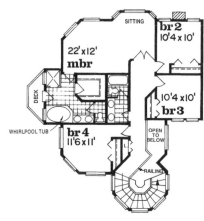

234

Design HPT860371

First Floor: 1,375 square feet
Second Floor: 1,087 square feet
Total: 2,462 square feet
Bonus Room: 156 square feet
Width: 59'-6" **Depth:** 39'-0"

A myriad of windows is topped by an impressive hipped roofline in this stately design. Fanlight and oxeye windows over a casement door light the two-story foyer, which leads to the U-shaped staircase. Columns decorate the formal dining hall. The kitchen includes a butler's pantry, corner window sink and snack bar.

Design HPT860373

First Floor: 1,737 square feet
Second Floor: 727 square feet
Total: 2,464 square feet
Bonus Room: 376 square feet
Width: 65'-6" **Depth:** 53'-0"

The beauty and warmth of a brick facade adds stately elegance to this traditional design. Its open floor plan is highlighted by a two-story living room and open dining room. The kitchen includes a central cooking island and opens to a bright breakfast area. The master suite offers an ample walk-in closet/dressing area and a bath featuring an exquisite double vanity and a tub with corner windows. A bonus room over the two-car garage offers room for expansion. Please specify basement or crawlspace foundation when ordering.

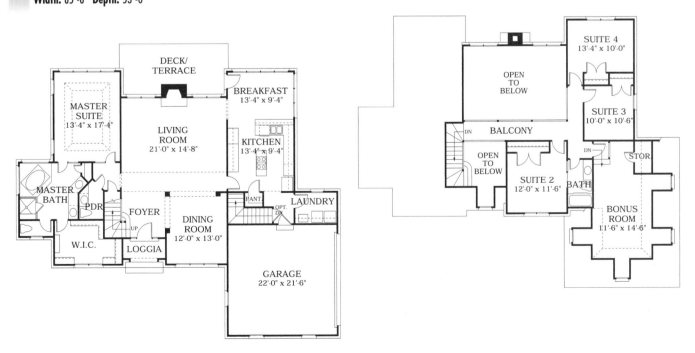

Design HPT860374

Main Level: 2,385 square feet
Lower Entry: 80 square feet
Total: 2,465 square feet
Bonus Space: 1,271 square feet
Width: 60'-4" **Depth:** 59'-4"

A classic pediment and low-pitched roof are topped by a cupola on this gorgeous coastal design. The great room features a wall of built-ins designed for even the most technology-savvy entertainment buff. Dazzling views through walls of glass are enlivened by the presence of a breezy porch. The master suite features a luxurious bath, a dressing area and two walk-in closets. Glass doors open to the portico and provide generous views of the seascape, while a nearby study offers an indoor retreat. Please specify pier or block foundation when ordering.

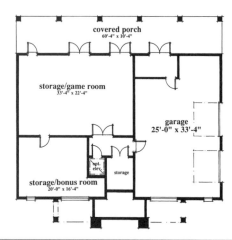

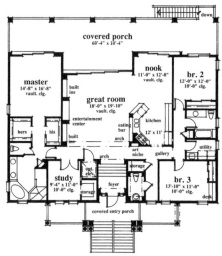

236

Design HPT860375

Square Footage: 2,465
Width: 65'-1" **Depth:** 64'-2"

This home boasts a well-laid-out design that promotes comfort and flow. The great room offers two sets of French doors to the rear porch, a fireplace, and a spacious layout that's perfect for entertaining. The open island kitchen shares an area with the breakfast room and connects to the dining room. The master suite delights in a room-sized sitting area, His and Hers walk-in closets and vanities, a compartmented toilet, and a separate tub and shower. Please specify basement, crawlspace or slab foundation when ordering.

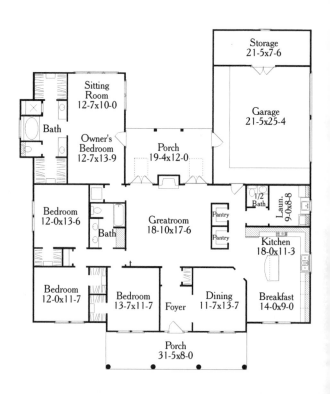

Design HPT860376

First Floor: 1,815 square feet
Second Floor: 650 square feet
Total: 2,465 square feet
Bonus Room: 124 square feet
Width: 55'-0" **Depth:** 55'-7"

Towering brick gables, arch-top windows and wooden shutters create excellent curb appeal in this traditional two-story design. A high-ceilinged entry reveals cedar posts around an inviting formal dining room and a long gallery paved with brick. Opposite is a comfortable study with full-wall bookshelves flanking an arch-top window. A wall of windows frames the spacious living room. A short hall leads to the even larger family room with a vaulted ceiling and brick fireplace. Secluded at the rear of the house, the master suite provides a high sloped ceiling and atrium doors that open to a private patio. Upstairs, three additional bedrooms with a full bath complete this marvelous home.

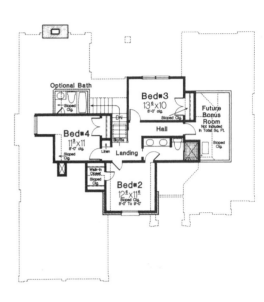

237

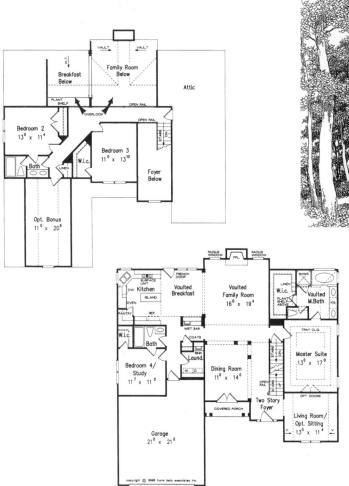

Design HPT860378

First Floor: 1,860 square feet
Second Floor: 612 square feet
Total: 2,472 square feet
Bonus Room: 244 square feet
Width: 54'-6" **Depth:** 56'-4"

Keystones, stucco arches and shutters add a French flavor to this traditional home. Inside, the formal dining room is defined by decorative columns. The gourmet kitchen has a work island and its own French door to the rear of the property. The secluded master suite features a tray ceiling, an optional sitting room and a sumptuous master bath. Two additional bedrooms share a full bath on the upper level, where an optional bonus room provides space to grow. Please specify basement or crawlspace foundation when ordering.

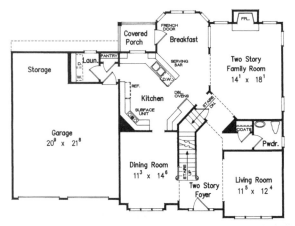

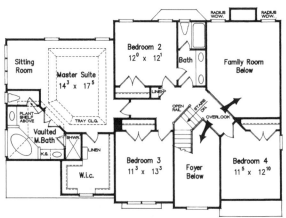

Design HPT860377

First Floor: 1,205 square feet
Second Floor: 1,277 square feet
Total: 2,482 square feet
Width: 53'-6" **Depth:** 39'-4"

A taste of Europe is reflected in the arched windows topped off by keystones in this traditional design. Formal rooms flank the foyer, which leads to a two-story family room with a focal-point fireplace. The sunny breakfast nook opens to a covered porch through a French door. A spacious, well-organized kitchen features angled wrapping counters, double ovens and a walk-in pantry. The master bedroom boasts a well-lit sitting area, a walk-in closet and a lavish bath with a vaulted ceiling. Please specify basement or crawlspace foundation when ordering.

Design HPT860379

First Floor: 1,831 square feet
Second Floor: 651 square feet
Total: 2,482 square feet
Bonus Room: 394 square feet
Width: 55'-0" **Depth:** 77'-0"

This beautiful country home characterizes all the charm of a rural lifestyle. From the covered entrance, the front door opens to a formal dining room and great room with a fireplace. A rear porch offers outdoor livability to the great room. The U-shaped kitchen and adjoining breakfast room are nearby and offer space for casual eating. Located on the first floor for privacy, the master suite features two large walk-in closets and a bath designed for relaxation. Upstairs are two family bedrooms—each with a walk-in closet—and a shared bath with separate dressing areas. This home is designed with a walkout basement foundation.

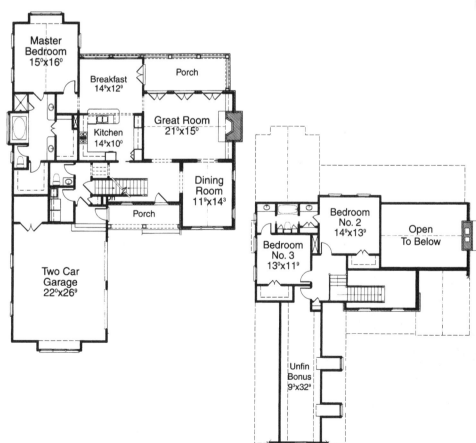

Master Bedroom 15⁰x16⁰
Breakfast 14⁹x12⁹
Porch
Great Room 21⁰x15⁰
Kitchen 14⁹x10⁰
Dining Room 11⁹x14³
Porch
Two Car Garage 22⁰x26⁹

Bedroom No. 2 14⁹x13⁹
Open To Below
Bedroom No. 3 13⁰x11⁹
Unfin Bonus 9³x32⁹

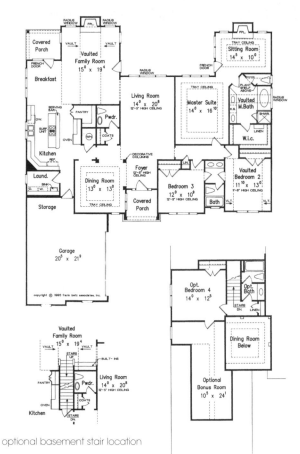

optional basement stair location

optional second floor

Design HPT860380

Square Footage: 2,491
Bonus Room: 588 square feet
Width: 64'-0" **Depth:** 72'-4"

European details bring charm and a bit of joie de vivre to this traditional home, and a thoughtful floor plan warms up to a myriad of lifestyles. Comfortable living space includes a vaulted family room with a centered fireplace. A sizable gourmet kitchen offers a walk-in pantry and a center cooktop island counter. The master suite offers a tray ceiling and a private sitting room, bright with windows and a warming hearth. Please specify basement or crawlspace foundation when ordering.

QUOTE ONE®
Cost to build? See page 454 to order complete cost estimate to build this house in your area!

Design HPT860381

First Floor: 1,269 square feet
Second Floor: 1,227 square feet
Total: 2,496 square feet
Width: 70'-0" **Depth:** 44'-5"

L

The two finely detailed outdoor living spaces found on this Victorian home add much to formal and informal entertaining options. Living and dining areas include a formal living room and dining room, a family room with a fireplace, a study and a kitchen with an attached breakfast nook. The second floor contains three family bedrooms and a luxurious master suite with a whirlpool spa and His and Hers walk-in closets.

Design HPT860382

Square Footage: 2,497
Bonus Space: 966 square feet
Width: 87'-0" **Depth:** 57'-3"

This symmetrical elegant home features a gabled porch complemented by columns. The breakfast room, adjacent to the kitchen, opens to a rear porch. The spacious great room provides a fireplace and a view of the patio. A lovely bayed window brightens the master suite, which includes a walk-in closet and a bath with a garden tub and a separate shower. Two secondary bedrooms each offer a private bath. A winding staircase leads to second-level future space. Please specify basement, crawlspace or slab foundation when ordering.

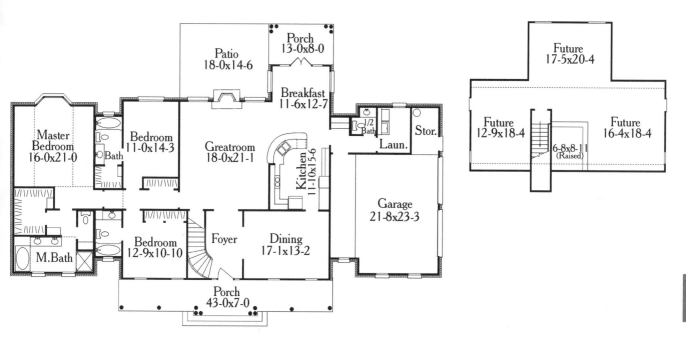

241

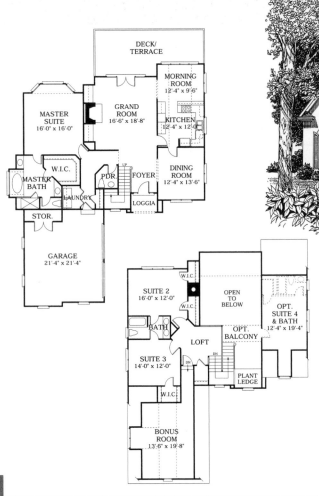

Design HPT860384

First Floor: 1,706 square feet
Second Floor: 791 square feet
Total: 2,497 square feet
Bonus Room: 644 square feet
Width: 53'-4" **Depth:** 63'-4"

Extremely cost-effective to build, this house makes great use of interior space. The foyer opens to a two-story grand room, which features a fireplace and an elegant Palladian window. A full kitchen connects the dining room and brightly lit morning room. The master suite overlooks the backyard through a bay window. An expansive walk-in closet and garden tub grace the master bath. A U-shaped staircase leads up to a loft and two additional suites that share a bath. Please specify basement or crawlspace foundation when ordering.

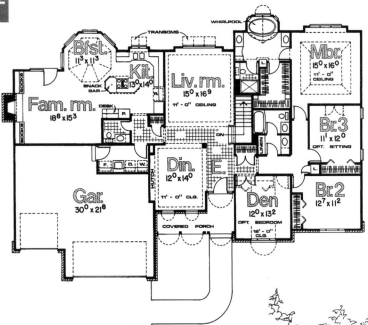

Design HPT860383

Square Footage: 2,498
Width: 76'-0" **Depth:** 55'-4"

Elegant arches at the covered entry of this home announce an exquisite floor plan with plenty of bays and niches. The tiled entry opens to the formal living and dining rooms, which enjoy open, soaring space defined by arches and a decorative column. A gourmet kitchen offers an island cooktop counter. The sleeping wing includes a master suite with a whirlpool bath, a sizable walk-in closet, two vanities and a box-bay window. Two family bedrooms share a full bath nearby.

Design HPT860385

First Floor: 1,910 square feet
Second Floor: 590 square feet
Total: 2,500 square feet
Bonus Room: 446 square feet
Width: 57'-4" **Depth:** 59'-0"

The porch is enjoying a revival in American home building, and this four-porch house is surely a prime example. In additional to a covered entry porch with a formal balustrade, this farmhouse design includes porches off the kitchen and the master bath as well as a porch and deck in the back. The entry hall in the front of the home is flanked by the formal living room and dining room. The peninsula in the kitchen opens to both the breakfast room and the large family room. The family room directly accesses the back porch and deck via doors on either side of the fireplace. The downstairs master suite is equipped with two walk-in closets. Please specify crawlspace or slab foundation when ordering.

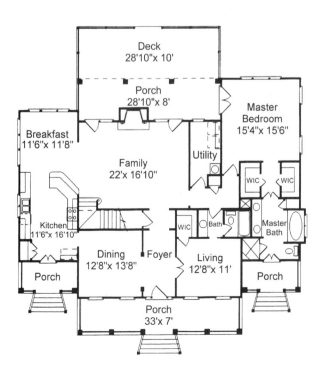

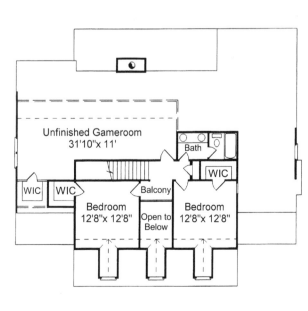

Design HPT860386

Square Footage: 2,500
Width: 73'-0" **Depth:** 65'-10"

Triple dormers highlight the roofline of this distinctive single-level French country design. The covered entryway leads to a grand open area. The large family room with a fireplace leads through double doors to the rear terrace. An L-shaped island kitchen opens to a breakfast area with a bay window. The master suite fills one wing and features a bay window, vaulted ceilings and access to the terrace. Two additional bedrooms on the opposite side of the house share a full bath.

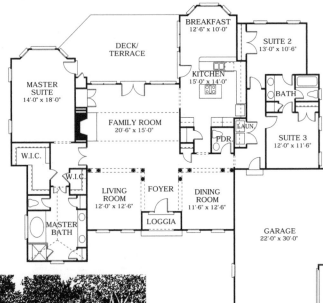

244

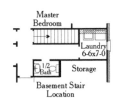

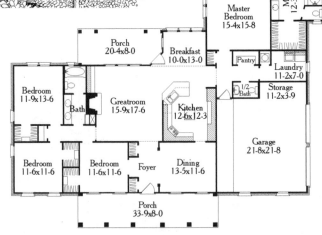

Design HPT860387

Square Footage: 2,506
Width: 72'-2" **Depth:** 66'-4"

A porch full of columns gives a relaxing emphasis to this country home. To the right of the foyer, the dining area resides conveniently near the efficient kitchen. Escape to the relaxing master suite featuring a private sun room/retreat and a luxurious bath set between His and Hers walk-in closets. The great room is complete with a warming fireplace and built-ins. Three family bedrooms enjoy private walk-in closets and share a fully appointed bath. Please specify basement, crawlspace or slab foundation when ordering.

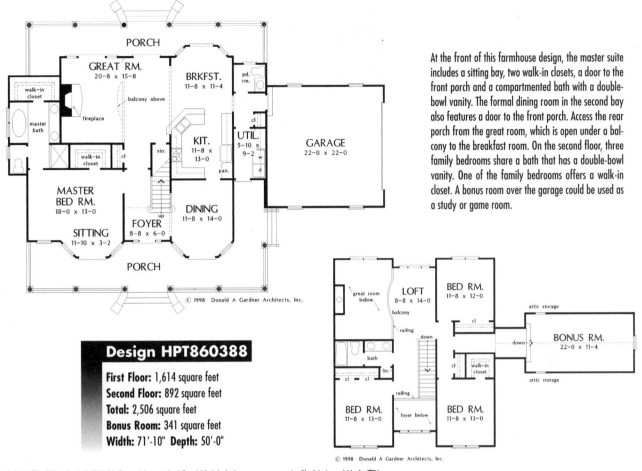

PORCH

GREAT RM.
20-8 x 15-8

BRKFST.
11-8 x 11-4

pd.
rm.

walk-in
closet

fireplace

balcony above

master
bath

KIT.
11-8 x
13-0

UTIL.
5-10 x
9-2

GARAGE
22-0 x 22-0

walk-in
closet

cl

sto.

pan.

w

d

cl

MASTER
BED RM.
18-0 x 13-0

up

DINING
11-8 x 14-0

FOYER
8-8 x 6-0

SITTING
11-10 x 3-2

PORCH

© 1998 Donald A Gardner Architects, Inc.

At the front of this farmhouse design, the master suite includes a sitting bay, two walk-in closets, a door to the front porch and a compartmented bath with a double-bowl vanity. The formal dining room in the second bay also features a door to the front porch. Access the rear porch from the great room, which is open under a balcony to the breakfast room. On the second floor, three family bedrooms share a bath that has a double-bowl vanity. One of the family bedrooms offers a walk-in closet. A bonus room over the garage could be used as a study or game room.

Design HPT860388

First Floor: 1,614 square feet
Second Floor: 892 square feet
Total: 2,506 square feet
Bonus Room: 341 square feet
Width: 71'-10" **Depth:** 50'-0"

great room
below

LOFT
8-8 x 14-0

BED RM.
11-8 x 12-0

balcony

railing

down

attic storage

cl

BONUS RM.
22-0 x 11-4

bath

down

cl

walk-in
closet

lin.

attic storage

cl cl

BED RM.
11-8 x 13-0

railing

foyer below

BED RM.
11-8 x 13-0

© 1998 Donald A Gardner Architects, Inc.

B. NATHAN

©1998 Donald A. Gardner Architects, Inc.

Design HPT860390

First Floor: 1,914 square feet
Second Floor: 597 square feet
Total: 2,511 square feet
Bonus Room: 487 square feet
Width: 79'-2" **Depth:** 51'-6"

Filled with the charm of farmhouse details, such as twin gables and bay windows, this design begins with a classic covered porch. The entry leads to a foyer flanked by columns that separate it from the formal dining and living rooms. The U-shaped kitchen separates the dining room from the bayed breakfast room. The first-floor master suite features a bedroom with a tray ceiling and a luxurious private bath.

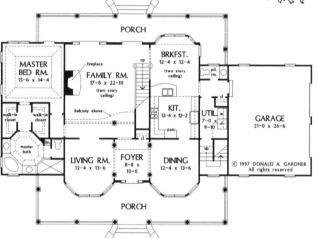

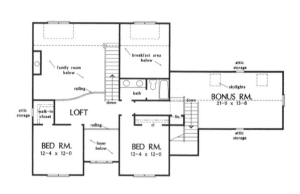

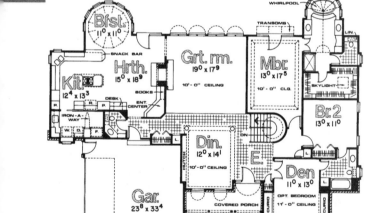

optional layout

Design HPT860389

Square Footage: 2,512
Width: 74'-0" **Depth:** 67'-8"

Repeating arches and striking brick detail complement this superb ranch-style home. Impressive tapered columns define the formal dining room. French doors open into the den with its twin curio cabinets—or convert the den into a third bedroom with a built-in desk. The great room's through-fireplace is shared with the open hearth room, the island kitchen and the gazebo-shaped breakfast nook. A curved wall invites you into the master bedroom, which features a skylit walk-in closet and a sumptuous bath with a step up to the curved whirlpool.

Quote One®
Cost to build? See page 454 to order complete cost estimate to build this house in your area!

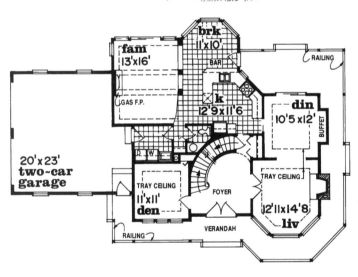

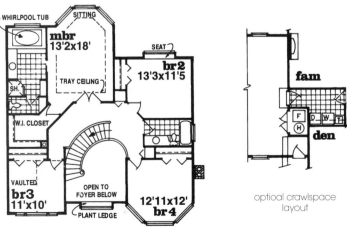

Design HPT860391

First Floor: 1,324 square feet
Second Floor: 1,192 square feet
Total: 2,516 square feet
Width: 67'-6" **Depth:** 47'-6"

A turret, wood detailing and a wraparound veranda signal desirable Victorian style for this home. The double-door entry opens to a foyer with a lovely curved staircase and leads into the living and dining rooms on the right and the den on the left. All three rooms have attractive tray ceilings; the living room boasts a fireplace; the formal dining room features a buffet alcove. Sliding glass doors in the dining room open to the veranda. Four bedrooms occupy the second floor. A tray ceiling highlights the master suite, and the private bath and walk-in closet give it a luxurious feel. Bedroom 2 includes a cozy window seat.

optioal crawlspace layout

Design HPT860392

First Floor: 1,305 square feet
Second Floor: 1,215 square feet
Total: 2,520 square feet
Bonus Space: 935 square feet
Width: 30'-6" **Depth:** 72'-2"

Louvered shutters, balustered railings and a slate-style roof complement a stucco-and-siding blend on this narrow design. Entry stairs lead up to the living areas, defined by arches and columns. A wall of built-ins and a fireplace highlight the contemporary great room, while four sets of French doors expand the living area to the wraparound porch. Second-floor sleeping quarters include a guest suite with a bayed sitting area, an additional bedroom and a full bath. The master suite features two walk-in closets, separate vanities and French doors to a private observation deck. The lower level offers bonus space for future use and another porch.

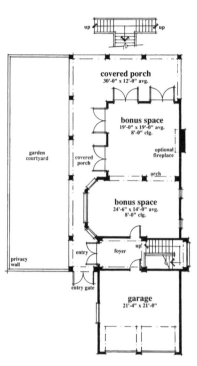

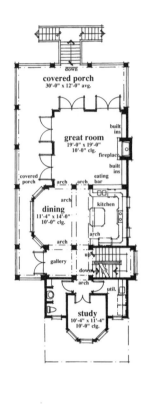

Design HPT860393

First Floor: 1,305 square feet
Second Floor: 1,215 square feet
Total: 2,520 square feet
Bonus Space: 935 square feet
Width: 30'-6" **Depth:** 72'-2"

This elegant Old Charleston Row design offers wraparound covered porches, a private sun deck and an observation deck. Four sets of French doors bring the outside in to the great room, which opens through archways framed by columns to the dining room and kitchen. The master suite, a family bedroom and a guest suite share the second floor. On the lower level, bonus space of 935 square feet opens to a garden courtyard.

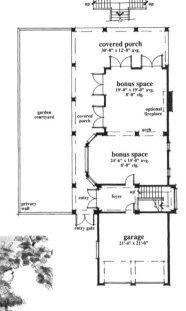

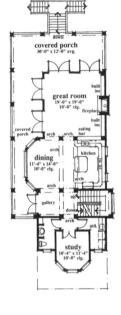

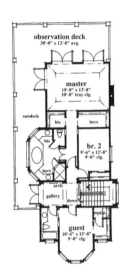

Design HPT860394

Square Footage: 2,526
Width: 64'-0" **Depth:** 81'-7"

Interesting angles and creative detailing characterize the exterior of this brick cottage. Inside, the formal dining room is just off the foyer. A gallery hall leads to the island kitchen, which opens to an informal dining area with access to two covered patios. Sleeping quarters include two family bedrooms to the right of the plan and another bedroom on the left. The left wing is dedicated to a lavish master suite, complete with a vaulted ceiling and a sumptuous bath with a whirlpool tub and separate shower.

Design HPT860395

First Floor: 1,676 square feet
Second Floor: 851 square feet
Total: 2,527 square feet
Width: 55'-0" **Depth:** 50'-0"

Muntin windows and gentle arches decorate the exterior of this traditional home. Living spaces consist of a formal dining room, a kitchen with an adjacent breakfast bay, and a great room with access to the rear veranda. A private study or guest suite in the rear left corner of the plan offers its own door to the veranda. The master suite enjoys a spacious bath with twin lavatories, a dressing area and two walk-in closets. A gallery hall on the second floor leads to a computer loft with built-ins for books and software.

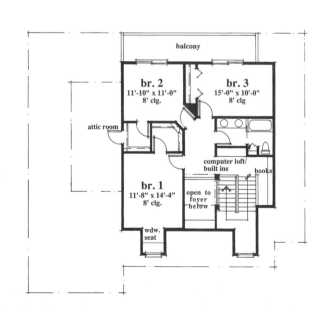

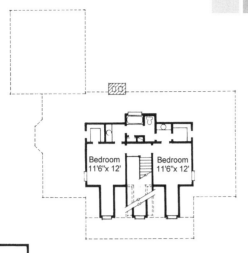

Design HPT860396

First Floor: 1,916 square feet
Second Floor: 617 square feet
Total: 2,533 square feet
Width: 66'-0" **Depth:** 66'-0"

This Southern cottage combines style and comfort and offers flexibility with an optional bedroom/study area. Nine-foot ceilings expand the plan throughout the first floor. The family chef will appreciate the large gourmet kitchen with an island cooktop, and there's room to relax with privacy in the spacious master suite. Upstairs, two family bedrooms enjoy private dressing areas. Please specify crawlspace or slab foundation when ordering.

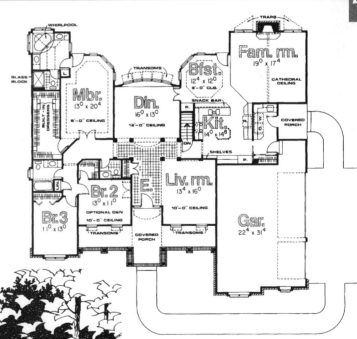

251

Design HPT860397

Square Footage: 2,538
Width: 68'-8" **Depth:** 64'-8"

The grand front porch gives this home a unique style and majestic curb appeal. Inside, the entry centers on the stately dining room with a bowed window. The island kitchen features abundant pantries and a snack bar. A sun-filled breakfast area opens to the large family room with a cathedral ceiling and fireplace. The bedroom wing has two family bedrooms and a master suite with a spacious walk-in closet and private access to the backyard.

Design HPT860399

Square Footage: 2,539
Width: 75'-2" **Depth:** 68'-8"

L

Exposed rafter tails, arched porch detailing, massive paneled front doors and stucco exterior walls enhance the character of this Western design. The sleeping zone takes an entire wing. The extra room could be used for a den or study. The family dining and kitchen activities are found in the other wing. A family/great room includes a fireplace and media built-ins. An open courtyard is accessible from each of the zones and leads to a quiet arbor.

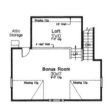

Design HPT860398

Square Footage: 2,539
Bonus Room: 639 square feet
Width: 98'-0" **Depth:** 53'-11"

Classic country character complements this home, complete with rustic stone corners, a covered front porch and interesting gables. The entry opens to the formal living areas that include a large dining room to the right, and straight ahead to a spacious living room warmed by a fireplace. Casual meals can be enjoyed overlooking the covered veranda and rear grounds from the connecting breakfast room. The other side of the gallery accesses the luxurious master suite and three second bedrooms—all with walk-in closets.

Design HPT860400

Square Footage: 2,540
Width: 70'-0" **Depth:** 65'-0"

L

A gabled stucco entry with oversized columns emphasizes the arched glass entry of this winsome one-story brick home. Arched windows on either side of the front door add symmetry and style to this pleasing exterior. An arched passage leads to the three family bedrooms and is flanked by twin bookcases and a plant ledge, providing focal interest to the living room. Bedroom 4 may also be used as a study and can be entered from double French doors off the living room. A large, efficient kitchen shares space with an octagonal breakfast area and a family room with a fireplace. Enter the master bedroom through angled double doors and view the cathedral ceiling. Attention centers immediately on the arched entry to the relaxing master bath and its central whirlpool tub. Please specify crawlspace or slab foundation when ordering.

253

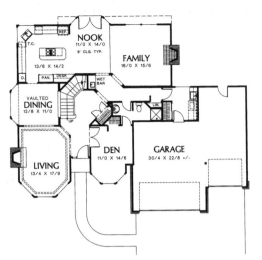

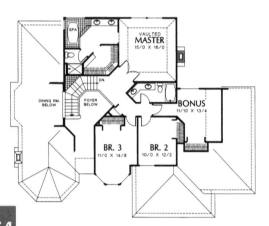

Design HPT860401

First Floor: 1,586 square feet
Second Floor: 960 square feet
Total: 2,546 square feet
Bonus Room: 194 square feet
Width: 63'-0" **Depth:** 50'-0"

L

This exquisite plan features two tower structures that enhance its dramatic facade. Inside, the living areas radiate around the central hallway which also contains the stairway to the second floor. The areas are large, open and convenient for both casual and formal occasions. Three bedrooms upstairs include two family bedrooms and a grand master suite with a bath fit for a king. An oversized walk-in closet and a vaulted ceiling are found here. Bonus space over the garage can be developed at a later time to suit changing needs.

Design HPT860402

Square Footage: 2,547
Width: 63'-10" **Depth:** 77'-5"

This stately Southern exterior welcomes guests in style with a raised porch. The magnificent foyer announces the living and dining areas with stunning decorative columns. The perfect marriage of style and comfort is made in the plush master suite, highlighted by a raised ceiling and voluminous bath with twin corner walk-in closets and separate dual lavatories. Please specify crawlspace or slab foundation when ordering.

Design HPT860403

Square Footage: 2,551
Bonus Room: 287 square feet
Width: 69'-8" **Depth:** 71'-4"

Shutters and multi-pane windows dress up the exterior of this lovely stucco home. Formal and informal areas flow easily, beginning with the dining room sized to accommodate large parties and function with the adjacent living room. A gourmet kitchen is complete with a walk-in pantry and a cozy breakfast nook. Double doors lead to the spacious master suite. The lavish master bath features His and Hers walk-in closets, a tub framed by a columned archway, and an oversized shower. Off the angular hallway are two bedrooms that share a Pullman-style bath and a study desk. A bonus room over the garage provides additional space.

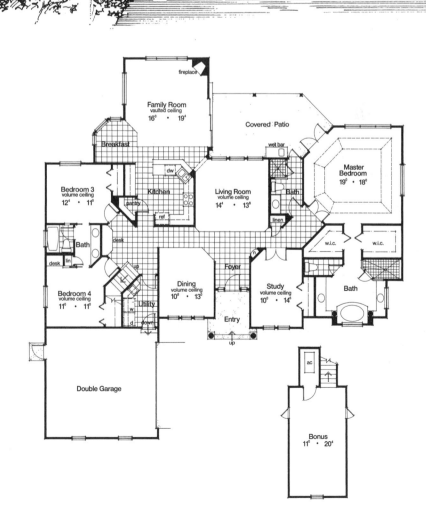

Two–car Garage
21'–4" X 22'–2"

Bath

Utility

Storage

Master Bedroom
17'–10" X 14'

Covered Porch

Breakfast
12'–4" X 12'

Bedroom
11' X 12'–6"

Ba.

Family Room
20' X 17'–6"

Kitchen
12'–4" X
12'–6"

Ba.

Bedroom
12'–2" X 13'

Living Room
13'–4" X 14'–6"

Foyer

Dining Room
13'–4" X 12'

Bedroom
12'–1" X 12'

Porch

Design HPT860404

Square Footage: 2,558
Width: 63'-6" **Depth:** 71'-6"

Heavy corner quoins make a rustic impression that is dressed up by a subtly asymmetrical design on this home. The centerpiece of the home is a magnificent family room with a tray ceiling, fireplace and built-in shelves. The breakfast room connects to the kitchen, which serves the formal dining room. Two secondary bedrooms on the right of the plan both provide private access to a full bath with twin vanities. To the far left are a third bedroom and the spacious master suite.

Design HPT860405

Square Footage: 2,561
Width: 70'-0" **Depth:** 65'-6"

L

Interesting window details and varying rooflines lend this split-bedroom home comfort and elegance. The angled foyer steps down into the living room. The family room and kitchen are conveniently grouped with the gazebo breakfast room to provide a large area for family gatherings and informal entertaining. Enter the master suite through angled double doors. Three family bedrooms with large walk-in closets and a roomy bath complete this best-selling plan. Please specify crawlspace or slab foundation when ordering.

MASTER BATH

PLANT LEDGE

PATIO

BREAKFAST

FAMILY ROOM

MASTER BEDROOM
CATHEDRAL CLG.
14'4" X 17'4"

BEDROOM 2

W.I.C.

BATH 2

W.I.C.

LIVING ROOM

KITCHEN

PDR.

REAR ENTRY

UTIL.

PLANT LEDGE

PAN.

FOYER

DINING ROOM

2 CAR GARAGE

BEDROOM 3
11' X 11'6"

BEDROOM 4/STUDY
COFFERED CLG.

W.I.C.

RAISED PORCH

PORCH

Design HPT860406

First Floor: 1,357 square feet
Second Floor: 1,204 square feet
Total: 2,561 square feet
Width: 80'-0" **Depth:** 57'-0"

This grand farmhouse features a double-gabled roof, a Palladian window and an intricately detailed brick chimney. The foyer opens to the living room for formal entertaining, while the family room offers a fireplace, wet bar and direct access to the porch. The lavish kitchen boasts a cooking island and serves the dining room, breakfast nook and porch. The master suite on the second level has a large walk-in closet and a master bath with a whirlpool tub, separate shower and double-bowl vanity. Three additional bedrooms share a full bath.

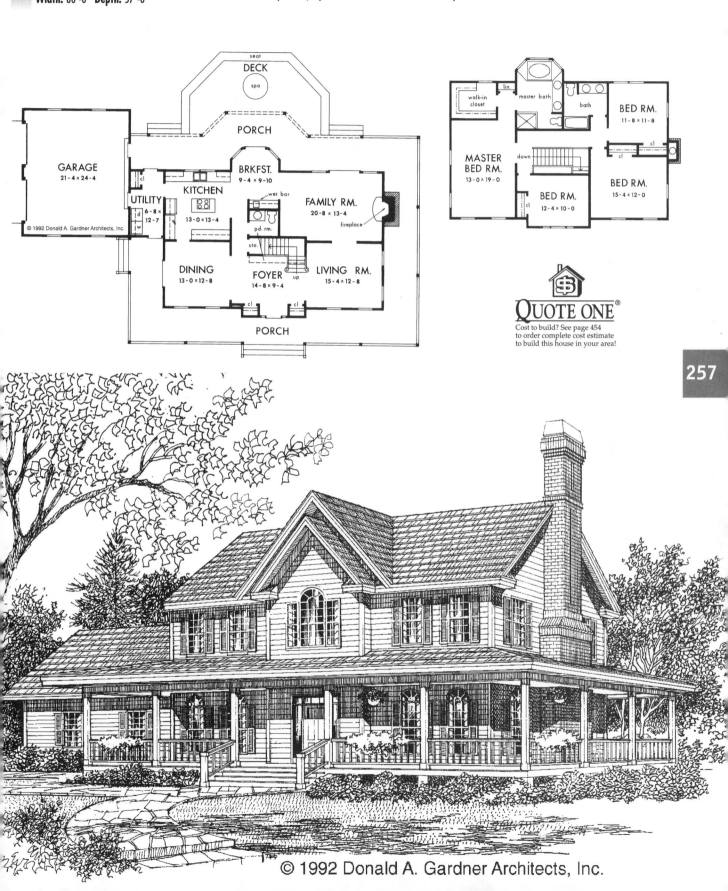

© 1992 Donald A. Gardner Architects, Inc.

QUOTE ONE®
Cost to build? See page 454
to order complete cost estimate
to build this house in your area!

257

© 1992 Donald A. Gardner Architects, Inc.

Design HPT860407

First Floor: 1,642 square feet
Second Floor: 927 square feet
Total: 2,569 square feet
Game Room/Storage: 849 square feet
Width: 60'-0" **Depth:** 44'-6"

L

Luxury abounds in this Floridian home. A game room greets you on the garage level. Up the stairs, an open grand room, a bayed nook and a deck stretch across the back of the plan. Two bedrooms occupy the right side of this level and share a full hall bath that includes dual lavatories and a separate tub and shower. The master retreat on the upper level pleases with its own reading room, a morning kitchen, a large walk-in closet and a pampering bath with a double-bowl vanity, a whirlpool tub and a shower that opens outside. A private deck allows outdoor enjoyments.

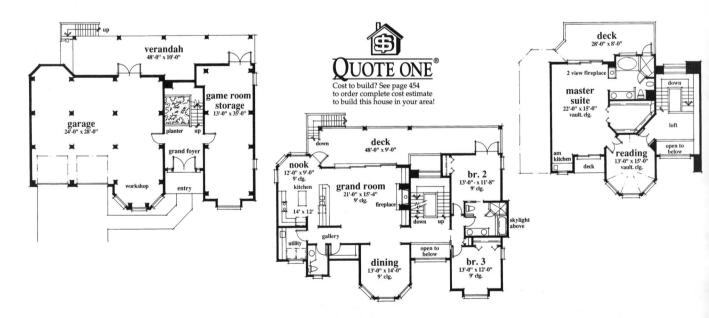

QUOTE ONE®

Cost to build? See page 454 to order complete cost estimate to build this house in your area!

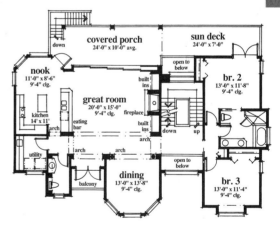

Design HPT860408

First Floor: 1,642 square feet
Second Floor: 927 square feet
Total: 2,569 square feet
Game Room/Storage: 849 square feet
Width: 60'-0" **Depth:** 44'-6"

This stunning Gulf Coast cottage features wide windows to take in gorgeous views, while cool outdoor spaces invite festive gatherings, or just a little light reading. The staircase from the ground-level foyer to the raised living area enjoys elaborate views that make a powerful "welcome home" statement. Sliding glass doors open the great room to the covered porch and sun deck, while a fireplace lends coziness. A columned archway announces the elegant dining room, while French doors open to a front balcony nearby. The gourmet kitchen is open to the bay-windowed morning nook and a single French door leads out to the covered porch. The upper level is dedicated to a spacious master suite and a bayed private study.

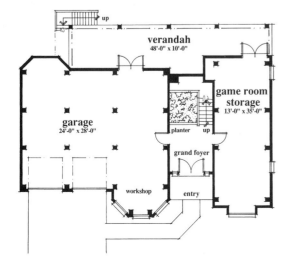

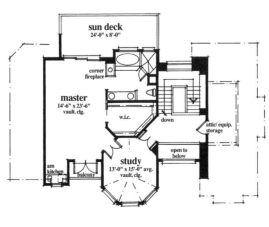

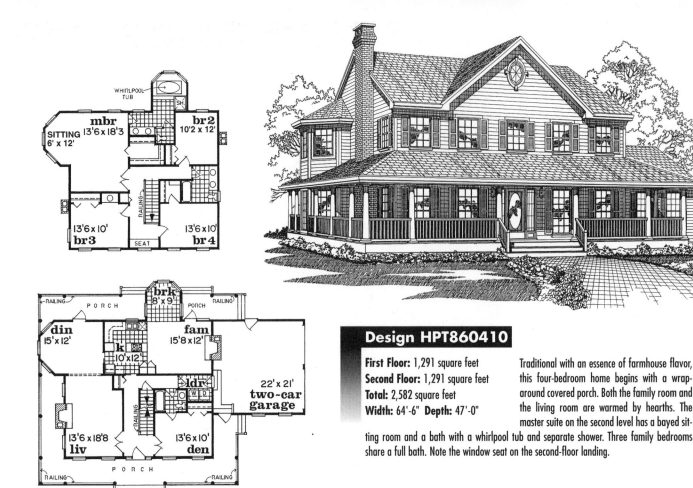

WHIRLPOOL TUB

mbr 13'6 x 18'3
SITTING 6' x 12'

SH

br 2 10'2 x 12'

br 3 13'6 x 10'

SEAT

br 4 13'6 x 10'

RAILING

RAILING   PORCH   **brk** 8' x 9'   PORCH   RAILING

din 15' x 12'

k 10' x 12'

fam 15'8 x 12'

ldr W D

22' x 21' two-car garage

liv 13'6 x 18'8

den 13'6 x 10'

RAILING   PORCH   RAILING

Design HPT860410

First Floor: 1,291 square feet
Second Floor: 1,291 square feet
Total: 2,582 square feet
Width: 64'-6" **Depth:** 47'-0"

Traditional with an essence of farmhouse flavor, this four-bedroom home begins with a wrap-around covered porch. Both the family room and the living room are warmed by hearths. The master suite on the second level has a bayed sitting room and a bath with a whirlpool tub and separate shower. Three family bedrooms share a full bath. Note the window seat on the second-floor landing.

Design HPT860409

Square Footage: 2,585
Bonus Room: 519 square feet
Width: 62'-6" **Depth:** 83'-10"

While designed to take full advantage of panoramic rear vistas, this house possesses some great visual effects of its own. Its unusual space plan, including an angled gathering room, expansive grand room and covered lanai, is perfect for entertaining. The master retreat features a sitting area and a bath, which includes His and Hers vanities and two walk-in closets. Please specify basement or crawlspace foundation when ordering.

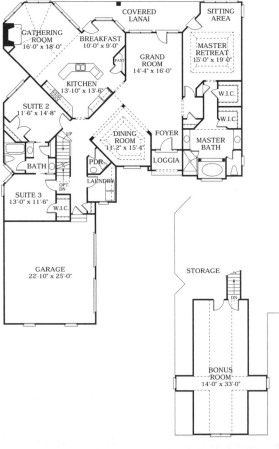

COVERED LANAI

SITTING AREA

GATHERING ROOM 16'-0" x 18'-0"

BREAKFAST 10'-0" x 9'-0"

MASTER RETREAT 15'-0" x 19'-0"

GRAND ROOM 14'-4" x 16'-0"

KITCHEN 13'-10" x 13'-6"

PANT.

W.I.C.

SUITE 2 11'-6" x 14'-8"

UP

W.I.C.

DINING ROOM 11'-2" x 15'-4"

FOYER

MASTER BATH

BATH

PDR

LOGGIA

OPT. DN

LAUNDRY

SUITE 3 13'-0" x 11'-6"

W.I.C.

GARAGE 22'-10" x 25'-0"

STORAGE

DN

BONUS ROOM 14'-0" x 33'-0"

Design HPT860412

First Floor: 2,028 square feet
Second Floor: 558 square feet
Total: 2,586 square feet
Bonus Room: 272 square feet
Width: 64'-10" **Depth:** 61'-0"

Double columns and an arch-top clerestory create an inviting entry to this fresh interpretation of traditional style. Decorative columns and arches open to the dining and great rooms. The C-shaped kitchen looks over an angled counter to a breakfast bay. A sitting area and a lavish bath set off the secluded master suite. A nearby secondary bedroom could be used as a guest suite while, upstairs, two family bedrooms share a full bath. Please specify basement, crawlspace or slab foundation when ordering.

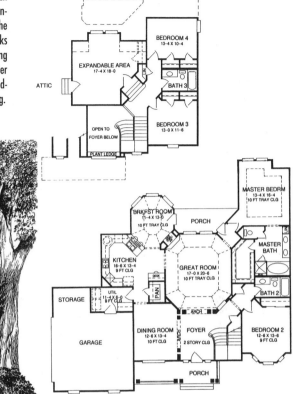

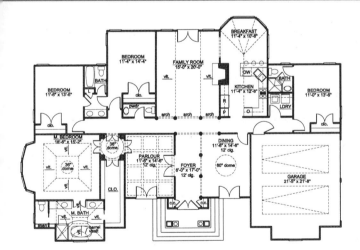

Design HPT860411

Square Footage: 2,588
Width: 77'-0" **Depth:** 52'-6"

A Mediterranean mansion or an Italian villa—these are the influences on the exterior of this grand one-story home. Double doors open to an elegant entry foyer which leads to the formal parlor and dining room. The family room is enhanced by a fireplace and double doors to the rear yard. A guest bedroom down the hall features a private bath. Two family bedrooms at the other end of the hall share a bath. The master suite may be accessed through a private foyer.

Design HPT860413

Square Footage: 2,590
Width: 73'-6" **Depth:** 64'-10"

With a solid exterior of rough cedar and stone, this new French Country design will stand the test of time. A wood-paneled study on the front features a large bay window. The heart of this home is a large open great room with a built-in entertainment center. The spacious master bedroom features a corner reading area, a whirlpool tub and access to an adjacent covered patio.

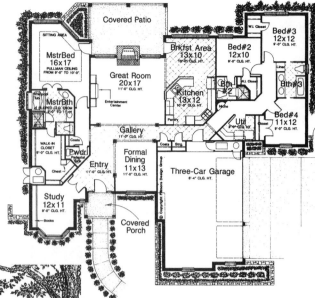

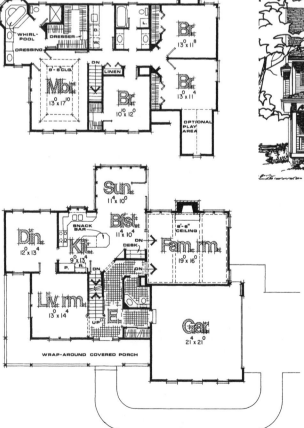

262

Quote One®

Cost to build? See page 454 to order complete cost estimate to build this house in your area!

Design HPT860414

First Floor: 1,322 square feet
Second Floor: 1,272 square feet
Total: 2,594 square feet
Width: 56'-0" **Depth:** 48'-0"

Here's the luxury you've been looking for — from the wraparound covered front porch to the bright sun room off the breakfast room. A sunken family room with a fireplace serves everyday casual gatherings, while the more formal living and dining rooms are reserved for special entertaining situations. The kitchen features a central island with a snack bar. Upstairs are four bedrooms and a lovely master suite with French doors to the private bath. Double vanities in the shared bath easily serves the three family bedrooms.

© 1997 Donald A. Gardner Architects, Inc.

Design HPT860415

First Floor: 1,939 square feet
Second Floor: 657 square feet
Total: 2,596 square feet
Bonus Room: 386 square feet
Width: 80'-10" **Depth:** 55'-8"

This country farmhouse offers an inviting wraparound porch for comfort and three gabled dormers for style. The foyer leads to a generous great room with an extended-hearth fireplace, cathedral ceiling and access to the back covered porch. The first-floor master suite enjoys a sunny bay window and features a private bath with a cathedral ceiling, large oval tub set near a window, separate shower and dual vanity sinks. Upstairs, two family bedrooms share an elegant bath that has a cathedral ceiling. An optional bonus room over the garage allows plenty of room to grow.

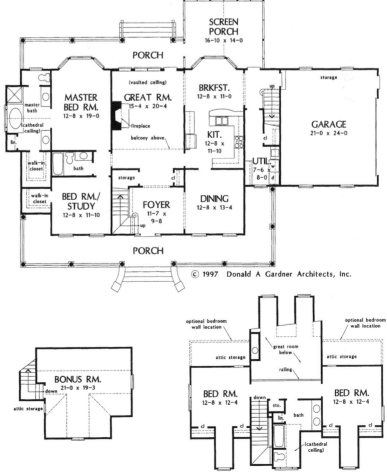

© 1997 Donald A Gardner Architects, Inc.

Design HPT860417

Square Footage: 2,597
Width: 96'-6" **Depth:** 50'-0"

The angles in this home create unlimited views and space. Inside, the foyer commands a special perspective on living areas, including the living room, dining room and den. The island kitchen serves the breakfast nook and the family room. Nearby, in the master suite, mitered glass and a private bath set the tone for simple luxury. Two secondary bedrooms share privacy and quiet at the front of the house. The den may also convert to a fourth bedroom, if desired.

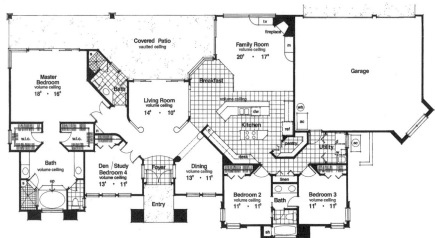

264

Design HPT860416

Square Footage: 2,600
Width: 87'-0" **Depth:** 60'-0"

Varied rooflines, shutters and multi-pane windows combine to make this one-story home a neighborhood showpiece. A tiled entry presents a grand view of the spacious great room. A den opens off the foyer through double doors. The island in the kitchen provides extra work space to an already well-equipped area. With direct access to both the formal dining room and the breakfast nook, the kitchen is a warm and bright place. A sumptuous master suite features a sitting bay, two walk-in closets and a lavish bath.

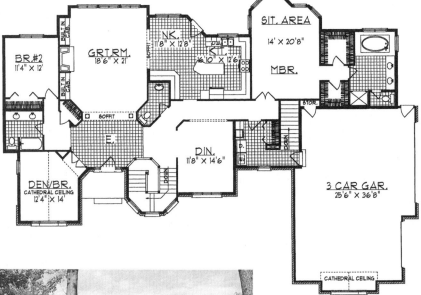

Photo courtesy of Ahmann Design

This home, as shown in the photograph, may differ from the actual blueprints. For more detailed information, please check the floor plans carefully.

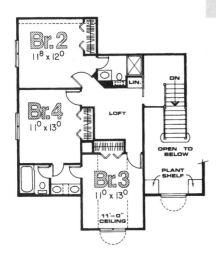

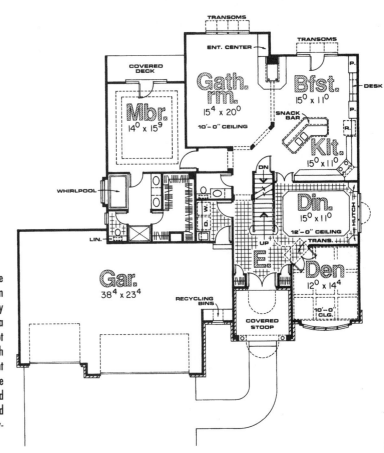

Design HPT860418

First Floor: 1,800 square feet
Second Floor: 803 square feet
Total: 2,603 square feet
Width: 62'-0" **Depth:** 60'-8"

Columns and double doors at the entry create a dash of European flavor for this fine 1½-story home. The tiled entry opens to a dining area with a twelve-foot ceiling and a cozy den with spider-beams and a bowed window. French doors in the dining room allow entry to the island kitchen. The adjacent breakfast area shares a three-sided fireplace with the gathering room. The secluded master suite boasts a private covered deck, whirlpool bath and large walk-in closet. Bedroom 2 has a private bath, while Bedrooms 3 and 4 share a compartmented bath. A popular three-car garage includes a recycling center and convenient laundry room access.

265

Design HPT860419

First Floor: 1,750 square feet
Second Floor: 855 square feet
Total: 2,605 square feet
Width: 77'-0" **Depth:** 56'-0"

Nine-foot ceilings and shady upper and lower porches make this a perfect retreat for long hot summers. The living room is cozy year-round with built-ins, a fireplace and a raised tray ceiling. The first-floor master suite furnishes its own porch retreat. Three family bedrooms share a full bath on the second floor. A storage room in the garage prevents the necessity of climbing up to the hot attic. Please specify basement, crawlspace or slab foundation when ordering.

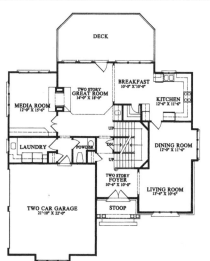

Quote One®

Cost to build? See page 454 to order complete cost estimate to build this house in your area!

Design HPT860420

First Floor: 1,395 square feet
Second Floor: 1,210 square feet
Total: 2,605 square feet
Bonus Room: 225 square feet
Width: 47'-0" **Depth:** 49'-6"

A gentle mix of stucco and stone, a box-bay window and a covered entry make this English country home very inviting. The two-story foyer opens to formal living and dining rooms. A spacious U-shaped kitchen adjoins a breakfast nook. This area flows to the two-story great room, which offers a through-fireplace shared with the media room. Upstairs, a plush retreat awaits the homeowner with a quiet sitting bay. This home is designed with a walkout basement foundation.

Design HPT860421

First Floor: 1,351 square feet
Second Floor: 1,257 square feet
Total: 2,608 square feet
Bonus Room: 115 square feet
Width: 60'-0" **Depth:** 46'-4"

Here's a new country home with a fresh face and a dash of Victoriana. Inside, the foyer leads to an elegant dining room and a spacious living room with French doors to the covered rear porch. The heart of the home is a two-story family room with a focal-point fireplace and views to the rear property. A breakfast room offers a walk-in pantry and shares a snack bar with the kitchen, which in turn leads to the formal dining room through a butler's pantry. The second-floor master suite features an optional sitting room and an impressive private bath with a vaulted ceiling.

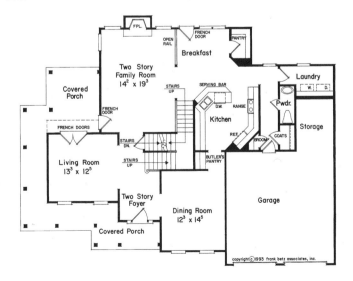

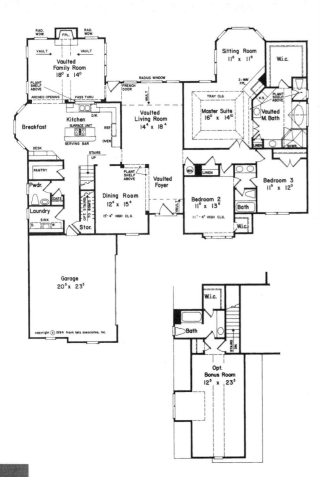

Design HPT860423

Square Footage: 2,622
Bonus Room: 478 square feet
Width: 69'-0" **Depth:** 71'-4"

Striking design and an open floor plan contribute to the gracious atmosphere of this one-story home. The gourmet kitchen features a cooktop island, a bayed breakfast nook and a pass-through to the cozy family room. A vaulted ceiling and a fireplace accent the family room. Sleeping quarters are headlined with a luxurious master suite that's designed for relaxing with a sunny sitting room. Two family bedrooms privately access a compartmented bath. Please specify basement or crawlspace foundation when ordering.

© 1994 Donald A. Gardner Architects, Inc.

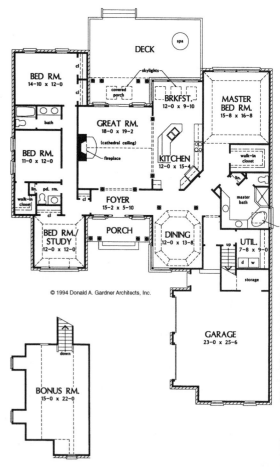

© 1994 Donald A. Gardner Architects, Inc.

Design HPT860422

Square Footage: 2,625
Bonus Room: 447 square feet
Width: 63'-1" **Depth:** 90'-2"

This stately brick facade features a covered columned porch that ushers visitors into the large foyer. An expansive great room with a fireplace and access to a covered rear porch awaits. The centrally located kitchen is within easy reach of the great room, formal dining room and skylit breakfast area. Split-bedroom planning places the master bedroom and elegant master bath to the right of the home. Two bedrooms reside to the left, while an optional bedroom or study faces the front.

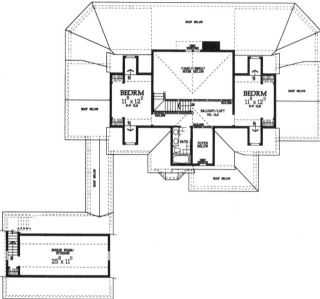

QUOTE ONE®
Cost to build? See page 454
to order complete cost estimate
to build this house in your area!

Design HPT860424

First Floor: 1,969 square feet
Second Floor: 660 square feet
Total: 2,629 square feet
Bonus Room: 360 square feet
Width: 90'-8" **Depth:** 80'-4"

L D

Varying roof planes, gables and dormers help create the unique character of this house. Inside, the family/great room gains attention with its high ceiling, fireplace/media-center wall, view of the upstairs balcony and French doors to the sun room. In the U-shaped kitchen, an island work surface, a planning desk and pantry are added conveniences. The spacious master suite can function with the home office, library or private sitting room. Its direct access to the huge raised veranda provides an ideal private outdoor haven for relaxation. The second floor contains two bedrooms and a bath. The garage features a workshop area and stairway to a second-floor storage or multi-purpose room.

269

Design HPT860425

First Floor: 1,362 square feet
Second Floor: 1,270 square feet
Total: 2,632 square feet
Width: 79'-0" **Depth:** 44'-0"

Rich with Victorian details—scalloped shingles, a wraparound veranda and turrets—this beautiful facade conceals a modern floor plan. Archways announce a distinctive living room with a lovely tray ceiling and help define the dining room. An octagonal den across the foyer provides a private spot for reading or studying. The U-shaped island kitchen holds an octagonal breakfast bay and a pass-through breakfast bar to the family room. Upstairs, three family bedrooms share a hall bath—one bedroom is within a turret. The master suite is complete with a bayed sitting room and a fancy bath set in another of the turrets.

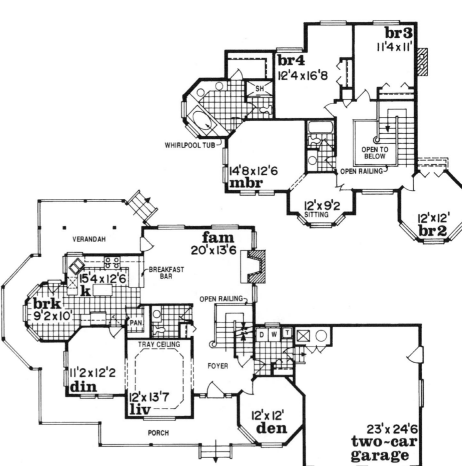

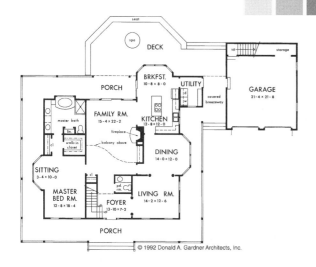

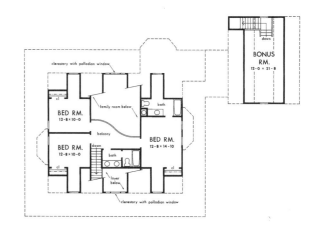

© 1992 Donald A. Gardner Architects, Inc.

A. Gardner Architects, Inc.

Design HPT860426

First Floor: 1,759 square feet
Second Floor: 888 square feet
Total: 2,647 square feet
Bonus Room: 324 square feet
Width: 85'-0" **Depth:** 67'-4"

This four-bedroom country farmhouse invites enjoyment of the outdoors with a true wraparound porch and a spacious deck and spa. Front and rear Palladian window dormers allow natural light to brighten the foyer and family room and lend sparkling accents to the country-style exterior. A gracefully curved balcony overlooks the two-story family room, warmed by a fireplace with an extended hearth. The master suite includes a large walk-in closet, a special sitting area and a master bath with a whirlpool tub, separate shower and twin vanities.

271

Design HPT860427

Square Footage: 2,648
Bonus Room: 266 square feet
Width: 68'-10" **Depth:** 77'-10"

This vintage elevation possesses all the extras desired by today's homeowner. Twelve-foot ceilings give a spacious feel in the study, dining room and great room. The kitchen has a cooktop work island, a pantry and a snack bar. The master suite includes His and Hers closets and an amenity-filled bath. Two family bedrooms contain roomy closets and share a private compartmented bath. Please specify basement, crawlspace or slab foundation when ordering.

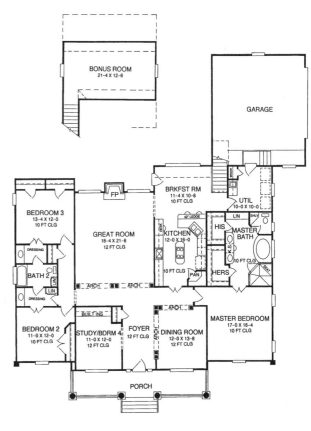

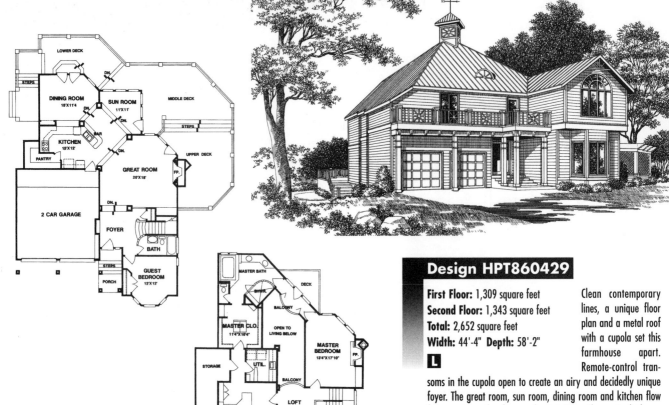

Floor plan labels (first floor, top left):
LOWER DECK
STEPS
DINING ROOM 18'X11'4
SUN ROOM 11'X11'
MIDDLE DECK
KITCHEN 15'X12'
BAR
PANTRY
STEPS
UPPER DECK
GREAT ROOM 20'X18'
FP.
DN.
2 CAR GARAGE
FOYER
DN.
BATH
STEPS
PORCH
GUEST BEDROOM 12'X12'

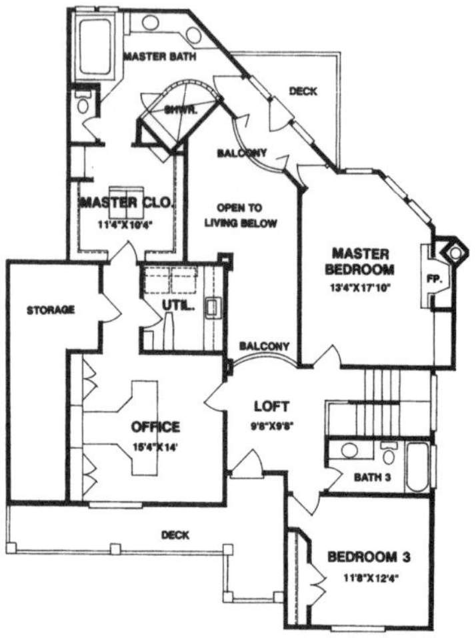

Floor plan labels (second floor):
MASTER BATH
SHWR.
DECK
BALCONY
MASTER CLO. 11'4"X10'4
OPEN TO LIVING BELOW
MASTER BEDROOM 13'4"X17'10"
FP.
STORAGE
UTIL.
BALCONY
OFFICE 16'4"X14'
LOFT 9'6"X9'8"
BATH 3
DECK
BEDROOM 3 11'8"X12'4"

Design HPT860429

First Floor: 1,309 square feet
Second Floor: 1,343 square feet
Total: 2,652 square feet
Width: 44'-4" **Depth:** 58'-2"

L

Clean contemporary lines, a unique floor plan and a metal roof with a cupola set this farmhouse apart. Remote-control transoms in the cupola open to create an airy and decidedly unique foyer. The great room, sun room, dining room and kitchen flow from one to another for casual entertaining. The master bedroom and bath upstairs are bridged by a pipe-rail balcony that also gives access to a rear deck.

Floor plan labels (lower left):
A/C
Window Seat
Bed Rm. 3 11'x 14'
Bed Rm. 2 12'x 11'
Bath
2 Car Garage 20'x 24'
36" fireplace
Family Rm. 21'x 17'
La.
Kit. 14'x 17'
DW
Nook 10'x 10'
covered patio
Dining Rm. 11'x 11'
Living Rm. 13'x 19'
Foyer
Entry
Master Suite 18'x 18'
Ma. Bath
A/C
Den/Study 11'x 11'

Design HPT860428

Square Footage: 2,656
Width: 92'-0" **Depth:** 69'-0"

A graceful design sets this charming home apart from the ordinary. The dining room branches off the sunny living room, setting a lovely backdrop for entertaining. Casual living is the focus in the oversized family room, where sliding doors open to the patio and the gourmet eat-in kitchen is open for easy conversation. Two family bedrooms are just off the family room. The master suite includes a cozy fireplace in the sitting area. A large covered patio adds to the living area.

© 1993 Donald A. Gardner Architects, Inc.

Quote One®
Cost to build? See page 454
to order complete cost estimate
to build this house in your area!

Design HPT860430

First Floor: 2,064 square feet
Second Floor: 594 square feet
Total: 2,658 square feet
Bonus Room: 483 square feet
Width: 92'-0" **Depth:** 57'-8"

You'll find country living at its best when meandering through this four-bedroom farmhouse with its wrap-around porch. A front Palladian dormer window and rear clerestory windows in the great room add exciting visual elements to the exterior while providing natural light to the interior. The large great room boasts a fireplace, bookshelves and a raised cathedral ceiling, allowing a curved balcony overlook above. The great room, master bedroom and breakfast room are accessible to the rear porch for greater circulation and flexibility. Special features such as the large cooktop island in the kitchen, the wet bar, the bedroom/study, the generous bonus room over the garage and ample storage space set this plan apart.

273

© 1993 Donald A. Gardner Architects, Inc.

Design HPT860431

First Floor: 1,752 square feet
Second Floor: 906 square feet
Total: 2,658 square feet
Width: 74'-0" **Depth:** 51'-7"

L D

Delightfully proportioned and superbly symmetrical, this Victorian farmhouse has lots of curb appeal. The wraparound porch offers rustic columns and railings, and broad steps present easy access to the front, rear and side yards. Archways, display niches and columns help define the great room, which offers a fireplace framed by views to the rear property. A formal parlor and a dining room flank the reception hall, and each offers a bay window. The master suite boasts two sets of French doors to the wraparound porch, and a private bath with a clawfoot tub, twin lavatories, a walk-in closet and a stall shower. Upstairs, a spacious office/den adjoins two family bedrooms, each with a private bath.

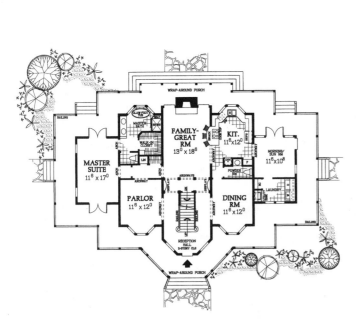

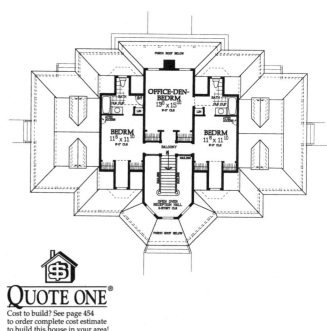

QUOTE ONE®

Cost to build? See page 454
to order complete cost estimate
to build this house in your area!

Design HPT860432

First Floor: 1,637 square feet
Second Floor: 1,022 square feet
Total: 2,659 square feet
Bonus Space: 532 square feet
Width: 50'-0" **Depth:** 53'-0"

Variable rooflines, a tower and a covered front porch all combine to give this home a wonderful ambiance. Enter through the mid-level foyer and head either up to the main living level or down to the garage. On the main level, find a spacious light-filled great room sharing a fireplace with the dining room. A study offers access to the rear covered veranda. The efficient island kitchen is open to the dining room, offering ease in entertaining. A guest suite with a private full bath completes this level. Upstairs, a second guest suite with its own bath and a deluxe master suite with a covered balcony, sun deck, walk-in closet and lavish bath are sure to please. This home is designed with a pier foundation.

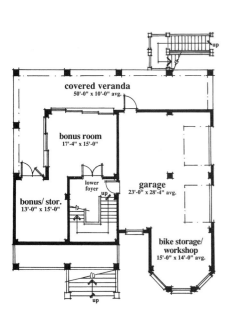

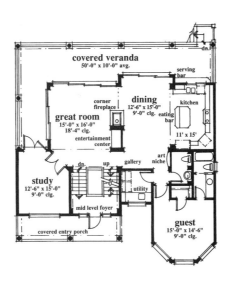

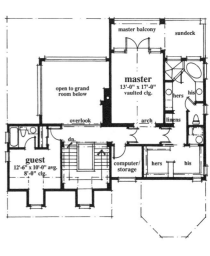

seat

DECK

SUN RM.
15-8 x 10-0
(cathedral ceiling)

arched window above door

fireplace

MASTER
BED RM.
14-0 x 19-4

master bath

lin

walk-in closet

BED RM.
13-0 x 12-0

GREAT RM.
18-0 x 21-0
(cathedral ceiling)

BRKFST.
12-0 x 11-0

VESTIBULE UTIL.
9-0 x 6-8

storage

d w

bath

fireplace

cabinets

KITCHEN
12-0 x 16-0

up

GARAGE
21-0 x 23-0

BED RM.
11-8 x 11-0

cl

cl

sto.

FOYER
12-0 x 5-8

storage

pd. rm.

cl

DINING
12-0 x 14-0

PORCH
15-0 x 5-2

BED RM./ STUDY
12-0 x 12-0

© 1993 Donald A. Gardner Architects, Inc.

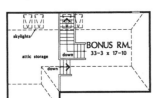

skylights

attic storage

BONUS RM.
33-3 x 17-10

down

down

©1993 Donald A. Gardner Architects, Inc.,
Photography courtesy of
Donald A. Gardner Architects, Inc.

This home, as shown in the photograph,
may differ from the actual blueprints.
For more detailed information, please
check the floor plans carefully.

Design HPT860434

Square Footage: 2,663
Bonus Room: 653 square feet
Width: 72'-7" **Depth:** 78'-0"

This home features large arched windows, round columns, a covered porch and brick veneer siding. The arched window in the clerestory above the entrance provides natural light to the interior. The great room boasts a cathedral ceiling, a fireplace and built-in cabinets and bookshelves. The L-shaped kitchen services the dining room, the breakfast area and the great room. The master suite, with a fireplace, uses a private passage to the deck. Three additional bedrooms are at the other end of the house for privacy.

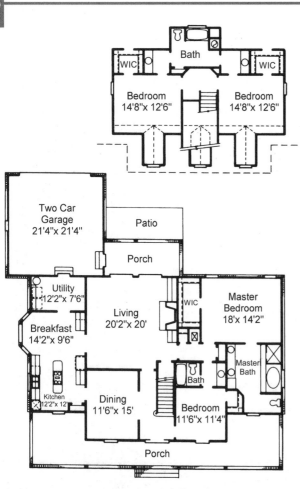

Bath

WIC

WIC

Bedroom
14'8"x 12'6"

Bedroom
14'8"x 12'6"

Two Car
Garage
21'4"x 21'4"

Patio

Porch

Utility
12'2"x 7'6"

Living
20'2"x 20'

WIC

Master
Bedroom
18'x 14'2"

Breakfast
14'2"x 9'6"

Master
Bath

Kitchen
12'2"x 12'

Dining
11'6"x 15'

Bath

Bedroom
11'6"x 11'4"

Porch

Design HPT860433

First Floor: 1,916 square feet
Second Floor: 749 square feet
Total: 2,665 square feet
Width: 63'-0" **Depth:** 63'-9"

Graceful French doors and tall shuttered windows combine to give this charming home its unique appeal. Walk through the elegant foyer to a grand living area, with a centered fireplace and built-in bookcase. The private master bedroom with a walk-in closet features a luxurious bath with a separate shower and tub and a compartmented toilet. Two second-floor family bedrooms share an expansive full bath. Please specify crawlspace or slab foundation when ordering.

Design HPT860435

First Floor: 1,765 square feet
Second Floor: 907 square feet
Total: 2,672 square feet
Width: 65'-0" **Depth:** 42'-6"

This stunning facade is ready for an ocean view or a beautiful suburb. Two-story windows with transoms allow natural light to fill the great room, which opens to the formal dining room. A grand kitchen has wrapping counters and a morning nook opening to a terrace. The upper-level master suite provides a double-bowl vanity, walk-in closet and fireplace. A nearby den boasts its own fireplace and plenty of space for computers and books. The lower-level four-car garage offers additional storage.

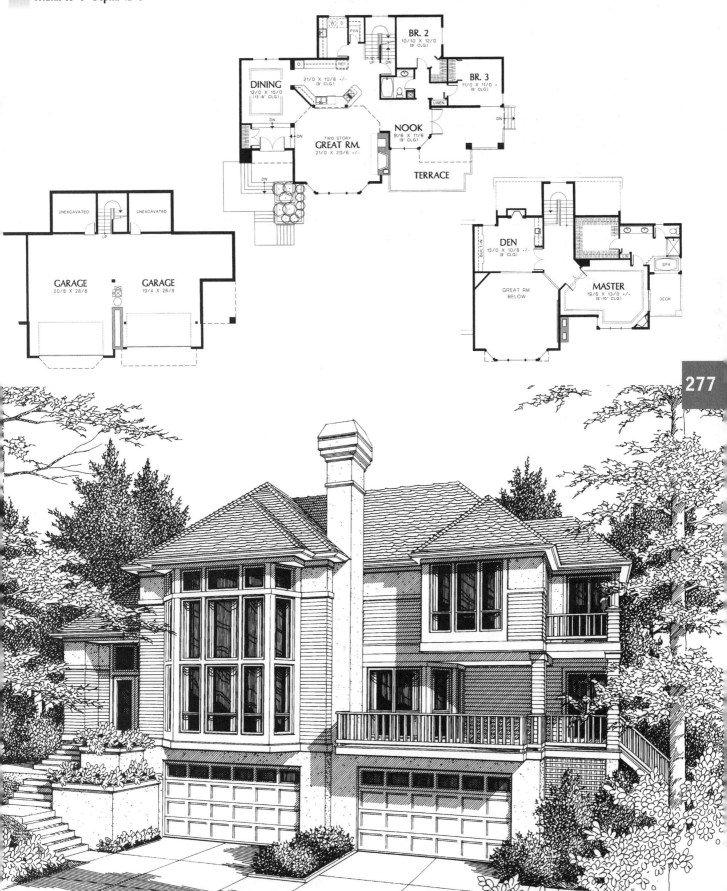

277

Design HPT860436

First Floor: 2,135 square feet
Second Floor: 538 square feet
Total: 2,673 square feet
Bonus Room: 225 square feet
Width: 62'-6" **Depth:** 70'-0"

Impressive rooflines and three dormer windows let this design shine with Southern charm. A splendid porch offers shade and a place to drink fresh lemonade on hot summer days. Inside, the formal dining and living rooms flank the foyer and offer front-porch views. The family room features a corner fireplace and rear-porch access. The spacious kitchen includes a cooktop island and breakfast room. A guest bedroom accesses a full bath, while the master suite features a corner tub, dual vanities, a walk-in closet and a separate shower. Upstairs, three family bedrooms share a full bath. Above the two-car garage, a future game room provides room to grow. Please specify crawlspace or slab foundation when ordering.

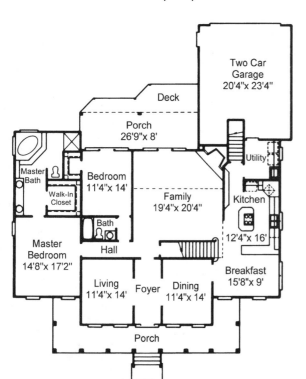

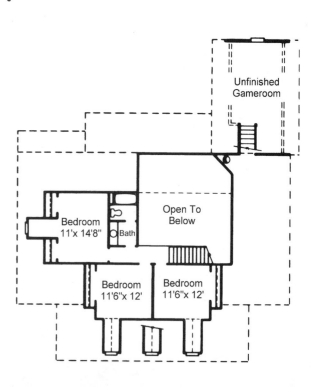

Design HPT860437

Square Footage: 2,678
Width: 76'-6" **Depth:** 77'-4"

L

This is it! The home you've been looking for—a stately stucco one-story home with a soaring entrance. For added flexibility, the guest room located to the front of the plan can be used as a home office. A spacious great room features a wall of windows, a warming fireplace and built-in niches. The master suite is separated from the family bedrooms for privacy. The island kitchen easily works with both the bay-windowed dining room and the sunny breakfast area.

Quote One®

Cost to build? See page 454 to order complete cost estimate to build this house in your area!

Design HPT860438

Square Footage: 2,678
Width: 70'-2" **Depth:** 67'-9"

Split sleeping arrangements enhance this lovely home. Two family bedrooms in the left wing have walk-in closets and share a bath that features a double-bowl vanity. The study or extra bedroom sits nearby. In the opposite wing, the master suite opens through French doors from a private hallway. The family room, kitchen and breakfast room comprise one open area in the rear of the home with access to two porches. Please specify slab or crawlspace foundation when ordering.

seat

DECK

spa

SUN RM.
16-2 × 10-4

skylights

clerestory above

fireplace

pass-thru

GREAT RM.
15-4 × 23-2
(high ceiling)

loft above

master bath

walk-in closet

BRKFST.
9-10 × 10-6

wash dry

UTIL.
8-0 × 8-6

sto.

KITCHEN

12-8 × 14-2

MASTER
BED RM.
12-8 × 16-4

sto.

cl

pd.
rm.

DINING
14-8 × 12-4

FOYER
11-10 × 7-0

up

PORCH   © 1990 Donald A. Gardner Architects, Inc.

Design HPT860439

First Floor: 1,734 square feet
Second Floor: 958 square feet
Total: 2,692 square feet
Width: 55'-0" **Depth:** 59'-10"

A wraparound covered porch at the front and sides of this home and the open deck with a spa and seating provide plenty of outside living area. A central great room features a high ceiling, a fireplace and clerestory windows above. The loft/study on the second floor overlooks this gathering area. Besides a formal dining room, kitchen, breakfast room and sun room on the first floor, there is also a generous master suite with a garden tub. Three second-floor bedrooms complete the sleeping accommodations.

clerestory with palladian window

bath

lin

walk-in closet

great room below

vaulted ceiling

railing

down

BED RM.
12-8 × 10-0

cl

bath

cl

BED RM.
12-8 × 16-4

LOFT/
STUDY
12-2 × 9-8

railing

vaulted ceiling

foyer below

BED RM.
12-8 × 10-0

clerestory with palladian window

© 1990 Donald A. Gardner Architects, Inc.

B. NATHAN.

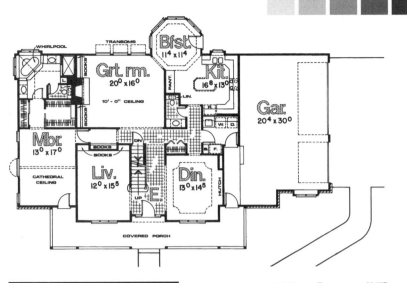

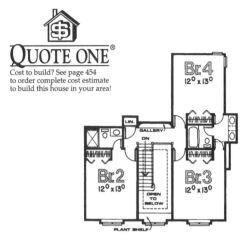

QUOTE ONE®

Cost to build? See page 454
to order complete cost estimate
to build this house in your area!

Design HPT860440

First Floor: 1,881 square feet
Second Floor: 814 square feet
Total: 2,695 square feet
Width: 72'-0" **Depth:** 45'-4"

Oval windows and an appealing covered porch lend character to this 1½-story home. Three large windows and a raised-hearth fireplace flanked by bookcases highlight a volume great room. An island kitchen with a huge pantry serves a gazebo dinette. In the master suite, a corner whirlpool tub and a roomy dressing area are featured. Each secondary bedroom conveniently accesses the bathrooms. This home's charm and blend of popular amenities will fit your lifestyle.

281

Design HPT860441

Square Footage: 2,696
Width: 80'-0" **Depth:** 64'-1"

A brick archway covers the front porch of this European-style home, creating a grand entrance. Situated beyond the entry, the living room takes center stage with a fireplace flanked by tall windows that overlook the rear yard. To the right is a bayed eating area and an efficient kitchen. Steps away, the formal dining room is perfect for holidays and special occasions. The master suite features a luxurious bath and private patio access.

2-CAR GARAGE
21'-6" X 21'-0"

LAUNDRY | STORAGE | VERANDA | MASTER BATH

BREAKFAST
13'-6" X 16'-0"

MASTER SUITE
15'-9" X 16'-0" | W.I.C.

UP

GREAT ROOM
20'-0" X 17'-6"

DN.

KITCHEN
16'-0" X 13'-6"

BEDROOM NO. 3
12'-0" X 13'-3"

POWDER

PANTRY

DINING ROOM
13'-3" X 14'-0"

FOYER

BEDROOM NO. 2
12'-6" X 13'-3"

BATH

PORTICO

Design HPT860443

Square Footage: 2,697
Width: 65'-3" **Depth:** 67'-3"

Dual chimneys (one is a false chimney for aesthetic effect) and a double stairway to the covered entry of this home create a balanced architectural statement. The sunlit foyer leads straight into the spacious great room, where French doors and large side windows provide a generous view of the covered veranda in back. This home is designed with a walkout basement foundation.

Design HPT860442

First Floor: 1,900 square feet
Second Floor: 800 square feet
Total: 2,700 square feet
Width: 63'-0" **Depth:** 51'-0"

A perfect blend of stucco and stacked stone sets off keystones, transoms and arches in this French country facade to inspire an elegant spirit. The foyer is flanked by the spacious dining room and the study, which is accented by a vaulted ceiling and a fireplace. A great room with a full wall of glass connects the interior with the outdoors. A first-floor master suite offers both style and intimacy with a coffered ceiling and a secluded bath. This home is designed with a walkout basement foundation.

BEDROOM NO. 4
13'-4" X 11'-4" | OPEN TO BELOW

BEDROOM NO. 3
15'-0" X 12'-6" | BATH | OPEN TO BELOW

BEDROOM NO. 2
12'-0" X 13'-2"

DECK

BREAKFAST
11'-0" X 10'-0"

MASTER BEDROOM
13'-4" X 17'-10"

KITCHEN
13'-0" X 16'-0"

GREAT ROOM
14'-4" X 19'-0"

LAUNDRY
8'-4" X 9'-6" | W.I.C. | MASTER BATH
10'-6" X 14'-8"

TWO CAR GARAGE
21'-4" X 21'-4"

DINING ROOM
12'-0" X 14'-0"

FOYER
7'-0" X 17'-0" | W.I.C.

STUDY
11'-4" X 13'-2"

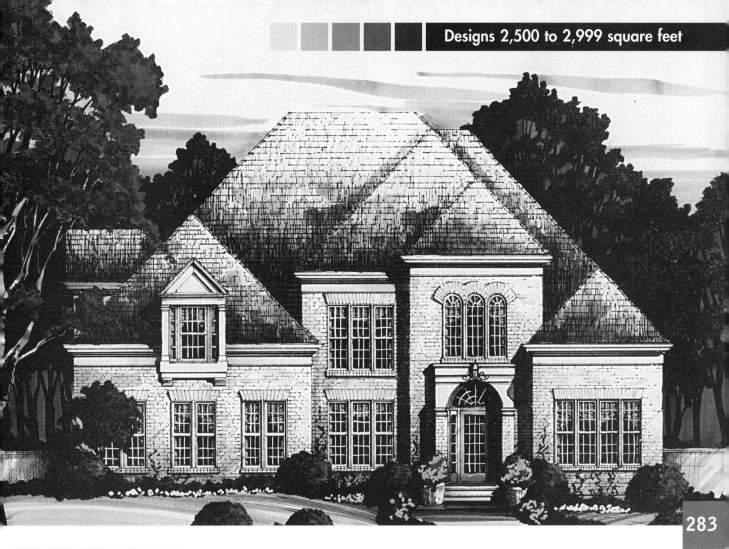

283

Design HPT860444

First Floor: 1,809 square feet
Second Floor: 898 square feet
Total: 2,707 square feet
Width: 54'-4" **Depth:** 46'-0"

Nested, hipped gables create a dramatic effect on this beautiful two-story brick home. The arched doorway is echoed in the triple clerestory window that lights the two-story foyer. Columns decorate the formal dining room, which is open to the two-story grand room with a fireplace. The master suite is located on the first floor for privacy, while upstairs, three secondary bedrooms are joined by a gallery overlooking the grand room.

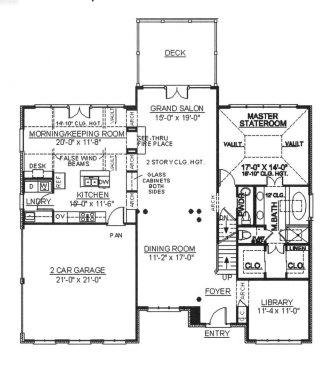

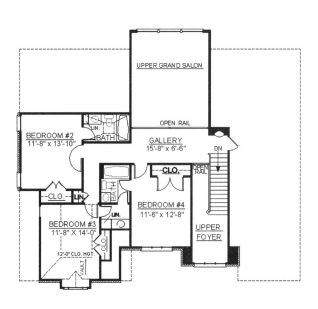

Design HPT860445

First Floor: 1,860 square feet
Second Floor: 848 square feet
Total: 2,708 square feet
Width: 56'-0" **Depth:** 59'-4"

The gorgeous entry of this traditional home opens to a formal dining room and to a volume living room with a see-through fireplace to the spacious family room. Adjacent is the bayed breakfast area and the island kitchen with a wraparound counter and a walk-in pantry. The master suite is highlighted by a formal ceiling in the bedroom and a bath with a two-person whirlpool tub. Upstairs, two bedrooms share private access to a compartmented bath; another bedroom includes a private bath.

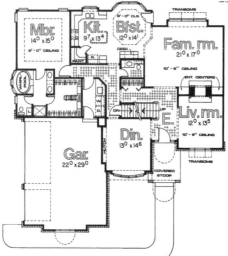

Design HPT860446

First Floor: 1,650 square feet
Second Floor: 1,060 square feet
Total: 2,710 square feet
Width: 53'-0" **Depth:** 68'-2"

This home, with its distinctive Georgian detailing, features brick jack arches that frame the arched front door and windows. Inside, the foyer opens directly to the large great room with a fireplace. Adjacent to the breakfast room is the keeping room with a corner fireplace. The master suite contains dual vanities and a spacious walk-in closet. Upstairs, two family bedrooms enjoy separate access to a shared bath while a fourth bedroom offers a private bath. This home is designed with a walkout basement foundation.

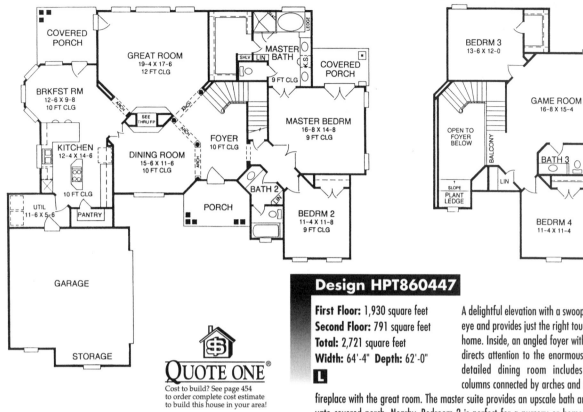

COVERED PORCH

GREAT ROOM
19-4 X 17-6
12 FT CLG

MASTER BATH
9 FT CLG

SHLV LIN

COVERED PORCH

BRKFST RM
12-6 X 9-8
10 FT CLG

SEE THRU FP

KITCHEN
12-4 X 14-6

DINING ROOM
15-6 X 11-6
10 FT CLG

FOYER
10 FT CLG

MASTER BEDRM
16-8 X 14-8
9 FT CLG

10 FT CLG

UTIL
11-6 X 5-6

PANTRY

PORCH

BATH 2

BEDRM 2
11-4 X 11-8
9 FT CLG

GARAGE

STORAGE

BEDRM 3
13-6 X 12-0

GAME ROOM
16-8 X 15-4

OPEN TO FOYER BELOW

BALCONY

BATH 3

LIN

SLOPE
PLANT LEDGE

BEDRM 4
11-4 X 11-4

Quote One®

Cost to build? See page 454
to order complete cost estimate
to build this house in your area!

Design HPT860447

First Floor: 1,930 square feet
Second Floor: 791 square feet
Total: 2,721 square feet
Width: 64'-4" **Depth:** 62'-0"
L

A delightful elevation with a swoop roof captures the eye and provides just the right touch for this inviting home. Inside, an angled foyer with a volume ceiling directs attention to the enormous great room. The detailed dining room includes massive round columns connected by arches and shares a through-fireplace with the great room. The master suite provides an upscale bath and access to a private covered porch. Nearby, Bedroom 2 is perfect for a nursery or home office/study. The kitchen features a large cooktop island and walk-in pantry. The second floor is dominated by an oversized game room. Two family bedrooms, a bath and a linen closet complete the upstairs. Please specify basement, crawlspace or slab foundation when ordering.

285

Design HPT860449

First Floor: 1,915 square feet
Second Floor: 823 square feet
Total: 2,738 square feet
Width: 63'-4" **Depth:** 48'-0"

A European feel is shown on the exterior facade of this exciting two-story home. The formal dining room is conveniently located for serving from the kitchen. The spacious breakfast room, wraparound bar in the kitchen and open hearth room offer a cozy gathering place for family members. The deluxe master suite boasts a sitting area and a garden bath. The second-floor balcony leads to a bedroom with a private bath and two additional bedrooms with private access to a shared bath.

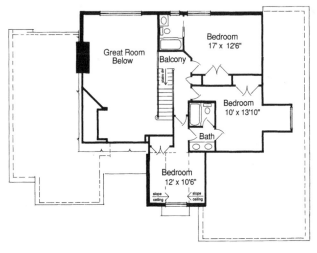

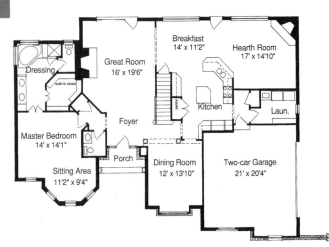

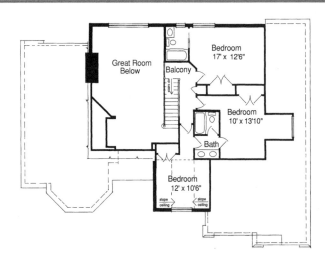

Design HPT860448

First Floor: 1,915 square feet
Second Floor: 823 square feet
Total: 2,738 square feet
Width: 63'-4" **Depth:** 48'-0"

A luxuriously styled exterior with wood and stone trim, a boxed window and an octagonal turret combine with a functional floor plan to create a home that will excite the most discriminating buyer. The spectacular view offered from the foyer includes high windows across the rear wall, a fireplace, open stairs with rich wood trim and a volume ceiling. The spacious breakfast room opens to the hearth room. The first-floor master suite boasts a sitting alcove.

Design HPT860450

First Floor: 1,932 square feet
Second Floor: 807 square feet
Total: 2,739 square feet
Width: 63'-0" **Depth:** 51'-6"

This sensational country Colonial exterior is set off by a cozy covered porch, just right for enjoying cool evenings outside. A two-story foyer opens to a quiet study with a centered fireplace. The gourmet kitchen features an island cooktop counter and a charming bayed breakfast nook. The great room soars two stories high, but is made cozy with an extended-hearth fireplace. Two walk-in closets, a garden tub and a separate shower highlight the master bath, while a coffered ceiling decorates the master bedroom. Three family bedrooms share a full bath upstairs. This home is designed with a walkout basement foundation.

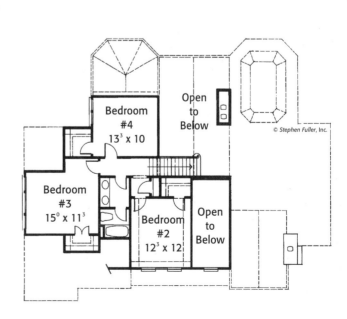

Design HPT860451

First Floor: 1,426 square feet
Second Floor: 1,315 square feet
Total: 2,741 square feet
Bonus Room: 200 square feet
Width: 57'-7" **Depth:** 44'-10"

The handsome facade of this outstanding two-story home is equaled by its efficient interior design. A library with multi-pane windows sits to the right of the entryway. The living room on the left adjoins a formal dining room with an octagonal tray ceiling. The island kitchen fills a bay window that looks out to the rear deck. A large breakfast room opens to the family room with a fireplace and hearth. The master suite with a cove ceiling, private bath and walk-in closet resides on the second floor along with the three family bedrooms and the bonus room.

Design HPT860453

First Floor: 1,462 square feet
Second Floor: 1,288 square feet
Total: 2,750 square feet
Width: 70'-8" **Depth:** 54'-0"

A touch of Victoriana enhances the facade of this home: a turret roof over a wrap-around porch with turned wood spindles. Special attractions on the first floor include a tray ceiling in the octagonal living room, fireplaces in the country kitchen and the living room, a coffered ceiling in the family room and double-door access to the cozy den. The master suite boasts a coffered ceiling, walk-in closet and whirlpool tub.

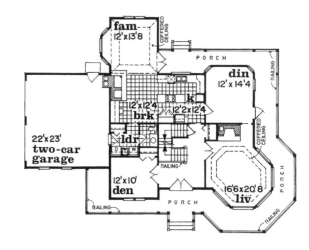

QUOTE ONE®

Cost to build? See page 454
to order complete cost estimate
to build this house in your area!

Photo by Dan Reaume Photography

This home, as shown in the photograph, may differ from the actual blueprints. For more detailed information, please check the floor plans carefully.

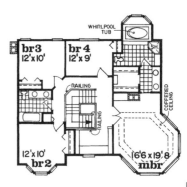

Design HPT860452

First Floor: 2,026 square feet
Second Floor: 726 square feet
Total: 2,752 square feet
Bonus Room: 277 square feet
Width: 61'-6" **Depth:** 56'-0"

This charming, two-story traditional home welcomes in an abundance of natural light with its multitude of windows. The two-story foyer with its grand staircase is flanked by the dining room to the left and the living room to the right. A study/bedroom is tucked away to the left, while the master suite finds privacy to the right. Please specify basement, crawlspace or slab foundation when ordering.

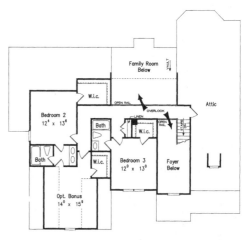

Floor plan labels:

GARAGE

PORCH

UTIL

PAN

KITCHEN
15-4 X 13-8
10 FT CLG

LIVING ROOM
17-0 X 16-4
12 FT CLG

BEDRM 4/STUDY
13-4 X 15-0
10 FT CLG

MASTER BEDROOM
15-6 X 15-0
12 FT TRAY CLG

MASTER BATH
10 FT CLG

BRKFST ROOM
15-4 X 9-4
14 FT CLG

DINING ROOM
12-4 X 14-4
12 FT CLG

FOYER
10 FT CLG

BATH 2

PWDR

SLOPE

FAMILY ROOM
15-4 X 14-0
14 FT CLG

FP

PORCH

BEDROOM 3
12-4 X 12-8
10 FT CLG

BEDROOM 2
12-6 X 12-8
10 FT CLG

Design HPT860455

Square Footage: 2,757
Width: 69'-6" **Depth:** 68'-3"

Country French appointments give this home an elegant Old World look. The foyer opens to the well-proportioned dining room, with a twelve-foot ceiling. A stairway is conveniently located to provide access to the optional basement below and the attic above. Double sets of French doors with transoms open to the rear porch. Three additional bedrooms include a flex room that easily converts to a home office or study. Please specify basement, crawlspace or slab foundation when ordering.

Floor plan labels:

TERRACE

GUEST SUITE
12-4 X 20-0

STOR.
7-0 X 7-0

W.I.C.

BATH

RECREATION ROOM
18-0 X 21-6

CRAWLSPACE STOR.

STOR.

DECK/TERRACE

MASTER SUITE
12-4 X 16-0

W.I.C.

MASTER BATH

MORNING ROOM
12-4 X 10-0

GRAND ROOM
18-6 X 21-0

KITCHEN
12-4 X 11-6

LAUNDRY

PDR

LIVING ROOM
14-6 X 12-6

FOYER

DINING ROOM
12-6 X 13-0

GARAGE
23-0 X 24-0

LOGGIA

OPEN TO BELOW

SUITE 2
12-4 X 10-8

W.I.C.

BATH

OPEN TO BELOW

SUITE 3
12-6 X 13-0

W.I.C.

BATH

W.I.C.

SUITE 4
11-6 X 13-4

DN

Design HPT860454

First Floor: 1,878 square feet
Second Floor: 886 square feet
Total: 2,764 square feet
Finished Basement: 942 square feet
Width: 67'-10" **Depth:** 56'-4"

This distinguished brick home with traditional stucco accents includes a spectacular two-story foyer and a grand room featuring a dramatic Palladian window. The master suite and morning room create matching bay wings to form a beautiful rear facade. The master suite features a bath with dual vanities and a garden tub. Upstairs, three additional suites share two baths. This design offers a basement plan that includes a guest suite and recreation area.

Design HPT860456

Square Footage: 2,765
Bonus Room: 367 square feet
Width: 66'-0" **Depth:** 82'-9"

Molded window facades and corner quoins join with triple gables to decorate the exterior of this three-bedroom plus bonus room plan. Entertain in the formal dining room, the grand room or the gracious gathering room with wraparound windows and a fireplace. Breakfast in the bayed nook that faces the covered lanai. The master suite stretches along the left wing of the house and features His and Hers walk-in closets, a compartmented toilet and a garden tub. Two additional bedrooms on the other side of the house share a full bath.

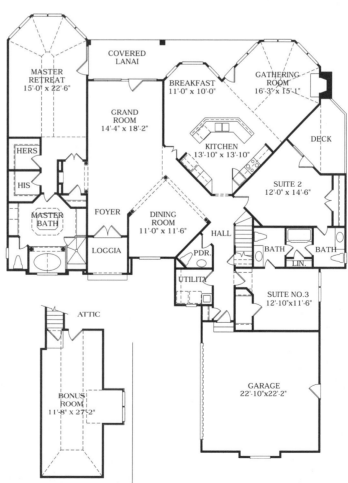

Floor plan labels (Design HPT860457):

DECK

SITTING 12'-0" x 12'-0"

W.I.C.

MASTER BATH

BREAKFAST 12'-0"x 13'-6"

DN.

GREAT ROOM 20'-6"x 18'-6"

MASTER SUITE 16'-6"x 15'-0"

W.I.C.

KITCHEN 14'-3"x 13'-6"

POWDER

BEDROOM NO.3 12'-0"x 12'-0"

FOYER

LAUNDRY 9'-0" X 8'-6"

DINING ROOM 13'-6" X 14'-6"

BEDROOM NO.2 12'-3"x 14'-0"

BATH

STORAGE

STOOP

TWO CAR GARAGE 21'-6"x 27'-6"

Design HPT860457

Square Footage: 2,770
Width: 73'-6" **Depth:** 78'-0"

This English cottage with a cedar shake exterior displays the best qualities of a traditional design. The foyer opens to both the dining room and the great room. The breakfast room opens to a gourmet kitchen. Two bedrooms with large closets are joined by a full bath with individual vanities. Through double doors at the end of a short hall, the master suite awaits with a tray ceiling and an adjoining sunlit sitting room. This home is designed with a walkout basement foundation.

292

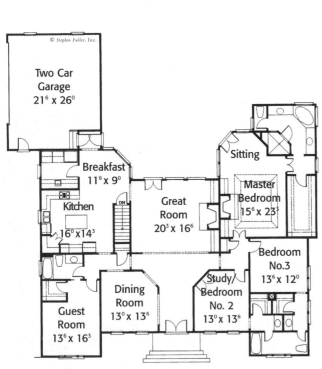

Floor plan labels (Design HPT860458):

© Stephen Fuller, Inc.

Two Car Garage 21⁶ x 26⁰

Breakfast 11⁶ x 9⁰

Kitchen 16⁰ x14³

DN

Sitting

Master Bedroom 15⁶ x 23³

Great Room 20³ x 16⁶

Bedroom No.3 13⁶ x 12⁰

Guest Room 13⁶ x 16³

Dining Room 13⁰ x 13⁶

Study/ Bedroom No. 2 13⁰ x 13⁶

Design HPT860458

Square Footage: 2,785
Width: 72'-0" **Depth:** 72'-0"

This elegant Colonial design boasts many European influences such as the stucco facade, corner quoins and arched windows. The foyer is flanked by a formal dining room and a study. Straight ahead, the great room accesses the rear-patio pool deck. The island kitchen opens to a breakfast nook. A guest bedroom is placed at the front of the home. The master suite on the opposite side of the home boasts a private fireplace and a bayed sitting area. This home is designed with a walkout basement foundation.

Design HPT860459

First Floor: 1,840 square feet
Second Floor: 950 square feet
Total: 2,790 square feet
Width: 58'-6" **Depth:** 62'-0"

The appearance of this early American home brings the past to mind with its wraparound porch, wood siding and flower-box detailing. Inside, columns frame the great room and the dining room. Left of the foyer lies the living room with a warming fireplace. The angular kitchen joins a sunny breakfast nook. The master bedroom has a spacious private bath and a walk-in closet. Stairs to the second level lead from the breakfast area to an open landing overlooking the great room. Three family bedrooms—two with walk-in closets and all three with private access to a bath—complete this level. This home is designed with a walkout basement foundation.

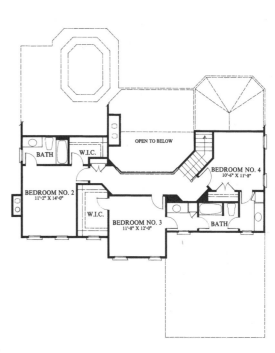

293

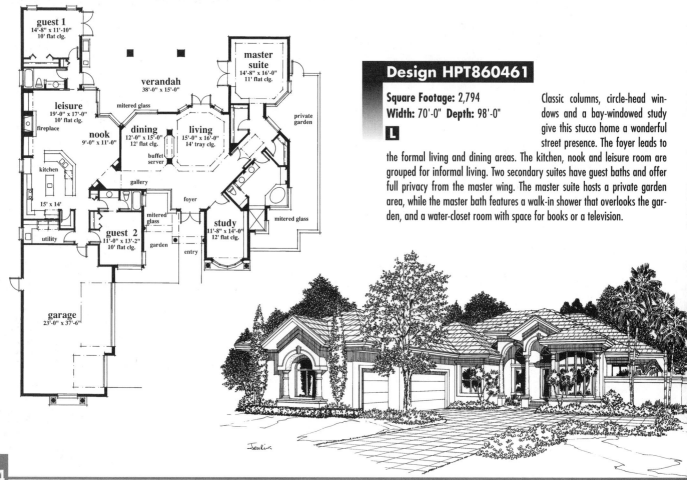

Design HPT860461

Square Footage: 2,794
Width: 70'-0" **Depth:** 98'-0"

L

Classic columns, circle-head windows and a bay-windowed study give this stucco home a wonderful street presence. The foyer leads to the formal living and dining areas. The kitchen, nook and leisure room are grouped for informal living. Two secondary suites have guest baths and offer full privacy from the master wing. The master suite hosts a private garden area, while the master bath features a walk-in shower that overlooks the garden, and a water-closet room with space for books or a television.

guest 1
14'-8" x 11'-10"
10' flat clg.

master suite
14'-8" x 16'-0"
11' flat clg.

verandah
38'-0" x 15'-0"

leisure
19'-0" x 17'-0"
10' flat clg.

mitered glass

fireplace

nook
9'-0" x 11'-0"

dining
12'-0" x 15'-0"
12' flat clg.

living
15'-0" x 16'-0"
14' tray clg.

private garden

buffet server

kitchen
15' x 14'

gallery

foyer

guest 2
11'-0" x 13'-2"
10' flat clg.

mitered glass

garden

study
11'-8" x 14'-0"
12' flat clg.

mitered glass

utility

entry

garage
23'-0" x 37'-6"

294

Design HPT860460

First Floor: 1,751 square feet
Second Floor: 1,043 square feet
Total: 2,794 square feet
Width: 45'-0" **Depth:** 69'-6"

Stately pilasters and a decorative balcony at a second-level window adorn this ornate four-bedroom design. Inside the recessed entryway, columns define the formal dining room. Ahead is a great room with a fireplace, built-in bookshelves and access to the rear deck. A breakfast nook nestles in a bay window and joins an island kitchen. The master suite with a tray ceiling features a walk-in closet and a pampering garden tub. A versatile loft and three additional bedrooms are found upstairs.

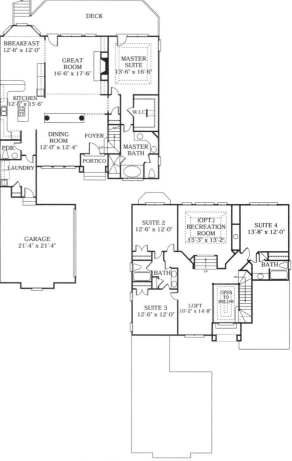

DECK

BREAKFAST
12'-6" x 12'-0"

GREAT ROOM
16'-6" x 17'-6"

MASTER SUITE
13'-6" x 16'-6"

KITCHEN
12'-6" x 15'-6"

W.I.C

DINING ROOM
12'-0" x 12'-4"

FOYER

MASTER BATH

PDR.

PORTICO

LAUNDRY

GARAGE
21'-4" x 21'-4"

SUITE 2
12'-6" x 12'-0"

(OPT.) RECREATION ROOM
15'-3" x 13'-2"

SUITE 4
13'-8" x 12'-0"

BATH

BATH

SUITE 3
12'-6" x 12'-0"

LOFT
10'-2" x 14'-8"

OPEN TO BELOW

295

Design HPT860462

First Floor: 1,355 square feet
Second Floor: 1,442 square feet
Total: 2,797 square feet
Width: 52'-2" **Depth:** 56'-6"

This Southern design begins with a spacious gathering room, complete with an extended-hearth fireplace and lovely French doors. The gathering room opens to a sunny breakfast area, with its own French door to the back terrace and deck. Upstairs, the master suite features a coffered ceiling, two walk-in closets and a lavish bath with separate vanities. Three family bedrooms, one with a private bath, share a hall that leads to a generous sitting area with space for books and computers.

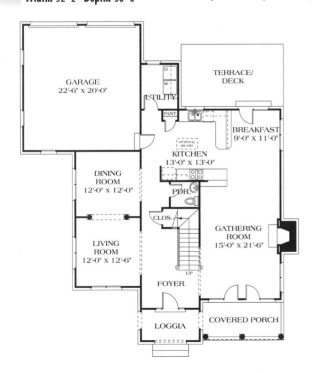

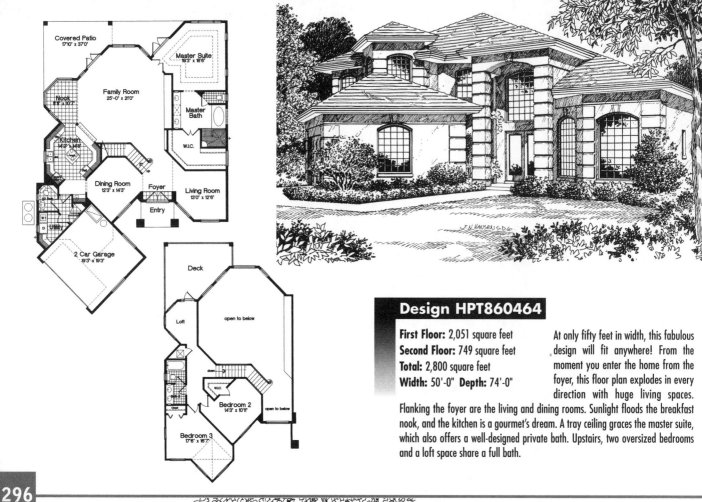

Covered Patio
17'0" x 37'0"

Master Suite
19'3" x 18'6"

Family Room
25'-0" x 21'0"

Master Bath

Nook

Kitchen
14'2" x 14'6"

W.I.C.

Dining Room
12'3" x 14'3"

Foyer

Living Room
13'0" x 12'6"

Entry

Utility

2 Car Garage
19'3" x 19'3"

Deck

Loft

open to below

down

W.I.C.

Closet

Bedroom 2
14'3" x 10'11"

open to below

Bedroom 3
17'6" x 16'7"

Design HPT860464

First Floor: 2,051 square feet
Second Floor: 749 square feet
Total: 2,800 square feet
Width: 50'-0" **Depth:** 74'-0"

At only fifty feet in width, this fabulous design will fit anywhere! From the moment you enter the home from the foyer, this floor plan explodes in every direction with huge living spaces. Flanking the foyer are the living and dining rooms. Sunlight floods the breakfast nook, and the kitchen is a gourmet's dream. A tray ceiling graces the master suite, which also offers a well-designed private bath. Upstairs, two oversized bedrooms and a loft space share a full bath.

Design HPT860463

First Floor: 1,483 square feet
Second Floor: 1,349 square feet
Total: 2,832 square feet
Bonus Room: 486 square feet
Width: 66'-10" **Depth:** 47'-8"

With two covered porches to encourage outdoor living, multi-pane windows and an open layout, this farmhouse has plenty to offer. Columns define the living room/study area. The family room is accented by a fireplace and accesses the rear porch. An adjacent sunny bayed breakfast room is convenient to the oversized island kitchen. Four bedrooms upstairs include a deluxe master suite with a lush bath and walk-in closet. Three family bedrooms have plenty of storage space and share a full hall bath.

QUOTE ONE®
Cost to build? See page 454 to order complete cost estimate to build this house in your area!

© 1995 Donald A. Gardner Architects, Inc.

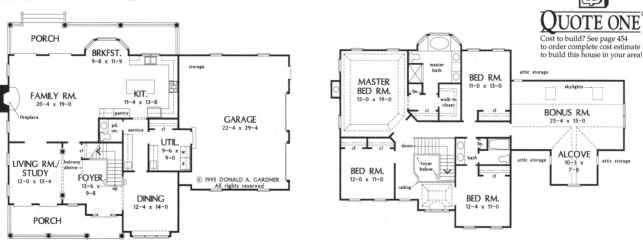

PORCH

BRKFST.
9-8 x 11-9

storage

FAMILY RM.
20-4 x 19-0

KIT.
11-4 x 13-8

fireplace

pantry

GARAGE
22-4 x 29-4

pd. rm.

service

cl

LIVING RM./
STUDY
12-0 x 13-4

balcony above

UTIL.
9-6 x 9-0

w
d

FOYER
13-6 x 9-8

up

© 1995 DONALD A. GARDNER
All rights reserved

DINING
12-4 x 14-0

PORCH

MASTER
BED RM.
15-0 x 19-0

master bath

lin.

walk-in closet

cl

BED RM.
11-0 x 13-0

attic storage

skylights

cl

BONUS RM.
25-4 x 15-0

cl

cl

down

lin.

bath

BED RM.
12-0 x 11-0

foyer below

railing

attic storage

ALCOVE
10-3 x 7-8

attic storage

cl

BED RM.
12-4 x 11-0

Design HPT860465

First Floor: 1,651 square feet
Second Floor: 1,150 square feet
Total: 2,801 square feet
Width: 46'-4" **Depth:** 79'-1"

Here's a new country home with a fresh face and a dash of Victoriana. Large rooms and beautiful bay windows enhance this functional five-bedroom plan, which boasts a game room on the second level. The entryway from the wraparound covered porch leads straight ahead to the large living room with a fireplace. A wall of windows looks out to the rear wraparound covered porch. Please specify crawlspace or slab foundation when ordering.

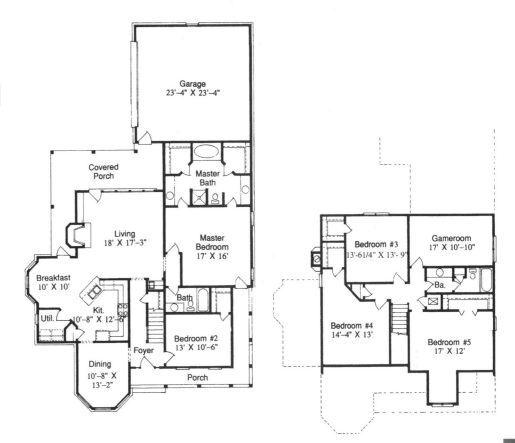

297

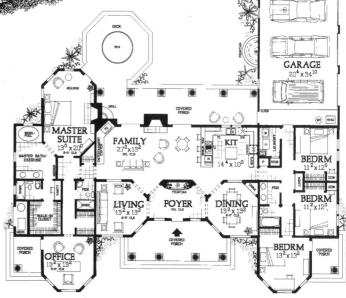

Design HPT860466

Square Footage: 2,831
Width: 84'-0" **Depth:** 77'-0"

L

Besides great curb appeal, this home has a wonderful floor plan. The foyer features a fountain and leads to a formal dining room on the right and a living room on the left. A large family room at the rear features a built-in entertainment center and a fireplace. To the right of the plan, three family bedrooms share a full bath. On the left side, the master suite has a large sitting area, an office and an amenity-filled bath. Outside the master suite is a deck with a spa.

298

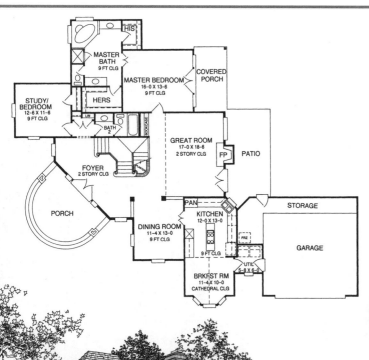

Design HPT860467

First Floor: 1,966 square feet
Second Floor: 872 square feet
Total: 2,838 square feet
Width: 63'-10" **Depth:** 79'-10"

This elegant two-story brick home, with its corner quoin brick detail, varied rooflines and multi-pane windows, has so many amenities to offer!

Enter into the two-story foyer. To the right, the formal dining room accesses the efficient island kitchen through double doors. The large great room is enhanced by direct access to the rear patio and a warming fireplace. The first-floor master suite contains a pampering spa-style bath. Upstairs, a balcony hall leads to the three family bedrooms. Please specify basement, crawlspace or slab foundation when ordering.

Design HPT860468

Square Footage: 2,846
Width: 84'-6" **Depth:** 64'-2"

L

This Southern Colonial home is distinguished by its columned porch and double dormers. Inside, columns and connecting arches define the angled foyer. The master suite, located away from the other bedrooms for privacy, includes a large master bath and a walk-in closet. Three additional bedrooms are located adjacent to the family room. The kitchen, breakfast area and family room are open — perfect for informal entertaining and family gatherings. The foyer, living room and dining room have twelve-foot ceilings. Please specify crawlspace or slab foundation when ordering.

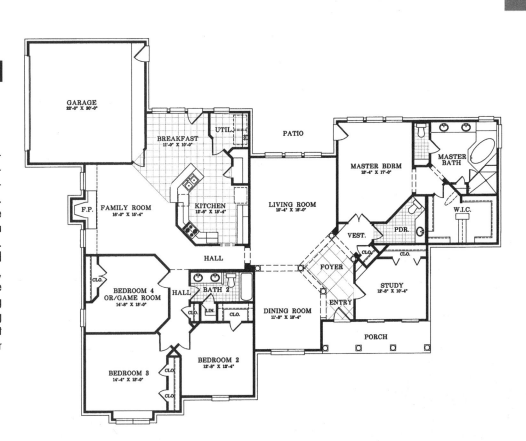

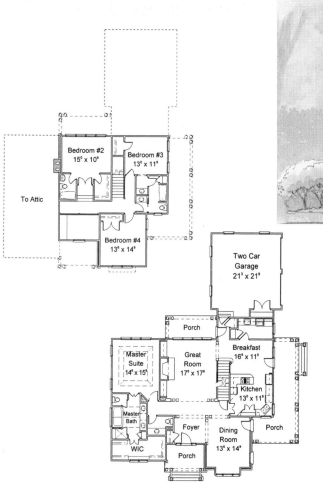

Bedroom #2
15⁰ x 10⁹

Bedroom #3
13⁰ x 11⁹

To Attic

Bedroom #4
13⁶ x 14⁹

Two Car Garage
21³ x 21⁶

Porch

Breakfast
16⁸ x 11⁹

Master Suite
14⁰ x 15⁰

Great Room
17⁸ x 17⁶

Kitchen
13⁰ x 11⁹

Master Bath

Foyer

Dining Room
13⁶ x 14⁹

Porch

WIC

Porch

Design HPT860470

First Floor: 1,804 square feet
Second Floor: 1,041 square feet
Total: 2,845 square feet
Width: 59'-10" **Depth:** 71'-0"

There's a feeling of old Charleston in this stately home—particularly on the quiet side porch that wraps around the kitchen and breakfast room. The interior of this home revolves around a spacious great room with a welcoming fireplace. The left wing is dedicated to the master suite, which boasts wide views of the rear property. The kitchen easily serves the dining room and breakfast area. Three family bedrooms are tucked upstairs. This home is designed with a basement foundation.

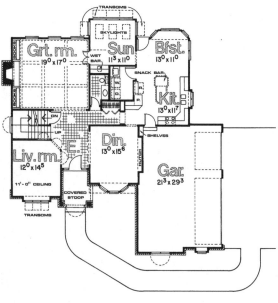

TRANSOMS

SKYLIGHTS

Grt. rm.
19⁰ x 17⁰

Sun
11³ x 11⁰

Bfst.
13⁰ x 11⁰

WET BAR

SNACK BAR

Kit.
13⁰ x 11⁷

DN

UP

Din.
13⁰ x 15⁶

SHELVES

Liv. rm.
12⁰ x 14⁵

11'-0" CEILING

Gar.
21³ x 29³

COVERED STOOP

TRANSOMS

Design HPT860469

First Floor: 1,520 square feet
Second Floor: 1,334 square feet
Total: 2,854 square feet
Width: 53'-4" **Depth:** 56'-8"

This stunning two-story home features an enormous great room with a spider-beam ceiling, built-in bookcases and a fireplace; it connects directly to the sun room with its attached wet bar. This skylit area leads to the breakfast room and island kitchen. Complementing these informal gathering areas are the formal living room and dining room. Upstairs, a luxurious master suite features His and Hers walk-in closets and a dressing area with an angled oval whirlpool tub. Generous bath arrangements are made for the three secondary bedrooms.

BOOKS

WHIRLPOOL

Mbr.
13⁰ x 17⁰
8'-0" CLG.

Br. 2
12⁰ x 13²

DRESSING

LINEN

LIN.

DN

OPEN TO BELOW

PLANT SHELF

Br. 3
12⁰ x 13⁰

Br. 4
13⁰ x 12⁰

10'-0" CEILING

TRANSOM

Design HPT860471

First Floor: 2,070 square feet
Second Floor: 790 square feet
Total: 2,860 square feet
Width: 58'-4" **Depth:** 54'-10"

The striking combination of wood framing, shingles and glass creates the exterior of this classic cottage. The foyer opens to the main-level layout. To the left of the foyer is a study with a warming hearth and vaulted ceiling, while to the right is a formal dining room. A great room with an attached breakfast area sits to the rear near the kitchen. A guest room is nestled in the rear of the plan for privacy. The master suite provides an expansive tray ceiling, a glass sitting area and easy passage to the outside deck. Upstairs, two bedrooms are accompanied by a loft for a quiet getaway. This home is designed with a walkout basement foundation.

QUOTE ONE®

Cost to build? See page 454
to order complete cost estimate
to build this house in your area!

Design HPT860472

First Floor: 2,070 square feet
Second Floor: 790 square feet
Total: 2,860 square feet
Width: 57'-6" **Depth:** 54'-0"

Wood shingles are a cozy touch on the exterior of this home. Interior rooms include a great room with a bay window and fireplace, a formal dining room, and a study with another fireplace. A guest room on the first floor contains a full bath and walk-in closet. The sumptuous master suite is on the first floor for privacy. The second floor holds two additional bedrooms, a loft area, and a gallery overlooking the central hall. This home is designed with a walkout basement foundation.

Design HPT860473

First Floor: 2,254 square feet
Second Floor: 608 square feet
Total: 2,862 square feet
Width: 66'-0" **Depth:** 78'-10"

Indoor and outdoor living are enhanced by the beautiful courtyard that decorates the center of this home. A gallery leads to a kitchen featuring a center work island and adjacent breakfast room. To the left, the gallery leads to the formal living room and master suite. The secluded master bedroom features a tray ceiling and double doors that lead to a covered patio. The second floor contains a full bath shared by two family bedrooms and a loft that provides flexible space.

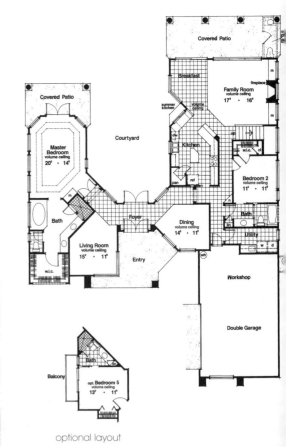

optional layout

Design HPT860474

First Floor: 2,172 square feet
Second Floor: 690 square feet
Total: 2,862 square feet
Bonus Room: 450 square feet
Width: 72'-0" **Depth:** 73'-0"

European details highlight this attractive compact exterior. Note the double-brick arches over the windows and entry, the wooden shutters and the stone exterior. The two-story foyer opens to a wide hallway with a coat closet and an elegant stairway. To the left, the den (or living room) features an unusual window and built-in cabinets. The dining room is to the right, just a short trip from the kitchen. Here, the family chef will appreciate a work island/snack bar combination, a walk-in pantry and a corner window sink. A bayed nook offers access to a screened porch. There's also a covered porch off the great room, which has an impressive fireplace flanked by cabinets. The master suite pampers with two closets, a garden tub and a dual-bowl vanity.

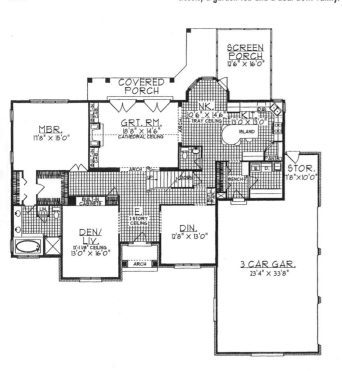

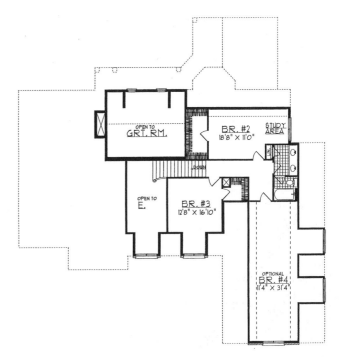

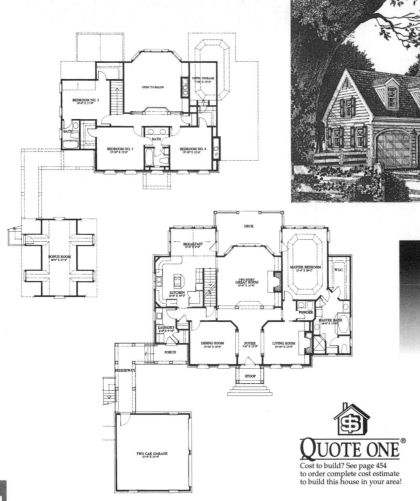

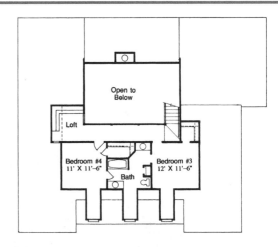

Design HPT860476

First Floor: 1,960 square feet
Second Floor: 905 square feet
Total: 2,865 square feet
Bonus Room: 297 square feet
Width: 61'-0" **Depth:** 70'-6"

Traditionalists will appreciate the classic styling of this Colonial home. The foyer opens to both a banquet-sized dining room and formal living room with a fireplace. The entire right side of the main level is taken up by the master suite. The left side includes a large kitchen and a breakfast room. Upstairs, each bedroom features ample closet space. The detached garage features an unfinished office or studio on its second level. This home is designed with a walkout basement foundation.

QUOTE ONE®
Cost to build? See page 454
to order complete cost estimate
to build this house in your area!

Design HPT860475

First Floor: 2,152 square feet
Second Floor: 717 square feet
Total: 2,869 square feet
Width: 62'-4" **Depth:** 53'-0"

Wonderful windows, sunburst transoms, French doors, dormers and Palladian windows flood the interior of this home with light. The formal areas of the home and the rear covered porch are wonderful for grand entertainment events. The master suite and one family bedroom occupy the left side of the plan. Preparing meals will be a breeze in the U-shaped kitchen. Upstairs, dormer windows adorn Bedrooms 3 and 4. Note the private loft. Please specify crawlspace or slab foundation when ordering.

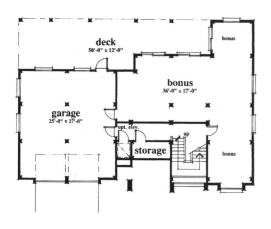

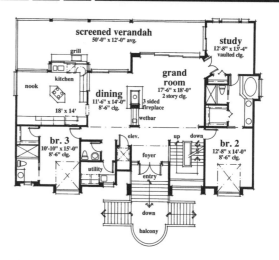

Design HPT860477

First Floor: 2,066 square feet
Second Floor: 810 square feet
Total: 2,876 square feet
Bonus Space: 1,260 square feet
Width: 64'-0" **Depth:** 45'-0"

L

This striking Floridian plan is designed for entertaining. A large open floor plan offers soaring, sparkling space for planned gatherings. The foyer leads to the grand room, highlighted by a glass fireplace, a wet bar and wide views of the outdoors. Both the grand room and the formal dining room open to a screened veranda. The first floor includes two spacious family bedrooms and a secluded study which opens from the grand room. The second-floor master suite offers sumptuous amenities, including a private deck and spa, a three-sided fireplace, a sizable walk-in closet and a gallery hall with an overlook to the grand room.

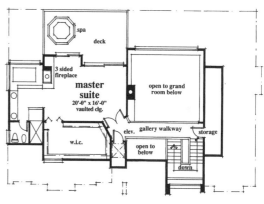

305

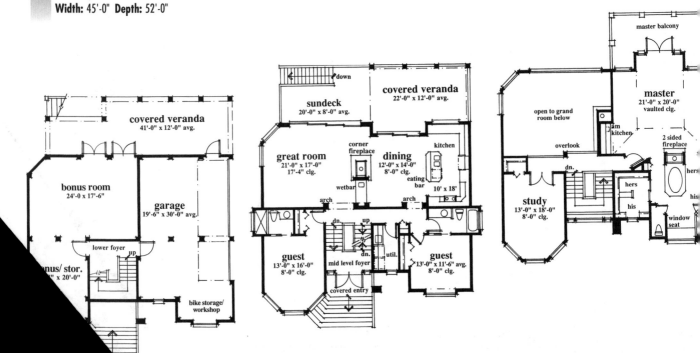

Design HPT860478

First Floor: 1,684 square feet
Second Floor: 1,195 square feet
Total: 2,879 square feet
Bonus Space: 674 square feet
Width: 45'-0" **Depth:** 52'-0"

Asymmetrical rooflines set off a grand turret and a two-story bay that allow glorious views from the front of this home. Arch-top clerestory windows bring natural light into the great room, which shares a corner fireplace and a wet bar with the dining room. Two guest suites are located on this floor. A winding staircase leads to a luxurious master suite that shares a fireplace with the bath and includes a morning kitchen, French doors to the balcony, and a double walk-in closet. Down the hall, a study and a balcony overlooking the great room complete the plan.

Design HPT860479

First Floor: 1,768 square feet
Second Floor: 1,120 square feet
Total: 2,888 square feet
Width: 72'-0" **Depth:** 58'-0"

The entry of this home is flanked by the formal dining room and a living room that boasts a fireplace and a multitude of windows. A large angled kitchen is nestled between the dining room and the bayed eating area. The master suite enjoys a bayed sitting area and a pampering private bath. Three additional bedrooms and a TV room are found on the second floor. Please specify basement, crawlspace or slab foundation when ordering.

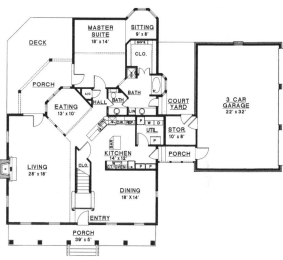

307

Design HPT860480

First Floor: 2,212 square feet
Second Floor: 675 square feet
Total: 2,887 square feet
Width: 70'-0" **Depth:** 74'-1"

As you drive up to the porte cochere entry of this home, the visual movement of the elevation is breathtaking. The foyer leads into the wide glass-walled living room. To the right, the formal dining room features a tiered pedestal ceiling. To the left is the guest and master suite wing of the home. The master bath comes complete with a columned vanity area, a soaking tub and a shower for two. Two large bedrooms on the second floor share a sun deck.

Design HPT860481

Square Footage: 2,888
Width: 68'-6" **Depth:** 78'-1"

Alternate exteriors— both European style! Stone quoins and shutters give one elevation the appearance of a French country cottage. The other, with keystone window treatment and a copper roof over the bay window, creates the impression of a stately French chateau. From the entry, formal living areas are accessed through graceful columned openings—living room to the left and dining room to the right. Straight ahead, the comfortable family room awaits with its warming fireplace and cathedral ceiling. The private master suite features a Pullman ceiling, a luxurious bath and twin walk-in closets. A private lanai is accessed from the master bath. Two family bedrooms with a connecting bath, a handy kitchen and breakfast room, and a utility room complete the floor plan.

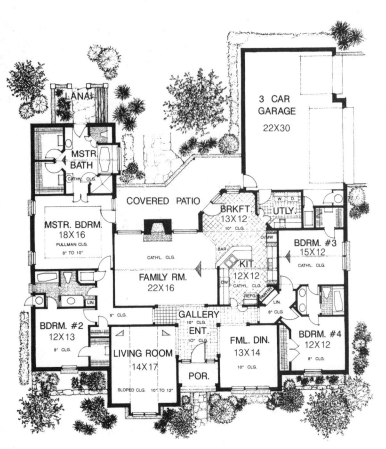

alternate elevation

Design HPT860483

First Floor: 2,181 square feet
Second Floor: 710 square feet
Total: 2,891 square feet
Bonus Room: 240 square feet
Width: 66'-4" **Depth:** 79'-0"

A barrel-vaulted entry and a two-story turret give an open, spacious feeling to this sophisticated home. A wall of built-ins and a fireplace adorn the grand room. A gourmet's delight, the kitchen easily serves the formal and informal living areas. If you desire, convert the study to a home office, library or exercise room. Pamper yourself in the master suite with a sitting area and step-up tub.

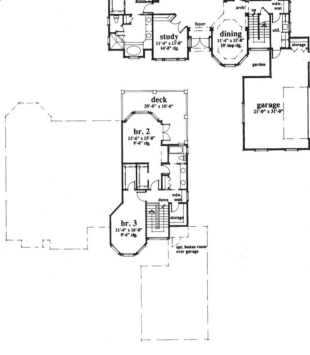

Design HPT860482

First Floor: 1,944 square feet
Second Floor: 954 square feet
Total: 2,898 square feet
Width: 51'-6" **Depth:** 73'-0"

This gracious home combines warm informal materials with a modern livable floor plan to create a true Southern classic. The dining room, study and great room work together to create one large, exciting space. Plenty of counter space and storage make the kitchen truly usable. The master suite is a welcome retreat. Upstairs, two additional bedrooms each have their own vanity within a shared bath, while the third bedroom includes its own bath. This home is designed with a walkout basement foundation.

QUOTE ONE®
Cost to build? See page 454
to order complete cost estimate
to build this house in your area!

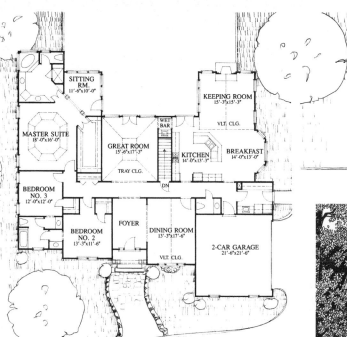

Design HPT860484

Square Footage: 2,902
Width: 71'-3" **Depth:** 66'-3"

Arches, transoms and sweeping rooflines blend artfully to highlight this French exterior. The interior starts with a great room that features a tray ceiling, a wet bar and French doors to the outside. Adjoining the kitchen and breakfast room, the spacious keeping room provides a fireplace. The master suite offers a sitting room and a sumptuous bath, while two family bedrooms share a connecting bath. This home is designed with a walkout basement foundation.

QUOTE ONE®
Cost to build? See page 454
to order complete cost estimate
to build this house in your area!

310

Design HPT860485

First Floor: 1,862 square feet
Second Floor: 1,044 square feet
Total: 2,906 square feet
Bonus Room: 259 square feet
Width: 60'-0" **Depth:** 60'-0"

A gently sloping high-pitched roof complements keystones, arch-top windows and a delicate balcony balustrade, and calls up a sense of cozy elegance. The foyer opens to a grand room with a focal-point fireplace. The gourmet kitchen offers a walk-in pantry and a morning room with outdoor flow. An island wardrobe highlights the master suite, which boasts a secluded lounge with a door to a private area of the veranda. Upstairs, two secondary bedrooms enjoy a balcony overlook to the foyer.

Photo by Living Concepts Home Planning

This home, as shown in the photograph, may differ from the actual blueprints. For more detailed information, please check the floor plans carefully.

Design HPT860486

First Floor: 2,076 square feet
Second Floor: 843 square feet
Total: 2,919 square feet
Width: 57'-6" **Depth:** 51'-6"

This lovely home's foyer opens to the formal dining room, defined by decorative columns, and leads to the two-story great room. The kitchen and breakfast room join the great room to create a casual family area. The master suite is finished with a coffered ceiling and a sumptuous bath. A guest suite with a private bath is located just off the kitchen. Upstairs, two family bedrooms share a compartmented bath and a raised loft. This home is designed with a walkout basement foundation.

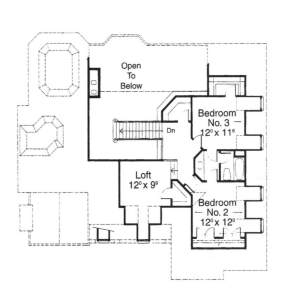

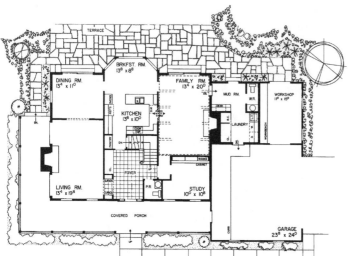

Design HPT860487

First Floor: 1,581 square feet
Second Floor: 1,344 square feet
Total: 2,925 square feet
Width: 74'-0" **Depth:** 46'-0"

L D

Here's a traditional farmhouse design that's made for down-home hospitality. The star attractions are the large covered porch and terrace, perfectly relaxing gathering points for family and friends.

Inside, the design is truly a hard worker: separate living and family rooms, each with their own fireplace; a formal dining room; and a large kitchen and breakfast area with a bay window. The second floor contains a master suite with twin closets and three family bedrooms that share a full bath.

QUOTE ONE®
Cost to build? See page 454
to order complete cost estimate
to build this house in your area!

Design HPT860488

Square Footage: 2,931
Width: 70'-8" **Depth:** 83'-0"

The corner quoins and keystone windows are just a few of this home's beautiful finishing touches. Inside, rich tile flows throughout for a beautiful decorating accent. The foyer opens to a large living room with a vaulted ceiling. The kitchen with a walk-in pantry opens up to the breakfast area and an immense family room. His and Hers walk-in closets, a compartmented toilet and a windowed tub make the master suite a study in elegance.

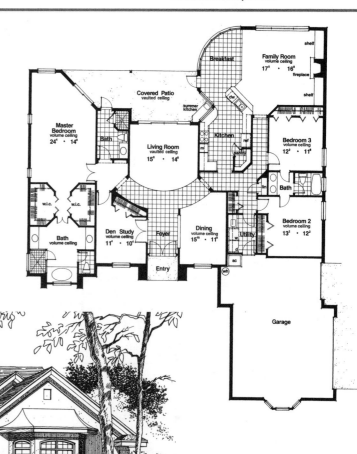

Design HPT860489

First Floor: 2,084 square feet
Second Floor: 848 square feet
Total: 2,932 square feet
Width: 68'-8" **Depth:** 60'-0"

The combination of brick, stucco and elegant detail provides this home with instant curb appeal. The entry is flanked by the formal dining room and the den, with a fireplace and an intriguing ceiling pattern. The great room offers a through-fireplace to the hearth room and French doors to a covered veranda. A sunny breakfast room and kitchen feature an island with a snack bar, wrapping counters and a pantry. The first-floor master suite affords luxury accommodations with two closets, a whirlpool tub, His and Hers vanities and access to the covered veranda. Three secondary bedrooms on the second floor offer walk-in closets and easy bathroom access.

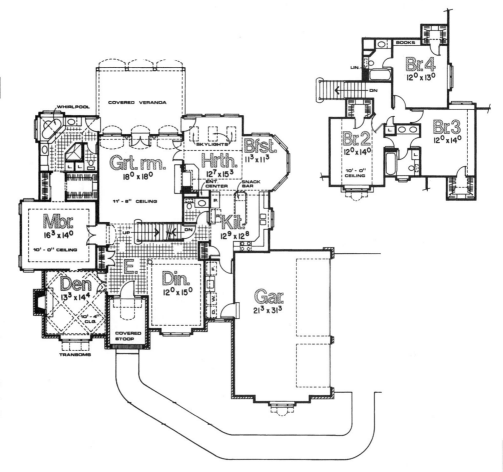

313

Design HPT860491

Square Footage: 2,935
Width: 71'-0" **Depth:** 66'-0"

This spacious one-story home easily accommodates a large family, providing all the luxuries and necessities for gracious living. For formal occasions, a grand dining room sits just off the entry foyer and features a vaulted ceiling. The great room offers a beautiful ceiling treatment and access to the rear deck. The spacious master suite is filled with amenities. Two family bedrooms share a full bath. This home is designed with a walkout basement foundation.

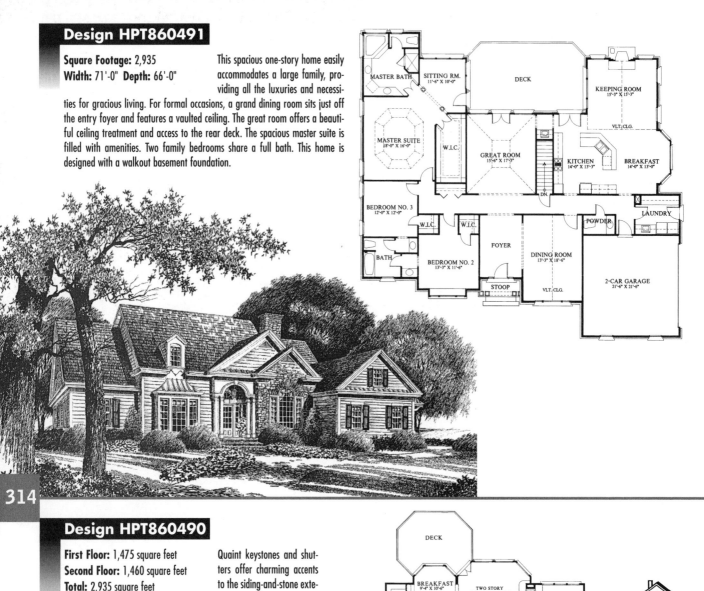

314

Design HPT860490

First Floor: 1,475 square feet
Second Floor: 1,460 square feet
Total: 2,935 square feet
Width: 57'-6" **Depth:** 46'-6"

Quaint keystones and shutters offer charming accents to the siding-and-stone exterior of this stately English country home. The two-story foyer opens through decorative columns to the formal living room. The nearby media room shares a through-fireplace with the two-story great room. The left wing of the second floor is dedicated to the rambling master suite, which boasts angled walls, a tray ceiling and a bayed sitting area. This home is designed with a walkout basement foundation.

Cost to build? See page 454 to order complete cost estimate to build this house in your area!

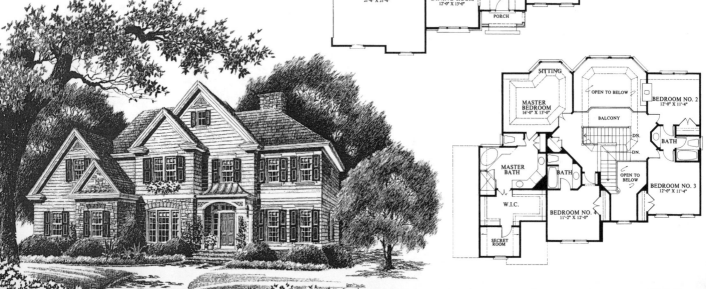

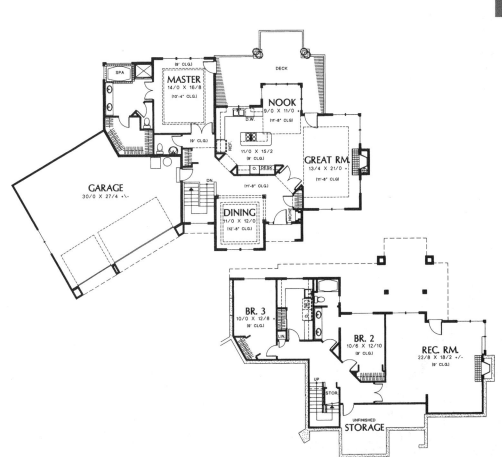

315

Design HPT860492

Main Level: 1,687 square feet
Lower Level: 1,251 square feet
Total: 2,938 square feet
Width: 82'-7" **Depth:** 54'-9"

This striking home is perfect for daylight basement lots. An elegant dining room fronts the plan. Nearby, an expansive kitchen features plenty of cabinet and counter space. A nook surrounded by a deck adds character. The comfortable great room, with a raised ceiling and a fireplace, shares space with these areas. The master bedroom suite includes private deck access and a superb bath with a spa tub and dual lavatories. Downstairs, two bedrooms, a laundry room with lots of counter space, and a rec room with a fireplace cap off the plan.

Second Floor Plan (Design HPT860493)

- Bedroom 2 — 14⁰ x 10¹⁰
- Family Room Below
- Bedroom 3 — 12⁷ x 12²
- Bedroom 4 — 13⁸ x 11⁵
- W.i.c.
- Bath
- Foyer Below
- Attic
- Opt. Bonus Room — 11⁰ x 17⁰

First Floor Plan (Design HPT860493)

- Breakfast
- Kitchen
- Two Story Family Room — 15⁵ x 18⁰
- Vaulted M.Bath
- W.i.c.
- Sitting Area
- Storage
- Laund.
- Dining Room — 13⁸ x 13⁰
- Master Suite — 16⁵ x 13⁵
- Garage — 21⁵ x 20⁸
- Covered Porch
- Two Story Foyer
- Living Room — 14⁵ x 14⁰
- Pwdr.

Design HPT860493

First Floor: 2,044 square feet
Second Floor: 896 square feet
Total: 2,940 square feet
Bonus Room: 197 square feet
Width: 63'-0" **Depth:** 54'-0"

Quote One®
Cost to build? See page 454
to order complete cost estimate
to build this house in your area!

A gracious front porch off the formal dining room and a two-story entry set the tone for this elegant home. The living room sits to the front of the plan. The two-story family room is accented with a fireplace and a serving bar. The first-floor master suite features a sitting area. Upstairs, two family bedrooms share a full bath while a third enjoys a private bath.

Floor Plan (Design HPT860494)

- Master Suite — 17⁰ x 13¹⁰
- Master Bath
- Bedrm — 12⁸ x 10⁰
- Kit — 11⁸ x 14⁸
- Morning Rm — 13⁰ x 14⁰
- Family Rm — 18⁰ x 12⁸
- Office-Den — 12⁰ x 12⁰
- Bedrm — 12⁸ x 10⁰
- Laundry Room
- Dining Rm — 11¹⁰ x 12⁰
- Living Rm — 14⁰ x 12¹⁰
- Guest Rm — 12⁰ x 10²
- Garage — 23¹⁰ x 21⁶
- Covered Porch

Design HPT860494

Square Footage: 2,946
Width: 94'-1" **Depth:** 67'-4"

L

Exquisite classical detailing includes delightfully proportioned columns below a modified pedimented gable and masses of brick punctuated by corner quoins. Formal and informal living areas are well defined by the living and family rooms. The family room has a complete media-center wall and a fireplace flanked by doors to the entertainment patio. Occupying the isolated end of the floor plan is the master suite and its adjacent office/den with a private porch.

Quote One®
Cost to build? See page 454
to order complete cost estimate
to build this house in your area!

Design HPT860495

First Floor: 2,063 square feet
Second Floor: 894 square feet
Total: 2,957 square feet
Width: 72'-8" **Depth:** 51'-4"

An elegant brick elevation and rows of shuttered windows lend timeless beauty to this two-story Colonial design. The volume entry opens to the formal dining and living rooms and the magnificent great room. Sparkling floor-to-ceiling windows flank the fireplace in the great room, which offers a cathedral ceiling. French doors, bay windows and a decorative ceiling, plus a wet bar, highlight the private den. Special lifestyle amenities in the kitchen and bayed breakfast area include a built-in desk, wrapping counters and an island. In the master bath/dressing area, note the large walk-in closet, built-in dresser, His and Hers vanities, oval whirlpool tub and plant shelves. Upstairs, each secondary bedroom contains a roomy closet and private bath.

Quote One®

Cost to build? See page 454
to order complete cost estimate
to build this house in your area!

317

G. MacDonald

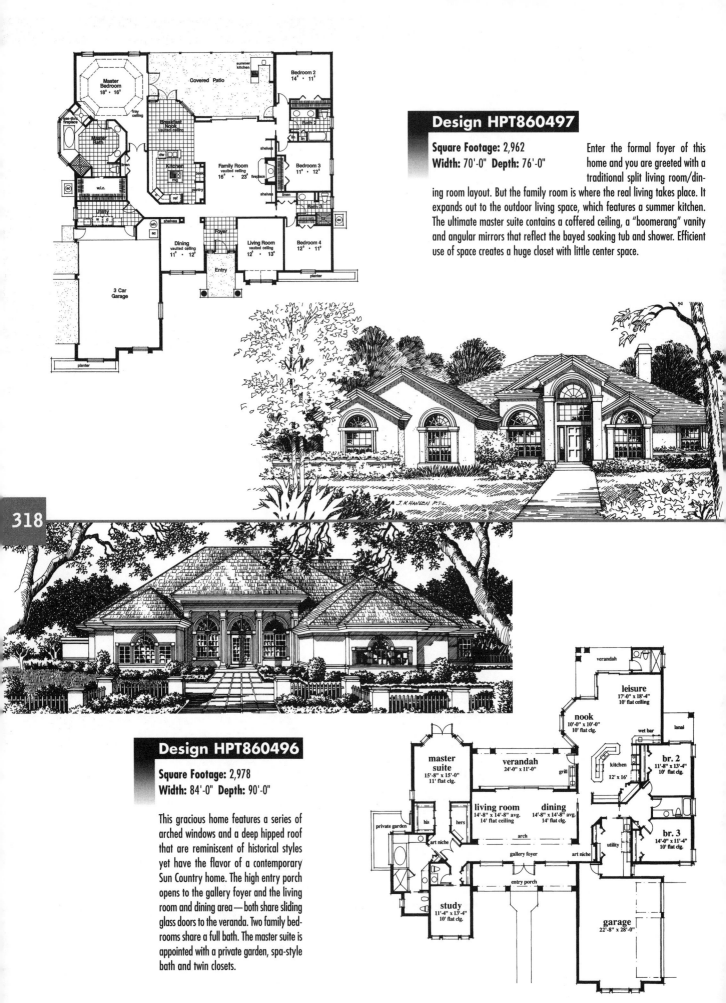

Master
Bedroom
18⁸ • 16⁰

Covered Patio

summer
kitchen

Bedroom 2
14⁴ • 11⁷

tray
ceiling

see-thru
fireplace

Breakfast
Nook
vaulted ceiling

Bath 2

Master
Bath

Kitchen

Family Room
vaulted ceiling
16⁰ • 23⁵

shelves

fireplace

Bedroom 3
11⁷ • 12⁵

w.l.c.

pantry

ref

shelves

Bath 3

linen

Utility
w d

shelves

Foyer

Dining
vaulted ceiling
11⁰ • 12²

Living Room
vaulted ceiling
12² • 13⁰

Bedroom 4
12⁸ • 11⁹

Entry

planter

3 Car
Garage

planter

Design HPT860497

Square Footage: 2,962
Width: 70'-0" **Depth:** 76'-0"

Enter the formal foyer of this home and you are greeted with a traditional split living room/dining room layout. But the family room is where the real living takes place. It expands out to the outdoor living space, which features a summer kitchen. The ultimate master suite contains a coffered ceiling, a "boomerang" vanity and angular mirrors that reflect the bayed soaking tub and shower. Efficient use of space creates a huge closet with little center space.

318

Design HPT860496

Square Footage: 2,978
Width: 84'-0" **Depth:** 90'-0"

This gracious home features a series of arched windows and a deep hipped roof that are reminiscent of historical styles yet have the flavor of a contemporary Sun Country home. The high entry porch opens to the gallery foyer and the living room and dining area — both share sliding glass doors to the veranda. Two family bedrooms share a full bath. The master suite is appointed with a private garden, spa-style bath and twin closets.

verandah

leisure
17'-0" x 18'-4"
10' flat ceiling

nook
10'-0" x 10'-0"
10' flat clg.

wet bar

lanai

master
suite
15'-8" x 15'-0"
11' flat clg.

verandah
24'-0" x 11'-0"

grill

kitchen
12' x 16'

br. 2
11'-8" x 13'-4"
10' flat clg.

his

private garden

hers

living room
14'-8" x 14'-8" avg.
14' flat ceiling

dining
14'-8" x 14'-8" avg.
14' flat clg.

art niche

arch

utility

br. 3
14'-0" x 11'-4"
10' flat clg.

gallery foyer

art niche

study
11'-4" x 13'-4"
10' flat clg.

entry porch

garage
22'-8" x 28'-0"

Design HPT860498

Square Footage: 2,985
Width: 80'-0" **Depth:** 68'-0"

A brick exterior, cast-stone trim and corner quoins make up this attractive single-living-area design. The entry introduces a formal dining room to the right and a living room with a wall of windows to the left. The hearth-warmed family room opens to the kitchen/dinette, both with ten-foot ceilings. A large bay window enhances the dinette with a full glass door to the covered patio. A large master suite with vaulted ceilings features a bayed sitting area, a luxurious master bath with double lavatories, and an oversized walk-in closet.

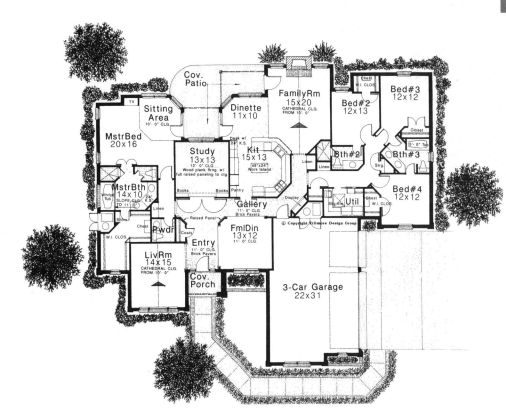

Design HPT860500

Square Footage: 2,987
Width: 74'-4" **Depth:** 82'-4"

Classic columns, a tiled roof and beautiful arched windows herald a gracious interior for this fine home. Arched windows also mark the entrance into the vaulted living room with a tiled fireplace. Filled with light from a wall of sliding glass doors, the family room leads to the covered patio. The master bedroom shares a through-fireplace with the master bath. A vaulted study/bedroom sits between two additional bedrooms—all share a full bath.

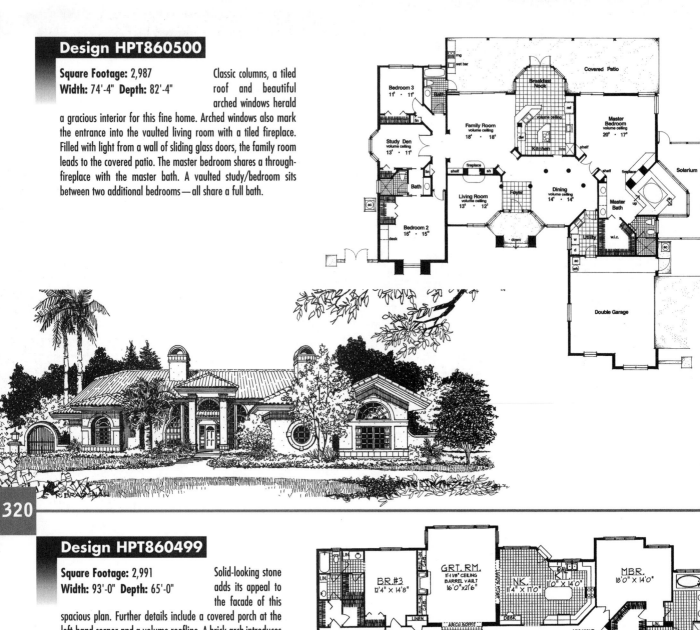

Design HPT860499

Square Footage: 2,991
Width: 93'-0" **Depth:** 65'-0"

Solid-looking stone adds its appeal to the facade of this spacious plan. Further details include a covered porch at the left-hand corner and a volume roofline. A brick arch introduces the recessed entry, which opens to a foyer with a barrel-vaulted ceiling. Beyond is the massive great room, also accented with a barrel-vaulted ceiling. The master suite sits protected at the rear of the home behind the three-car garage. Two family bedrooms share a full bath.

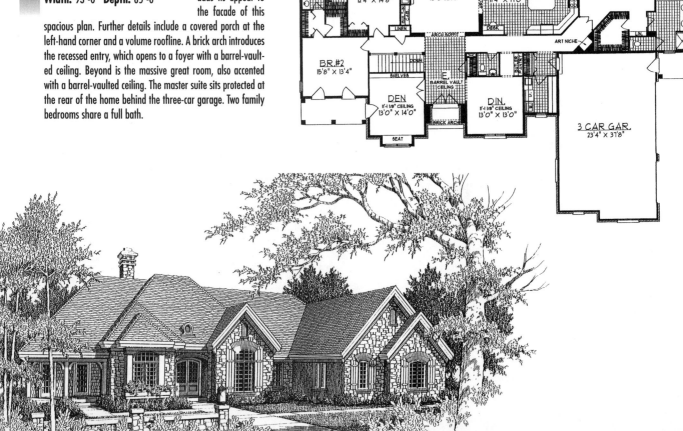

Design HPT860501

First Floor: 2,369 square feet
Second Floor: 624 square feet
Total: 2,993 square feet
Width: 65'-6" **Depth:** 84'-0"

Large columns and decorative stonework are eye-catching details as you approach this house. Inside, the foyer is flanked by the formal living and dining rooms, both featuring large multi-pane windows. The family room is in the center of the house, with a fireplace, built-in shelves and access to the covered back porch. A large kitchen, with a U-shaped counter and an island work area, will receive light and warmth from the fireplace and natural light from the cheery breakfast area. The master suite provides its own door to the porch. Two family bedrooms upstairs hold walk-in closets and dressing rooms that open to the shared hall bath. Please specify crawlspace or slab foundation when ordering.

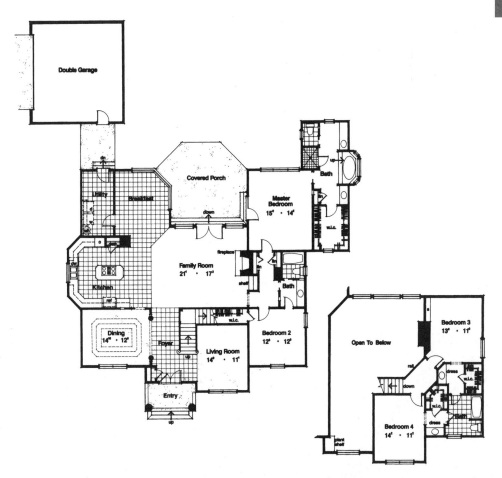

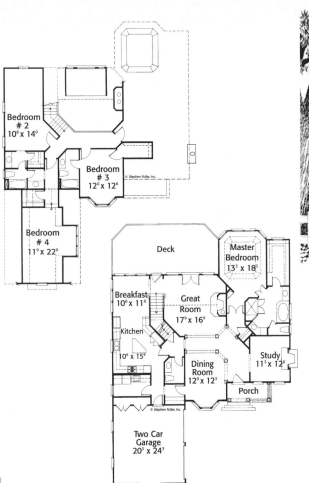

Bedroom
2
10⁶ x 14⁰

Bedroom
3
12⁰ x 12⁶

© Stephen Fuller, Inc.

Bedroom
4
11⁰ x 22⁰

Deck

Master
Bedroom
13³ x 18³

Breakfast
10⁶ x 11⁰

Great
Room
17⁹ x 16⁵

Kitchen
10⁶ x 15⁹

Dining
Room
12⁰ x 12⁵

Study
11³ x 12⁶

Porch

© Stephen Fuller, Inc.

Two Car
Garage
20³ x 24³

Design HPT860503

First Floor: 1,944 square feet
Second Floor: 1,055 square feet
Total: 2,999 square feet
Width: 51'-6" **Depth:** 72'-0"

Interesting rooflines and a two-story bay window create a unique cottage farmhouse appearance. The foyer leads to the dining room and great room, both graced with columns. The great room features a fireplace and opens to the deck. The right wing is devoted to an amenity-filled master suite with convenient access to the study. The second floor contains three bedrooms and two baths. This home is designed with a walkout basement foundation.

Design HPT860502

First Floor: 1,581 square feet
Second Floor: 1,415 square feet
Total: 2,996 square feet
Width: 55'-0" **Depth:** 52'-0"

Classical details and a stately brick exterior accentuate the grace and timeless elegance of this home. The two-story great room awaits, featuring a wet bar and warming fireplace. To the left is the sunlit breakfast room and efficient kitchen. Upstairs, the master suite features a sun deck, while two large family bedrooms offer separate vanities and share a bath. This home is designed with a walkout basement foundation.

QUOTE ONE®
Cost to build? See page 454 to order complete cost estimate to build this house in your area!

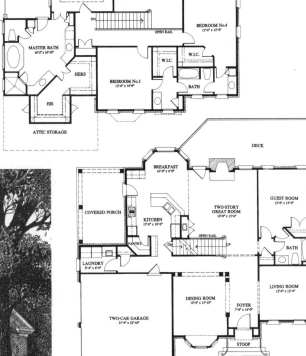

SITTING AREA
10'-0" x 4'-4"

SUN DECK

MASTER SUITE
14'-2" x 15'-6"

OPEN TO
GREAT ROOM
BELOW

ATTIC STORAGE

DN

OPEN RAIL

BEDROOM No.4
12'-6" x 12'-0"

MASTER BATH
10'-7" x 16'-10"

HERS

W.I.C.

W.I.C.

BEDROOM No.3
12'-6" x 14'-0"

BATH

HIS

ATTIC STORAGE

DECK

BREAKFAST
10'-0" x 4'-0"

COVERED PORCH

KITCHEN
12'-8" x 10'-0"

TWO-STORY
GREAT ROOM
16'-0" x 17'-0"

GUEST ROOM
12'-4" x 13'-0"

PANTRY

DN

OPEN RAIL

UP

BATH

LAUNDRY
5'-4" x 6'-0"

LIVING ROOM
12'-6" x 12'-0"

DINING ROOM
12'-4" x 15'-10"

FOYER
7'-0" x 16'-0"

TWO-CAR GARAGE
21'-4" x 22'-10"

STOOP

Design HPT860504

Square Footage: 3,034
Width: 112'-0" **Depth:** 74'-6"

L

A grand entry enhances the exterior of this elegant stucco home. The office located at the front of the plan makes this design ideal for a home-based business. Formal areas combine to provide lots of space for entertaining. The kitchen, complete with a snack bar and a breakfast nook, opens to the family room which connects to the media room. The private master suite includes two retreats—one is a multi-windowed sitting area, the other contains a spa for outdoor enjoyment. A walk-in closet and a luxurious bath complete this area. Two family bedrooms share a full bath.

QUOTE ONE®
Cost to build? See page 454 to order complete cost estimate to build this house in your area!

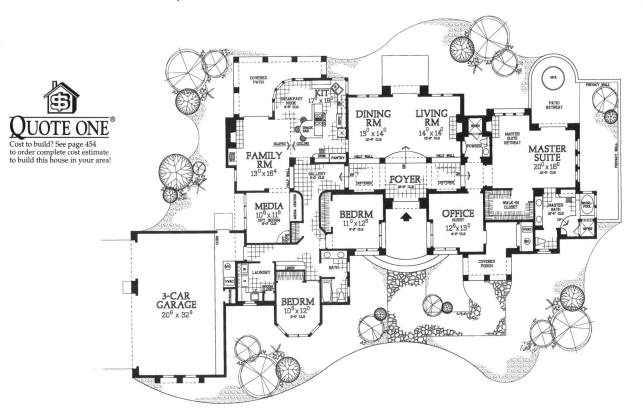

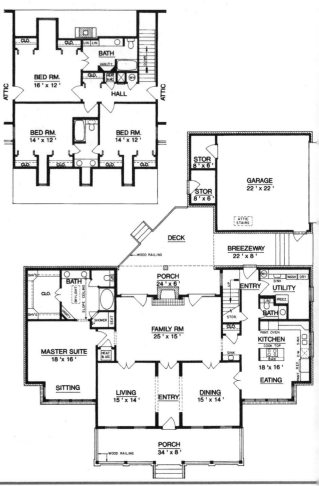

Design HPT860506

First Floor: 2,008 square feet
Second Floor: 1,027 square feet
Total: 3,035 square feet
Width: 66'-0" **Depth:** 74'-0"

A porch with wood railings borders the facade of this plan, lending a farmhouse or country feel. The family room includes a fireplace and doors to access the back porch. The master suite is filled with luxuries, from the walk-in closet with shelves, the full bath with a skylight, sloped ceiling and double vanity, to the shower with a convenient seat. Three additional bedrooms upstairs share two full baths between them. Please specify basement, crawlspace or slab foundation when ordering.

© 1993 Donald A. Gardner Architects, Inc.

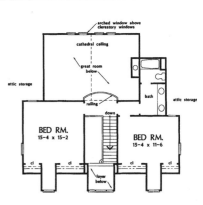

Design HPT860505

First Floor: 2,316 square feet
Second Floor: 721 square feet
Total: 3,037 square feet
Bonus Room: 545 square feet
Width: 95'-4" **Depth:** 54'-10"

Cost to build? See page 454 to order complete cost estimate to build this house in your area!

The entrance to this farmhouse enjoys a Palladian clerestory window, lending an abundance of natural light to the foyer. The great room furthers this feeling of airiness with a balcony above and two sets of sliding glass doors leading to the back porch. For privacy, the master suite occupies the right side of the first floor. A sitting bay and roomy bath adds to the luxury in this suite. Two more bedrooms and a double-vanity bath are located upstairs.

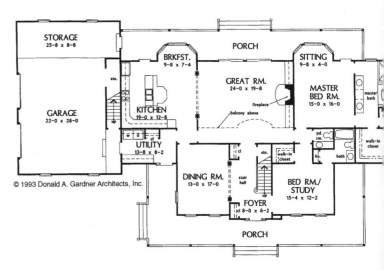

© 1993 Donald A. Gardner Architects, Inc.

Design HPT860507

First Floor: 1,370 square feet
Second Floor: 1,673 square feet
Total: 3,043 square feet
Width: 73'-6" **Depth:** 49'-0"

Quote One®
Cost to build? See page 454
to order complete cost estimate
to build this house in your area!

This English Georgian home exhibits a dramatic brick exterior. Enter the two-story foyer—the unusually shaped staircase and balcony overlook create a tremendous first impression. Separated only by a classical colonnade detail, the living and dining rooms are perfect for entertaining. The great room features a fireplace on the outside wall. This room opens to the breakfast room and angled kitchen with plenty of cabinets and counter space. Upstairs is a guest room, a children's den area, two family bedrooms and the master suite. Look for the cozy fireplace, tray ceiling and sumptuous bath in the master suite. This home is designed with a walkout basement foundation.

Design HPT860508

First Floor: 1,591 square feet
Second Floor: 1,457 square feet
Total: 3,048 square feet
Bonus Room: 324 square feet
Width: 66'-4" **Depth:** 43'-4"

The two-story pedimented porch adds drama to this Georgian-style home. French doors open the family room to a spacious terrace. A walk-in pantry and a snack counter highlight the kitchen. Bay windows brighten the living room and formal dining room. Upper-level sleeping quarters include a deluxe master suite with an oversized shower and a whirlpool tub. A gallery hall leads to an unfinished recreation room.

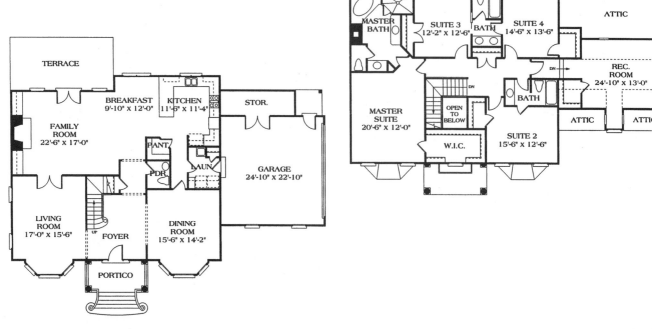

TERRACE

BREAKFAST
9'-10" x 12'-0"

KITCHEN
11'-6" x 11'-4"

STOR.

FAMILY
ROOM
22'-6" x 17'-0"

PANT.

GARAGE
24'-10" x 22'-10"

PDR.

LAUN.

LIVING
ROOM
17'-0" x 15'-6"

UP FOYER

DINING
ROOM
15'-6" x 14'-2"

PORTICO

MASTER
BATH

SUITE 3
12'-2" x 12'-6"

BATH

SUITE 4
14'-6" x 13'-6"

ATTIC

MASTER
SUITE
20'-6" x 12'-0"

OPEN
TO
BELOW

DN

DN

BATH

REC.
ROOM
24'-10" x 13'-0"

ATTIC

ATTIC

W.I.C.

SUITE 2
15'-6" x 12'-6"

Design HPT860509

Square Footage: 3,056
Width: 80'-0" **Depth:** 79'-0"

Depending on European and French influences for its exterior beauty, this regal home possesses plenty of curb appeal. There are more than enough living areas in this plan: formal living and dining rooms, a huge family room with a fireplace, and a study with a bay window. The kitchen features an attached light-filled breakfast area. Two family bedrooms on the right side of the plan share a full bath, while the third family bathroom has a private bath. The master suite offers a private covered patio, two walk-in closets and a bath fit for a king.

327

Design HPT860510

First Floor: 1,925 square feet
Second Floor: 1,134 square feet
Total: 3,059 square feet
Width: 78'-0" **Depth:** 52'-0"

This four-bedroom traditional beauty presents the quaint look of an older home. The two-story den has a fireplace and a large rear porch accessible via French doors. The kitchen includes a large pantry and is located directly between the eating area and the formal dining room. The master suite is situated for convenience and features a plush bath. The two bedrooms on the upper level each include huge walk-in closets. Please specify crawlspace or slab foundation when ordering.

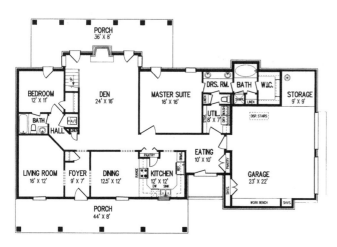

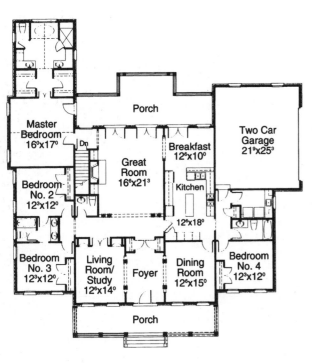

Design HPT860511

Square Footage: 3,066
Width: 73'-0" **Depth:** 70'-6"

Descended from the architecture that developed in America's Tidewater country, this updated adaptation retains the insouciant charm of a coastal cottage. Central to the social flow in the house, the great room opens to the kitchen, the breakfast room and the rear porch that runs across the back. The left wing contains a private master suite. This home is designed with a walkout basement foundation.

Design HPT860512

First Floor: 2,429 square feet
Second Floor: 654 square feet
Total: 3,083 square feet
Bonus Room: 420 square feet
Width: 63'-6" **Depth:** 71'-4"

Keystones that cap each window, a terrace that dresses up the entrance, and a bay-windowed turret add up to a totally refined exterior of this home. Inside, open planning employs columns to define the foyer, dining room and two-story family room. The first-floor master suite is designed with every amenity to answer your needs. Rounding out the first floor are the kitchen, breakfast nook and keeping room. The second floor contains two bedrooms, each with a private bath and walk-in closet, and an optional bonus room. Please specify basement or crawlspace foundation when ordering.

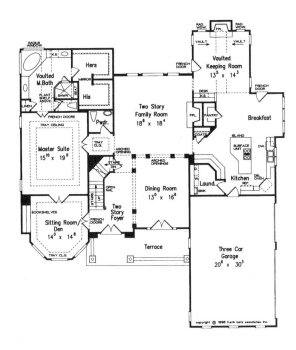

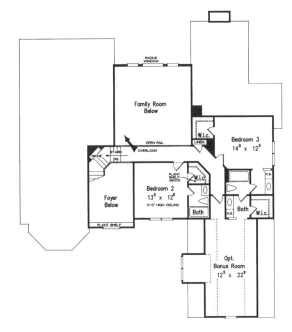

329

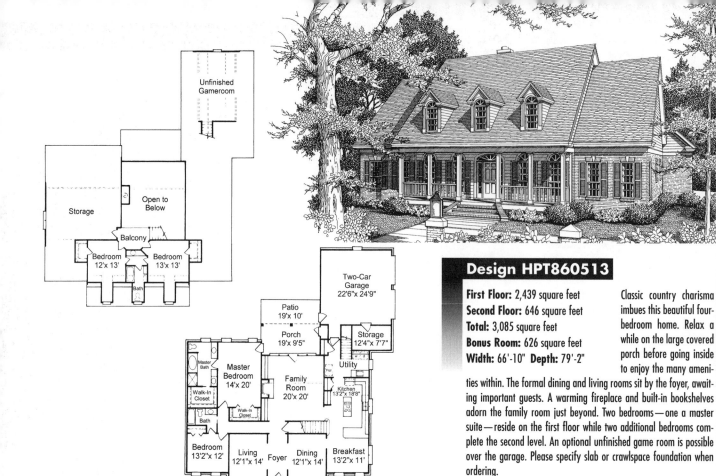

Unfinished Gameroom

Storage

Open to Below

Balcony

Bedroom 12'x 13'

Bedroom 13'x 13'

Bath

Two-Car Garage 22'6"x 24'9"

Patio 19'x 10'

Porch 19'x 9'5"

Storage 12'4"x 7'7"

Master Bath

Master Bedroom 14'x 20'

Family Room 20'x 20'

Utility

Walk-In Closet

Walk-In Closet

Bath

Kitchen 13'2"x 18'8"

Bedroom 13'2"x 12'

Living 12'1"x 14'

Foyer

Dining 12'1"x 14'

Breakfast 13'2"x 11'

Porch 32'10"x 6'

Design HPT860513

First Floor: 2,439 square feet
Second Floor: 646 square feet
Total: 3,085 square feet
Bonus Room: 626 square feet
Width: 66'-10" **Depth:** 79'-2"

Classic country charisma imbues this beautiful four-bedroom home. Relax a while on the large covered porch before going inside to enjoy the many amenities within. The formal dining and living rooms sit by the foyer, awaiting important guests. A warming fireplace and built-in bookshelves adorn the family room just beyond. Two bedrooms—one a master suite—reside on the first floor while two additional bedrooms complete the second level. An optional unfinished game room is possible over the garage. Please specify slab or crawlspace foundation when ordering.

Design HPT860514

First Floor: 1,455 square feet
Second Floor: 1,649 square feet
Total: 3,104 square feet
Width: 53'-0" **Depth:** 46'-0"

The double wings, twin chimneys and center portico of this home work in concert to create a classic architectural statement. The two-story foyer is flanked by the spacious dining room and formal living room, each containing its own fireplace. This home is designed with a walkout basement foundation.

COVERED PORCH

SITTING 9'-0" x 4'-6"

MASTER BATH 17'-4" x 15'-10"

BEDROOM No.4 16'-10" x 11'-10"

MASTER BEDROOM 15'-6" x 16'-0"

MASTER CLOSET

BATH

BATH

BEDROOM No.2 13'-4" x 12'-0"

OPEN TO FOYER BELOW

BEDROOM No.3 13'-2" x 12'-0"

QUOTE ONE®
Cost to build? See page 454 to order complete cost estimate to build this house in your area!

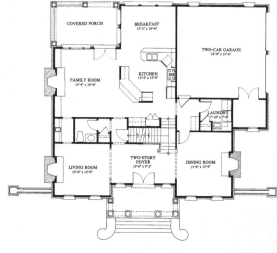

COVERED PORCH

BREAKFAST 13'-2" x 10'-0"

TWO-CAR GARAGE 22'-0" x 21'-0"

FAMILY ROOM 15'-6" x 16'-0"

KITCHEN 13'-2" x 12'-0"

LAUNDRY 7'-10" x 7'-4"

LIVING ROOM 13'-4" x 12'-0"

TWO-STORY FOYER 13'-2" x 9'-2"

DINING ROOM 13'-4" x 15'-0"

331

Design HPT860515

First Floor: 1,919 square feet
Second Floor: 1,190 square feet
Total: 3,109 square feet
Bonus Room: 286 square feet
Width: 64'-6" **Depth:** 55'-10"

Flower boxes, arches and multi-pane windows all combine to create the elegant facade of this four-bedroom home. Inside, the two-story foyer introduces a formal dining room to its right and leads to a two-story living room that is filled with light. An efficient kitchen has a bayed breakfast room and shares a snack bar with a cozy family room. Located on the first floor for privacy, the master suite is graced with a luxurious bath. Upstairs, three secondary bedrooms share two full baths and access a large game room. For future growth there is an expandable area accessed through the game room. Please specify basement, crawlspace or slab foundation when ordering.

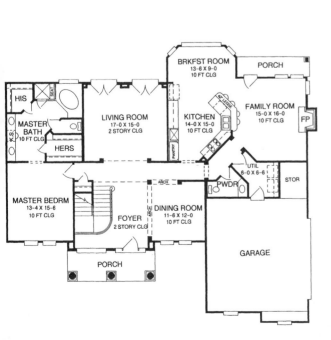

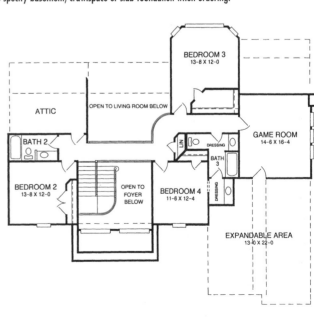

Design HPT860516

First Floor: 2,422 square feet
Second Floor: 714 square feet
Total: 3,136 square feet
Width: 77'-8" **Depth:** 62'-0"

L

This Southwestern contemporary home offers a distinctive look for any neighborhood—both inside and out. The formal living areas are concentrated in the center of the plan, perfect for entertaining. To the right, the kitchen and family room function well together as a working and living area. The first-floor sleeping wing includes a guest suite and a master suite. Upstairs, two family bedrooms are reached by a balcony overlooking the living room. Each bedroom has a walk-in closet and a dressing area with a vanity, while sharing a compartmented bath with a linen closet.

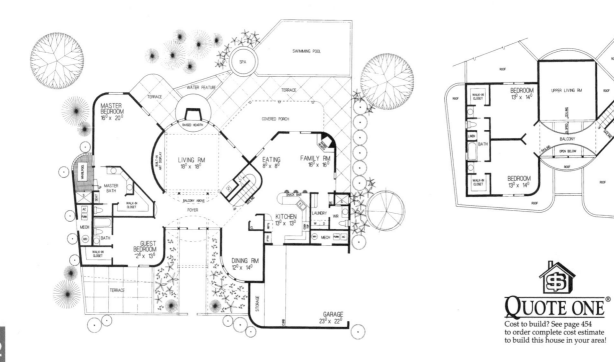

QUOTE ONE®

Cost to build? See page 454
to order complete cost estimate
to build this house in your area!

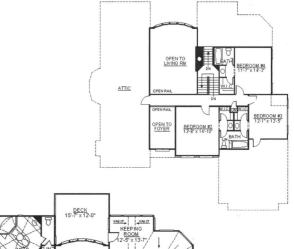

Design HPT860517

First Floor: 2,253 square feet
Second Floor: 890 square feet
Total: 3,143 square feet
Width: 61'-6" **Depth:** 64'-0"

This grand house begins with a double-door entry topped by a beautiful arched window. Inside, the foyer opens to the two-story living room, which features a wide bow window overlooking the rear property. The kitchen serves both the formal dining room and the breakfast area adjoining the bright keeping room. The master suite, secluded on the first floor, is large and opulent. Three more bedrooms and two baths are upstairs for family and friends.

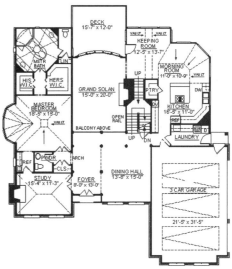

333

Design HPT860518

Square Footage: 3,144
Width: 139'-10" **Depth:** 63'-8"

L

In classic Santa Fe style, this home strikes a beautiful combination of historic exterior detailing and open floor planning on the inside. A covered porch running the width of the facade leads to an entry foyer that connects to a huge gathering room with a fireplace and a formal dining room. The family kitchen allows special space for casual gatherings. The right wing of the home holds two family bedrooms and a full bath. The left wing is devoted to the master suite and a guest room or study.

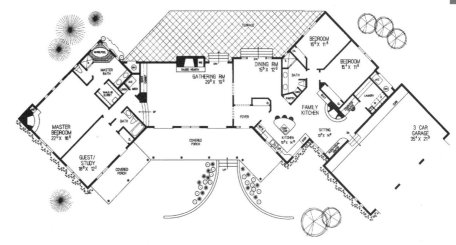

QUOTE ONE®
Cost to build? See page 454
to order complete cost estimate
to build this house in your area!

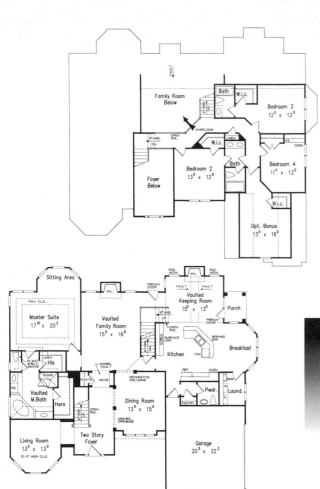

Design HPT860520

First Floor: 2,302 square feet
Second Floor: 845 square feet
Total: 3,147 square feet
Bonus Room: 247 square feet
Width: 64'-0" **Depth:** 59'-4"

The arched front doorway bids a warm welcome to this spacious home. The formal dining room opens to the right. Both the family and keeping rooms feature fireplaces and vaulted ceilings, while the large kitchen offers a work island and a serving bar. On the left side of the plan are a gazebo-shaped formal living room and the elegant master suite with a bayed sitting area. Two staircases lead to three family bedrooms and the optional bonus room upstairs. Please specify basement or crawlspace foundation when ordering.

Design HPT860519

First Floor: 2,033 square feet
Second Floor: 1,116 square feet
Total: 3,149 square feet
Width: 71'-0" **Depth:** 56'-0"

This large Southern-style home offers luxury to spare, inside and out. Decorative columns and tall arched windows along a raised porch welcome guests and introduce a grand two-story foyer. Custom archways define both the entry and the great room. Luxury abounds in the opulent master suite, complete with a sitting room, a private rear porch and deck, a separate front porch and a master bath with a corner whirlpool tub. Please specify crawlspace or slab foundation when ordering.

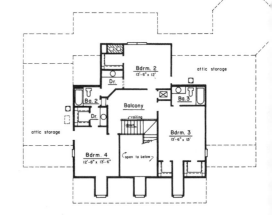

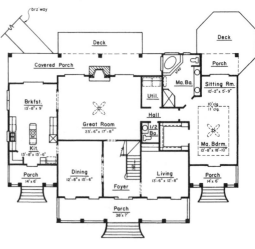

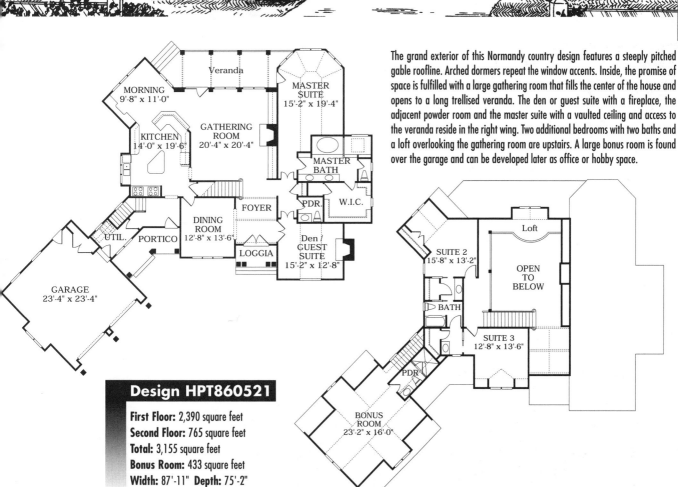

The grand exterior of this Normandy country design features a steeply pitched gable roofline. Arched dormers repeat the window accents. Inside, the promise of space is fulfilled with a large gathering room that fills the center of the house and opens to a long trellised veranda. The den or guest suite with a fireplace, the adjacent powder room and the master suite with a vaulted ceiling and access to the veranda reside in the right wing. Two additional bedrooms with two baths and a loft overlooking the gathering room are upstairs. A large bonus room is found over the garage and can be developed later as office or hobby space.

Design HPT860521

First Floor: 2,390 square feet
Second Floor: 765 square feet
Total: 3,155 square feet
Bonus Room: 433 square feet
Width: 87'-11" **Depth:** 75'-2"

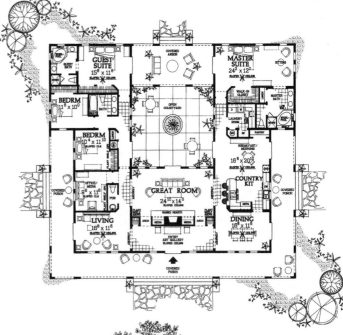

Design HPT860522

Square Footage: 3,158
Width: 72'-0" **Depth:** 70'-0"

The entry of this transitional home leads into a family room with a thirteen-foot ceiling, fireplace and built-in entertainment center. Beyond the family room are the breakfast room and sun room, where a skylight and a bar with a wine rack, sink and glass shelves can be found. The kitchen includes a pantry, skylight and snack bar. The master suite is a study in spaciousness with its large walk-in closet, sloped bathroom ceiling, skylight, linen closets, vanity and glass-surrounded spa tub. Please specify crawlspace or slab foundation when ordering.

Design HPT860523

Square Footage: 3,163
Width: 75'-2" **Depth:** 68'-8"

L

An open courtyard takes center stage in this home, providing a happy marriage of indoor/outdoor relationships. The formal dining room accommodates special occasions, while casual mealtimes are enjoyed in the adjacent country kitchen. The centrally located great room supplies the nucleus for formal and informal entertaining. A raised-hearth fireplace flanked by built-in media centers adds a special touch. The master suite provides a private retreat where you can relax.

Quote One®
Cost to build? See page 454 to order complete cost estimate to build this house in your area!

Design HPT860524

First Floor: 2,086 square feet
Second Floor: 1,077 square feet
Total: 3,163 square feet
Bonus Room: 403 square feet
Width: 81'-10" **Depth:** 51'-8"

This beautiful farmhouse with its prominent twin gables and bays adds just the right amount of country style. The master suite is quietly tucked away downstairs with no rooms directly above. The family cook will love the spacious U-shaped kitchen and adjoining bayed breakfast nook. A bonus room is easily accessible from the back stairs or from the second floor, where three large bedrooms share two full baths.

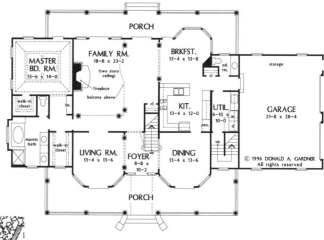

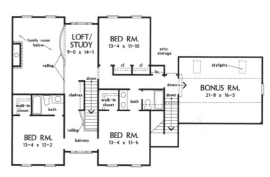

Design HPT860525

First Floor: 2,294 square feet
Second Floor: 869 square feet
Total: 3,163 square feet
Bonus Room: 309 square feet
Width: 63'-6" **Depth:** 63'-0"

A turreted living room adds a special touch to this four-bedroom home. From the pleasing covered porch, the two-story foyer leads through an arched opening to the formal dining room and also to the charming bayed living room. The master suite is tucked away on the first floor, with its own vaulted sitting room, walk-in closet and spacious bath. The two-story family room with a fireplace and rear views rounds out the main level. Three more bedrooms and two baths, plus an optional bonus room, complete the upper level. Please specify basement or crawlspace foundation when ordering.

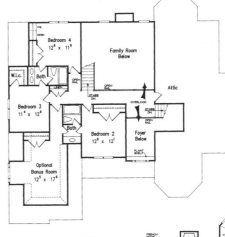

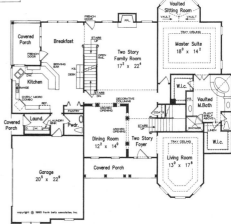

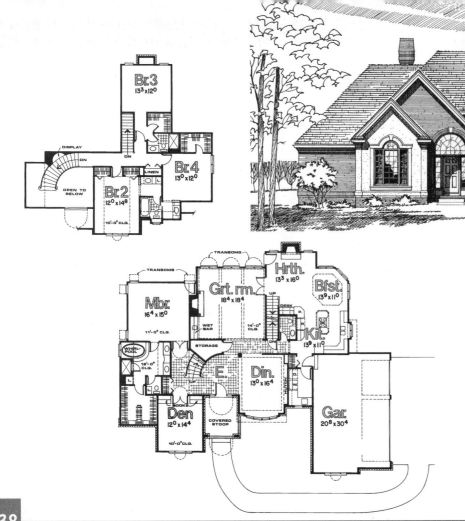

Br3
13³ x 12⁰

DISPLAY

DN   DN

Br.4
13⁰ x 12⁰

LINEN

OPEN TO BELOW

Br.2
12⁰ x 14⁸

10'-0" CLG.

TRANSOMS

TRANSOMS

Hrth.
13³ x 16⁰

Grt. rm.
18⁴ x 18⁴

Bfst.
13⁹ x 11⁰

UP

DESK

Mbr.
16⁴ x 15⁰

WET BAR

11'-0" CLG.

STORAGE

Kit.
13⁹ x 11⁰

WHIRL-POOL

18'-0" CLG.

E.

Din.
13⁰ x 16⁴

BOOKS

UP

Den
12⁰ x 14⁴

COVERED STOOP

Gar.
20⁸ x 30⁴

10'-0" CLG.

Design HPT860526

First Floor: 2,252 square feet
Second Floor: 920 square feet
Total: 3,172 square feet
Width: 73'-4" **Depth:** 57'-4"

A curving staircase graces the entry to this beautiful home and hints at the wealth of amenities found in the floor plan. Besides an oversized great room with a fireplace and arched windows, there's a cozy hearth room with its own fireplace. A secluded den contains bookcases and an arched transom above double doors. The master suite sits on the first floor, thoughtfully separated from three family bedrooms upstairs.

338

Design HPT860527

First Floor: 2,502 square feet
Second Floor: 677 square feet
Total: 3,179 square feet
Bonus Room: 171 square feet
Width: 71'-2" **Depth:** 56'-10"

Stone and stucco bring a chateau welcome to this Mediterranean-style home. A sensational sun room lights up the rear of the plan and flows to the bayed breakfast nook. The living area opens to the formal dining room. A master suite with rear-deck access leads to a family or guest bedroom with a private bath. Upstairs, two secondary bedrooms and a full bath enjoy easy kitchen access down a side stairway. This home is designed with a walkout basement foundation.

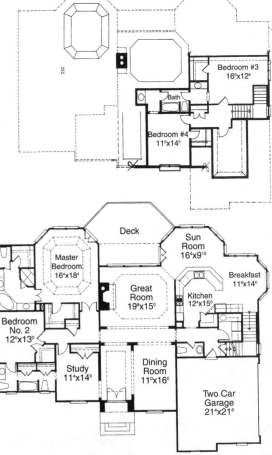

Bedroom #3
16⁰ x 12⁶

Bath

Bedroom #4
11⁰ x 14⁰

Deck

Master Bedroom
16⁴ x 18⁴

Sun Room
16⁴ x 9¹⁰

Great Room
19⁸ x 15⁰

Breakfast
11⁶ x 14⁰

Kitchen
12⁴ x 15⁰

Bedroom No. 2
12⁰ x 13⁰

Study
11⁴ x 14⁰

Dining Room
11⁰ x 16⁰

Two Car Garage
21⁴ x 21⁶

Breakfast 13³ x 8⁰

Deck

Master Bedroom 13³ x 22⁶

Kitchen 14⁰ x 16⁶

Great Room 19⁰ x 19⁶

Foyer

Dining Room 13⁹ x 12⁰

Living Room 13⁹ x 12⁰

Two Car Garage 21³ x 22⁰

BEDROOM NO.2 14'-0" X 11'-0"

OPEN TO BELOW

UNFINISHED STORAGE 7'-10" X 12'-2"

DN.

BATH

BATH

BEDROOM NO.3 13'-10" X 12'-0"

BEDROOM NO.4 12'-4" X 12'-0"

QUOTE ONE®
Cost to build? See page 454
to order complete cost estimate
to build this house in your area!

Design HPT860528

First Floor: 2,081 square feet
Second Floor: 1,105 square feet
Total: 3,186 square feet
Width: 69'-9" **Depth:** 65'-0"

From its pediment to the columned porch, this Georgian facade is impressive. Inside, classical symmetry balances the living and dining rooms on either side of the foyer. The two-story great room features built-in cabinetry, a fireplace and a large bay window. The island kitchen opens to the breakfast area. The master suite boasts a tray ceiling, a wall of glass and access to the rear deck, as well as a private bath. This home is designed with a walkout basement foundation.

339

Design HPT860530

First Floor: 2,293 square feet
Second Floor: 901 square feet
Total: 3,194 square feet
Bonus Room: 265 square feet
Width: 82'-6" **Depth:** 67'-2"

From its dramatic front entry to its rear twin-bay turrets, this design is as traditional as its history. A two-story foyer opens through a gallery into an expansive gathering room. A formal living room or study offers a coffered ceiling and a private door to the gallery hall that leads to the master suite.

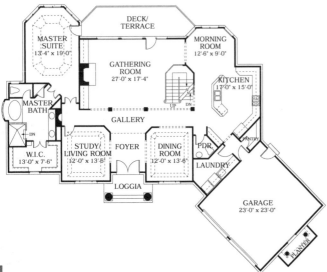

Design HPT860529

First Floor: 2,127 square feet
Second Floor: 1,069 square feet
Total: 3,196 square feet
Width: 66'-0" **Depth:** 62'-0"

Victorian detailing accents the charm of this fine four-bedroom home. A covered front porch ushers you into the two-story foyer that leads to the formal dining room on the left and a spacious great room directly ahead. Located on the first floor for privacy, the master suite is lavish with its luxuries. A guest suite is found on the second floor and offers its own amenities. A three-car garage is available for the family fleet.

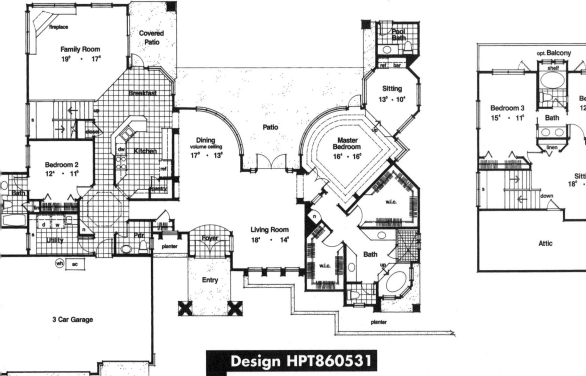

Design HPT860531

First Floor: 2,531 square feet
Second Floor: 669 square feet
Total: 3,200 square feet
Width: 82'-4" **Depth:** 72'-0"

This exquisite brick-and-stucco contemporary home takes its cue from the tradition of Frank Lloyd Wright. The formal living and dining areas combine to provide a spectacular view of the rear grounds. Unique best describes the private master suite, highlighted by a multitude of amenities. The family living area encompasses the left portion of the plan, featuring a spacious family room with a corner fireplace, access to the covered patio from the breakfast area and a step-saving kitchen. Bedroom 2 connects to a private bath. Upstairs, two bedrooms share a balcony, a sitting room and a full bath.

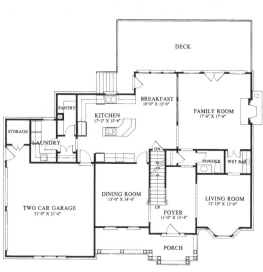

Quote One®

Cost to build? See page 454 to order complete cost estimate to build this house in your area!

Design HPT860532

First Floor: 1,570 square feet
Second Floor: 1,630 square feet
Total: 3,200 square feet
Width: 59'-10" **Depth:** 43'-4"

This classic Americana design employs wood siding, a variety of window styles and a detailed front porch. Inside, the large two-story foyer flows into the formal dining room with arched window accents and the living room highlighted by a bay window. This home is designed with a walkout basement foundation.

Design HPT860533

First Floor: 2,200 square feet
Second Floor: 1,001 square feet
Total: 3,201 square feet
Bonus Room: 694 square feet
Width: 70'-4" **Depth:** 74'-4"

A wide, welcoming front porch and three dormer windows lend Southern flair to this charming farmhouse. Inside, three fireplaces—found in the living, dining and family rooms—create a cozy atmosphere. The family room opens to the covered rear porch, while the breakfast area opens to a small side porch. Sleeping quarters include a luxurious first-floor master suite—with a private bath and two walk-in closets—as well as three family bedrooms upstairs.

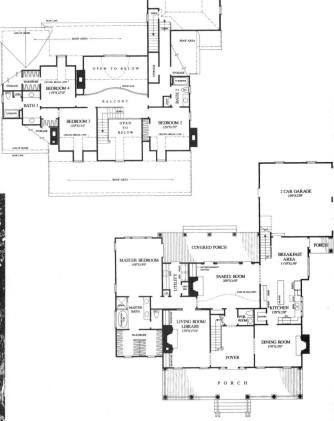

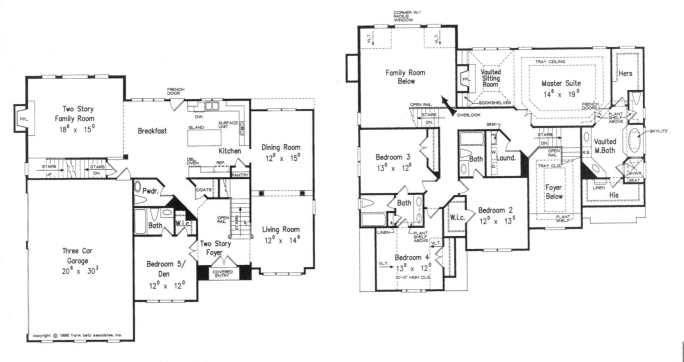

Design HPT860534

First Floor: 1,583 square feet
Second Floor: 1,632 square feet
Total: 3,215 square feet
Width: 58'-4" **Depth:** 50'-0"

From outside to inside, the decorative details on this stucco two-story home make it very special. Ceiling adornments are particularly interesting: the two-story foyer and the master bedroom have tray ceilings. The dining room and living room are separated by columns; another column graces the two-story family room. A den is reached through double doors just to the left of the foyer. Use it for an additional bedroom if needed—it has a private bath. There are four upstairs bedrooms in this plan. The master suite includes a fireplace in the vaulted sitting room.

Two Story
Family Room
18⁶ x 15⁰

Breakfast

FRENCH DOOR

DW.

ISLAND

SURFACE UNIT

Kitchen

Dining Room
12⁰ x 15⁰

FPL

STAIRS UP

STAIRS DN.

Pwdr.

Bath

W.i.c.

DBL. OVEN

REF.

COATS

PANTRY

OPEN RAIL

STAIRS

Living Room
12⁰ x 14⁶

Three Car
Garage
20⁶ x 30³

Bedroom 5/
Den
12⁰ x 12⁰

Two Story
Foyer

COVERED ENTRY

copyright © 1996 frank betz associates, inc.

DORMER W/ RADIUS WINDOW

VLT.

VLT.

Family Room
Below

Vaulted
Sitting
Room

FPL

TRAY CEILING

Master Suite
14⁶ x 19⁰

Hers

BOOKSHELVES

FRENCH DOORS

PLANT SHELF ABOVE

OPEN RAIL

STAIRS DN.

OVERLOOK

SINK

STAIRS DN.

Bedroom 3
13⁰ x 12⁰

Bath

Laund.

OPEN RAIL

Vaulted
M.Bath

SKYLITE

Bath

W.i.c.

Bedroom 2
12⁰ x 13⁵

TRAY CLG.

Foyer
Below

His

PLANT SHELF

LINEN

LINEN

PLANT SHELF ABOVE

VLT.

W.i.c.

Bedroom 4
13⁰ x 12⁰
10'-0" HIGH CLG.

VLT.

Design HPT860535

First Floor: 2,351 square feet
Second Floor: 866 square feet
Total: 3,217 square feet
Apartment: 596 square feet
Width: 113'-7" **Depth:** 57'-5"

If you've ever dreamed of living in a castle, this could be the home for you. The interior is also fit for royalty, from the formal dining room to the multi-purpose grand room to the comfortable sitting area off the kitchen. The master suite has its own fireplace, two walk-in closets and a compartmented bath with dual vanities and a garden tub. Two stairways lead to the second floor. One, housed in the turret, leads to a sitting area and a balcony overlooking the grand room. The balcony leads to two more bedrooms and a recreation room (or apartment) with a deck.

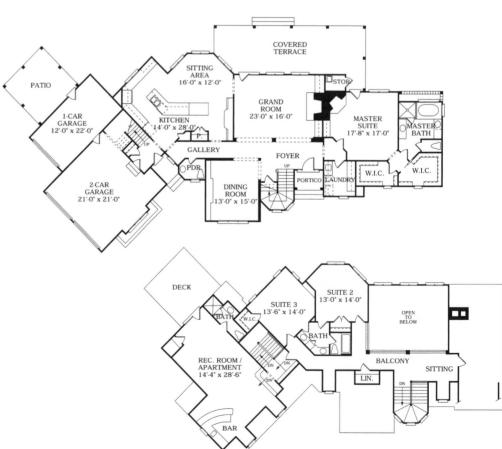

Design HPT860536

First Floor: 1,665 square feet
Second Floor: 1,554 square feet
Total: 3,219 square feet
Width: 58'-6" **Depth:** 44'-10"

This stately transitional home focuses on family living. The formal living areas are traditionally placed flanking the two-story foyer. The two-story family room has a lovely fireplace and windows to the rear yard. The remarkable kitchen features wraparound counters, a breakfast nook and a cooktop island/serving bar. A bedroom and full bath would make a comfortable guest suite or a quiet den. A balcony hall leads to two bedrooms that share a bath; a third bedroom has its own bath and walk-in closet. The master suite is designed with a tray ceiling and a sitting room with a through-fireplace to the vaulted bath. Please specify basement or crawlspace foundation when ordering.

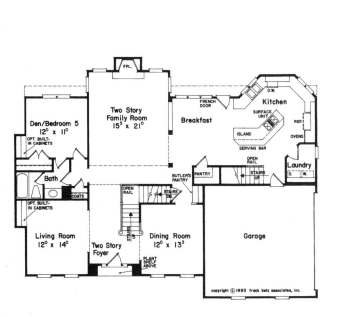

Quote One®

Cost to build? See page 454
to order complete cost estimate
to build this house in your area!

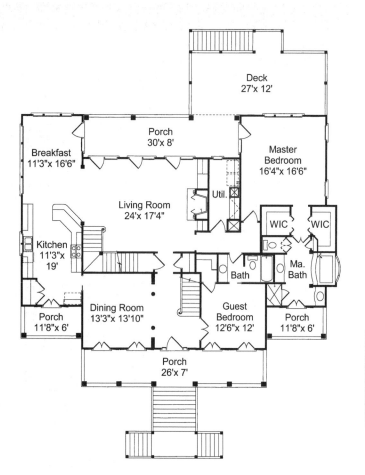

Deck
27'x 12'

Porch
30'x 8'

Breakfast
11'3"x 16'6"

Master
Bedroom
16'4"x 16'6"

Living Room
24'x 17'4"

Util.

Kitchen
11'3"x
19'

WIC

WIC

Bath

Ma.
Bath

Porch
11'8"x 6'

Dining Room
13'3"x 13'10"

Guest
Bedroom
12'6"x 12'

Porch
11'8"x 6'

Porch
26'x 7'

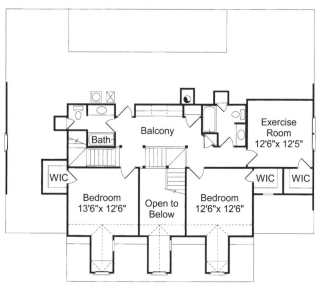

Bath

Balcony

Exercise
Room
12'6"x 12'5"

WIC

Bedroom
13'6"x 12'6"

Open to
Below

Bedroom
12'6"x 12'6"

WIC

WIC

Design HPT860537

First Floor: 2,213 square feet
Second Floor: 1,010 square feet
Total: 3,223 square feet
Width: 61'-4" **Depth:** 67'-0"

A raised porch welcomes guests and home-owners to relax in this four-bedroom design. French doors let in fresh breezes and allow entry to the dining room and guest bedroom on the first floor. The master bedroom sits to the right of the plan and enjoys deck and rear-porch access as well as a private front porch. The kitchen also features a private porch and adjoins a sunlit breakfast nook. A fireplace with built-ins adorns the living room. Two family bedrooms, two baths and an exercise room fill the second floor.

Design HPT860538

Main Level: 1,887 square feet
Lower Level: 1,338 square feet
Total: 3,225 square feet
Width: 65'-4" **Depth:** 52'-8"

A majestic window and a brick exterior provide an extra measure of style to this handsome traditional home. Straight ahead, upon entering the foyer, is the spacious great room. The kitchen and breakfast area are integrated with the gathering room. Entertaining is easy in the adjacent dining room. The large master suite is highlighted by double doors opening to the private dressing area. The lower level features a fabulous family room and two family bedrooms and offers a second fireplace.

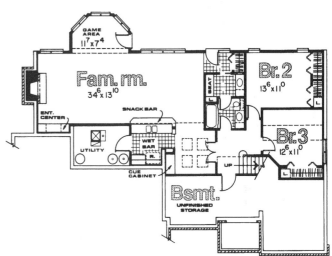

347

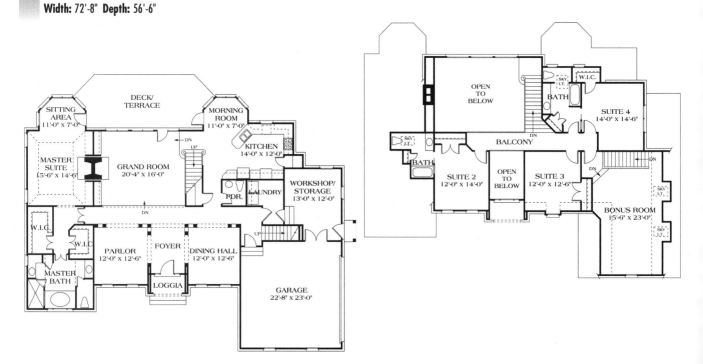

Design HPT860539

First Floor: 2,198 square feet
Second Floor: 1,028 square feet
Total: 3,226 square feet
Bonus Room: 466 square feet
Width: 72'-8" **Depth:** 56'-6"

Designed for active lifestyles, this home caters to homeowners who enjoy dinner guests, privacy, luxurious surroundings and open spaces. The foyer, parlor and dining hall are defined by sets of columns and share a gallery hall that runs through the center of the plan. The grand room opens to the deck/terrace, which is also accessed from the sitting area and morning room. The right wing of the plan contains the well-appointed kitchen. The left wing is dominated by the master suite with its sitting bay, fireplace, two walk-in closets and compartmented bath.

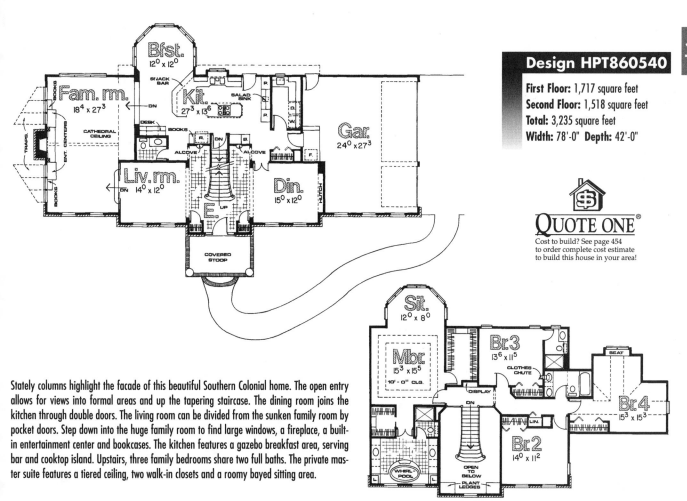

Design HPT860540

First Floor: 1,717 square feet
Second Floor: 1,518 square feet
Total: 3,235 square feet
Width: 78'-0" **Depth:** 42'-0"

QUOTE ONE®

Cost to build? See page 454
to order complete cost estimate
to build this house in your area!

Stately columns highlight the facade of this beautiful Southern Colonial home. The open entry allows for views into formal areas and up the tapering staircase. The dining room joins the kitchen through double doors. The living room can be divided from the sunken family room by pocket doors. Step down into the huge family room to find large windows, a fireplace, a built-in entertainment center and bookcases. The kitchen features a gazebo breakfast area, serving bar and cooktop island. Upstairs, three family bedrooms share two full baths. The private master suite features a tiered ceiling, two walk-in closets and a roomy bayed sitting area.

OFFICE
15'-4" x 19'-10"

COVERED
TERRACE

GUEST
SUITE
14'-0" x 18'-6"

BATH

RECREATION
ROOM
24'-0" x 17'-0"

UNFIN.
STOR.

BAR

UP

WINE
CELLAR

UNFIN.
STOR.

MASTER
SUITE
16'-0" x 20'-8"

TERRACE/
DECK

SUNROOM
14'-10" x 14'-5"

GREAT
ROOM
19'-10" x 17'-2"

DINING
ROOM
12'-4" x 15'-0"

BREAKFAST
14'-10" x 12'-9"

MASTER
BATH

W.I.C.

BAR

PDR.

FOYER

UP

BATH

STUDY/GUEST/
LIBRARY
13'-0" x 14'-2"

LOGGIA

OPT.
DN

KITCHEN
15'-4" x 16'-0"

W.I.C.

LAUNDRY

PANT

GARAGE
24'-2" x 25'-6"

STOR.

OPEN
TO
BELOW

SUITE 4
13'-0" x 13'-0"

BATH

W.I.C.

OPEN
TO
BELOW

BALCONY

DN

SUITE 3
15'-4" x 11'-4"

W.I.C.

DN

BONUS
ROOM
14'-4" x 24'-3"

Design HPT860541

First Floor: 2,520 square feet
Second Floor: 723 square feet
Total: 3,243 square feet
Finished Basement: 1,021 square feet
Bonus Room: 321 square feet
Width: 72'-10" **Depth:** 73'-3"

Grand luxury abounds in this stucco rendition. Corner quoins, high arched windows and a sensational entry all spell classic estate details. Note the multi-purpose room just off the foyer that can be used as a study, library or guest room. The great room is separated from the dining room by columns and is warmed by a hearth flanked by bookcases. The U-shaped island kitchen opens to the breakfast room and its adjoining sun room. Placement of the master suite on the first floor guarantees privacy. The private master bath holds a spa tub in a bay window, a separate shower and double sinks.

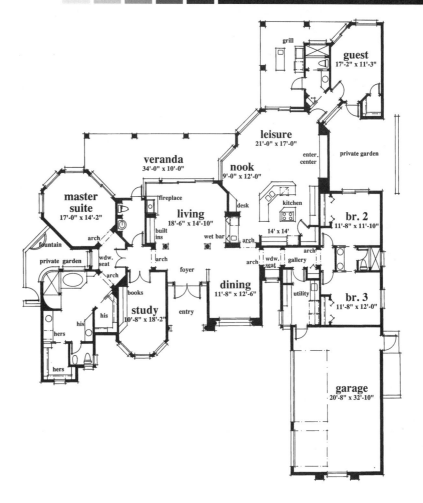

grill

guest
17'-2" x 11'-3"

leisure
21'-0" x 17'-0"

enter. center

private garden

veranda
34'-0" x 10'-0"

nook
9'-0" x 12'-0"

Design HPT860542

Square Footage: 3,265
Width: 80'-0" **Depth:** 103'-8"

A turret study and a raised entry add elegance to this marvelous stucco home. A guest suite includes a full bath, porch access and a private garden entry, making it perfect for use as an in-law suite. Secondary bedrooms share a full bath. The master suite has a foyer with a window seat overlooking another private garden and fountain area; the private master bath holds dual closets, a garden tub and a curved-glass shower.

master suite
17'-0" x 14'-2"

fireplace

living
18'-6" x 14'-10"

desk

kitchen

14' x 14'

br. 2
11'-8" x 11'-10"

built ins

wet bar

arch

arch

arch

fountain

private garden

wdw. seat

arch

foyer

wdw. seat

gallery

br. 3
11'-8" x 12'-0"

books

study
10'-8" x 18'-2"

his

his

dining
11'-8" x 12'-6"

utility

entry

hers

hers

garage
20'-8" x 32'-10"

351

Design HPT860544

Square Footage: 3,268
Width: 98'-0" **Depth:** 67'-3"

Brick, with accents of stone, define the stately facade of this home. The entry hall provides convenient access to the study (or make it a bedroom), the formal dining room, the formal living room and the kitchen. Living spaces to the rear include a breakfast nook with a snack bar and the angled family room. Three family bedrooms dominate the right side of the plan—one has a private bath. The master suite sits on the left side and accesses the rear patio and an amenity-filled bath.

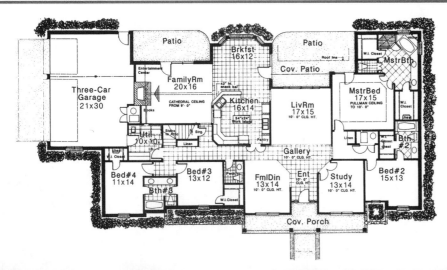

Design HPT860543

Square Footage: 3,270
Width: 101'-0" **Depth:** 48'-1"

A distinctive exterior, a cathedral ceiling in the large family room, and room to expand make this country contemporary home a good choice. A study and formal dining room flank the entryway; three family bedrooms align across the front. The master suite offers plenty of seclusion, and two patio areas add outdoor livability to this plan.

Design HPT860545

First Floor: 1,598 square feet
Second Floor: 1,675 square feet
Total: 3,273 square feet
Bonus Room: 534 square feet
Width: 54'-8" **Depth:** 68'-0"

First- and second-level covered porches, accompanied by intricate detailing, and many multi-pane windows create a splendid Southern mansion. The prominent entry opens to formal dining and living rooms. The grand family room is warmed by a fireplace and views a screened porch with a cozy window seat. The roomy breakfast area provides access to the porch and the three-car garage. French doors open to the second-floor master suite, which features decorative ceiling details, His and Hers walk-in closets, a large dressing area, dual lavs, a whirlpool bath and a separate shower area.

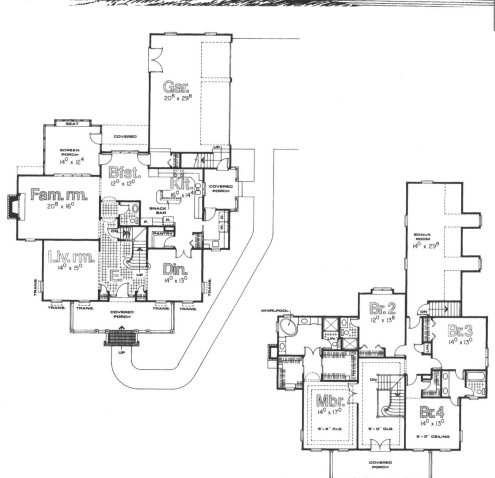

Design HPT860546

Square Footage: 3,278
Width: 75'-10" **Depth:** 69'-4"

L

Form follows function as dual gallery halls lead from formal areas to split sleeping quarters in this Prairie adaptation. At the heart of the plan, the grand-scale great room offers a raised-hearth fireplace framed by built-in cabinetry and plant shelves. Open planning combines the country kitchen with an informal dining space and adds an island counter with a snack bar. A lavish master suite harbors a sitting area with private access to the covered pergola. The secondary sleeping wing includes a spacious guest suite. A fifth bedroom or home office offers its own door to the wrap-around porch.

QUOTE ONE®
Cost to build? See page 454
to order complete cost estimate
to build this house in your area!

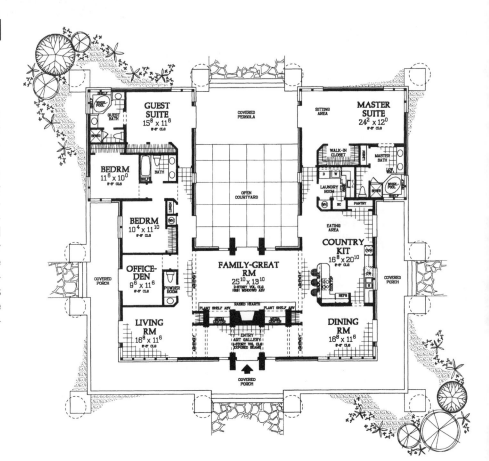

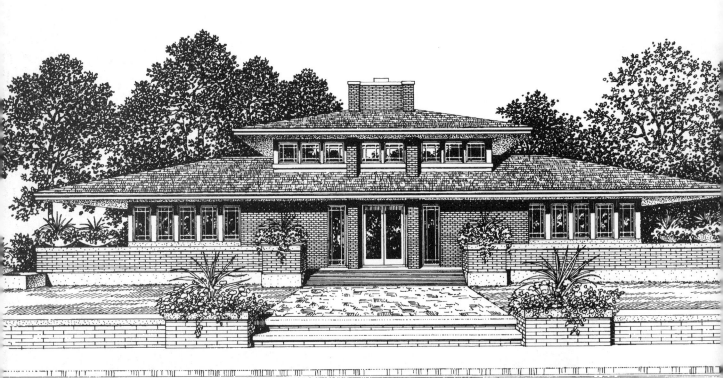

Design HPT860547

First Floor: 1,700 square feet
Second Floor: 1,585 square feet
Total: 3,285 square feet
Bonus Room: 176 square feet
Width: 60'-0" **Depth:** 47'-6"

The covered front stoop of this two-story traditionally styled home gives way to the foyer and formal areas inside. A cozy living room with a fireplace sits on the right and an elongated dining room is on the left. For fine family living, a great room and a kitchen/breakfast area account for the rear of the first-floor plan. A guest room with a nearby full bath finishes off the accommodations. Upstairs, four bedrooms include a master suite fit for a king. A bonus room rests near Bedroom 3 and would make a great office or additional bedroom. This home is designed with a walkout basement foundation.

QUOTE ONE®

Cost to build? See page 454
to order complete cost estimate
to build this house in your area!

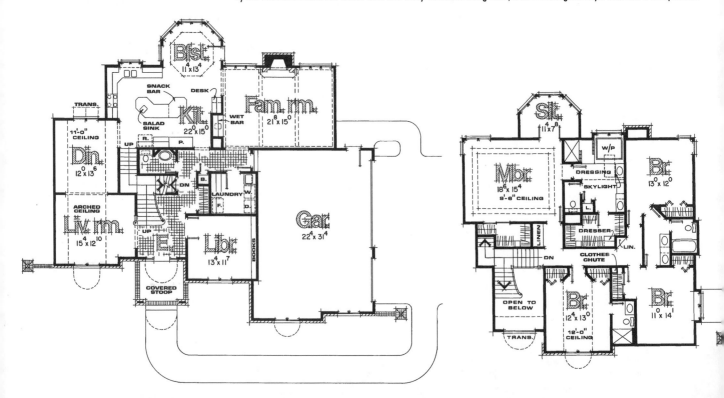

Design HPT860548

First Floor: 1,709 square feet
Second Floor: 1,597 square feet
Total: 3,306 square feet
Width: 62'-0" **Depth:** 55'-4"

An attractive facade and amenity-filled interior make this home a showplace both outside and in. Immediately off the two-story foyer is the living room and formal dining room, both with interesting ceiling details, and the quiet library with built-in bookcases. The enormous gourmet kitchen features a large island work counter/snack bar, pantry, desk and gazebo breakfast room. Just steps away is the spacious family room with a grand fireplace and windows overlooking the backyard. Upstairs are three family bedrooms served by two baths and a luxurious master suite with a bay-windowed sitting room, detailed ceiling and skylit bath with a whirlpool tub.

357

Design HPT860549

First Floor: 2,391 square feet
Second Floor: 922 square feet
Total: 3,313 square feet
Finished Basement: 1,964 square feet
Bonus Room: 400 square feet
Width: 63'-10" **Depth:** 85'-6"

Here's an upscale multi-level plan with expansive rear views. The first floor provides an open living and dining area, defined by decorative columns and enhanced by natural light from tall windows. A breakfast area with a lovely triple window opens to a sun room, which allows light to pour into the gourmet kitchen. The master wing features a tray ceiling in the bedroom, two walk-in closets and an elegant private vestibule leading to a lavish bath. Upstairs, a reading loft overlooks the great room and leads to a sleeping area with two suites. A recreation room, exercise room, office, guest suite and additional storage are available in the finished basement.

Design HPT860550

Main Level: 1,096 square feet
Upper Level: 1,115 square feet
Lower Level: 1,104 square feet
Total: 3,315 square feet
Width: 40'-0" **Depth:** 58'-0"

L

A splendidly asymmetrical design, this clean-lined, open-planned contemporary home is a great place for the outdoor minded. The gathering room (with a fireplace), dining room and breakfast room all lead out to a deck off the main level. Similarly, the lower-level activity room, complete with another fireplace, hobby room and guest bedroom, contain separate doors to the backyard terrace. Upstairs reside three bedrooms, including a master suite with a through-fireplace, private balcony, walk-in closet, dressing room and whirlpool tub.

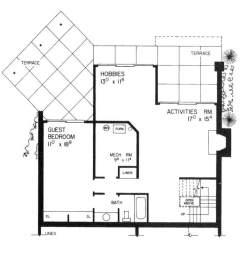

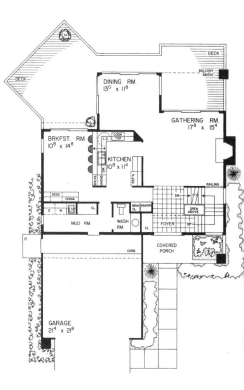

Cost to build? See page 454 to order complete cost estimate to build this house in your area!

QUOTE ONE®

358

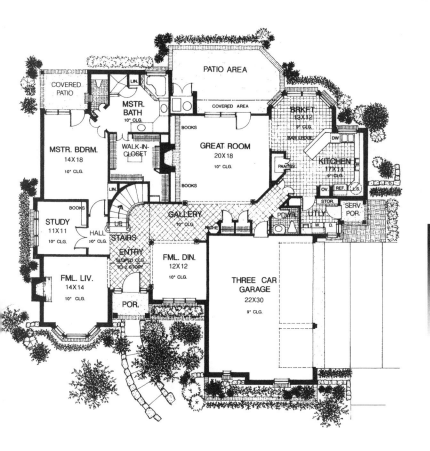

Design HPT860551

First Floor: 2,438 square feet
Second Floor: 882 square feet
Total: 3,320 square feet
Bonus Room: 230 square feet
Width: 70'-0" **Depth:** 63'-2"

Wonderful rooflines top a brick exterior with cedar and stone accents and lots of English country charm. The two-story entry reveals a graceful curving staircase and opens to the formal living and dining rooms. Fireplaces are found in the living room as well as the great room, which also boasts built-in bookcases and access to the rear patio. The kitchen and breakfast room add to the informal area and include a snack bar. A private patio is part of the master suite, which also offers a lavish bath, a large walk-in closet and a nearby study. Three family bedrooms and a bonus room comprise the second floor.

359

Design HPT860552

First Floor: 2,129 square feet
Second Floor: 1,206 square feet
Total: 3,335 square feet
Finished Basement: 435 square feet
Width: 59'-4" **Depth:** 64'-0"

French style embellishes this dormered country home. Stepping through French doors to the foyer, the dining area is immediately to the left. To the right is a set of double doors leading to a study or secondary bedroom. A lavish master bedroom provides privacy and plenty of storage space. The living room sports three doors to the rear porch and a lovely fireplace with built-ins. A secluded breakfast nook adjoins an efficient kitchen. Upstairs, two of the three family bedrooms boast dormer windows. Plans include a basement-level garage that adjoins a game room and two handy storage areas.

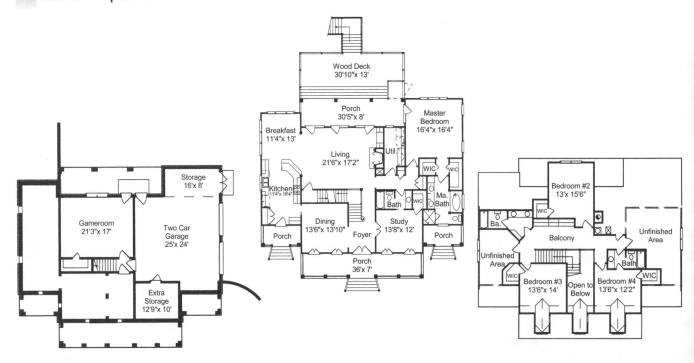

Design HPT860553

First Floor: 2,432 square feet
Second Floor: 903 square feet
Total: 3,335 square feet
Width: 90'-0" **Depth:** 53'-10"

The elegant symmetry of this four-bedroom Southern traditional plan makes it a joy to own. Six columns frame the covered porch, and two chimneys add interest to the exterior roofline. The two-story foyer opens to the right to a formal living room with a built-in wet bar and a fireplace. A massive family room with a cathedral ceiling leads outside to a large covered patio or to the breakfast room and kitchen. A side-entry, three-car garage provides room for a golf cart and separate workshop area. The first-floor master bedroom features vaulted ceilings, a secluded covered patio and a plant ledge in the master bath. The three bedrooms upstairs share two baths.

Design HPT860554

First Floor: 1,989 square feet
Second Floor: 1,349 square feet
Total: 3,338 square feet
Lower Entry: 105 square feet
Bonus Room: 487 square feet
Width: 63'-0" **Depth:** 48'-0"

Dramatic balconies and spectacular window treatments enhance this stunning luxury home. Inside, a through-fireplace warms the formal living room and a restful den. Both living spaces open to a balcony that invites quiet reflection on starry nights. The banquet-sized dining room is easily served from the adjacent kitchen. Here, space is shared with an eating nook that provides access to the rear grounds and a family room with a corner fireplace—perfect for casual gatherings. The upper level contains two family bedrooms and a luxurious master suite that enjoys its own private balcony. The lower level accommodates a shop and a bonus room for future development.

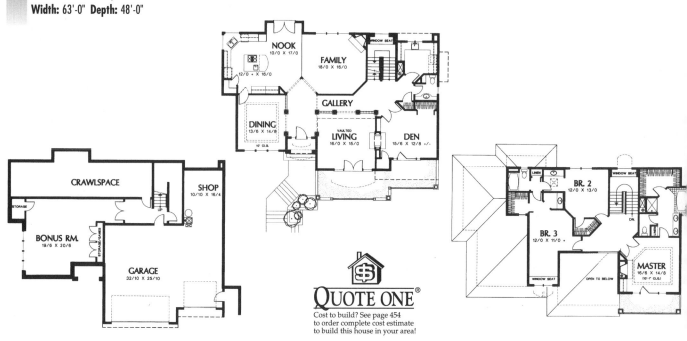

Quote One®
Cost to build? See page 454
to order complete cost estimate
to build this house in your area!

362

Design HPT860555

First Floor: 2,159 square feet
Second Floor: 1,179 square feet
Total: 3,338 square feet
Bonus Room: 360 square feet
Width: 68'-0" **Depth:** 69'-0"

This attractive Plantation-style home exhibits a floor plan that is completely up-to-date, beginning with the secluded master suite and its lavish bath. The foyer is flanked by the living room and the dining room and leads ahead to the morning room. The family chef will enjoy the open kitchen and its nearby pantry and wet bar. The family room features a fireplace and built-ins. The second floor contains three bedrooms, two baths, a bonus room and attic storage.

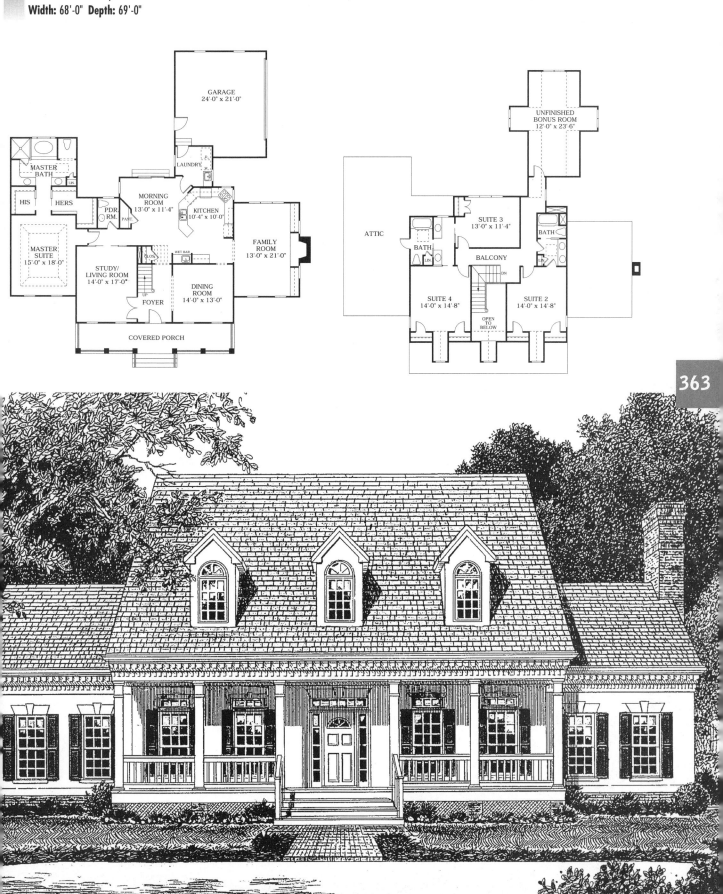

363

Design HPT860556

First Floor: 2,355 square feet
Second Floor: 987 square feet
Total: 3,342 square feet
Width: 61'-6" **Depth:** 52'-6"

The front of this traditional home is characterized by the arch pattern evident in the windows, doorway and above the columned front porch. The master suite includes a vaulted study that also opens from the foyer. The study's two-sided fireplace also warms the bedroom. Through the master suite and beyond two walk-in closets is a bath with dual vanities. Upstairs, there are three more bedrooms and two full baths. This home is designed with a walkout basement foundation.

QUOTE ONE®
Cost to build? See page 454
to order complete cost estimate
to build this house in your area!

Design HPT860557

Square Footage: 3,352
Width: 91'-0" **Depth:** 71'-9"

From the nicely detailed covered porch, enter the formal dining room to the right and the living room to the rear. The arched gallery leads past the kitchen with an island and bar to the family room with a fireplace and built-in entertainment center. Adjoining the kitchen and family room is the bay-windowed breakfast nook which looks out to the rear patio. Three family bedrooms are located to the front. Bedroom 4 offers a private full bath, while Bedrooms 2 and 3 have private vanities in the shared full bath. The left side of the plan is comprised of the master suite and the double-door, bay-windowed study with built-ins.

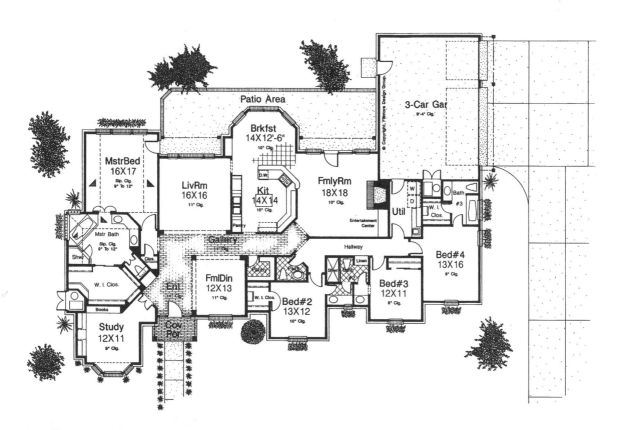

Design HPT860558

First Floor: 1,678 square feet
Second Floor: 1,677 square feet
Total: 3,355 square feet
Width: 50'-0" **Depth:** 50'-6"

This English manor home features a dramatic brick-and-stucco exterior. Inside, the foyer opens to the formal living room accented with a vaulted ceiling and box-bay window. The dining room flows directly off the living room and features its own angled bay window. An entire wall of glass, accented by a central fireplace, spans from the family room through to the breakfast area and kitchen. For your guests, a bedroom and bath are located on the main level. The second floor provides two additional bedrooms and a bath for children. The master suite is a pleasant retreat. This home is designed with a walkout basement foundation.

Design HPT860559

First Floor: 2,384 square feet
Second Floor: 1,023 square feet
Total: 3,407 square feet
Bonus Room: 228 square feet
Width: 63'-4" **Depth:** 57'-0"

The covered front porch of this stucco home opens to a two-story foyer and one of two staircases. Arched openings lead into both the formal dining room and the vaulted living room. The efficient kitchen features a walk-in pantry, built-in desk, work island and separate snack bar. Nearby, the large breakfast area opens to the family room. Lavish in its amenities, the master suite offers a separate vaulted sitting room with a fireplace, among other luxuries. Three bedrooms, along with optional bonus space and attic storage, are found on the second floor. Please specify basement or crawlspace foundation when ordering.

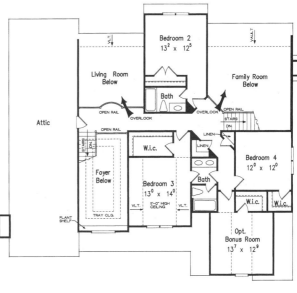

367

Design HPT860560

First Floor: 2,026 square feet
Second Floor: 1,386 square feet
Total: 3,412 square feet
Width: 84'-0" **Depth:** 65'-8"

L

This two-story design faithfully recalls the 18th-Century homestead of Secretary of Foreign Affairs John Jay. First-floor livability includes a grand living room with a fireplace and a music alcove. The nearby library also sports a fireplace and convenient built-ins. A large country kitchen delights with another fireplace and a snack bar. A large clutter room has an attached half-bath and allows plenty of space for hobbies or a workshop. Three upstairs bedrooms include a large master suite with a walk-in closet, vanity seating and double sinks. Each family bedroom contains a double closet.

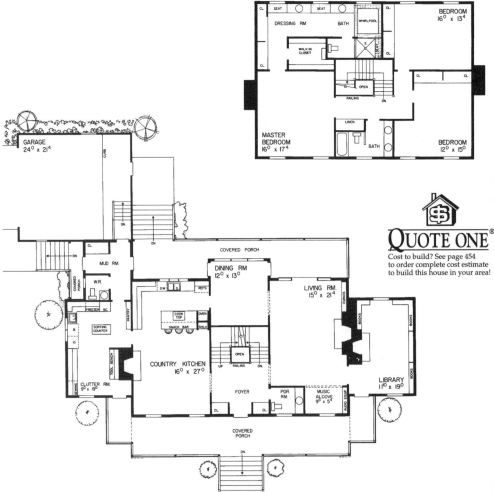

QUOTE ONE®

Cost to build? See page 454 to order complete cost estimate to build this house in your area!

Design HPT860561

First Floor: 2,347 square feet
Second Floor: 1,087 square feet
Total: 3,434 square feet
Width: 93'-6" **Depth:** 61'-0"

L

Dutch-gable rooflines and a gabled wraparound porch provide an extra measure of farmhouse style. The foyer opens on the left to the study or guest bedroom that leads to the master suite. To the right is the formal dining room; the massive great room is in the center. The kitchen combines with the great room, the breakfast nook and the dining room for entertaining options. The master suite includes access to the covered patio, a spacious walk-in closet and a full bath with a whirlpool tub.

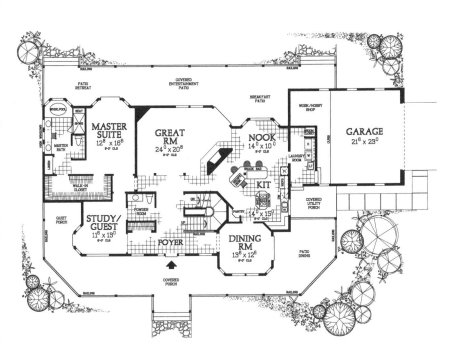

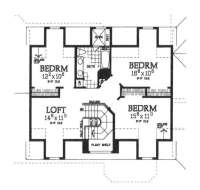

QUOTE ONE®

Cost to build? See page 454
to order complete cost estimate
to build this house in your area!

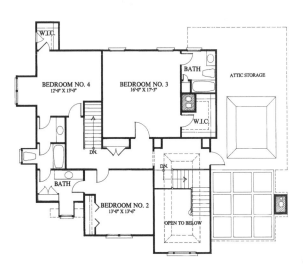

Design HPT860562

First Floor: 2,208 square feet
Second Floor: 1,250 square feet
Total: 3,458 square feet
Width: 60'-6" **Depth:** 60'-0"

Quaint, yet majestic, this European-style stucco home enjoys the enchantment of arched windows to underscore its charm. The two-story foyer leads through French doors to the study with its own hearth and coffered ceiling. Coupled with this cozy sanctuary is the master suite with a tray ceiling and large accommodating bath. The large sunken great room is highlighted by a fireplace, built-in bookcases, lots of glass and easy access to a back stair and large gourmet kitchen. Three secondary bedrooms reside upstairs. One upstairs bedroom gives guests a private bath and walk-in closet. This home is designed with a walkout basement foundation.

370

Design HPT860563

First Floor: 2,470 square feet
Second Floor: 1,000 square feet
Total: 3,470 square feet
Width: 79'-0" **Depth:** 58'-0"

Double columns flank the elegant entry to this four-bedroom home. Inside, the two-story foyer leads to a cozy study on the right and a formal dining room on the left. The kitchen features a cooktop island, snack bar into the nook and access to the nearby sun room. The first-floor master bedroom is full of amenities: a bayed sitting area, a walk-in closet and a cathedral ceiling in the lavish bath. Upstairs, a balcony overlooks the family room and the foyer and leads to three secondary bedrooms—each with walk-in closets. The four-car garage will easily shelter the family fleet and also features plenty of storage space.

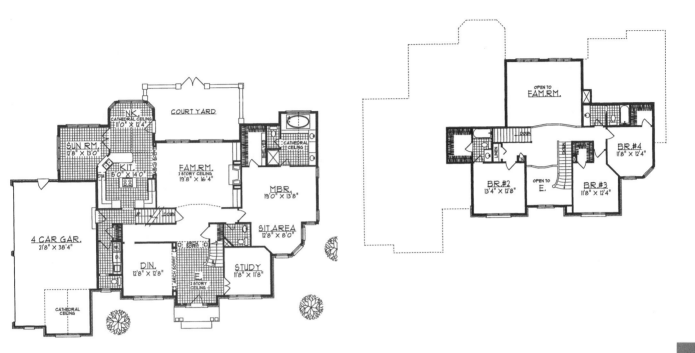

371

FREILING

Design HPT860564

First Floor: 2,500 square feet
Second Floor: 973 square feet
Total: 3,473 square feet
Width: 84'-0" **Depth:** 52'-0"

Step between the columns and into the entry of this grand design. Large living and dining rooms flank a formal staircase. The great room features a fourteen-foot beamed ceiling, a fireplace and wonderful views. Nearby sits the octagon-shaped breakfast nook and the kitchen with abundant counter space. This house incorporates four bedrooms, with the master bedroom on the first floor. A tiered ceiling, two walk-in closets and a luxurious bath with His and Hers vanities, a shower and a spa tub all characterize this suite. On the second floor, you'll find three bedrooms: two share a full bath and one has a private bath.

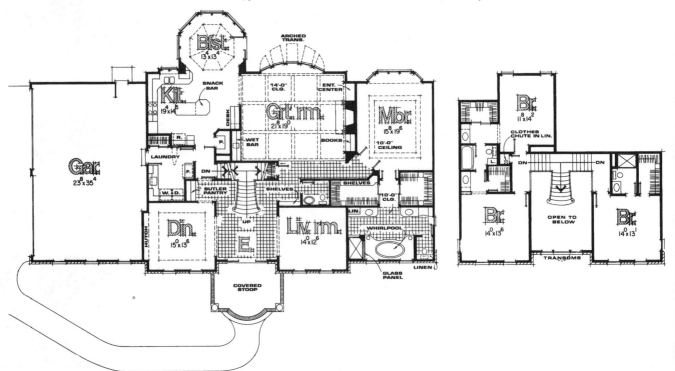

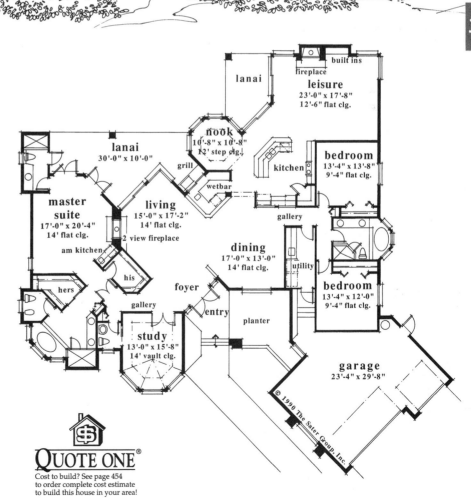

Design HPT860565

Square Footage: 3,477
Width: 95'-0" **Depth:** 88'-8"

Make dreams come true with this fine sunny design. An octagonal study provides a nice focal point both inside and outside. The living areas remain open to each other and access outdoor areas. A wet bar makes entertaining a breeze, especially with a window pass-through to a grill area on the lanai. The kitchen enjoys shared space with a lovely breakfast nook and a bright leisure room. Two bedrooms are located near the family living center. In the master bedroom suite, luxury abounds with a two-way fireplace, a morning kitchen, two walk-in closets and a compartmented bath. Another full bath accommodates a pool area.

QUOTE ONE®

Cost to build? See page 454
to order complete cost estimate
to build this house in your area!

Design HPT860566

First Floor: 2,302 square feet
Second Floor: 1,177 square feet
Total: 3,479 square feet
Width: 66'-3" **Depth:** 57'-9"

Gently arched cornices and keystones call up a sense of history with this traditional home. Formal rooms flank the two-story foyer, which leads to comfortably elegant living space with an extended-hearth fireplace. A sizable kitchen serves the formal dining room through a butler's pantry and overlooks the breakfast room. A secluded home office is a quiet place for business conversations. The master suite nestles to the rear of the plan and offers many amenities. Upstairs, Bedrooms 3 and 4 share a full bath that includes two lavatories, while Bedroom 2 enjoys a private bath. This home is designed with a walkout basement foundation.

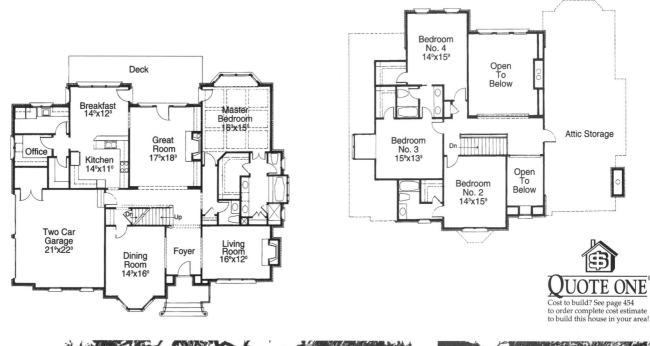

Quote One®
Cost to build? See page 454
to order complete cost estimate
to build this house in your area!

374

Design HPT860567

First Floor: 2,853 square feet
Second Floor: 627 square feet
Total: 3,480 square feet
Guest House: 312 square feet
Width: 80'-0" **Depth:** 96'-0"

L

A unique courtyard provides a happy marriage of indoor/outdoor relationships for this design. Inside, the foyer opens to a grand salon with a wall of glass, providing unobstructed views of the backyard. Informal areas include a leisure room with an entertainment center and glass doors that open to a covered poolside lanai. An outdoor fireplace enhances casual gatherings. The master suite is filled with amenities that include a bayed sitting area, access to the rear lanai, His and Hers closets and a soaking tub. Upstairs, two family bedrooms—both with private decks—share a full bath. A detached guest house has a cabana bath and an outdoor grill area.

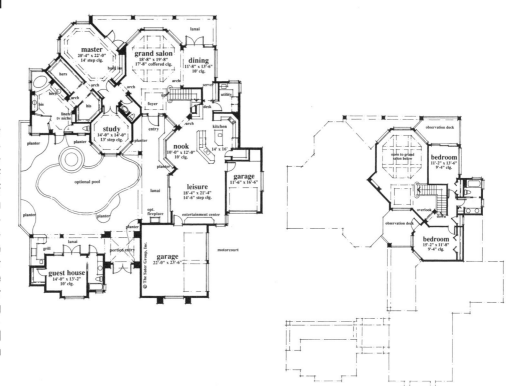

375

Design HPT860568

First Floor: 2,469 square feet
Second Floor: 1,025 square feet
Total: 3,494 square feet
Bonus Room: 320 square feet
Width: 67'-8" **Depth:** 74'-2"

L

A lovely double arch gives this European-style home a commanding presence. Once inside, a two-story foyer provides an open view directly through the formal living room to the rear grounds beyond. The spacious kitchen with a work island and the bayed breakfast area share space with the family room. The private master suite features dual sinks, twin walk-in closets, a corner garden tub and a separate shower. A large game room completes this wonderful family home. Please specify basement, crawlspace or slab foundation when ordering.

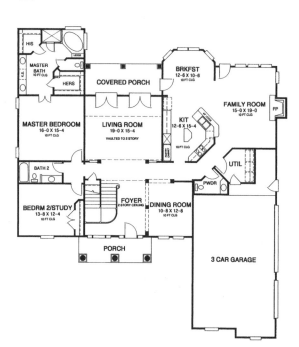

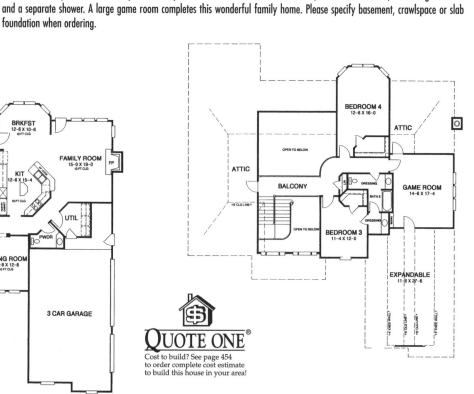

QUOTE ONE®

Cost to build? See page 454
to order complete cost estimate
to build this house in your area!

Design HPT860569

First Floor: 2,315 square feet
Second Floor: 1,200 square feet
Total: 3,515 square feet
Width: 77'-4" **Depth:** 46'-8"

Dormer windows and a traditional brick and siding exterior create a welcoming facade on this home. Inside, the entry foyer opens to a formal zone consisting of a living room to the left and a dining room to the right. The kitchen enjoys a pass-through to the breakfast area—the great room is just a step away. Double doors grant passage to the backyard. Beyond the first-floor gallery, the master bedroom boasts a tray ceiling, bay window and lavish bath. Upstairs, three family bedrooms all have walk-in closets. This home is designed with a walkout basement foundation.

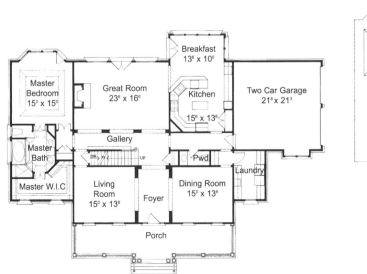

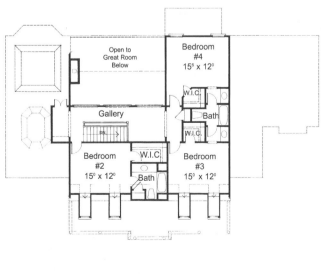

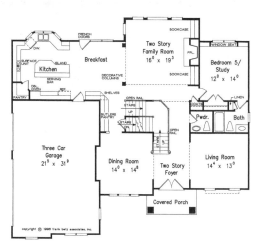

Design HPT860570

First Floor: 1,786 square feet
Second Floor: 1,739 square feet
Total: 3,525 square feet
Width: 59'-0" **Depth:** 53'-0"

European details dress up this home that includes a two-story family room with a centered fireplace. A butler's pantry eases serving in the dining room. The second floor contains a generous master suite and three family bedrooms—one with a private bath. Please specify basement or crawlspace foundation when ordering.

Design HPT860571

First Floor: 2,660 square feet
Second Floor: 914 square feet
Total: 3,574 square feet
Bonus Room: 733 square feet
Width: 114'-8" **Depth:** 75'-10"

Gently curved arches and dormers contrast with the straight lines of gables and wooden columns on this French-style stone exterior. Inside, a spacious gathering room, with a fireplace, opens to a cheery morning room. The kitchen is a delight, with a beam ceiling, triangular work island, walk-in pantry and angular counter with a snack bar. The first-floor master suite boasts a bay-windowed sitting nook and a handy study. The second floor includes two bedroom suites and a large guest area.

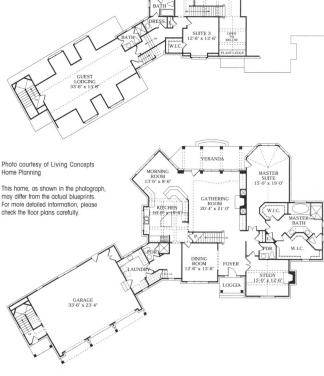

Photo courtesy of Living Concepts Home Planning

This home, as shown in the photograph, may differ from the actual blueprints. For more detailed information, please check the floor plans carefully.

A myriad of glass and ornamental stucco detailing complements the asymmetrical facade of this two-story home. Inside, the striking two-story foyer provides a dramatic entrance. To the right is the formal dining room. An efficient L-shaped kitchen and bayed breakfast nook are conveniently located near the dining area. The living room, with its welcoming fireplace, opens through double doors to the rear terrace. The private master suite provides access to the rear terrace and adjacent study. The master bath is sure to please with its many amenities. The second floor contains three large bedrooms, one with a private bath, while the others share a bath. This home is designed with a walkout basement foundation.

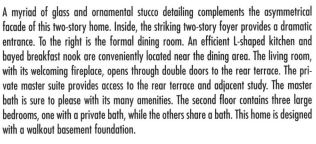

QUOTE ONE®

Cost to build? See page 454
to order complete cost estimate
to build this house in your area!

Design HPT860572

First Floor: 2,461 square feet
Second Floor: 1,114 square feet
Total: 3,575 square feet
Width: 84'-4" **Depth:** 63'-0"

379

Design HPT860573

First Floor: 2,603 square feet
Second Floor: 1,020 square feet
Total: 3,623 square feet
Width: 76'-8" **Depth:** 68'-0"

Perhaps the most notable characteristic of this traditional house is its masterful use of space. The glorious great room, open dining room and handsome den serve as the heart of the home. A cozy hearth room with a fireplace rounds out the kitchen and breakfast area. The master bedroom opens up to a private sitting room with a fireplace. Three family bedrooms occupy the second floor, each one with a private bath. Other special features include a four-car garage, a corner whirlpool tub in the master bath, a walk-in pantry and snack bar in the kitchen, and transom windows in the dining room.

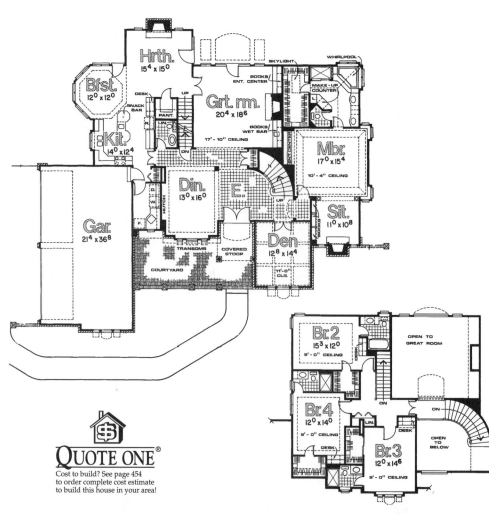

QUOTE ONE®
Cost to build? See page 454
to order complete cost estimate
to build this house in your area!

Design HPT860574

First Floor: 2,380 square feet
Second Floor: 1,295 square feet
Total: 3,675 square feet
Width: 77'-4" **Depth:** 58'-4"

Finely crafted porches—front, side and rear—make this home a classic in traditional Southern living. Past the large French doors, the impressive foyer is flanked by the formal living and dining rooms. Beyond the stair is a vaulted great room with an expanse of windows, a fireplace and built-in bookcases. From here, the breakfast room and kitchen are easily accessible and open to a private side porch. The master suite provides a large bath, two spacious closets and a fireplace. The second floor contains three bedrooms with private bath access and a playroom. This home is designed with a walkout basement foundation.

QUOTE ONE®
Cost to build? See page 454
to order complete cost estimate
to build this house in your area!

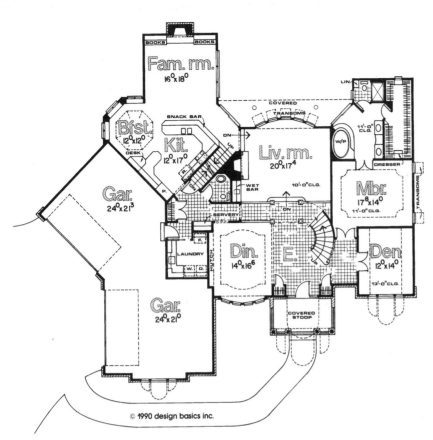

Fam. rm.
16⁰ x 18⁰

BOOKS   BOOKS

Bfst.
12⁰ x 12⁰

DESK

SNACK BAR

Kit.
12⁰ x 17⁰

COVERED
TRANSOMS

LIN.

11'-0"
CLG.

Gar.
24⁰ x 21³

WET
BAR

Liv. rm.
20⁰ x 17⁴

10'-0"CLG.

Mbr.
17⁸ x 14⁰

11'-0" CLG.

DRESSER

SERVERY

P.

DN

TRANSOMS

LAUNDRY

Din.
14⁰ x 16⁶

E.

Den
12⁰ x 14⁰

13'-0" CLG.

R.

W. D.

Gar.
24⁰ x 21⁰

COVERED
STOOP

© 1990 design basics inc.

382

Design HPT860575

First Floor: 2,617 square feet
Second Floor: 1,072 square feet
Total: 3,689 square feet
Width: 83'-5" **Depth:** 73'-4"

A spectacular volume entry with a curving staircase opens through columns to the formal areas of this home. The sunken living room contains a fireplace, a wet bar and a bowed window, while the front-facing dining room offers a built-in hutch. The family room, with bookcases surrounding a fireplace, is open to a bayed breakfast nook, and both are easily served from the nearby kitchen. Placed away from the living area of the home, the den provides a quiet retreat. The master suite on the first floor contains an elegant bath and a huge walk-in closet. Second-floor bedrooms also include walk-in closets and private baths.

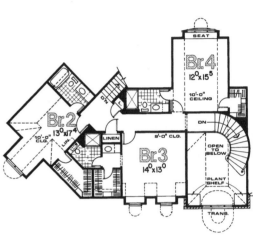

SEAT

Br. 4
12⁰ x 15⁵

Br. 2
13⁰ x 17⁴

10'-0"
CLG.

10'-0"
CEILING

DN

LINEN

LIN.

9'-0" CLG.

DN

Br. 3
14⁰ x 13⁰

OPEN
TO
BELOW

PLANT
SHELF

TRANS.

G. MACDONALD

Design HPT860576

First Floor: 2,700 square feet
Second Floor: 990 square feet
Total: 3,690 square feet
Bonus Room: 365 square feet
Width: 76'-0" **Depth:** 74'-1"

This cottage-style home looks as if it was nestled in the French countryside. The combination of brick, stone and rough cedar, and multiple chimneys add to the charm of the facade. The gracious two-story entry leads to all areas of the home. A beautiful curving staircase leads to an upper balcony overlooking the entry. The second floor consists of three bedrooms, each with a connecting bath and walk-in closet. Space for a future playroom is located above the garage. Downstairs, the family area with a cathedral ceiling is open to the large kitchen and breakfast area. A large pantry is located near the kitchen. The cozy study has its own marble fireplace and a vaulted ceiling.

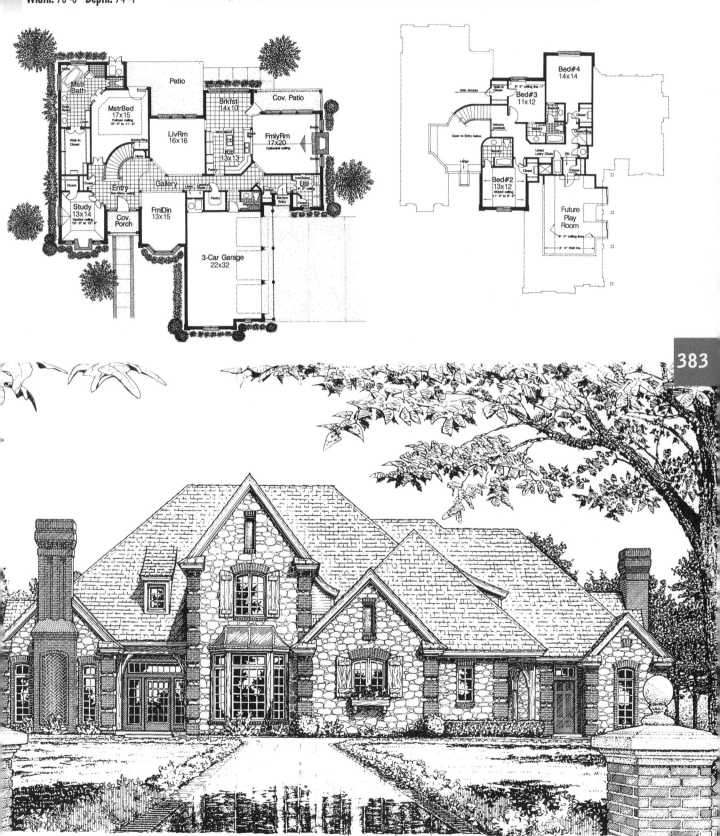

383

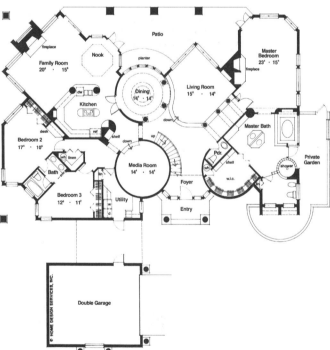

Design HPT860577

First Floor: 3,236 square feet
Second Floor: 494 square feet
Total: 3,730 square feet
Width: 80'-0" **Depth:** 89'-10"

If you want to build a home light years ahead of most other designs, non-traditional, yet addresses every need for your family, this showcase home is for you. From the moment you walk into this home, you are confronted with wonderful interior architecture that reflects modern, yet refined taste. The exterior says contemporary; the interior creates special excitement. Note the special rounded corners found throughout the home and the many amenities. The master suite is especially appealing with a fireplace and grand bath. Upstairs are a library/sitting room and a very private den or guest bedroom.

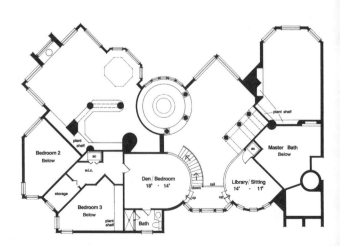

385

Design HPT860578

Main Level: 2,196 square feet
Lower Level: 1,542 square feet
Total: 3,738 square feet
Width: 72'-0" **Depth:** 56'-0"

This refined hillside home is designed for lots that fall off toward the rear and works especially well with a view out the back. The kitchen and eating nook wrap around the vaulted family room where arched transom windows flank the fireplace. Formal living is graciously centered in the living room and the adjoining dining room. A grand master suite is located on the main level for convenience and privacy. Downstairs, three family bedrooms share a compartmented hall bath. This home may also be built with a crawlspace foundation.

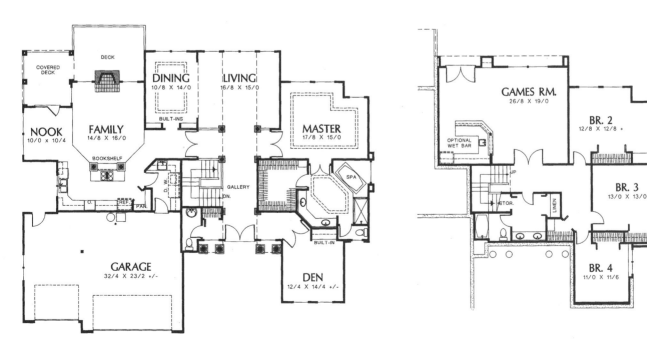

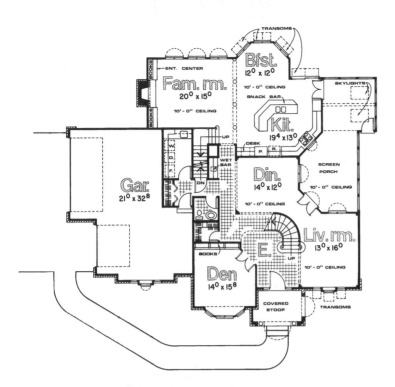

Breathtaking details and bright windows highlight this luxurious two-story home. Just off the spectacular entry is an impressive private den. The curved hall between the living and dining rooms offers many formal entertaining options. In the family room, three arched windows, a built-in entertainment center and a fireplace flanked by bookcases enhance daily comfort. After ascending the front staircase and overlooking the dramatic entry, four large bedrooms are presented. Three secondary bedrooms include generous closet space and private access to a bath. A sumptuous master suite awaits the homeowners with its built-in entertainment center and His and Hers walk-in closets.

Design HPT860579

First Floor: 1,923 square feet
Second Floor: 1,852 square feet
Total: 3,775 square feet
Width: 70'-0" **Depth:** 60'-0"

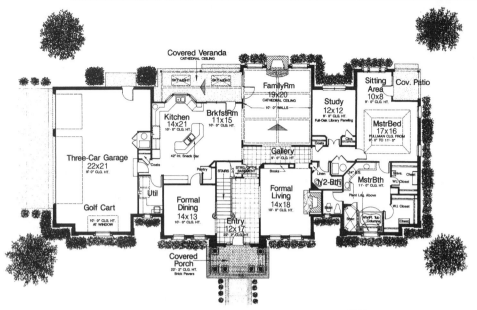

Design HPT860580

First Floor: 2,814 square feet
Second Floor: 979 square feet
Total: 3,793 square feet
Width: 98'-0" **Depth:** 45'-10"

A covered, columned porch and symmetrically placed windows welcome you to this elegant brick home. The formal living room offers built-in bookshelves and one of two fireplaces, the other being found in the spacious family room. A gallery running between these rooms leads to the sumptuous master suite, which includes a sitting area, a private covered patio, and a bath with two walk-in closets, dual vanities, a large shower and a garden tub. The step-saving kitchen features a work island and a snack bar. The breakfast and family rooms offer doors to the large covered veranda. Upstairs you'll find three bedrooms and attic storage space. The three-car garage even has room for a golf cart.

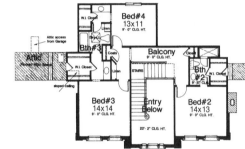

387

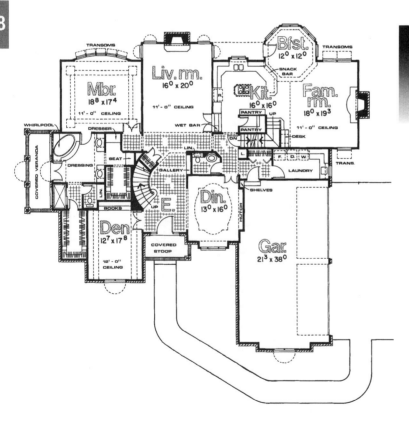

Design HPT860581

First Floor: 2,789 square feet
Second Floor: 1,038 square feet
Total: 3,827 square feet
Width: 78'-0" **Depth:** 73'-8"

The sophisticated lines and brick details of this house are stunning enhancements. The entry surveys a dramatic curved staircase. French doors open to the den, where a tiered ceiling and a bookcase wall provide a lofty ambiance. Large gatherings are easily accommodated in the dining room. The living room enjoys an eleven-foot ceiling and a fireplace flanked by transom windows. For more casual living, the family room includes a raised-hearth fireplace and a built-in desk. The gourmet kitchen provides two pantries, an island cooktop, a wrapping counter, a snack bar and private stairs to the second level. Four bedrooms include a pampering master suite on the first floor and three family bedrooms upstairs.

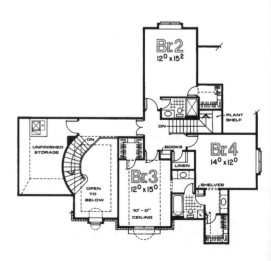

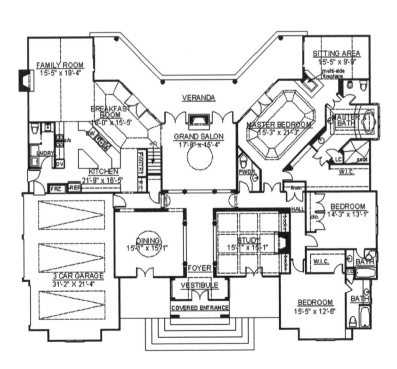

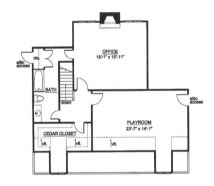

Design HPT860582

Square Footage: 3,828
Bonus Space: 1,018 square feet
Width: 80'-6" **Depth:** 70'-8"

This neoclassical home has plenty to offer! The elegant entrance is flanked by a formal dining room on the left and a beam-ceilinged study—complete with a fireplace—on the right. An angled kitchen is sure to please with a work island, plenty of counter and cabinet space, and a snack counter that it shares with the sunny breakfast room. A family room with a second fireplace is nearby. The lavish master suite features many amenities, including a huge walk-in closet, a three-sided fireplace and a lavish bath. Two secondary bedrooms have private baths. Finish the second-floor bonus space to create an office, a play room and a full bath. A three-car garage easily shelters the family fleet.

Fam. rm.
16⁰ x 19⁴

Bfst.
12⁰ x 12⁰

SNACK BAR

Kit.
12⁰ x 17⁰

DESK

Gar.
24⁰ x 21³

Liv. rm.
20⁰ x 17⁴

10'-0" CEILING

WHIRLPOOL

DRESSING

Mbr.
19⁸ x 15⁰

10'-0" CEILING

WET BAR

PANT.

SERVERY

Din.
14⁰ x 15⁶

HUTCH

Gar.
24⁰ x 21⁰

STOOP

COVERED STOOP

Den
12⁰ x 13⁸

11'-0" CEILING

BOOKS

Sit.
10⁴ x 13⁰

BOOKS

TRANS.

TRANS.

Keystone lintels and an arched transom over the entry spell classic design for this four-bedroom home. The tiled foyer offers entry to any room you choose, whether it be the secluded den with its built-in bookshelves, the formal dining room, the formal living room with its fireplace, or the spacious rear family room and kitchen area with a sunny breakfast nook. The first-floor master suite features a sitting room with bookshelves, two walk-in closets and a private bath with a corner whirlpool tub. Upstairs, two family bedrooms share a bath and enjoy separate vanities. A third family bedroom features its own full bath and a built-in window seat in a box-bay window.

Br. 2
13⁰ x 17⁴

10'-0" CLG.

BOOKS

LINEN

SEAT

Br. 4
12⁰ x 15⁶

10'-0" CEILING

DN

Br. 3
14⁰ x 15⁶

OPEN TO BELOW

TRANSOMS

Design HPT860583

First Floor: 2,813 square feet
Second Floor: 1,091 square feet
Total: 3,904 square feet
Width: 85'-5" **Depth:** 74'-8"

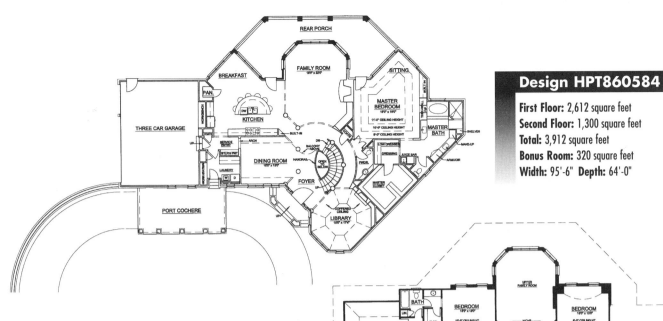

Design HPT860584

First Floor: 2,612 square feet
Second Floor: 1,300 square feet
Total: 3,912 square feet
Bonus Room: 320 square feet
Width: 95'-6" **Depth:** 64'-0"

Lovely stucco columns and a copper standing-seam roof highlight this stone-and-brick facade. An elegant New World interior starts with a sensational winding staircase, a carved handrail and honey-hued hardwood floor. An open two-story formal dining room enjoys front-property views and leads to the gourmet kitchen through the butler's pantry, announced by an archway. Beyond the foyer, tall windows brighten the two-story family room and bring in a sense of the outdoors, while a fireplace makes the space cozy and warm. The center food-prep island counter overlooks a breakfast niche that offers wide views through walls of windows and access to the rear porch.

391

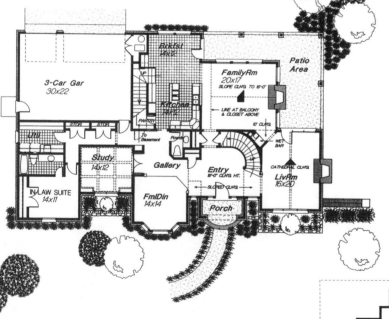

This stately two-story home with a gracious exterior features a large arched entryway as its focal point. The large two-story family area is adjacent to the living room with its cathedral ceiling and formal fireplace—a convenient arrangement for entertaining large groups, or just a cozy evening at home. A wrapping patio area allows for dining outdoors. The large kitchen is centrally located, with a second stairway leading to the second floor. The master suite features a volume ceiling and a sitting area overlooking the rear yard. The huge master bath includes two walk-in closets.

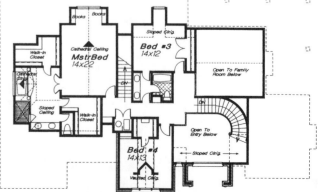

Design HPT860585

First Floor: 2,506 square feet
Second Floor: 1,415 square feet
Total: 3,921 square feet
Width: 80'-5" **Depth:** 50'-4"

Design HPT860586

First Floor: 2,985 square feet
Second Floor: 938 square feet
Total: 3,923 square feet
Width: 86'-0" **Depth:** 68'-6"

This French country design, decorated with brick and stone, begins with a cedar-beamed entry. Fireplaces enhance the study and the family room, and the living room and family room both open to patios. The island kitchen works well with both the formal bayed dining room as well as the casual dining area to the back of the home. A secluded bedroom with a private bath can serve as a guest suite. The first-floor master suite is designed to pamper, with a huge walk-in closet, a lavish bath and private access to the backyard. Upstairs, find two family bedrooms, a playroom and bonus space.

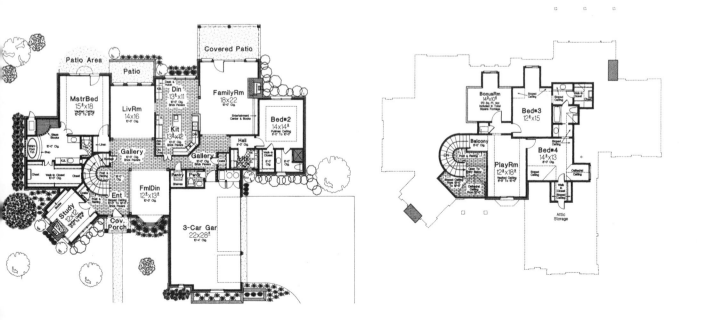

Design HPT860587

First Floor: 2,565 square feet
Second Floor: 1,375 square feet
Total: 3,940 square feet
Width: 88'-6" **Depth:** 58'-6"

A symmetrical facade with twin chimneys makes a grand statement. A covered porch welcomes visitors and provides a pleasant place to spend a mild evening. The entry foyer is flanked by formal living areas—a dining room and a living room—each with a fireplace. A third fireplace is the highlight of the expansive great room to the rear. An L-shaped kitchen offers a work island and a walkin pantry as amenities and easily serves the nearby breakfast and sun rooms. The master suite provides lavish luxuries. This home is designed with a walkout basement foundation.

QUOTE ONE®
Cost to build? See page 454
to order complete cost estimate
to build this house in your area!

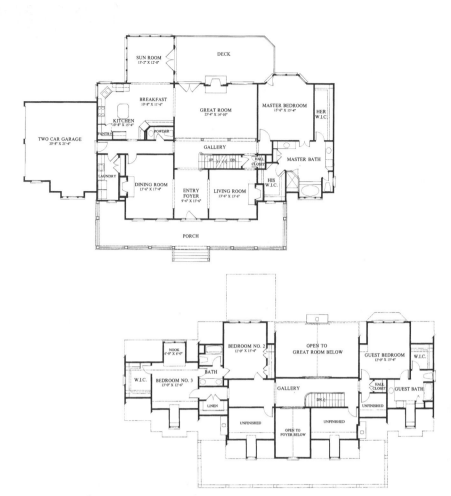

Design HPT860588

First Floor: 2,839 square feet
Second Floor: 1,111 square feet
Total: 3,950 square feet
Width: 95'-9" **Depth:** 70'-2"

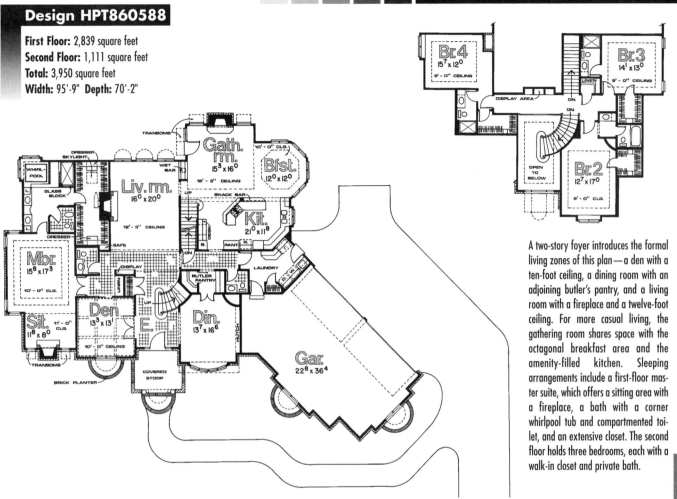

A two-story foyer introduces the formal living zones of this plan—a den with a ten-foot ceiling, a dining room with an adjoining butler's pantry, and a living room with a fireplace and a twelve-foot ceiling. For more casual living, the gathering room shares space with the octagonal breakfast area and the amenity-filled kitchen. Sleeping arrangements include a first-floor master suite, which offers a sitting area with a fireplace, a bath with a corner whirlpool tub and compartmented toilet, and an extensive closet. The second floor holds three bedrooms, each with a walk-in closet and private bath.

395

Design HPT860589

First Floor: 2,588 square feet
Second Floor: 1,375 square feet
Total: 3,963 square feet
Bonus Room: 460 square feet
Width: 91'-4" **Depth:** 51'-10"

Though there are two entrances to this fine home, the one on the right is where friends and family should enter to truly absorb the grandeur of this design. The foyer is flanked by a bayed formal dining room and a bayed formal living room. Directly ahead is the lake gathering room, a spacious room with a welcoming fireplace and access to the rear veranda. Located on the first floor for privacy, the master suite is complete with a huge dressing closet, access to the veranda, and a lavish bath.

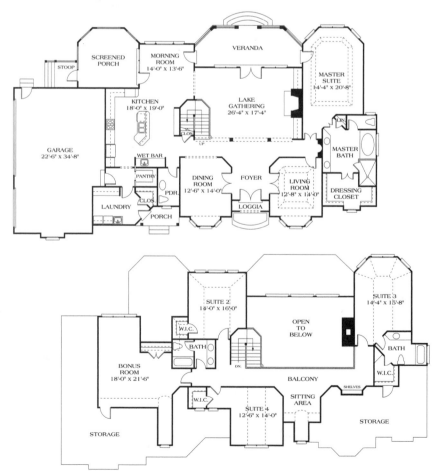

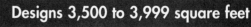

397

Design HPT860590

Main Level: 2,773 square feet
Lower Level: 1,214 square feet
Total: 3,987 square feet
Width: 70'-8" **Depth:** 91'-2"

An understated stucco facade creates an elegant picture from the curb of this sloping-lot home. The grand foyer features a barrel-vaulted ceiling, which ties into the arched opening leading to the enormous great room and its fourteen-foot ceiling. Created for outdoor living, the ground floor provides views for the master suite, the great room, the kitchen and the breakfast room. All of these areas provide access to the large deck that wraps the rear of the home. Downstairs, the basement includes two roomy bedrooms with private baths. Nine-foot ceilings in the basement give the rooms an open, spacious feeling. This home is also available with a slab foundation. Please specify when ordering.

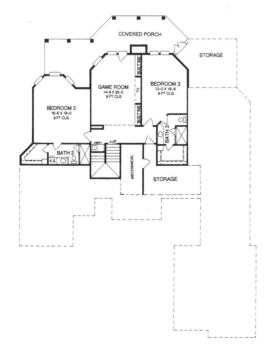

Design HPT860591

First Floor: 2,997 square feet
Second Floor: 983 square feet
Total: 3,980 square feet
Play Room: 208 square feet
Width: 89'-4" **Depth:** 71'-1"

The distinctive covered entry to this stunning manor leads to a gracious entry with impressive two-story semi-circular fanlights. The entry leads to a study, formal dining, formal living room and master suite. The numerous amenities in the kitchen include an island workstation and built-in pantry. The breakfast room features a cone ceiling. The luxurious master bath, secluded in its own wing, is complete with a covered patio. The master bedroom also contains a huge walk-in closet. Upstairs are three bedrooms, two baths and a future playroom.

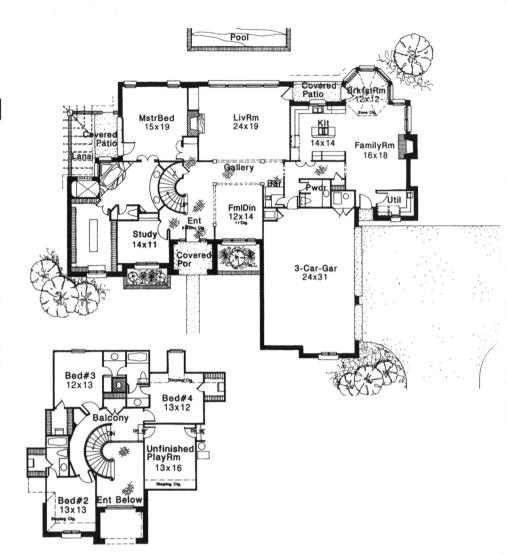

398

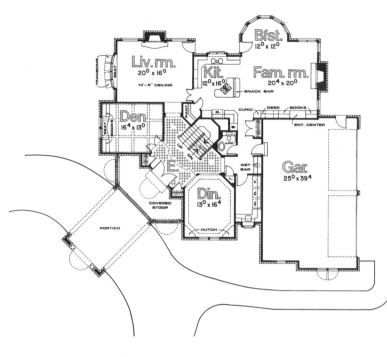

This stately brick home offers a magnificent elevation from every angle. The spacious formal dining room includes two built-in china cabinets and is easily reached from the living room. Between them is a den with floor-to-ceiling cabinetry, a window seat and a spider-beam ceiling. A gourmet kitchen with a walk-in pantry and an island cooktop/snack bar opens to a family room featuring a built-in roll-top desk, an entertainment center and a raised-hearth fireplace. The nearby breakfast nook offers views to the outside. Upstairs, a lavish master suite includes a sitting room with a fireplace framed by bookcases, a whirlpool tub and two walk-in closets. Two of the family bedrooms feature window seats for added storage.

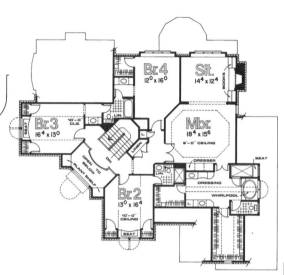

Design HPT860592

First Floor: 2,040 square feet
Second Floor: 1,952 square feet
Total: 3,992 square feet
Width: 68'-0" **Depth:** 66'-0"

399

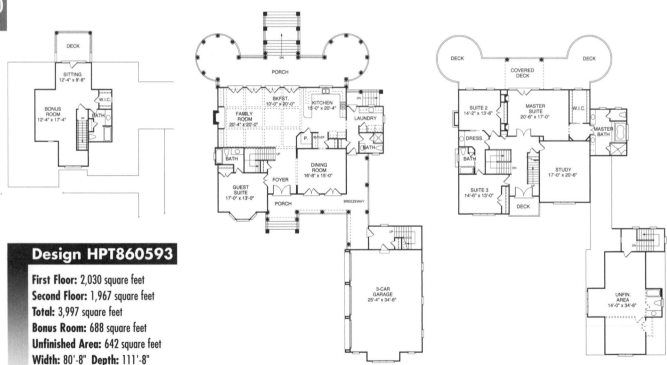

Design HPT860593

First Floor: 2,030 square feet
Second Floor: 1,967 square feet
Total: 3,997 square feet
Bonus Room: 688 square feet
Unfinished Area: 642 square feet
Width: 80'-8" **Depth:** 111'-8"

This Northwest coastal/country-style home extends livability outside with its front and back porches and elevated deck. The first floor flows from the open family room and breakfast nook to the kitchen with U-shaped counters. The dining room opens to the kitchen and the foyer. In the front, a guest suite contains a private bath. Upstairs, the spacious master bedroom has a walk-in closet and access to the deck. The family bedrooms share a bath with the study. Attached to the main house by a breezeway, the garage includes an unfinished area above that can be converted to an apartment.

Design HPT860594

First Floor: 2,126 square feet
Second Floor: 1,882 square feet
Total: 4,008 square feet
Width: 92'-0" **Depth:** 64'-4"

L **D**

This historical Georgian home has its roots in the 18th Century. The full two-story center section is delightfully complemented by the 1½-story wings. An elegant gathering room, three steps down from the rest of the house, provides ample space for entertaining on a grand scale. The study and the formal dining room flank the foyer. Each of these rooms has a fireplace as its highlight. The breakfast room, kitchen, powder room and laundry room are arranged for maximum efficiency. The second floor houses the family bedrooms. Take special note of the spacious master suite.

QUOTE ONE®

Cost to build? See page 454
to order complete cost estimate
to build this house in your area!

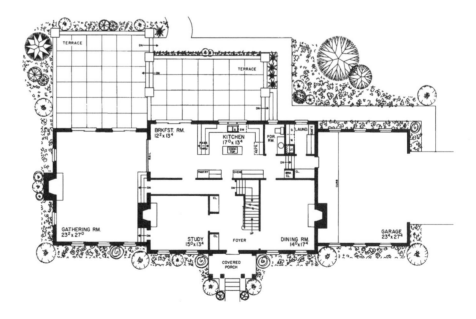

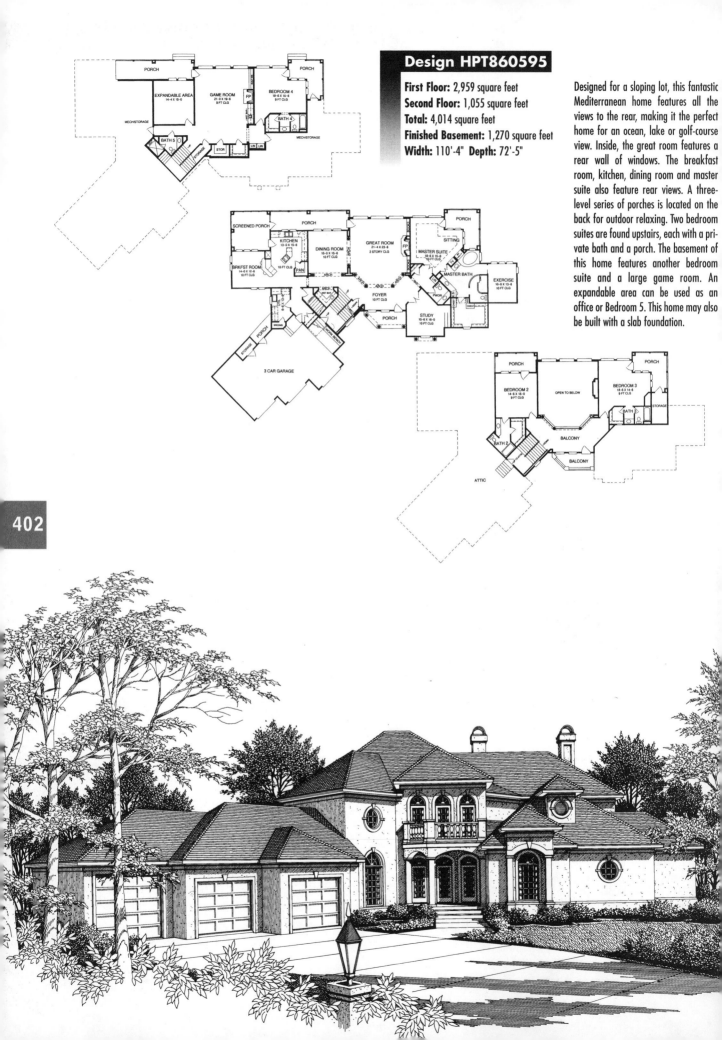

Design HPT860595

First Floor: 2,959 square feet
Second Floor: 1,055 square feet
Total: 4,014 square feet
Finished Basement: 1,270 square feet
Width: 110'-4" **Depth:** 72'-5"

Designed for a sloping lot, this fantastic Mediterranean home features all the views to the rear, making it the perfect home for an ocean, lake or golf-course view. Inside, the great room features a rear wall of windows. The breakfast room, kitchen, dining room and master suite also feature rear views. A three-level series of porches is located on the back for outdoor relaxing. Two bedroom suites are found upstairs, each with a private bath and a porch. The basement of this home features another bedroom suite and a large game room. An expandable area can be used as an office or Bedroom 5. This home may also be built with a slab foundation.

Design HPT860596

Square Footage: 4,038
Width: 98'-0" **Depth:** 90'-0"

Reminiscent of the old Newport mansions, this luxury house has volume ceilings, a glamorous master suite with a hearth-warmed sitting area, a glassed-in sun room, a home office, three porches with a deck, and a gourmet kitchen with a pantry. Graceful French doors are used for all the entrances and in the formal living and dining rooms. The magnificent kitchen boasts a large pantry. A centrally-positioned family room is graced with a large fireplace and is accessed by the rear porch, living room and dining room. Please specify basement, crawlspace or slab foundation when ordering.

403

Design HPT860597

First Floor: 2,608 square feet
Second Floor: 1,432 square feet
Total: 4,040 square feet
Width: 89'-10" **Depth:** 63'-8"

A distinctively French flair is the hall-mark of this European design. Inside, the two-story foyer provides views to the huge great room beyond. A well-placed study off the foyer provides space for a home office. The kitchen, breakfast room and sun room are adjacent to lend a spacious feel. The great room is visible from this area through decorative arches. The master suite includes a roomy sitting area and a lovely bath with a centerpiece whirlpool tub flanked by half-columns. Upstairs, Bedrooms 2 and 3 share a bath that includes separate dressing areas. Please specify crawlspace or slab foundation when ordering.

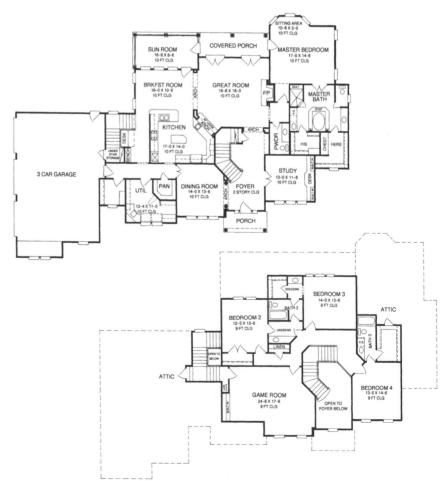

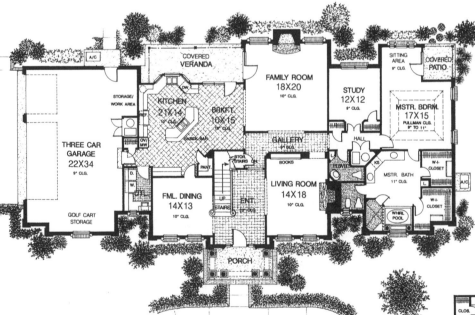

Design HPT860598

First Floor: 2,814 square feet
Second Floor: 1,231 square feet
Total: 4,045 square feet
Width: 98'-0" **Depth:** 45'-10"

This very formal Georgian home was designed to be admired, but also to be lived in. It features handsome formal areas in a living room and formal dining room, but also an oversized family room with a focal fireplace. The master suite sits on the first floor, as is popluar with most homeowners today. Besides its wealth of amenities, it is located near a cozy study. Don't miss the private patio and sitting area with glass in the master bedroom. Upstairs, there are four family bedrooms with great closet space. A three-car garage contains space for a golf cart and a work bench.

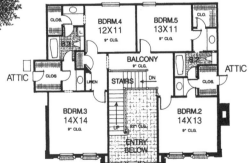

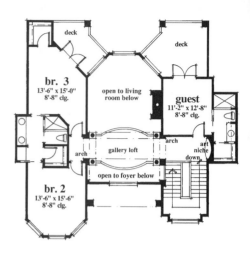

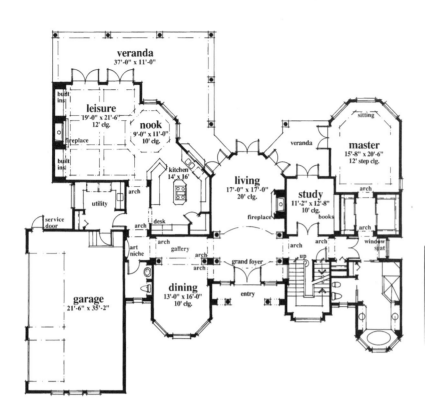

Floor plan labels (first floor):

veranda
37'-0" x 11'-0"

leisure
19'-0" x 21'-6"
12' clg.

nook
9'-0" x 11'-0"
10' clg.

built ins
fireplace
built ins

kitchen
14' x 16'

utility

arch

service door

art niche

gallery

arch

desk

living
17'-0" x 17'-0"
20' clg.

fireplace

grand foyer

entry

dining
13'-0" x 16'-0"
10' clg.

garage
21'-6" x 35'-2"

up

veranda

sitting

master
15'-8" x 20'-6"
12' step clg.

study
11'-2" x 12'-8"
10' clg.

arch

books

arch

window seat

Floor plan labels (second floor):

deck

deck

br. 3
13'-6" x 15'-0"
8'-8" clg.

open to living room below

guest
11'-2" x 12'-8"
8'-8" clg.

arch

gallery loft

arch

art niche

down

open to foyer below

br. 2
13'-6" x 15'-6"
8'-8" clg.

Design HPT860599

First Floor: 3,027 square feet
Second Floor: 1,079 square feet
Total: 4,106 square feet
Width: 87'-4" **Depth:** 80'-4"

The inside of this design is just as majestic as the outside. The grand foyer opens to a two-story living room with a fireplace and magnificent views. Dining in the bayed formal dining room will be a memorable experience. A well-designed kitchen is near a sunny nook and a leisure room with a fireplace and outdoor access. The master wing includes a separate study and an elegant private bath. The second level features a guest suite with its own bath and deck, two family bedrooms (Bedroom 3 also has its own deck) and a gallery loft with views to the living room below.

406

Design HPT860600

First Floor: 3,166 square feet
Second Floor: 950 square feet
Total: 4,116 square feet
Width: 154'-0" **Depth:** 94'-8"

L

A long low-pitched roof distinguishes this Southwestern-style farmhouse design. The tiled entrance leads to a grand dining room and opens to a formal parlor secluded by half-walls. A country kitchen with a cooktop island overlooks the two-story gathering room with its full wall of glass, fireplace and built-in media shelves. The master suite satisfies the most discerning tastes with a raised hearth, an adjacent study or exercise room, access to the wraparound porch, and a bath with corner whirlpool tub. Rooms upstairs can serve as secondary bedrooms for family members, be converted to home office space or used as guest bedrooms.

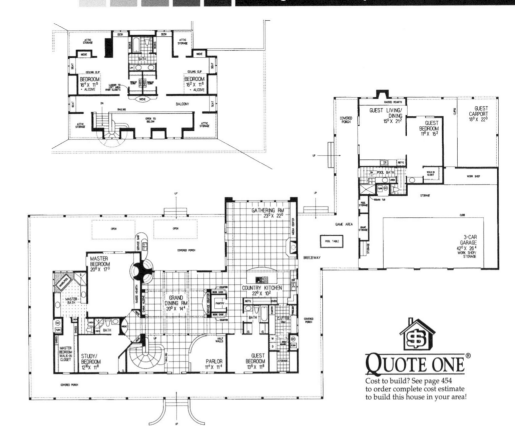

QUOTE ONE®

Cost to build? See page 454
to order complete cost estimate
to build this house in your area!

Design HPT860601

First Floor: 2,098 square feet
Second Floor: 2,037 square feet
Total: 4,135 square feet
Width: 68'-6" **Depth:** 53'-0"

This two-story farmhouse has much to offer, with the most exciting feature being the opulent master suite, which takes up almost the entire width of the upper level. French doors access the large master bedroom with its coffered ceiling. Steps lead to a separate sitting room with a fireplace and sun-filled bay window. On the first floor, an island kitchen and a bayed breakfast room flow into a two-story family room with a raised-hearth fireplace, built-in shelves and French-door access to the rear yard. Please specify basement or crawlspace foundation when ordering.

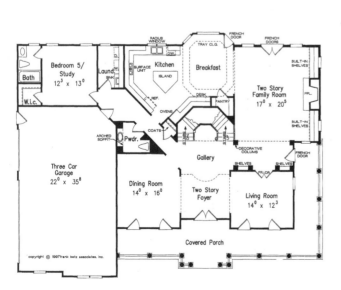

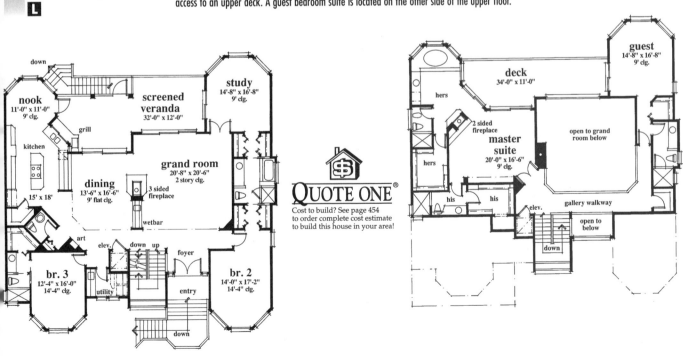

Design HPT860602

First Floor: 2,725 square feet
Second Floor: 1,418 square feet
Total: 4,143 square feet
Width: 61'-4" **Depth:** 62'-0"

L

Florida living takes off in this grand design. A grand room gains attention as a superb entertaining area. A see-through fireplace here connects this room to the dining room. In the study, quiet time is assured—or slip out the doors and onto the veranda for a breather. A full bath connects the study and Bedroom 2. Bedroom 3 sits on the opposite side of the house and enjoys its own bath. The kitchen features a large work island and a connecting breakfast nook. Upstairs, the master bedroom suite contains His and Hers baths, a see-through fireplace and access to an upper deck. A guest bedroom suite is located on the other side of the upper floor.

Quote One®

Cost to build? See page 454
to order complete cost estimate
to build this house in your area!

Design HPT860603

First Floor: 2,340 square feet
Second Floor: 1,806 square feet
Total: 4,146 square feet
Finished Basement: 1,608 square feet
Bonus Space: 442 square feet
Width: 117'-6" **Depth:** 74'-5"

Upper floor plan labels: PORCH, PORCH, WORK SHOP 22-6 X 28-0 10 FT CLG, GAME ROOM 14-4 X 17-6 10 FT CLG, MASONRY FP ABOVE, HOBBY ROOM 17-4 X 18-4 10 FT CLG, SITTING 9-6 X 12-6 10 FT CLG, STORAGE, PWDR, LOWER FOYER, MECHANICAL 14-6 X 12-0 10 FT CLG

First floor plan labels: STUDY 15-8 X 14-8 10 FT CLG, GREAT ROOM 17-0 X 17-0 2 STORY CLG, HEARTH ROOM 15-0 X 14-6 10 FT CLG, FP, FP, PORCH, MEDIA ROOM 13-8 X 14-0 10 FT CLG, KITCHEN 15-0 X 20-6, BRKFST RM 12-0 X 12-6 10 FT CLG, PWDR, FOYER 2 STORY CLG, STEP, SHELVS, DOWN, PORCH, PAN, BATH 2, BREEZEWAY, GARAGE, UTIL 16-6 X 10-6 10 FT CLG

Second floor plan labels: SITTING, OPEN TO BELOW, MASTER SUITE 15-6 X 18-0 10 FT TRAY CLG, BEDROOM 2 15-4 X 12-0, WINDOW SEAT, MASTER BATH, BALCONY, DRESSING, BATH 3, DRESSING, BEDROOM 3 12-6 X 16-6 CLG COFFERED TO 10 FT, WINDOW SEAT, LIN, OPEN TO BELOW, BEDROOM 4 15-0 X 14-6, BATH 4, WINDOW SEAT

Expandable area plan: EXPANDABLE AREA 16-8 X 25-0 10 FT CLG

Full of amenities, this country estate includes a media room and a study. The two-story great room is perfect for formal entertaining. Family and friends will enjoy gathering in the large kitchen, the hearth room and the breakfast room. The luxurious master suite is located upstairs. Bedrooms 2 and 3 share a bath that includes dressing areas for both bedrooms. Bedroom 4 features a private bath. The rear stair is complete with a dumbwaiter, which goes down to a walkout basement, where you'll find an enormous workshop, a game room and a hobby room. This home may also be built with a slab foundation. Please specify your preference when ordering.

410

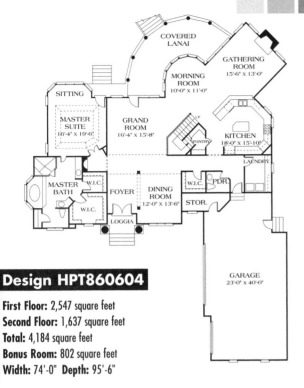

COVERED LANAI

GATHERING ROOM
15'-6" x 13'-0"

MORNING ROOM
10'-0" x 11'-0"

SITTING

MASTER SUITE
16'-4" x 19'-6"

GRAND ROOM
16'-4" x 15'-8"

PANTRY

KITCHEN
18'-0" x 15'-10"

LAUNDRY

MASTER BATH

W.I.C.

FOYER

DINING ROOM
12'-0" x 13'-6"

W.I.C.

PDR

W.I.C.

STOR.

LOGGIA

GARAGE
23'-0" x 40'-0"

EVENING DECK

SUITE 3
15'-6" x 12'-8"

CAPTAINS QUARTERS
22'-0" x 19'-0"

SUITE 2
12'-2" x 19'-4"

OPEN TO BELOW

W.I.C.

BATH

DN

BATH

SUITE 4
14'-4" x 11'-10"

OPEN TO BELOW

DINING ROOM VOLUME

WET BAR

W.I.C.

DN

ACCESS

UNFIN. REC. RM./ STORAGE
12'-0" x 39'-4"

ACCESS

ACCESS

Design HPT860604

First Floor: 2,547 square feet
Second Floor: 1,637 square feet
Total: 4,184 square feet
Bonus Room: 802 square feet
Width: 74'-0"   **Depth:** 95'-6"

Double columns flank a raised loggia that leads to a beautiful two-story foyer. Flanking this elegance to the right is a formal dining room. Straight ahead, under a balcony and defined by yet more pillars, is the spacious grand room. A bow-windowed morning room and a gathering room feature a full view of the rear lanai and beyond. The master bedroom suite is lavish with its amenities, which include a bayed sitting area, direct access to the rear terrace, a walk-in closet and a sumptuous bath.

411

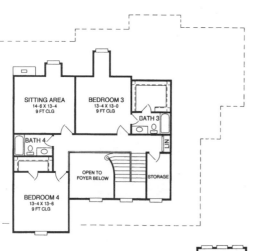

SITTING AREA
14-6 X 13-4
9 FT CLG

BEDROOM 3
13-4 X 13-0
9 FT CLG

BATH 3

BATH 4

LIN

OPEN TO
FOYER BELOW

STORAGE

BEDROOM 4
13-4 X 13-6
9 FT CLG

Design HPT860605

First Floor: 3,120 square feet
Second Floor: 1,083 square feet
Total: 4,203 square feet
Width: 118'-1" **Depth:** 52'-2"

The blending of natural materials and a nostalgic farmhouse look give this home its unique character. Inside, a sophisticated floor plan includes all the amenities demanded by today's upscale family. Three large covered porches—one on the front and two on the rear—provide outdoor entertaining areas. The kitchen features a built-in stone fireplace visible from the breakfast and sun rooms. The master suite includes a large sitting area and a luxurious bath. Upstairs, two additional bedrooms and a large sitting room will please family and guests. Please specify crawlspace or slab foundation when ordering.

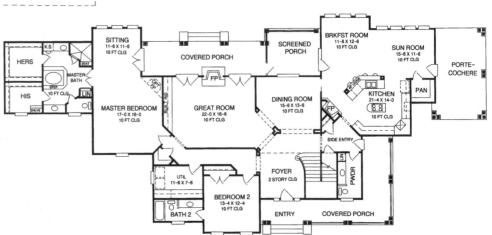

K.S.

HERS

MASTER
BATH
SEAT
STEP
10 FT CLG

HIS

LIN

SHLVS

SITTING
11-6 X 11-6
10 FT CLG

COVERED PORCH

SCREENED
PORCH

BRKFST ROOM
11-8 X 12-6
10 FT CLG

SUN ROOM
15-6 X 11-6
10 FT CLG

PORTE-
COCHERE

BUILT-INS

FP

MASTER BEDROOM
17-0 X 18-0
10 FT CLG

GREAT ROOM
22-0 X 16-6
10 FT CLG

DINING ROOM
15-6 X 13-6
10 FT CLG

KITCHEN
21-4 X 14-0
10 FT CLG

PAN

FP

SIDE ENTRY

UTIL
11-6 X 7-6

BEDROOM 2
13-4 X 12-4
10 FT CLG

FOYER
2 STORY CLG

LIN

PWDR

BATH 2

ENTRY

COVERED PORCH

The magnificent entry of this elegant traditional home makes a grand impression. The soaring ceiling of the foyer looks over a curved staircase that leads to secondary sleeping quarters. The first-floor master suite offers an expansive retreat for the homeowner, with mitered windows and a see-through fireplace shared with the spacious spa-style bath. Formal rooms open from the foyer, while a gallery hall leads to the casual living area, with a two-story family room and French doors to the outside. The three-car garage offers wardrobe space for cloaks.

Design HPT860606

First Floor: 3,098 square feet
Second Floor: 1,113 square feet
Total: 4,211 square feet
Bonus Room: 567 square feet
Width: 112'-0" **Depth:** 69'-9"

Design HPT860607

Square Footage: 4,222
Bonus Room: 590 square feet
Width: 83'-10" **Depth:** 112'-0"

The striking facade of this magnificent estate is just the beginning of the excitement you will encounter inside. The entry foyer passes the formal dining room on the way to the columned gallery. The formal living room opens to the rear patio and has easy access to a wet bar. The contemporary kitchen has a work island and all the amenities for gourmet preparation. The family room will be a favorite for casual entertainment. The family sleeping wing begins with an octagonal vestibule and has three bedrooms with private baths. The master wing features a private garden and an opulent bath.

Design HPT860608

First Floor: 2,639 square feet
Second Floor: 1,625 square feet
Total: 4,264 square feet
Width: 73'-8" **Depth:** 58'-6"
L

This home speaks of luxury and practicality and is abundant in attractive qualities. A study and dining room flank the foyer, while the great room offers a warming fireplace and double French-door access to the rear yard. A butler's pantry acts as a helpful buffer between the kitchen and the columned dining room. Double bays at the rear of the home form the keeping room and the breakfast room on one side and the master bedroom on the other. Three family bedrooms and two baths grace the second floor. A game room is perfect for casual family time. Please specify basement, crawlspace or slab foundation when ordering.

Photo by Exposures Unlimited Ron & Donna Kolb, Builder Credit to Sanneman Homes

This home, as shown in the photograph, may differ from the actual blueprint
For more detailed information, please check the floor plans carefully

Design HPT860609

Main Level: 2,582 square feet
Lower Level: 1,746 square feet
Total: 4,328 square feet
Width: 70'-8" **Depth:** 64'-0"

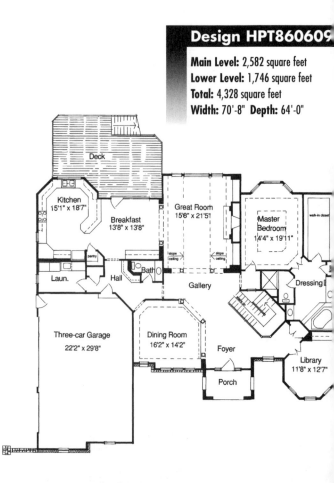

Stone accents provide warmth and character to the exterior of this home. An arched entry leads to the interior, where elegant window styles and dramatic ceiling treatments create an impressive showplace. The gourmet kitchen and breakfast room offer a spacious area for chores and family gatherings, while providing a striking view through the great room to the fireplace wall. An extravagant master suite and a library with built-in shelves round out the main level. On the lower level, two additional bedrooms, a media room, a billiards room and an exercise room complete the home.

© HOME DESIGN SERVICES, INC.

J.N.HANSEN P.T.L.

417

Design HPT860610

First Floor: 2,899 square feet
Second Floor: 1,472 square feet
Total: 4,371 square feet
Width: 69'-4" **Depth:** 76'-8"

Finished with French country adornments, this estate home is comfortable in just about any setting. Main living areas are sunken down just a bit from the entry foyer, providing them with soaring ceilings and sweeping views. The family room features a focal fireplace. A columned entry gains access to the master suite where separate sitting and sleeping areas are defined by a three-sided fireplace. There are three bedrooms upstairs; one has a private bath. The sunken media room on this level includes storage space. Look for the decks on the second level.

optional basement
stair location

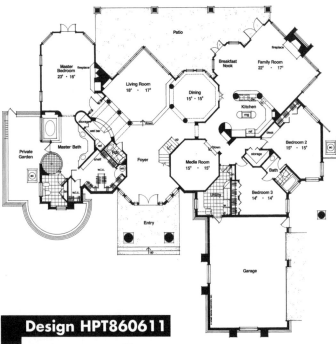

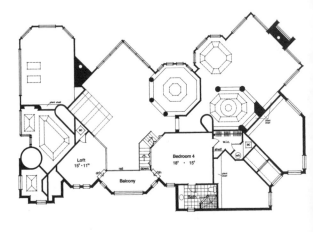

Design HPT860611

First Floor: 3,770 square feet
Second Floor: 634 square feet
Total: 4,404 square feet
Width: 87'-0" **Depth:** 97'-6"

This fresh and innovative design creates unbeatable ambiance. The breakfast nook and family room both open to a patio—a perfect arrangement for informal entertaining. The dining room is sure to please with elegant pillars separating it from the sunken living room. A media room delights both with its shape and by being convenient to the nearby kitchen—great for snack runs. A private garden surrounds the master bath and its spa tub and enormous walk-in closet. The master bedroom is enchanting with a fireplace and access to the outdoors. Additional family bedrooms come in a variety of different shapes and sizes; Bedroom 4 reigns over the second floor and features its own full bath. pass-through to the family room, which is highlighted by a wing-shaped hearth and a greenhouse window. A bayed turret encloses a media room with plenty of built-ins. The second-floor master suite boasts His and Hers walk-in closets, a fireplace and a whirlpool tub. Three other bedrooms have private adjoining baths. Two steps down on this floor is a mother-in-law suite with a bedroom, living room and full bath.

Design HPT860612

First Floor: 3,219 square feet
Second Floor: 1,202 square feet
Total: 4,421 square feet
Width: 86'-1" **Depth:** 76'-10"

Timeless sophistication characterizes this lovely home that's designed for entertaining and family. The columned dining room and the vaulted living room, with a striking two-story window wall, welcome all to this sensational home. The master bedroom is a dream with a cozy sitting room that includes a corner fireplace. A dramatic curved staircase leads upstairs to the secondary sleeping quarters. Here, two bedrooms with private baths, a computer room and a large game room complete the plan.

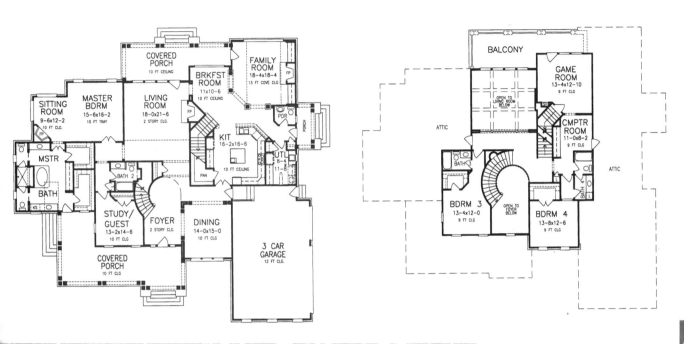

419

Design HPT860613

First Floor: 3,218 square feet
Second Floor: 1,240 square feet
Total: 4,458 square feet
Bonus Room: 656 square feet
Width: 76'-0" **Depth:** 73'-10"

This design features a breathtaking elevation all around, with an upper rear balcony, four covered porches and an inconspicuous side garage. The foyer is flanked by the dining room and the two-story library, which includes a fireplace and built-in bookcases. The elegant master bath provides dual vanities, a bright radius window and a separate leaded-glass shower. A unique double-decker walk-in closet provides plenty of storage. Nearby, a home office offers stunning views of the backyard. Upstairs, two family bedrooms share a compartmented bath and a covered porch, while a third bedroom offers a private bath. A bonus room is included for future expansion.

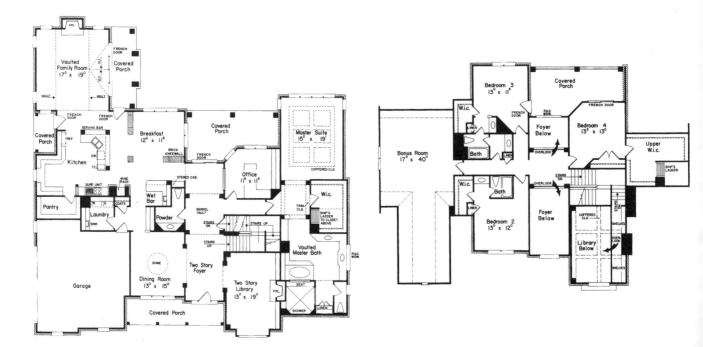

Design HPT860614

First Floor: 3,739 square feet
Second Floor: 778 square feet
Total: 4,517 square feet
Width: 105'-0" **Depth:** 84'-0"

This estate embraces the style of an elegant region—Southern France. Double doors open to a formal columned foyer and give views of the octagonal living room beyond. To the left is the formal dining room that connects to the kitchen via a butler's pantry. To the right is an unusual den with octagonal reading space. The master wing is immense. It features a wet bar, private garden and exercise area. Two secondary bedrooms have private baths; Bedroom 2 has a private terrace. An additional bedroom with a private bath resides on the second floor, making it a perfect student's retreat. Also on the second floor is a game loft and storage area.

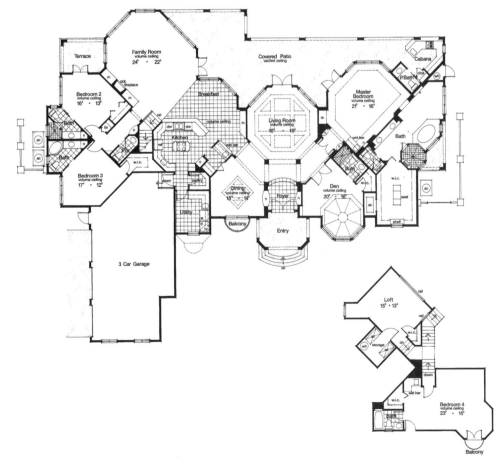

Design HPT860615

First Floor: 3,364 square feet
Second Floor: 1,198 square feet
Total: 4,562 square feet
Width: 98'-6" **Depth:** 61'-5"

The richness of natural stone and brick sets the tone for the warmth and charm of this transitional home. The expansive entry is adorned with an angled stairway, a grand opening to the formal dining room and a view of the spectacular great room. A deluxe bath and a dressing area with a walk-in closet complement the master suite. The spacious island kitchen opens to the breakfast room and the cozy hearth room. Stairways in both the foyer and the kitchen provide convenient access to the second floor. A dramatic view greets you at the second-floor balcony. Two family bedrooms share a tandem bath that includes separate vanities, and a third bedroom holds a private bath.

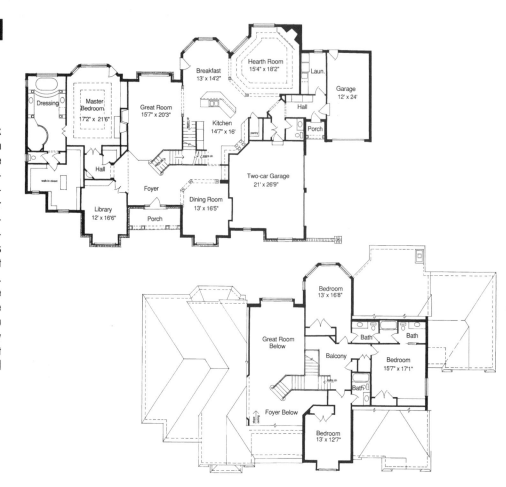

Design HPT860616

First Floor: 3,103 square feet
Second Floor: 1,482 square feet
Total: 4,585 square feet
Bonus Room: 786 square feet
Width: 106'-0" **Depth:** 56'-6"

The opulence of this fine home extends from the circular stairway that floats in front of the grand salon and floor-to-ceiling windows. The dining hall can easily seat twelve with additional furnishings. There is also a butler's pantry on the way to the octagonal kitchen, near a vaulted family room and a vaulted breakfast area. The master suite features all the finest appointments expected in a large home, including built-in dressers, cedar closets, study access and a fireplace. The second floor contains a large stateroom with a sitting room and bath. Two additional staterooms feature private baths.

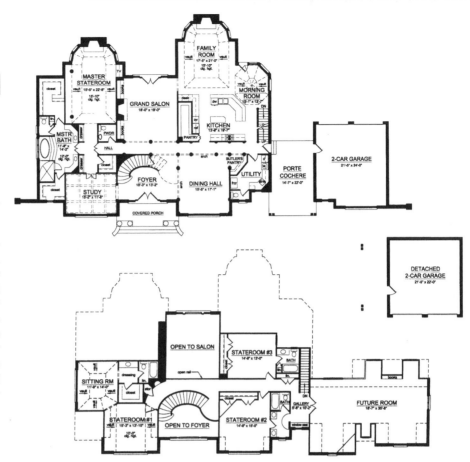

423

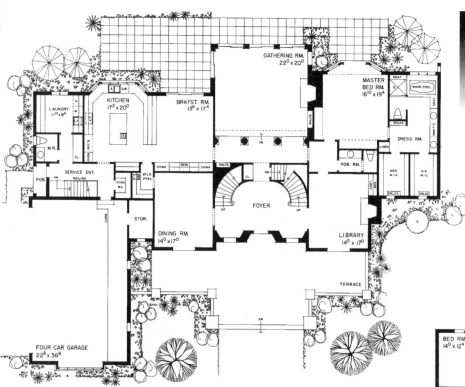

Design HPT860617

First Floor: 3,350 square feet
Second Floor: 1,298 square feet
Total: 4,648 square feet
Width: 97'-0" **Depth:** 74'-4"

Reminiscent of a Mediterranean villa, this grand manor is sure to please. An elegant receiving hall boasts a double staircase and is flanked by the formal dining room and the library. A huge gathering room at the back is graced by a fireplace and a wall of sliding glass doors to the rear terrace. The lavish master bedroom resides on the first floor for privacy. Upstairs are four additional bedrooms with ample storage space, a large balcony overlooking the gathering room and two full baths.

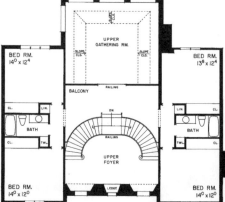

QUOTE ONE®

Cost to build? See page 454
to order complete cost estimate
to build this house in your area!

Design HPT860618

First Floor: 3,248 square feet
Second Floor: 1,426 square feet
Total: 4,674 square feet
Width: 99'-10" **Depth:** 74'-10"

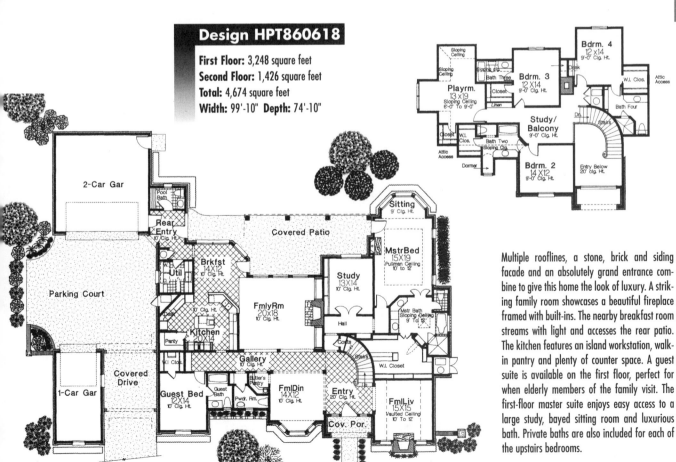

Multiple rooflines, a stone, brick and siding facade and an absolutely grand entrance combine to give this home the look of luxury. A striking family room showcases a beautiful fireplace framed with built-ins. The nearby breakfast room streams with light and accesses the rear patio. The kitchen features an island workstation, walk-in pantry and plenty of counter space. A guest suite is available on the first floor, perfect for when elderly members of the family visit. The first-floor master suite enjoys easy access to a large study, bayed sitting room and luxurious bath. Private baths are also included for each of the upstairs bedrooms.

Design HPT860619

First Floor: 2,559 square feet
Second Floor: 2,140 square feet
Total: 4,699 square feet
Width: 80'-0" **Depth:** 67'-0"

Accommodate your life's diverse pattern of formal occasions and casual times with this spacious home. The exterior of this estate presents a palatial bearing, while the interior is both comfortable and elegant. Formal areas are graced with amenities to make entertaining easy. Casual areas are kept intimate, but no less large. The solarium serves both with skylights and terrace access. Guests will appreciate a private guest room and a bath with loggia access on the first floor. Family bedrooms and the master suite are upstairs. Note the gracious ceiling treatments in the master bedroom, its sitting room and Bedroom 2.

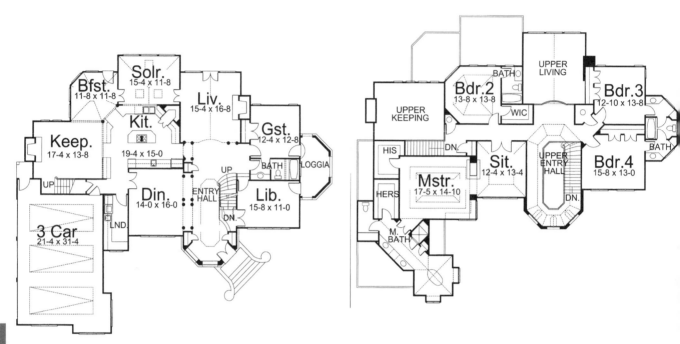

Design HPT860620

First Floor: 3,546 square feet
Second Floor: 1,213 square feet
Total: 4,759 square feet
Width: 95'-4" **Depth:** 83'-0"

This grand traditional home offers an elegant, welcoming residence. Beyond the grand foyer, the spacious living room provides views of the rear grounds and opens to the veranda and rear yard through three pairs of French doors. An arched galley hall leads past the formal dining room to the family areas. Here, an ample gourmet kitchen easily serves the nook and the leisure room. The homeowner's wing includes a study or home office. Upstairs, each of three secondary bedrooms features a walk-in closet, and two bedrooms offer private balconies.

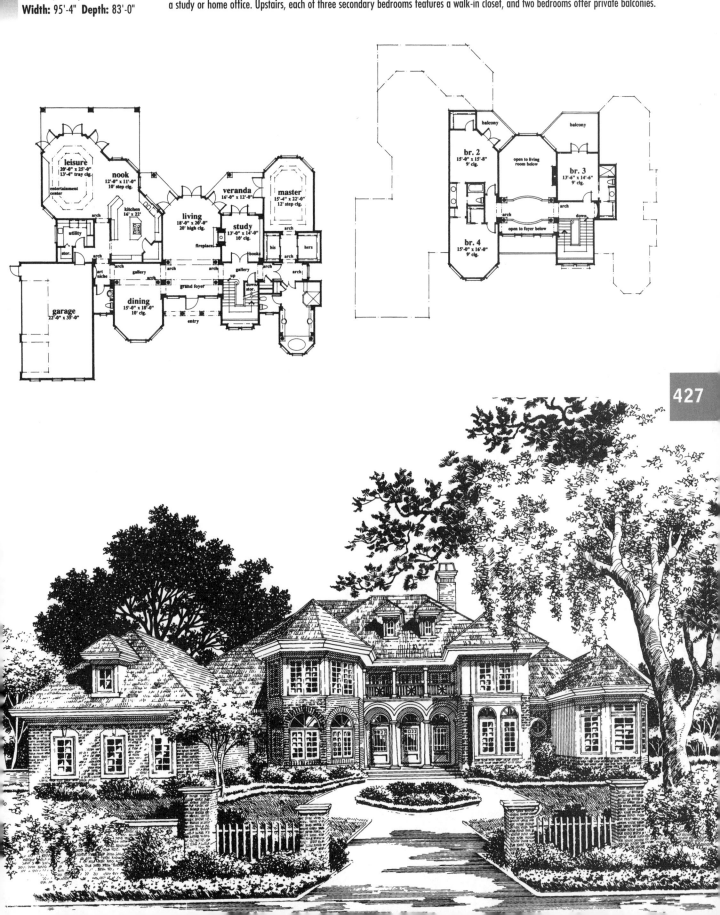

427

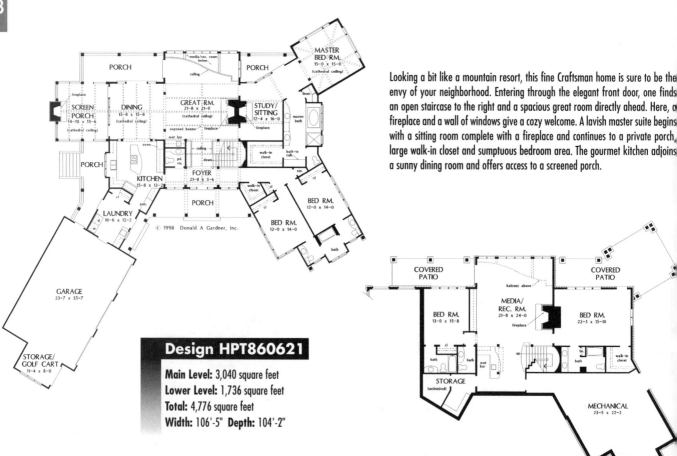

Looking a bit like a mountain resort, this fine Craftsman home is sure to be the envy of your neighborhood. Entering through the elegant front door, one finds an open staircase to the right and a spacious great room directly ahead. Here, a fireplace and a wall of windows give a cozy welcome. A lavish master suite begins with a sitting room complete with a fireplace and continues to a private porch, large walk-in closet and sumptuous bedroom area. The gourmet kitchen adjoins a sunny dining room and offers access to a screened porch.

MASTER BED RM.
15-0 x 15-0
(cathedral ceiling)

PORCH

PORCH

media/rec. room below

railing

linen

master bath

SCREEN PORCH
14-10 x 15-6
(cathedral ceiling)

fireplace

DINING
15-8 x 15-8
(cathedral ceiling)

GREAT RM.
21-8 x 21-0
(cathedral ceiling)

exposed beams

STUDY/SITTING
12-4 x 16-0

fireplace

fireplace

walk-in closet

built-in cab.

PORCH

wet bar

oven

pd. rm.

railing

down

KITCHEN
15-8 x 13-2

FOYER
21-8 x 5-6

walk-in closet

cl

cl

LAUNDRY
10-6 x 12-2

pan.

PORCH

© 1998 Donald A Gardner, Inc.

BED RM.
12-0 x 14-0

BED RM.
12-0 x 14-0

bath

GARAGE
23-7 x 35-7

STORAGE/GOLF CART
11-4 x 8-0

Design HPT860621

Main Level: 3,040 square feet
Lower Level: 1,736 square feet
Total: 4,776 square feet
Width: 106'-5" **Depth:** 104'-2"

COVERED PATIO

COVERED PATIO

balcony above

MEDIA/REC. RM.
21-8 x 24-0

fireplace

BED RM.
13-0 x 15-8

BED RM.
22-3 x 15-10

cl

bath

bath

wet bar

up

bath

walk-in closet

STORAGE
(unfinished)

MECHANICAL
23-5 x 22-2

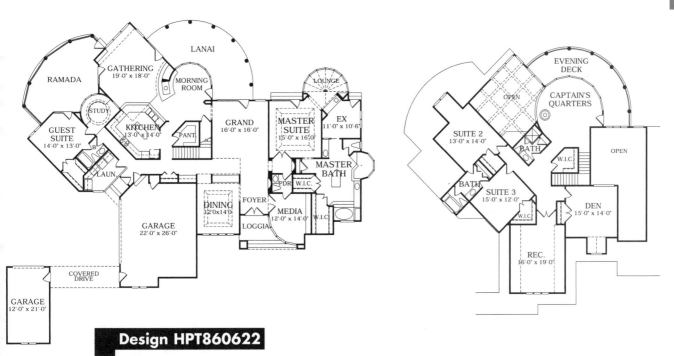

Design HPT860622

First Floor: 3,329 square feet
Second Floor: 1,485 square feet
Total: 4,814 square feet
Bonus Room: 300 square feet
Width: 106'-6" **Depth:** 89'-10"

A curved wall of windows leads to the entrance of this fine home. The lavish master suite features two walk-in closets, a deluxe bath with a separate tub and shower and two vanities, a separate lounge and an exercise room. On the other end of the home, find the highly efficient kitchen, a spacious gathering room, a round morning room and study and a quiet guest suite. The second level is equally deluxe with two suites, a recreation room, a quiet den and a large open area called the captain's quarters that opens to an evening deck.

Design HPT860623

Square Footage: 4,825
Width: 155'-6" **Depth:** 60'-4"

In this English country design, a series of hip roofs covers an impressive brick facade accented by fine wood detailing. Formal living and dining rooms flank the foyer, while the nearby media room is designed for home theater and surround sound. Fireplaces warm the living room and the family room, which also boasts a cathedral ceiling. The kitchen offers plenty of work space, a bright breakfast nook and access to two covered patios. Convenient to all areas of the house, the barrel-vaulted study has a wall of windows and French doors that can be closed for private meetings or quiet relaxing. All four bedrooms have private baths and walk-in closets. The master suite has the added luxury of a glass-enclosed sitting area.

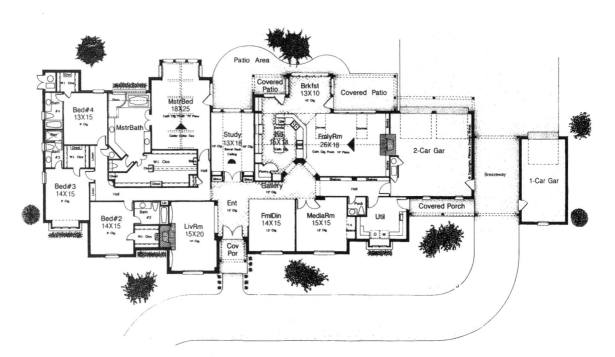

Design HPT860624

First Floor: 2,995 square feet
Second Floor: 1,831 square feet
Total: 4,826 square feet
Width: 95'-0" **Depth:** 99'-3"

L D

A magnificent covered porch wraps around this impressive Victorian estate home. The two-story foyer provides a direct view into the great room with a large central fireplace. To the left of the foyer is a bookshelf-lined library and to the right is an octagonal dining room. The island cooktop serves as a convenient work space in the kitchen, and a pass-through connects this room with the morning room. A luxurious master suite on the first floor opens to the rear covered porch. Four uniquely designed bedrooms, three full baths and a lounge with a fireplace are located on the second floor.

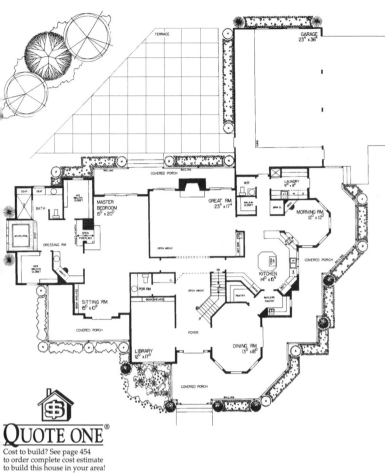

QUOTE ONE®
Cost to build? See page 454
to order complete cost estimate
to build this house in your area!

431

Design HPT860625

First Floor: 3,307 square feet
Second Floor: 1,642 square feet
Total: 4,949 square feet
Bonus Room: 373 square feet
Pool House: 761 square feet
Width: 132'-6" **Depth:** 74'-0"

This French country estate has plenty to offer. Inside, features include: formal living and dining rooms, a casual gathering room and a sunny breakfast room. But this home adds a study or parlor that is flexible enough to suit your needs. The master suite is on the first floor—you've never seen a bath quite like this one! Upstairs are three family bedrooms, plus an immense bonus room with a balcony. Don't miss the additional suite over the garage. The pool house can easily be used as a guest house. It includes a fireplace, a full bath and a dressing area.

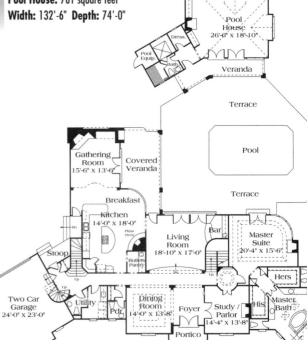

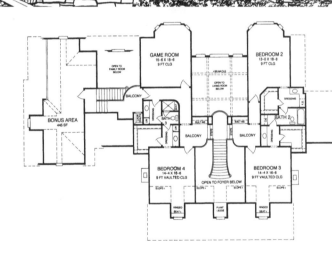

Design HPT860626

First Floor: 3,170 square feet
Second Floor: 1,914 square feet
Total: 5,084 square feet
Bonus Room: 445 square feet
Width: 100'-10" **Depth:** 65'-5"

This elegantly appointed home is a beauty inside and out. A centerpiece stair rises gracefully from the two-story grand foyer. The kitchen, breakfast room and family room provide open space for the gathering of family and friends. The beam-ceilinged study and the dining room flank the grand foyer and each includes a fireplace. The master bedroom features a cozy sitting area and a luxury master bath with His and Hers vanities and walk-in closets. Three large bedrooms and a game room complete the second floor. A large expandable area is available at the top of the rear stair.

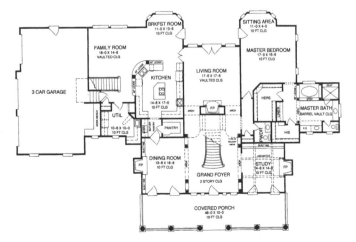

Design HPT860627

First Floor: 3,703 square feet
Second Floor: 1,427 square feet
Total: 5,130 square feet
Bonus Space: 1,399 square feet
Width: 125'-2" **Depth:** 58'-10"

This magnificent estate is detailed with exterior charm: a porte cochere connecting the detached garage to the house, a covered terrace and oval windows. The first floor consists of a lavish master suite, a cozy library with a fireplace, a grand room/solarium combination and an elegant formal dining room with another fireplace. Three bedrooms dominate the second floor—each features a walk-in closet. For the kids, there is a playroom and up another flight of stairs is a room for future expansion into a deluxe studio with a fireplace. Over the three-car garage, there is a room for a future mother-in-law or maid's suite. This home is designed with a walkout basement foundation.

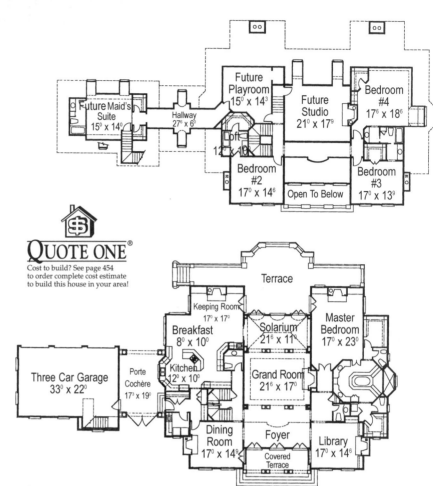

Quote One®

Cost to build? See page 454 to order complete cost estimate to build this house in your area!

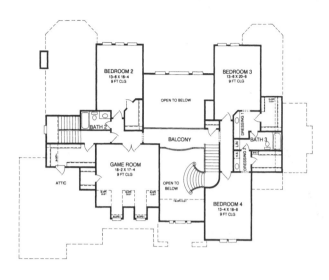

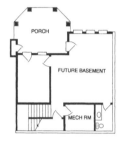

Design HPT860628

First Floor: 3,261 square feet
Second Floor: 1,920 square feet
Total: 5,181 square feet
Finished Basement: 710 square feet
Width: 86'-2"   **Depth:** 66'-10"

This home is elegantly styled in the French country tradition. A large dining room and a study open off the two-story grand foyer. The large formal living room accesses the covered patio. A more informal family room is conveniently located off the kitchen and breakfast room. The roomy master suite includes a sitting area, a luxurious private bath and its own entrance to the study. The second floor can be reached from the formal front stair or a well-placed rear staircase. Three large bedrooms and a game room are located on this floor. The walkout basement can be expanded to provide more living space. A crawlspace foundation is also available.

435

COPYRIGHT LARRY E. BELK

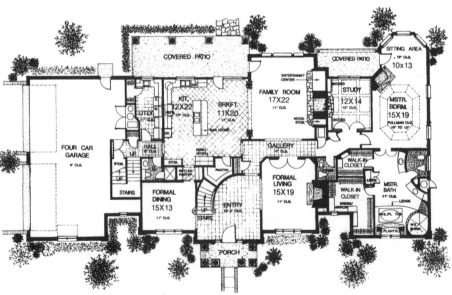

Design HPT860629

First Floor: 3,599 square feet
Second Floor: 1,621 square feet
Total: 5,220 square feet
Bonus Room: 356 square feet
Width: 108'-10" **Depth:** 53'-10"

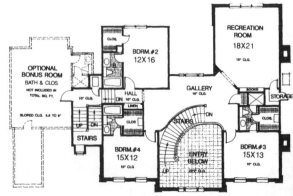

A grand facade detailed with brick corner quoins, stucco flourishes, arched windows and an elegant entrance presents this home. A spacious foyer is accented by curving stairs and flanked by a formal living room and a formal dining room. For cozy times, a through-fireplace is located between a large family room and a quiet study. The master bedroom is designed to pamper, with two walk-in closets, a two-sided fireplace, a bayed sitting area and a lavish private bath. Upstairs, three secondary bedrooms each have a private bath and walk-in closet. Also on this level is a spacious recreation room, perfect for a game room or children's playroom.

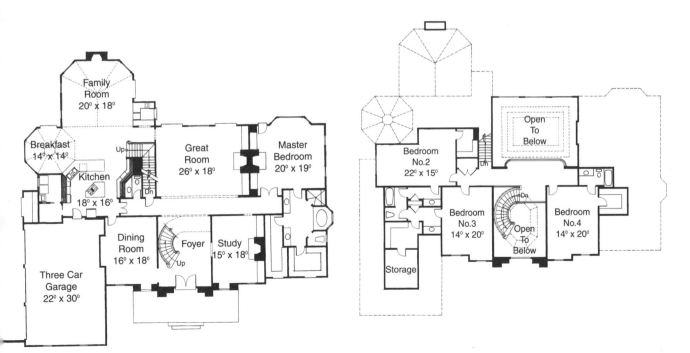

437

Design HPT860630

First Floor: 3,568 square feet
Second Floor: 1,667 square feet
Total: 5,235 square feet
Width: 86'-8" **Depth:** 79'-0"

The ornamental stucco detailing on this home creates an Old World Mediterranean charm. The two-story foyer with a sweeping curved stair opens to the large formal dining room and study. The master suite is complete with a fireplace, His and Hers walk-in closets and a bath with twin vanities and a separate shower and tub. The two-story great room overlooks the rear patio. A large kitchen with an island workstation opens to an octagonal-shaped breakfast room and the family room. A staircase located off the family room provides additional access to the three second-floor bedrooms that each offer walk-in closets. This home is designed with a walkout basement foundation.

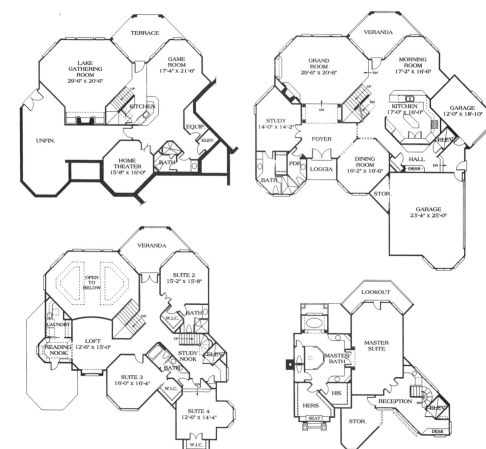

Design HPT860631

First Floor: 2,347 square feet
Second Floor: 1,800 square feet
Third Floor: 1,182 square feet
Total: 5,329 square feet
Finished Basement: 1,688 square feet
Width: 75'-5" **Depth:** 76'-4"

A level for everyone! On the first floor, there's a study with a full bath, a formal dining room, a grand room with a fireplace, and a fabulous kitchen with an adjacent morning room. The second floor contains three suites—each with walk-in closets—two full baths, a loft and a reading nook. A lavish master suite on the third floor is full of amenities, including His and Hers walk-in closets, a huge private bath and a balcony. In the basement, casual entertaining takes off with a large gathering room, a home theater and a spacious game room.

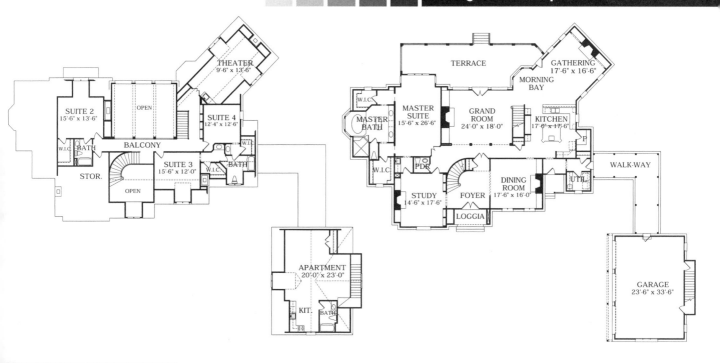

THEATER
9'-6" x 13'-6"

SUITE 2
15'-6" x 13'-6"

OPEN

SUITE 4
12'-4" x 12'-6"

W.I.C.

BALCONY

W.I.C.

BATH

STOR.

SUITE 3
15'-6" x 12'-0"

W.I.C.

BATH

W.I.C.

OPEN

APARTMENT
20'-0" x 23'-0"

KIT.

BATH

TERRACE

GATHERING
17'-6" x 16'-6"

MORNING
BAY

W.I.C.

MASTER
SUITE
15'-6" x 26'-6"

GRAND
ROOM
24'-0" x 18'-0"

KITCHEN
17'-6" x 17'-6"

MASTER
BATH

W.I.C.

PDR.

WALK-WAY

STUDY
14'-6" x 17'-6"

FOYER

DINING
ROOM
17'-6" x 16'-0"

UTIL.

LOGGIA

GARAGE
23'-6" x 33'-6"

Design HPT860632

First Floor: 3,560 square feet
Second Floor: 1,783 square feet
Total: 5,343 square feet
Apartment: 543 square feet
Width: 121'-2" **Depth:** 104'-4"

Multi-pane windows and a natural stone facade complement this French country estate. A two-story foyer leads to a central grand room. A formal dining room to the front offers a fireplace. To the left, a cozy study with a second fireplace features built-in cabinetry. The sleeping quarters offer luxurious amenities. The master bath includes a whirlpool tub in a bumped-out bay, twin lavatories and two walk-in closets. Upstairs, three suites, each with a walk-in closet and one with its own bath, share a balcony hall that leads to a home theater. An apartment over the garage will house visiting or live-in relatives, or may be used as a maid's quarters.

Design HPT860633

First Floor: 5,183 square feet
Second Floor: 238 square feet
Total: 5,421 square feet
Width: 93'-5" **Depth:** 113'-0"

Contemporary styling coupled with traditional finishes of brick and stucco make this home a standout that caters to the discriminating few. The entry, with a two-story ceiling, steps down into an enormous great room with a see-through fireplace. A formal living room opens from the entry and begins one wing of the home. The bedroom wing provides three bedrooms, each with a large amenity-filled bath, as well as a study area and a recreation room. The opposite wing houses the dining room, kitchen, breakfast room and two more bedrooms. A stair leads to a loft overlooking the great room and entry.

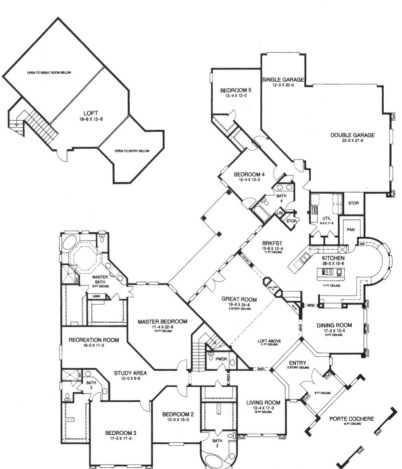

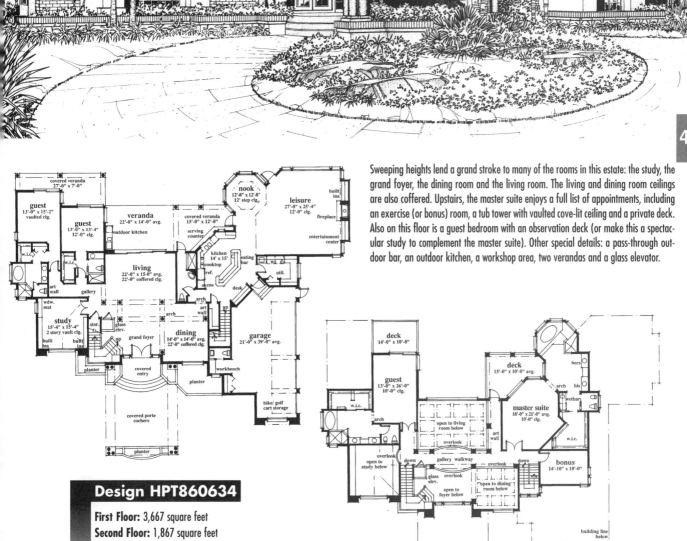

441

Sweeping heights lend a grand stroke to many of the rooms in this estate: the study, the grand foyer, the dining room and the living room. The living and dining room ceilings are also coffered. Upstairs, the master suite enjoys a full list of appointments, including an exercise (or bonus) room, a tub tower with vaulted cove-lit ceiling and a private deck. Also on this floor is a guest bedroom with an observation deck (or make this a spectacular study to complement the master suite). Other special details: a pass-through outdoor bar, an outdoor kitchen, a workshop area, two verandas and a glass elevator.

Design HPT860634

First Floor: 3,667 square feet
Second Floor: 1,867 square feet
Total: 5,534 square feet
Bonus Room: 140 square feet
Width: 102'-0" **Depth:** 87'-0"

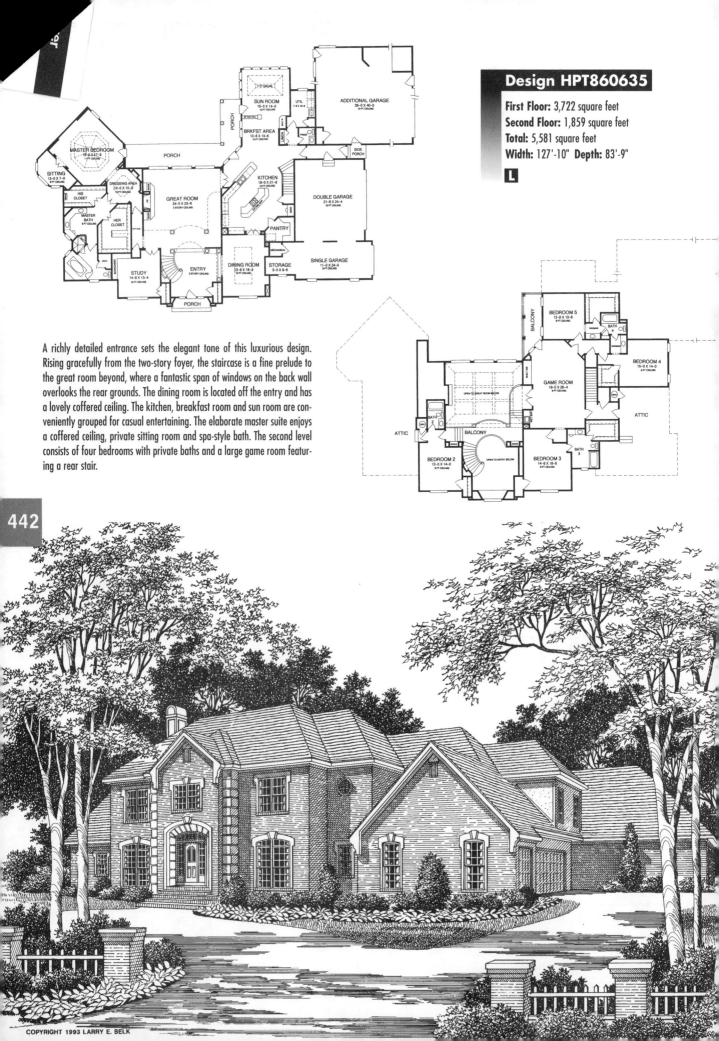

Design HPT860635

First Floor: 3,722 square feet
Second Floor: 1,859 square feet
Total: 5,581 square feet
Width: 127'-10" **Depth:** 83'-9"

L

A richly detailed entrance sets the elegant tone of this luxurious design. Rising gracefully from the two-story foyer, the staircase is a fine prelude to the great room beyond, where a fantastic span of windows on the back wall overlooks the rear grounds. The dining room is located off the entry and has a lovely coffered ceiling. The kitchen, breakfast room and sun room are conveniently grouped for casual entertaining. The elaborate master suite enjoys a coffered ceiling, private sitting room and spa-style bath. The second level consists of four bedrooms with private baths and a large game room featuring a rear stair.

442

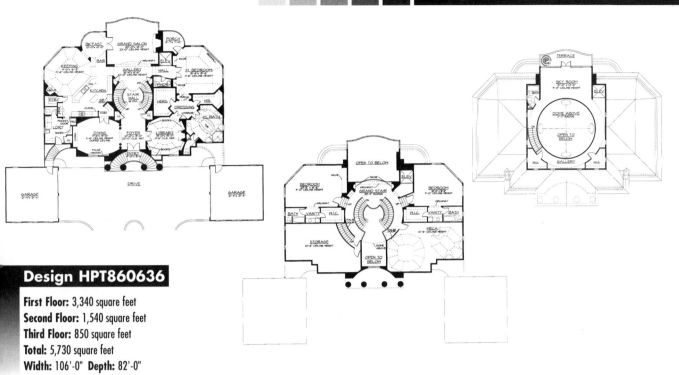

Design HPT860636

First Floor: 3,340 square feet
Second Floor: 1,540 square feet
Third Floor: 850 square feet
Total: 5,730 square feet
Width: 106'-0" **Depth:** 82'-0"

This is a grand design—there is no denying it. Symmetrical, ornate, historical and complex, it speaks to those with the discretion to investigate a very particular kind of estate home. Interior spaces are adorned with distinctive details. The entry and gallery focus on circular stairs with double access to the second-floor landing. Each of the living areas has a unique and decorative ceiling treatment. Even the master bath is enhanced beyond the ordinary. Aspects to appreciate: a formal library, two walk-in pantries, a master bedroom vestibule, double garages, a private master bedroom porch, an elevator, and a gigantic storage area on the second floor.

443

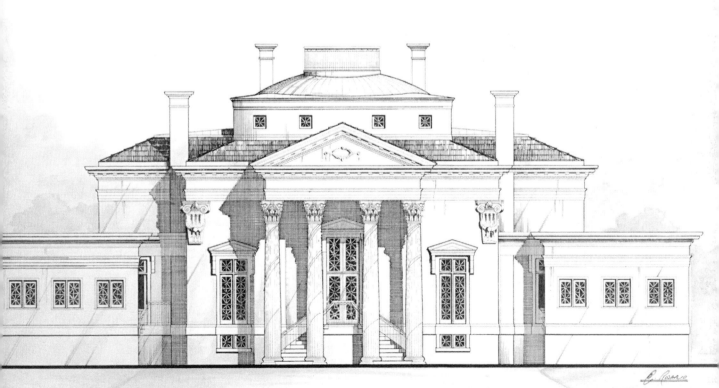

Design HPT860637

First Floor: 5,152 square feet
Second Floor: 726 square feet
Total: 5,878 square feet
Width: 146'-7" **Depth:** 106'-7"

Luxury abounds in this graceful manor. The formal living and dining rooms bid greeting as you enter and the impressive great room awaits more casual times with its cathedral ceiling and raised-hearth fireplace. A gallery hall leads to the kitchen and the family sleeping wing on the right and to the study, guest suite and master suite on the left. The large island kitchen offers a sunny breakfast nook. The master suite includes a bayed sitting area, a dual fireplace shared with the study, and a luxurious bath. Each additional bedroom features its own bath and sitting area. Upstairs is a massive recreation room with a sunlit studio area and a bridge leading to an attic over the garage.

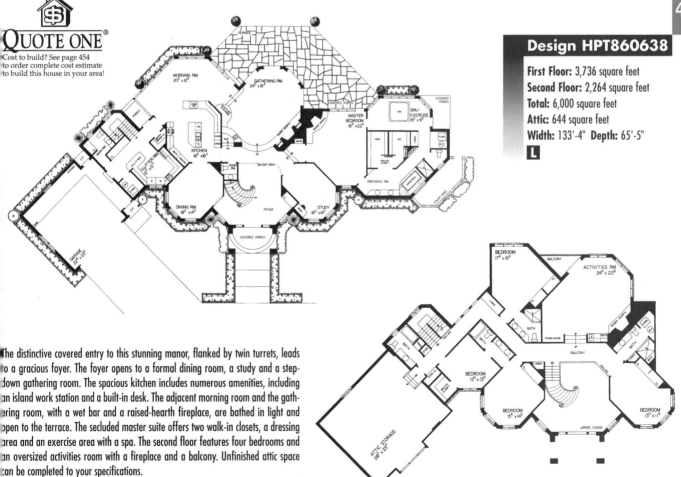

Quote One®

Cost to build? See page 454
to order complete cost estimate
to build this house in your area!

Design HPT860638

First Floor: 3,736 square feet
Second Floor: 2,264 square feet
Total: 6,000 square feet
Attic: 644 square feet
Width: 133'-4" **Depth:** 65'-5"

L

The distinctive covered entry to this stunning manor, flanked by twin turrets, leads to a gracious foyer. The foyer opens to a formal dining room, a study and a step-down gathering room. The spacious kitchen includes numerous amenities, including an island work station and a built-in desk. The adjacent morning room and the gathering room, with a wet bar and a raised-hearth fireplace, are bathed in light and open to the terrace. The secluded master suite offers two walk-in closets, a dressing area and an exercise area with a spa. The second floor features four bedrooms and an oversized activities room with a fireplace and a balcony. Unfinished attic space can be completed to your specifications.

Design HPT860639

First Floor: 3,902 square feet
Second Floor: 2,159 square feet
Total: 6,061 square feet
Width: 85'-3"   **Depth:** 74'-0"

The entry to this classic home is framed with a sweeping double staircase and four large columns topped with a pediment. The two-story foyer is flanked by spacious living and dining rooms. The two-story family room, which has a central fireplace, opens to the study and a solarium. A spacious U-shaped kitchen features a central island cooktop. An additional staircase off the breakfast room offers convenient access to the second floor. The impressive master suite features backyard access and a bath fit for royalty. Four bedrooms upstairs enjoy large proportions. This home is designed with a walkout basement foundation.

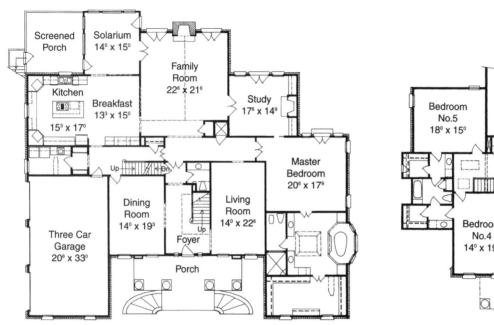

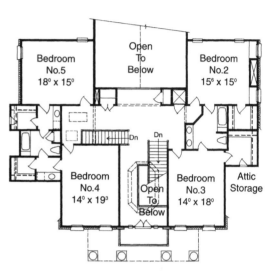

446

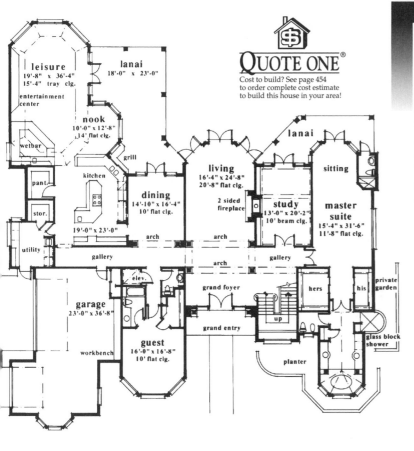

Quote One®

Cost to build? See page 454
to order complete cost estimate
to build this house in your area!

Design HPT860640

First Floor: 4,760 square feet
Second Floor: 1,552 square feet
Total: 6,312 square feet
Width: 98'-0" **Depth:** 103'-8"

L

This home features a spectacular blend of arch-top windows, French doors and balusters. An impressive informal leisure room has a sixteen-foot tray ceiling, an entertainment center and a grand ale bar. The large gourmet kitchen is well appointed and easily serves the nook and formal dining room. The master suite has a large bedroom and a bayed sitting area. His and Hers vanities and walk-in closets and a curved glass-block shower are highlights in the bath. The staircase leads to the deluxe secondary guest suites, two of which have observation decks to the rear and each with their own full baths.

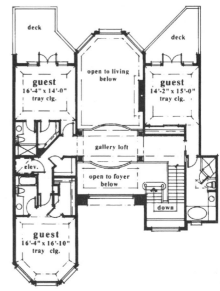

Shake-covered dormers and stone accents highlight this brick country
home. Tall chimneys support three fireplaces—in the gathering room, the
grand room and the study. Distinctive features include built-ins flanking
the fireplaces, a large work island and walk-in pantry in the kitchen, and
a laundry room with plenty of counter space for sorting and folding. The
master suite offers private access to the terrace, two huge walk-in closets
and His and Hers baths sharing only the tub and shower area. Three flights
of stairs lead upstairs to four family bedroom suites with private baths, a
home theater and bonus space over one of the two-car garages.

First-floor plan labels:
- TERRACE
- GATHERING ROOM 17'-0" x 17'-6"
- BKFST. 11'-0" x 9'-6"
- KITCHEN 21'-0" x 18'-0"
- SCREENED PORCH
- GRAND ROOM 24'-0" x 17'-0"
- MASTER SUITE 16'-0" x 21'-6"
- DRESS.
- MASTER BATH
- W.I.C.
- GALLERY
- FALSE
- PDR.
- DRESS.
- 2-CAR GARAGE 23'-0" x 23'-6"
- LAUNDRY
- DINING ROOM 15'-0" x 16'-0"
- PDR.
- FOYER
- STUDY 17'-0" x 16'-0"
- W.I.C.
- PORTICO
- STOR.
- 2-CAR GARAGE 23'-6" x 22'-8"

Second-floor plan labels:
- SUITE 3 18'-10" x 19'-6"
- OPEN TO BELOW
- SUITE 4 18'-0" x 16'-0"
- W.I.C.
- BATH
- W.I.C.
- BALCONY
- BATH
- BUILT-IN THEATER
- HOME THEATER 20'-6" x 23'-6"
- BATH
- SUITE 2 15'-0" x 12'-6"
- OPEN TO BELOW
- SUITE 5 17'-0" x 17'-6"
- BATH
- KITCHEN
- BATH
- BONUS ROOM

Design HPT860641

First Floor: 3,767 square feet
Second Floor: 2,602 square feet
Total: 6,369 square feet
Bonus Room: 677 square feet
Width: 131'-0" **Depth:** 99'-11"

449

Design HPT860642

First Floor: 3,874 square feet
Second Floor: 2,588 square feet
Total: 6,462 square feet
Width: 137'-8" **Depth:** 91'-7"

An oversized front entry beckons your attention to the wonderful amenities inside this home: a raised marble vestibule with a circular stair; a formal library and dining hall with views to the veranda and pool beyond; and a family gathering hall, open to the kitchen and connected to the outdoor grill. The master suite is embellished with a nature garden, His and Hers wardrobes, a fireplace and an elegant bath. The second floor offers more living space; a media presentation room and game room. Each of the family bedrooms features a private bath—one suite is reached via a bridge over the porte cochere.

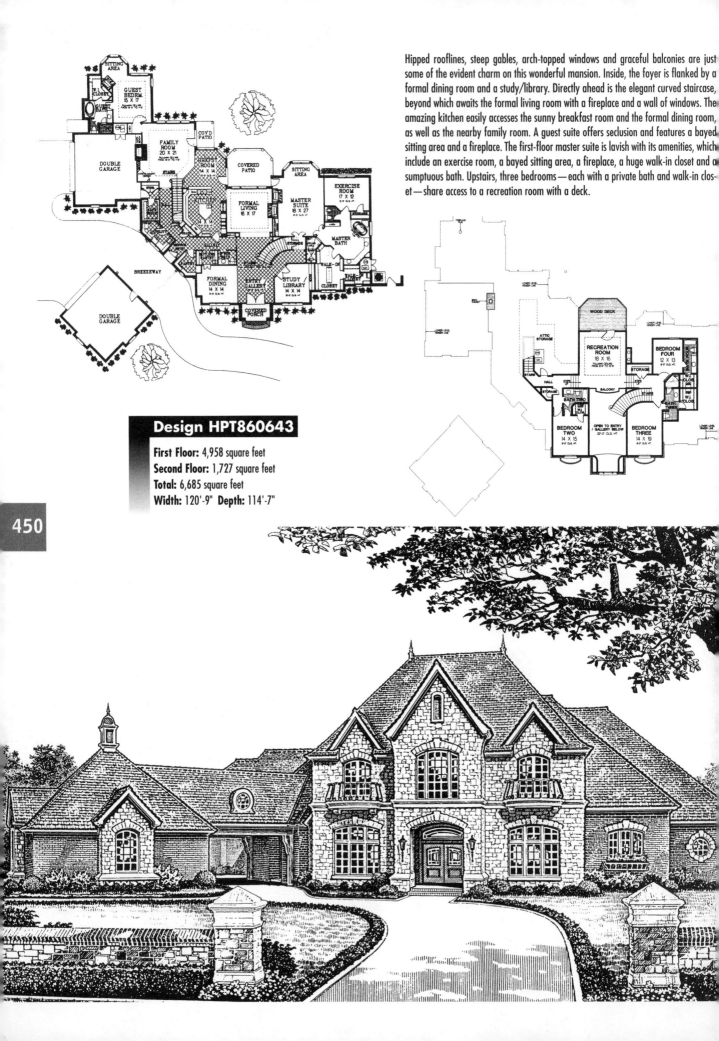

Hipped rooflines, steep gables, arch-topped windows and graceful balconies are just some of the evident charm on this wonderful mansion. Inside, the foyer is flanked by a formal dining room and a study/library. Directly ahead is the elegant curved staircase, beyond which awaits the formal living room with a fireplace and a wall of windows. The amazing kitchen easily accesses the sunny breakfast room and the formal dining room, as well as the nearby family room. A guest suite offers seclusion and features a bayed sitting area and a fireplace. The first-floor master suite is lavish with its amenities, which include an exercise room, a bayed sitting area, a fireplace, a huge walk-in closet and a sumptuous bath. Upstairs, three bedrooms—each with a private bath and walk-in closet—share access to a recreation room with a deck.

Design HPT860643

First Floor: 4,958 square feet
Second Floor: 1,727 square feet
Total: 6,685 square feet
Width: 120'-9" **Depth:** 114'-7"

450

This elegant French Country estate features a plush world of luxury within. A beautiful curved staircase cascades into the welcoming foyer, which is flanked by a formal living room and the dining room with a fireplace. A butler's pantry leads to the island kitchen, which is efficiently enhanced by a walk-in storage pantry. The kitchen easily serves the breakfast room. The covered rear porch is accessed from the media/family room and the great room warmed by a fireplace. The master suite is a sumptuous retreat highlighted by its lavish bath and two huge walk-in closets. Next door, double doors open to a large study. All family bedrooms feature walk-in closets. Bedrooms 2 and 3 share a bath. Upstairs, Bedrooms 4 and 5 share another hall bath. A home office is located above the three-car garage.

Design HPT860644

First Floor: 5,394 square feet
Second Floor: 1,305 square feet
Total: 6,699 square feet
Width: 124'-10" **Depth:** 83'-2"

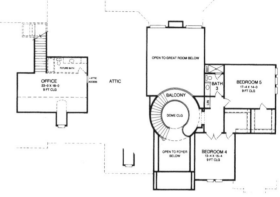

451

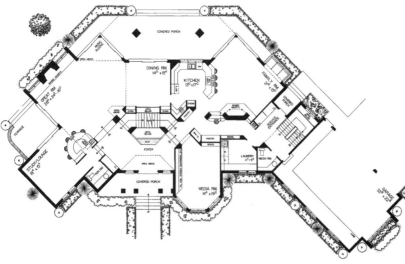

Arched windows and ultra-high roof and ceiling spaces make a bold statement on this imposing Norman design. The living area begins in the great room with a two-story music alcove, a raised-hearth fireplace and a curved bar shared with a study/lounge. The great room opens to the formal dining room, which has built-in china storage. Sliding glass doors in the dining, music and family rooms lead to the covered porch. The U-shaped kitchen features a snack bar pass-through to the family room, which is highlighted by a wing-shaped hearth and a greenhouse window. A bayed turret encloses a media room with plenty of built-ins. The second-floor master suite boasts His and Hers walk-in closets, a fireplace and a whirlpool tub. Three other bedrooms have private adjoining baths. Two steps down on this floor is a mother-in-law suite with a bedroom, living room and full bath.

Design HPT860645

First Floor: 3,202 square feet
Second Floor: 3,612 square feet
Total: 6,814 square feet
Width: 122'-0" **Depth:** 72'-4"

L

LET US SHOW YOU OUR HOME BLUEPRINT PACKAGE.

BUILDING A HOME? PLANNING A HOME?

OUR BLUEPRINT PACKAGE HAS NEARLY EVERYTHING YOU NEED TO GET THE JOB DONE RIGHT,

whether you're working on your own or with help from an architect, designer, builder or subcontractors. Each Blueprint Package is the result of many hours of work by licensed architects or professional designers.

QUALITY

Hundreds of hours of painstaking effort have gone into the development of your blueprint plan. Each home has been quality-checked by professionals to insure accuracy and buildability.

VALUE

Because we sell in volume, you can buy professional quality blueprints at a fraction of their development cost. With our plans, your dream home design costs substantially less than the fees charged by architects.

SERVICE

Once you've chosen your favorite home plan, you'll receive fast, efficient service whether you choose to mail or fax your order to us or call us toll free at 1-800-521-6797. After you have received your order, call for customer service toll free 1-888-690-1116.

SATISFACTION

Over 50 years of service to satisfied home plan buyers provide us unparalleled experience and knowledge in producing quality blueprints.

ORDER TOLL FREE 1-800-521-6797

After you've looked over our Blueprint Package and Important Extras, call toll free on our Blueprint Hotline: 1-800-521-6797, for current pricing and availability prior to mailing the order form on page 463. We're ready and eager to serve you. After you have received your order, call for customer service toll free 1-888-690-1116.

Each set of blueprints is an interrelated collection of detail sheets which includes components such as floor plans, interior and exterior elevations, dimensions, cross-sections, diagrams and notations. These sheets show exactly how your house is to be built.

SETS MAY INCLUDE:

FRONTAL SHEET
This artist's sketch of the exterior of the house gives you an idea of how the house will look when built and landscaped. Large floor plans show all levels of the house and provide an overview of your new home's livability, as well as a handy reference for deciding on furniture placement.

FOUNDATION PLANS
This sheet shows the foundation layout including support walls, excavated and unexcavated areas, if any, and foundation notes. If slab construction rather than basement, the plan shows footings and details for a monolithic slab. This page, or another in the set, may include a sample plot plan for locating your house on a building site.

DETAILED FLOOR PLANS
These plans show the layout of each floor of the house. Rooms and interior spaces are carefully dimensioned and keys are given for cross-section details provided later in the plans. The positions of electrical outlets and switches are shown.

HOUSE CROSS-SECTIONS
Large-scale views show sections or cut-aways of the foundation, interior walls, exterior walls, floors, stairways and roof details. Additional cross-sections may show important changes in floor, ceiling or roof heights or the relationship of one level to another. Extremely valuable for construction, these sections show exactly how the various parts of the house fit together.

INTERIOR ELEVATIONS
Many of our drawings show the design and placement of kitchen and bathroom cabinets, laundry areas, fireplaces, bookcases and other built-ins. Little "extras," such as mantelpiece and wainscoting drawings, plus molding sections, provide details that give your home that custom touch.

EXTERIOR ELEVATIONS
These drawings show the front, rear and sides of your house and give necessary notes on exterior materials and finishes. Particular attention is given to cornice detail, brick and stone accents or other finish items that make your home unique.

MATERIALS LIST

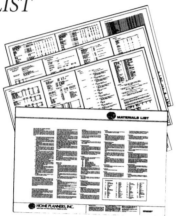

(Note: Because of the diversity of local building codes, our Materials List does not include mechanical materials.)

For many of the designs in our portfolio, we offer a customized materials take-off that is invaluable in planning and estimating the cost of your new home. This Materials List outlines the quantity, type and size of materials needed to build your house (with the exception of mechanical system items). Included are framing lumber, windows and doors, kitchen and bath cabinetry, rough and finish hardware, and much more. This handy list helps you or your builder cost out materials and serves as a reference sheet when you're compiling bids. Some Materials Lists may be ordered before blueprints are ordered, call for information.

SPECIFICATION OUTLINE

This valuable 16-page document is critical to building your house correctly. Designed to be filled in by you or your builder, this book lists 166 stages or items crucial to the building process. It provides a comprehensive review of the construction process and helps in choosing materials. When combined with the blueprints, a signed contract, and a schedule, it becomes a legal document and record for the building of your home.

QUOTE ONE®

SUMMARY COST REPORT   **MATERIAL COST REPORT**

A product for estimating the cost of building select designs, the Quote One® system is available in two separate stages: The Summary Cost Report and the Material Cost Report.

The **Summary Cost Report** is the first stage in the package and shows the total cost per square foot for your chosen home in your zip-code area and then breaks that cost down into various categories showing the costs for building materials, labor and installation. The report includes three grades: Budget, Standard and Custom. These reports allow you to evaluate your building budget and compare the costs of building a variety of homes in your area.

Make even more informed decisions about your home-building project with the second phase of our package, our **Material Cost Report.** This tool is invaluable in planning and estimating the cost of your new home. The material and installation (labor and equipment) cost is shown for each of over 1,000 line items provided in the Materials List (Standard grade), which is included when you purchase this estimating tool. It allows you to determine building costs for your specific zip-code area and for your chosen home design. Space is allowed for additional estimates from contractors and subcontractors, such as for mechanical materials, which are not included in our packages. This invaluable tool includes a Materials List. A Material Cost Report cannot be ordered before blueprints are ordered. Call for details. In addition, ask about our Home Planners Estimating Package.

If you are interested in a plan that is not indicated as Quote One®, please call and ask our sales reps. They will be happy to verify the status for you. To order these invaluable reports, use the order form.

CONSTRUCTION INFORMATION

*IF YOU WANT TO KNOW MORE ABOUT TECHNIQUES—
and deal more confidently with subcontractors —
we offer these useful sheets. Each set is an excellent
tool that will add to your understanding of these
technical subjects. These helpful details provide
general construction information and
are not specific to any single plan.*

PLUMBING

The Blueprint Package includes locations for all the plumbing fixtures, including sinks, lavatories, tubs, showers, toilets, laundry trays and water heaters. However, if you want to know more about the complete plumbing system, these Plumbing Details will prove very useful. Prepared to meet requirements of the National Plumbing Code, these fact-filled sheets give general information on pipe schedules, fittings, sump-pump details, water-softener hookups, septic system details and much more. Sheets also include a glossary of terms.

ELECTRICAL

The locations for every electrical switch, plug and outlet are shown in your Blueprint Package. However, these Electrical Details go further to take the mystery out of household electrical systems. Prepared to meet requirements of the National Electrical Code, these comprehensive drawings come packed with helpful information, including wire sizing, switch-installation schematics, cable-routing details, appliance wattage, doorbell hook-ups, typical service panel circuitry and much more. A glossary of terms is also included.

CONSTRUCTION

The Blueprint Package contains information an experienced builder needs to construct a particular house. However, it doesn't show all the ways that houses can be built, nor does it explain alternate construction methods. To help you understand how your house will be built—and offer additional techniques—this set of Construction Details depicts the materials and methods used to build foundations, fireplaces, walls, floors and roofs. Where appropriate, the drawings show acceptable alternatives.

MECHANICAL

These Mechanical Details contain fundamental principles and useful data that will help you make informed decisions and communicate with subcontractors about heating and cooling systems. Drawings contain instructions and samples that allow you to make simple load calculations, and preliminary sizing and costing analysis. Covered are the most commonly used systems from heat pumps to solar fuel systems. The package is filled with illustrations and diagrams to help you visualize components and how they relate to one another.

THE HANDS-ON HOME FURNITURE PLANNER

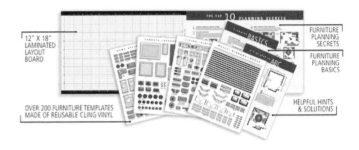

Effectively plan the space in your home using The **Hands-On Home Furniture Planner**. It's fun and easy—no more moving heavy pieces of furniture to see how the room will go together. And you can try different layouts, moving furniture at a whim.

The kit includes reusable peel and stick furniture templates that fit onto a 12" x 18" laminated layout board—space enough to layout every room in your home.

Also included in the package are a number of helpful planning tools. You'll receive:

- ✓ Helpful hints and solutions for difficult situations.
- ✓ Furniture planning basics to get you started.
- ✓ Furniture planning secrets that let you in on some of the tricks of professional designers.

The **Hands-On Home Furniture Planner** is the one tool that no new homeowner or home remodeler should be without. It's also a perfect housewarming gift!

To Order, Call Toll Free
1-800-521-6797

After you've looked over our Blueprint Package and Important Extras on these pages, call for current pricing and availability prior to mailing the order form. We're ready and eager to serve you. After you have received your order, call for customer service toll free 1-888-690-1116.

THE DECK BLUEPRINT PACKAGE

Many of the homes in this book can be enhanced with a professionally designed Home Planners Deck Plan. Those homes marked with a **D** have a complementary Deck Plan, sold separately, which includes a Deck Plan Frontal Sheet, Deck Framing and Floor Plans, Deck Elevations and a Deck Materials List. A Standard Deck Details Package, also available, provides all the how-to information necessary for building *any* deck. Our Complete Deck Building Package contains one set of Custom Deck Plans of your choice, plus one set of Standard Deck Building Details, all for one low price. Our plans and details are carefully prepared in an easy-to-understand format that will guide you through every stage of your deck-building project. This page shows a sample Deck layout to match your favorite house. See Blueprint Price Schedule for ordering information.

THE LANDSCAPE BLUEPRINT PACKAGE

For the homes marked with an **L** in this book, Home Planners has created a front-yard Landscape Plan that is complementary in design to the house plan. These comprehensive blueprint packages include a Frontal Sheet, Plan View, Regionalized Plant & Materials List, a sheet on Planting and Maintaining Your Landscape, Zone Maps and Plant Size and Description Guide. These plans will help you achieve professional results, adding value and enjoyment to your property for years to come. Each set of blueprints is a full 18" x 24" in size with clear, complete instructions and easy-to-read type. A sample Landscape Plan is shown below. See Blueprint Price Schedule for ordering information.

CONTEMPORARY LEISURE DECK
Deck ODA021

CAPE COD COTTAGE
Landscape OLA003

REGIONAL ORDER MAP

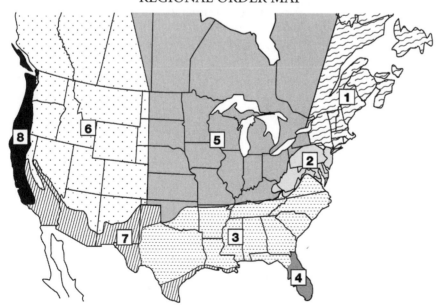

Most Landscape Plans are available with a Plant & Materials List adapted by horticultural experts to 8 different regions of the country. Please specify the Geographic Region when ordering your plan. See Blueprint Price Schedule for ordering information and regional availability.

Region	1	Northeast
Region	2	Mid-Atlantic
Region	3	Deep South
Region	4	Florida & Gulf Coast
Region	5	Midwest
Region	6	Rocky Mountains
Region	7	Southern California & Desert Southwest
Region	8	Northern California & Pacific Northwest

BLUEPRINT PRICE SCHEDULE

Prices guaranteed through December 31, 2003

TIERS	1-SET STUDY PACKAGE	4-SET BUILDING PACKAGE	8-SET BUILDING PACKAGE	1-SET REPRODUCIBLE*
P1	$20	$50	$90	$140
P2	$40	$70	$110	$160
P3	$70	$100	$140	$190
P4	$100	$130	$170	$220
P5	$140	$170	$210	$270
P6	$180	$210	$250	$310
A1	$440	$480	$520	$660
A2	$480	$520	$560	$720
A3	$530	$575	$615	$800
A4	$575	$620	$660	$870
C1	$620	$665	$710	$935
C2	$670	$715	$760	$1000
C3	$715	$760	$805	$1075
C4	$765	$810	$855	$1150
L1	$870	$925	$975	$1300
L2	$945	$1000	$1050	$1420
L3	$1050	$1105	$1155	$1575
L4	$1155	$1210	$1260	$1735
SQ1				.35/SqFt

* Requires a fax number

OPTIONS FOR PLANS IN TIERS A1–L4

Additional Identical Blueprints
...same order for "A1–L4" price plans ....$50 per set
Reverse Blueprints (mirror image)
...with 4- or 8-set order for "A1–L4" plans...$50 fee per order
Specification Outlines...$10 each
Materials Lists for "A1–C3" plans ....$60 each
Materials Lists for "C4–L4" plans..$70 each

OPTIONS FOR PLANS IN TIERS P1–P6

Additional Identical Blueprints
...same order for "P1–P6" price plans..$10 per set
Reverse Blueprints (mirror image) for "P1–P6" price plans ....$10 fee per order
...set of Deck Construction Details ....$14.95 each
Deck Construction Package ....**add $10 to Building Package price**
(Includes 1 set of "P1–P6" plans, plus 1 set Standard Deck Construction Details)

IMPORTANT NOTES

Q one-set building package includes one set of reproducible vellum construction drawings plus, one set of study blueprints.
The 1-set study package is marked "not for construction."
Prices for 4- or 8-set Building Packages honored only at time of original order.
Some foundations carry a $225 surcharge.
Right-reading reverse blueprints, if available, will incur a $165 surcharge.
Additional identical blueprints may be purchased within 60 days of original order.

TO USE THE INDEX, refer to the design number listed in numerical order (a helpful page reference is also given). Note the price tier and refer to the Blueprint Price Schedule above for the cost of one, four or eight sets of blueprints or the cost of a reproducible drawing. Additional prices are shown for identical and reverse blueprint sets, as well as a very useful Materials List for some of the plans. Also note in the Plan Index those plans that have Deck Plans or Landscape Plans. Refer to the schedules above for prices of these plans. The letter "Y" identifies plans that are part of our Quote One® estimating service and those that offer Materials Lists.

TO ORDER, Call toll free 1-800-521-6797 for current pricing and availability prior to mailing the order form. FAX: 1-800-224-6699 or 520-544-3086.

PLAN INDEX

DESIGN	PRICE	PAGE	MATERIALS LIST	QUOTE ONE®	DECK	DECK PRICE	LANDSCAPE	LANDSCAPE PRICE	REGIONS
HPT860001	A2	4	Y	Y					
HPT860002	A4	5	Y	Y	ODA012	P3	OLA008	P4	1234568
HPT860003	A4	6	Y	Y					
HPT860004	C2	7	Y	Y					
HPT860005	C1	8	Y	Y					
HPT860006	C3	9							
HPT860007	C1	10	Y				OLA004	P3	123568
HPT860008	C1	11	Y				OLA004	P3	123568
HPT860009	C1	12							
HPT860010	C2	13							
HPT860011	C2	14							
HPT860012	C4	15							
HPT860013	C4	16	Y				OLA008	P4	1234568
HPT860014	A1	17	Y						
HPT860015	A3	18	Y						
HPT860016	A1	18	Y						
HPT860017	A1	19	Y						
HPT860018	A1	20	Y						
HPT860019	A1	20	Y						
HPT860020	A1	21	Y						
HPT860021	A1	22	Y						
HPT860022	A2	22	Y						
HPT860023	A2	23	Y						
HPT860024	A2	24	Y						
HPT860025	A2	24	Y						
HPT860026	A2	25	Y						
HPT860027	A2	26	Y						
HPT860028	A2	26	Y						
HPT860029	A3	27	Y	Y					
HPT860030	A2	28							
HPT860031	A2	28	Y						
HPT860032	A2	29	Y						
HPT860033	A2	30							
HPT860034	A3	30	Y	Y	ODA016	P2			
HPT860035	A3	31	Y						
HPT860036	A4	32	Y						
HPT860037	A3	32	Y	Y					
HPT860038	A2	33	Y						
HPT860039	A2	34							
HPT860040	A3	35	Y	Y			OLA001	P3	123568
HPT860041	A2	36	Y						
HPT860042	A4	36							
HPT860043	A2	37	Y						
HPT860044	A3	38	Y						
HPT860045	A2	38	Y						
HPT860046	A3	39	Y						
HPT860047	A4	40	Y						
HPT860048	A2	40							
HPT860049	C3	41	Y						
HPT860050	A3	42	Y						
HPT860051	A3	43	Y						
HPT860052	C4	44	Y						
HPT860053	A2	45	Y	Y			OLA012	P3	12345678
HPT860054	A2	45							
HPT860055	A3	46	Y						
HPT860056	A2	47	Y						
HPT860057	A2	47	Y						
HPT860058	A3	48	Y						
HPT860059	A3	49							
HPT860060	A4	50	Y						
HPT860061	A3	50							
HPT860062	A3	51							
HPT860063	A3	52	Y	Y					
HPT860064	A3	52	Y						
HPT860065	A3	53							
HPT860066	A4	53							
HPT860067	A4	54	Y	Y					
HPT860068	A3	54	Y	Y					
HPT860069	A4	55	Y						

PLAN INDEX

DESIGN	PRICE	PAGE	MATERIALS LIST	QUOTE ONE®	DECK	DECK PRICE	LANDSCAPE	LANDSCAPE PRICE	REGIONS
HPT860070	A3	55							
HPT860071	A3	56	Y						
HPT860072	A3	56	Y						
HPT860073	A3	57							
HPT860074	A3	57							
HPT860075	A4	58	Y	Y					
HPT860076	A4	59	Y	Y					
HPT860077	A3	59							
HPT860078	A4	60	Y						
HPT860079	A4	60	Y	Y					
HPT860080	A4	61	Y						
HPT860081	A3	61							
HPT860082	A4	62	Y						
HPT860083	A3	62	Y						
HPT860084	A4	63	Y						
HPT860085	A3	63	Y						
HPT860086	A3	64	Y						
HPT860087	A3	64	Y						
HPT860088	A4	65	Y	Y					
HPT860089	A3	65	Y						
HPT860090	A3	66	Y						
HPT860091	A4	66							
HPT860092	A3	67							
HPT860093	A4	68	Y	Y	ODA012	P3	OLA083	P3	12345678
HPT860094	A3	68	Y	Y					
HPT860095	A4	69	Y	Y	ODA012	P3	OLA083	P3	12345678
HPT860096	A4	69	Y	Y	ODA011	P2	OLA024	P4	123568
HPT860097	A3	70							
HPT860098	A3	71	Y						
HPT860099	A3	71	Y						
HPT860100	A4	72	Y						
HPT860101	A3	72							
HPT860102	A4	73	Y	Y					
HPT860103	C1	73	Y	Y					
HPT860104	A3	74	Y	Y					
HPT860105	A4	74	Y						
HPT860106	A3	75	Y						
HPT860107	A3	75	Y						
HPT860108	C1	76	Y	Y					
HPT860109	A3	76							
HPT860110	A3	77	Y				OLA001	P3	123568
HPT860111	A3	77	Y						
HPT860112	A3	78	Y						
HPT860113	A3	78							
HPT860114	A3	79	Y	Y					
HPT860115	C1	79							
HPT860116	A3	80							
HPT860117	A3	80	Y						
HPT860118	A3	81							
HPT860119	A4	81							
HPT860120	A3	82							
HPT860121	A3	82					OLA004	P3	123568
HPT860122	A3	83	Y						
HPT860123	A3	84							
HPT860124	A3	84							
HPT860125	A3	85							
HPT860126	A3	85							
HPT860127	C1	86	Y						
HPT860128	A4	87					OLA024	P4	123568
HPT860129	A3	88	Y						
HPT860130	A3	88							
HPT860131	A3	89	Y						
HPT860132	C1	89							
HPT860133	C1	90							
HPT860134	A4	91					OLA024	P4	123568
HPT860135	A3	92							
HPT860136	A4	92	Y	Y					
HPT860137	A4	93	Y						
HPT860138	A3	93							
HPT860139	A4	94	Y						
HPT860140	A3	94	Y						
HPT860141	C1	95	Y						
HPT860142	A3	96	Y						
HPT860143	A3	96	Y						
HPT860144	A4	97	Y						
HPT860145	A4	97	Y	Y					
HPT860146	A4	98	Y	Y					
HPT860147	C1	98	Y	Y					
HPT860148	A3	99							
HPT860149	A4	100	Y	Y					
HPT860150	A3	101	Y						
HPT860151	A4	101							
HPT860152	A4	102	Y	Y					
HPT860153	A4	102							
HPT860154	A3	103	Y				OLA004	P3	123568
HPT860155	A4	103	Y	Y					
HPT860156	A4	104							
HPT860157	A4	104	Y						
HPT860158	A4	105	Y						
HPT860159	A3	105	Y	Y					
HPT860160	A4	106	Y	Y					
HPT860161	A4	107	Y						
HPT860162	A3	108	Y	Y					
HPT860163	A3	108	Y						
HPT860164	A4	109	Y						
HPT860165	A3	109	Y						
HPT860166	A4	110	Y	Y					
HPT860167	A4	110							
HPT860168	A4	111	Y	Y					
HPT860169	A3	111							
HPT860170	A3	112							
HPT860171	A4	112							
HPT860172	A4	113	Y	Y					
HPT860173	A3	113	Y						
HPT860174	A4	114							
HPT860175	A3	115							
HPT860176	A3	115	Y						
HPT860177	A3	116	Y						
HPT860178	A4	116							
HPT860179	A4	117							
HPT860180	C1	117							
HPT860181	A3	118	Y						
HPT860182	A3	118	Y						
HPT860183	A3	119	Y						
HPT860184	A4	119	Y						
HPT860185	A3	120	Y						
HPT860186	A3	120							
HPT860187	A3	121							
HPT860188	A4	121	Y	Y					
HPT860189	A4	122							
HPT860190	A4	122	Y	Y	ODA014	P2	OLA003	P3	123568
HPT860191	A4	123	Y	Y					
HPT860192	A3	123							
HPT860193	A3	124	Y						
HPT860194	A3	125	Y						
HPT860195	A3	125	Y						
HPT860196	A4	126	Y						
HPT860197	A3	126							
HPT860198	A4	127	Y	Y					
HPT860199	A4	127							
HPT860200	A4	128	Y	Y			OLA088	P4	12345678
HPT860201	C1	128	Y						
HPT860202	C1	129							
HPT860203	A3	130	Y						
HPT860204	A3	130	Y	Y					
HPT860205	A4	131	Y						
HPT860206	A4	132							
HPT860207	A3	133							
HPT860208	A3	133							
HPT860209	A4	134	Y	Y					
HPT860210	A3	134							
HPT860211	A4	135							
HPT860212	A3	135							
HPT860213	A3	136	Y						

461

Before filling out

the order form,

please call us on

our Toll-Free

Blueprint Hotline

1-800-521-6797.

You may want to

learn more about

our services and

products. Here's

some information

you will find helpful.

OUR EXCHANGE POLICY

With the exception of reproducible plan orders, we will exchange your entire first order for an equal or greater number of blueprints within our plan collection within 90 days of the original order. The entire content of your original order must be returned before an exchange will be processed. Please call our customer service department for your return authorization number and shipping instructions. If the returned blueprints look used, redlined or copied, we will not honor your exchange. Fees for exchanging your blueprints are as follows: 20% of the amount of the original order...plus the difference in cost if exchanging for a design in a higher price bracket or less the difference in cost if exchanging for a design in a lower price bracket. **(Reproducible blueprints are not exchangeable or refundable.)** Please call for current postage and handling prices. Shipping and handling charges are not refundable.

ABOUT REPRODUCIBLES

When purchasing a reproducible you may be required to furnish a fax number. The designer will fax documents that you must sign and return to them before shipping will take place.

ABOUT REVERSE BLUEPRINTS

Although lettering and dimensions will appear backward, reverses will be a useful aid if you decide to flop the plan. See Price Schedule and Plans Index for pricing.

REVISING, MODIFYING AND CUSTOMIZING PLANS

Like many homeowners who buy these plans, you and your builder, architect or engineer may want to make changes to them. We recommend purchase of a reproducible plan for any changes made by your builder, licensed architect or engineer. As set forth below, we cannot assume any responsibility for blueprints which have been changed, whether by you, your builder or by professionals selected by you or referred to you by us, because such individuals are outside our supervision and control.

ARCHITECTURAL AND ENGINEERING SEALS

Some cities and states are now requiring that a licensed architect or engineer review and "seal" a blueprint, or officially approve it, prior to construction due to concerns over energy costs, safety and other factors. Prior to application for a building permit or the start of actual construction, we strongly advise that you consult your local building official who can tell you if such a review is required.

ABOUT THE DESIGNS

The architects and designers whose work appears in this publication are among America's leading residential designers. Each plan was designed to meet the requirements of a nationally recognized model building code in effect at the time and place the plan was drawn. Because national building codes change from time to time, plans may not comply with any such code at the time they are sold to a customer. In addition, building officials may not accept these plans as final construction documents of record as the plans may need to be modified and additional drawings and details added to suit local conditions and requirements. We strongly advise that purchasers consult a licensed architect or engineer, and their local building official, before starting any construction related to these plans.

LOCAL BUILDING CODES AND ZONING REQUIREMENTS

At the time of creation, our plans are drawn to specifications published by the Building Officials and Code Administrators (BOCA) International, Inc.; the Southern Building Code Congress (SBCCI) International, Inc.; the International Conference of Building Officials (ICBO); or the Council of American Building Officials (CABO). Our plans are designed to meet or exceed national building standards. Because of the great differences in geography and climate throughout the United States and Canada, each state, county and municipality has its own building codes, zone requirements, ordinances and building regulations. Your plan may need to be modified to comply with local requirements regarding snow loads, energy codes, soil and seismic conditions and a wide range of other matters. In addition, you may need to obtain permits or inspections from local governments before and in the course of construction. Prior to using blueprints ordered from us, we strongly advise that you consult a licensed architect or engineer—and speak with your local building official—before applying for any permit or beginning construction. We authorize the use of our blueprints on the express condition that you strictly comply with all local building codes, zoning requirements and other applicable laws, regulations, ordinances and requirements. Notice: Plans for homes to be built in Nevada must be re-drawn by a Nevada-registered professional. Consult your building official for more information on this subject.

TOLL FREE
1-800-521-6797

REGULAR OFFICE HOURS:
8:00 a.m.-9:00 p.m. EST, Monday-Friday

If we receive your order by 3:00 p.m. EST, Monday-Friday, we'll process it and ship within **two business days**. When ordering by phone, please have your credit card or check information ready. We'll also ask you for the Order Form Key Number at the bottom of the order form.

By FAX: Copy the Order Form on the next page and send it on our FAX line: 1-800-224-6699 or 520-544-3086.

Canadian Customers
Order Toll Free 1-877-223-6389

DISCLAIMER

The designers we work with have put substantial care and effort into the creation of their blueprints. However, because they cannot provide on-site consultation, supervision and control over actual construction, and because of the great variance in local building requirements, building practices and soil, seismic, weather and other conditions, WE CANNOT MAKE ANY WARRANTY, EXPRESS OR IMPLIED, WITH RESPECT TO THE CONTENT OR USE OF THE BLUEPRINTS, INCLUDING BUT NOT LIMITED TO ANY WARRANTY OF MERCHANTABILITY OR OF FITNESS FOR A PARTICULAR PURPOSE. ITEMS, PRICES, TERMS AND CONDITIONS ARE SUBJECT TO CHANGE WITHOUT NOTICE. REPRODUCIBLE PLAN ORDERS MAY REQUIRE A CUSTOMER'S SIGNED RELEASE BEFORE SHIPPING.

TERMS AND CONDITIONS

These designs are protected under the terms of United States Copyright Law and may not be copied or reproduced in any way, by any means, unless you have purchased Reproducibles which clearly indicate your right to copy or reproduce. We authorize the use of your chosen design as an aid in the construction of one single family home only. You may not use this design to build a second or multiple dwellings without purchasing another blueprint or blueprints or paying additional design fees.

HOW MANY BLUEPRINTS DO YOU NEED?

Although a standard building package may satisfy many states, cities and counties, some plans may require certain changes. For your convenience, we have developed a Reproducible plan which allows a local professional to modify and make up to 10 copies of your revised plan. As our plans are all copyright protected, with your purchase of the Reproducible, we will supply you with a Copyright release letter. The number of copies you may need: 1 for owner; 3 for builder; 2 for local building department and 1-3 sets for your mortgage lender.

ORDER TOLL FREE!

For information about any of our services or to order call
1-800-521-6797

Browse our website:
www.eplans.com

BLUEPRINTS ARE NOT REFUNDABLE EXCHANGES ONLY

For Customer Service, call toll free
1-888-690-1116.

 HOME PLANNERS, LLC wholly owned by Hanley-Wood, LLC
3275 WEST INA ROAD, SUITE 110 • TUCSON, ARIZONA • 85741

THE BASIC BLUEPRINT PACKAGE

Rush me the following (please refer to the Plans Index and Price Schedule in this section):

____ Set(s) of reproducibles*, plan number(s) _____ $_____
    indicate foundation type _____ surcharge (if applicable): $_____
____ Set(s) of blueprints, plan number(s) _____ $_____
    indicate foundation type _____ surcharge (if applicable): $_____
____ Additional identical blueprints (standard or reverse) in same order @ $50 per set $_____
____ Reverse blueprints @ $50 fee per order. Right-reading reverse @ $165 surcharge $_____

IMPORTANT EXTRAS

Rush me the following:

____ Materials List: $60 (Must be purchased with Blueprint set.) Add $10 for Schedule C4–L4 plans $_____
____ **Quote One**® Summary Cost Report @ $29.95 for one, $14.95 for each additional,
    for plans _____ $_____
    Building location: City _____ Zip Code _____
____ **Quote One**® Material Cost Report @ $120 Schedules P1–C3; $130 Schedules C4–L4,
    for plan _____ (Must be purchased with Blueprints set.) $_____
    Building location: City _____ Zip Code _____
____ Specification Outlines @ $10 each $_____
____ Detail Sets @ $14.95 each; any two $22.95; any three $29.95; all four for $39.95 (save $19.85) $_____
____ ❑ Plumbing ❑ Electrical ❑ Construction ❑ Mechanical
____ Home Furniture Planner @ $15.95 each $_____

DECK BLUEPRINTS

(Please refer to the Plans Index and Price Schedule in this section)

____ Set(s) of Deck Plan _____ $_____
____ Additional identical blueprints in same order @ $10 per set. $_____
____ Reverse blueprints @ $10 fee per order. $_____
____ Set of Standard Deck Details @ $14.95 per set. $_____
____ Set of Complete Deck Construction Package (Best Buy!) Add $10 to Building Package.
    Includes Custom Deck Plan _____ Plus Standard Deck Details

LANDSCAPE BLUEPRINTS

(Please refer to the Plans Index and Price Schedule in this section.)

____ Set(s) of Landscape Plan _____ $_____
____ Additional identical blueprints in same order @ $10 per set $_____
____ Reverse blueprints @ $10 fee per order $_____

Please indicate appropriate region of the country for Plant & Material List. Region _____

POSTAGE AND HANDLING *SIGNATURE IS REQUIRED FOR ALL DELIVERIES.*	1–3 sets	4+ sets
DELIVERY No CODs (Requires street address—No P.O. Boxes)		
•Regular Service (Allow 7–10 business days delivery)	❑ $20.00	❑ $25.00
•Priority (Allow 4–5 business days delivery)	❑ $25.00	❑ $35.00
•Express (Allow 3 business days delivery)	❑ $35.00	❑ $45.00
OVERSEAS DELIVERY	fax, phone or mail for quote	

Note: All delivery times are from date Blueprint Package is shipped.

POSTAGE (From box above) $_____
SUBTOTAL $_____
SALES TAX (AZ & MI residents, please add appropriate state and local sales tax.) $_____
TOTAL (Subtotal and tax) $_____

YOUR ADDRESS (please print legibly)

Name _____

Street _____

City _____ State _____ Zip _____

Daytime telephone number (required) (_____) _____

* Fax number (required for reproducible orders) _____
TeleCheck® Checks By Phone℠ available

FOR CREDIT CARD ORDERS ONLY

Credit card number _____ Exp. Date: (M/Y) _____

Check one ❑ Visa ❑ MasterCard ❑ Discover Card ❑ American Express

Order Form Key

Signature (required) _____ | HPT86 |

Please check appropriate box: ❑ Licensed Builder-Contractor ❑ Homeowner

 **ORDER TOLL FREE!**
1-800-521-6797

BY FAX: Copy the order form above and send it on our FAXLINE: 1-800-224-6699 OR 520-544-3086

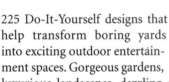
464